現代建築家による
"水"建築

企画　マリアロザリア タリアフェッリ
翻訳　乙須 敏紀

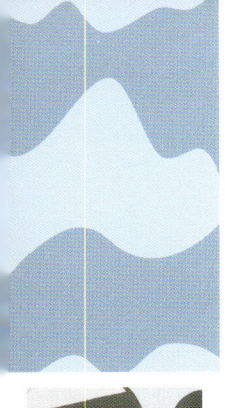

目次
CONTENTS

水と建築との交流 4

視覚としての水 10

◆フローティングハウス・ムソカ 12
　シム＆サットクリフ・アーキテクツ

◆ランドバーグ・キャビン 18
　ランドバーグ・デザイン

◆メゾン・ペレ 22
　L-アルシテクト

◆バジル邸 30
　ウラジミール・ジュロヴィッチ・ランドスケープ・アーキテクチュア

◆ハウス・ペイフェ 38
　クラエ＆ジャメイン・ソシエ・アルシテクト

◆レイクサイド・レジデンス 44
　オーバーランド・パートナーズ

◆サマーハウス 50
　トット・サンダース＆トミー・ウィルヘルムセン

◆チキンポイント・キャビン 54
　オルソン・サンドバーグ＆クンディック・アレン・アーキテクツ

◆ボート・ドック 58
　ミロ・リベラ・アーキテクツ

◆ゲストハウス 62
　ミロ・リベラ・アーキテクツ

◆ザ・スフィンクス 68
　ノイトリング・リーダイク・アーキテクツ

◆桟橋の家 74
　オニキス

◆缶詰工場ロフト 78
　ターナーヘクト・アーキテクチュア

◆X氏邸 84
　バークレイ＆クラウス・アーキテクチュア

◆ヴィラ＋ 88
　ハイメ・サナウーハ・アソシアードス

◆クロナキルティーの家 94
　ナイアル・マクラフリン・アーキテクツ

◆ポルタス・ノヴァス 98
　ファン・ロカ／アクアート、ヴィクトール・カニャス

◆水平線の家 106
　小川　晋一　都市建築設計事務所

◆サ・リエラ 112
　アルフォンソ・モラレス

◆ナムリー通りの家 118
　ベドマール＆シー

◆アイランド・モダン 122
　ジャングルズ・ランドスケープ・アーキテクチュア

◆カサ・マルドナド 124
　アルベルト・ブルクハルト

◆カブリー邸 128
　ハビエル・プラナス／プラナス―トーレス建築設計事務所

◆ピエリーノ邸 132
　アルベルト・ブルクハルト

◆エリー・サーブ邸 136
　ウラジミール・ジュロヴィッチ・ランドスケープ・アーキテクチュア

◆カルデラ湖のある家 …………………… 142	◆コーナー・オブ・ピース ………………… 220
GADアーキテクチュア	アルベルト・ブルクハルト
◆カサ・トーロ ………………………………… 146	◆復活した伝統 ………………………………… 224
アルヴァロ・レイト・シザ・ヴィエイラ	クラーソン・コイヴィスト・ルーネ・アルキテクトコントロール
◆ウッドサイド・レジデンス ……………… 152	◆メディテーション ………………………… 228
ラツコー建築設計事務所	ボネッティ・コザルスキー・スタジオ
◆リューティ …………………………………… 158	◆オリエンタル・リラクゼーション …… 232
ドナルド・ヤコブ／ヤコブ・ラントシャフツアルヒテクテン	バーバラ・シンドリュー／CADインテリオリスモ
◆シューベルト邸 …………………………… 162	◆ピース・イン・ザ・マウンテンズ …… 236
ホルガー・シューベルト	マルシオ・コーガン
◆プライベート・レジデンス ……………… 166	◆ミニマリストの泉 ………………………… 240
ウラジミール・ジュロヴィッチ・ランドスケープ・アーキテクチュア	岡田憲史建築都市計画研究所
◆チューリッヒの家 ………………………… 170	◆幸福の感覚 …………………………………… 244
クリスチャン・ビュートリッヒ	ギレム・ルスタン
◆デザイナーの家 …………………………… 172	◆スパ・フォー・ザ・ファミリー ……… 248
ブッジ・ラユグ／ブッジリビング・バンコク	アロハ・プールズ、クリエイティブ・アウトドア・ソリューションズ
◆ナムリー通りの家 ………………………… 176	◆アーバン・オアシス ……………………… 250
ベドマール＆シー	フォータナー＆チャップマン・ランドスケープ・アーキテクツ
◆ブドウ畑の池 ……………………………… 180	◆ウォークウェイ・オン・ザ・ウォーター …… 254
ラツコー建築設計事務所	ジャンダルズ・ランドスケープ・アーキテクチュア
◆歩道橋 ………………………………………… 186	◆沈黙の庭 ……………………………………… 260
ミロ・リベラ・アーキテクツ	ダルデレ

体感としての水 …………………………………… 192

◆グラスハウス ……………………………… 194	
ファン・ロカ／アクアート、ヴィクトール・カニャス	
◆風景のあるラウンジ ……………………… 198	
デイヴィット・ラック・アーキテクチュア	
◆風景のあるバスルーム …………………… 200	
小川 晋一 都市建築設計事務所	
◆ネクサスを繋ぐ …………………………… 204	
NATアーキテクテン	
◆大西洋への窓 ……………………………… 208	
製作者不詳	
◆マジック・イン・ザ・ウォーター …… 214	
D&Dアクアリウム・ソリューションズ	

夢としての水 ……………………………………… 264

◆ウォーキング・オン・ザ・ウォーター …… 266
スタファン・ストリンドベリ
◆デイリーライフ・オン・ザ・ウォーター …… 272
バネケ、ファン・デル・ホーベン・アルヒテクテン
◆ウォーター・フォー・ライフ …………… 276
ジェニファー・ランドール建築設計事務所
◆概念の見直し ……………………………… 280
ドリュー・ヘス

作品・建築家一覧 ……………………………… 286

水と建築との交流

　水はこの惑星で最も豊富に存在する元素だ。水は生命の源であり、水なくしてはいかなる生物も生きていくことはできない。この惑星から水を取りさると、すべての生物が消滅する。

　人類文明の夜明け、人々は水の傍で生活した。川の岸辺、オアシス、湖や小川のほとりに集落が生まれ発展した。

　やがて人間は水を貯留し輸送するためのより複雑で、より効率的なシステムを開発し、水を多種多様な目的に利用した。

　例えば古代ローマ人は水道橋を建設し、アラブ人は灌漑システムを発明した。現在では、供給網、浄化施設、淡水化設備などの複雑なネットワークがさまざまな用途に応えながら、人々のもとへと水を供給している。

foreword

Water is the most plentiful element on the planet. It is the source of life, without which no living thing could survive. Practically nothing would exist on the planet without water.
At the dawn of civilization, man lived
close to water; towns grew around rivers, oasis, next to lakes or streams.
In time man developed more complex
and efficient systems for the conservation or transportation of water, and to adapt
it for its different uses.
The Romans, for example built aqueducts, and the Arabs invented irrigation systems. Today, complex supply, purification
and desalination networks manipulate water to adapt and distribute
it to the people.

水は日常生活に欠くことのできない要素だ。それゆえ最も発展した、最も幸運な国々とは、水が最も容易に手に入る位置にある国々だった。この惑星では水は不公平に分配されている。

　ただでさえ貧しい発展途上国は、飲料水の確保という面でも苦難を強いられている。現在ユネスコなどの国際的組織が、これらの国々がもっと容易に水を確保することができるように、また水の使用がより持続可能なものになるように活動している。

　住宅建築のなかに水を組み込み、それと交流する可能性は無限にある。これから紹介するプロジェクトは、いずれも実際に水と人とが生き生きと交流しており、斬新で表現力に富んだ可能性を提示することにおいて抜きん出ている。どのプロジェクトにおいても、水は視覚的、建築的に住宅と関係を結び、その主要なエレメントとして住宅のなかに巧みに統合されている。

Water is a necessary element for our daily lives, and the most developed, fortunate countries are those that have easiest access to this resource, which is shared unequally throughout the planet.
Poor and developing countries have the added difficulty of accessing drinking water. International organizations such as Unesco are working to give these countries easier access to water and
to make the use of water more sustainable.

There are lots of possibilities to interact with water in residential architecture.
The expressive possibilities stand
out in these projects, since as well
as its practicalities, there is a visual
and architectural relation with water,
which integrates with each project
as one of the main elements.

本書を開くと、どのページからも臨場感溢れる写真が飛び込んでき、水と建築のコラボレーションが創りだす魅力溢れる住宅が眼前に現れる。あるものは海洋の傍にあり、あるものは湖や運河の傍にある。

　本書はまた、室内池、プール、アクアリウムなど、水を住宅のインテリアとして、あるいはエクステリアとして、華やかに、より装飾的に用いたプロジェクトも紹介する。プールは住宅にレクリエーションと水浴の空間をもたらし、庭の水の流れは安息と蘇生の気をもたらす。またスパのある住宅など、心と身体の再生を主題にしたプロジェクトも多く収載している。最後に夢がそのまま現実化した建築、フローティングハウスを紹介する。

　本書に満載している心を呼び覚ますイメージは、読者を異次元の世界へと誘い、水と建築の新しい関係を探求する終わりなき旅へと連れ立つ。

This book reveals the relation water
has with residential architecture, presenting houses from all
over the world, next to the sea, lakes or canals.
There are also projects that use water
in more of a festive or decorative way,
both in interiors and exteriors of houses: indoor ponds,
swimming pools, aquariums, etc. Swimming pools provide
recreational and bathing areas, while gardens allow
for exclusive projects with relaxing, evocative environments.
Other pages harbor projects dedicated to the body
and soul, such as spas and finally,
a chapter straight out of a dream:
floating houses.
This volume, full of evocative images, transports the reader
to other places
and attempts to present new ideas,
which continue to develop the relation between water and
architecture.

この章に登場する住宅はどれもみな、水が建築にもたらす無限の可能性を提示する。フォルム、1本1本の線、ヴォリューム、すべてが水と接しているという優位性を最大限生かすためにデザインされている。住宅は水際に寄り添って立ち、海や湖に開けた大きな窓やテラスからは、心をのびやかにする美しい景観が眺望できる。プールや水のある庭はユニークな屋外空間を形成し、自然へと開かれた私的世界を創造する。人はそこで環境とより親密な関係を結ぶ。

The homes that appear in this chapter show the infinite possibilities that water offers; their forms, lines and the volumes that compose them were designed considering the close proximity of water. The houses are situated close to the water's edge, with large windows and terraces facing the sea or a lake that provide excellent views. Swimming pools and gardens form unique exterior spaces where private worlds can be created, allowing for a more personal relationship with the environment.

視覚としての水

フローティング・ハウス・ムソカ　シム＆サットクリフ・アーキテクツ
船屋、瀟洒な隠れ家　*A SOPHISTICATED REFUGE*

ムソカ湖―オンタリオ州―カナダ　撮影：ジェームズ・ダウ, エドワード・バーティンスキー

　トロントから車で約2時間、ムソカ湖の湖畔に背後を山に守られながらこの住宅は佇んでいる。伝統的なカナディアン建築様式にのっとり、住宅は完璧に風景と統合されている。水に浸かる木の軸組によって構造が造られ、伝統的な継手で接合された種々の再生板が壁や屋根を覆っている。このすっきりと洗練された船屋は、安らぎに満ちた楽園のような環境のなかの瀟洒な隠れ家になっている。

The design of this residence situated between the mountains and the banks
of lake Musoka, about two hours drive from Toronto, follows traditional Canadian architecture and integrates perfectly with the landscape. A wooden framework submerged in the water forms the structure of the house, which has been roofed and clad with different recycled woods joined according to traditional methods. The result is a simple and elegant house that provides refuge in a paradisiacal environment full of peace.

水と建築は非常に親密な関係で結ばれている。住宅には室内に2本、室外に屋根付きのものが1本、あわせて3本の桟橋があり、いつでも好きな時にボート遊びができる。

The relationship between architecture and water is very close. The house includes two interior jetties and a covered exterior one, offering the possibility of boating around the lake at any time.

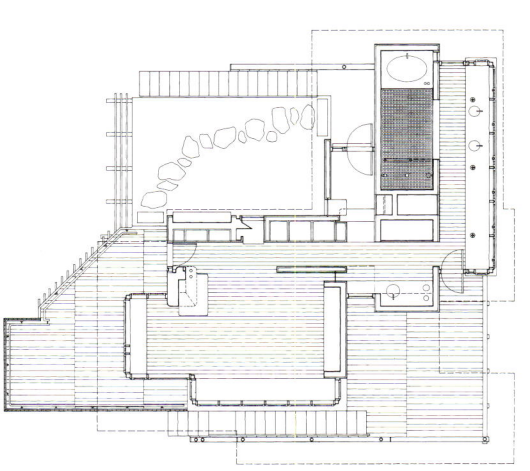
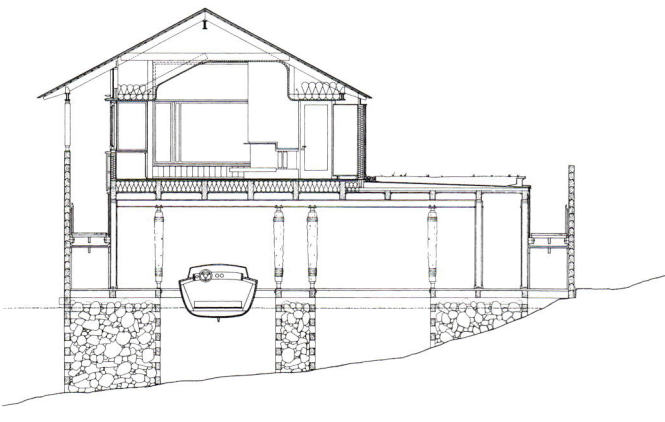

16 | 視覚としての水 | See it

ランドバーグ・キャビン　ランドバーグ・デザイン

山と山のはざまに　*BETWEEN MOUNTAINS*

ソノマ―カリフォルニア州―アメリカ　撮影：J D・ピーターソン

　サンフランシスコから車で2時間程の山あいに位置するこの山小屋は、使われていなかったものを建築家が自分と家族の安息の場として再生したもの。材料はすべて他のプロジェクトで出た廃材を利用し、現在も改築は継続している。古い貯水タンクは屋外プールに生まれ変わり、周囲の環境との高い次元での統合を体現している。大きい方のタンクはスイミングプールで、家族は昼でも夜でも好きな時に自然と一体化し、心と身体を全面的に解放する。小さい方のタンクは温めることができ、プライベートな露天風呂となる。

This refuge, situated just two hours from San Francisco, has been transformed into a place of rest for the architect and his family. It has been built from materials left over from other projects and is in continual transformation. The outdoor pools were built with old water tanks and their arrangement allows a high level of integration with the surroundings.
The swimming pools, surrounded by nature, can be refreshing and relaxing at any time of the day or night.
The small one is heated.

スイミングプールの水面とテラスのレベルが等しくされ、地面からかなり高い位置に持ち上げられている。テラスで食事を楽しんでいるときもプールで泳いでいるときも、視界をさえぎるものはなく、風景を心ゆくまで満喫できる。

The swimming pools are in the terrace area, which is raised above ground level. This means the views can be appreciated both from the outdoor dining area and the water.

メゾン・ペレ L-アルシテクト

レマン湖を見下ろして　*ON THE LAKE*

ラヴォー──スイス　撮影：ジャン・ミッシェル・ランデシー

　ユネスコが指定する自然保護区のなかにこの簡潔な住宅は位置している。ラヴォー地区の地形的特徴である急峻な斜面を生かして設計されたテラスは、まるで空中に浮かんでいるかのように眼下にレマン湖を見下ろし、雄大な景観をほしいままにしている。構造は周囲の景観と自然保護区の建築規制を考慮して決定されたが、その結果、自由と自然をこよなく愛するクライアントにとっての最高の隠れ場所となった。全面を木で覆われたこの小さな住宅からは、レマン湖の穏やかな水面と、その向こうに美しい山影を見せるアルプスの峰々が望める。

This simple house is located in a natural space protected by Unesco. The steep slope that defines the topography allowed for the installation of a terrace with magnificent views of Lake Leman.
The environment and the regulations
of the natural space determined
the characteristics of the construction
and the client, a lover of freedom
and nature, found his perfect refuge here. The small house clad in wood enjoys
the calm water of the lake and the fantastic views of the Alpine peaks.

24 | 視覚としての水 | See it

住宅はプレハブ構法で建てられたが、現場でさらにいくつかの仕上げが行われた。テラスは見る者と湖の間に何ものも介在しないように設計されている。

The house was prefabricated, although some of the finishes was done on site.
The design of the terrace is such that nothing comes between the spectator and the views of the lake.

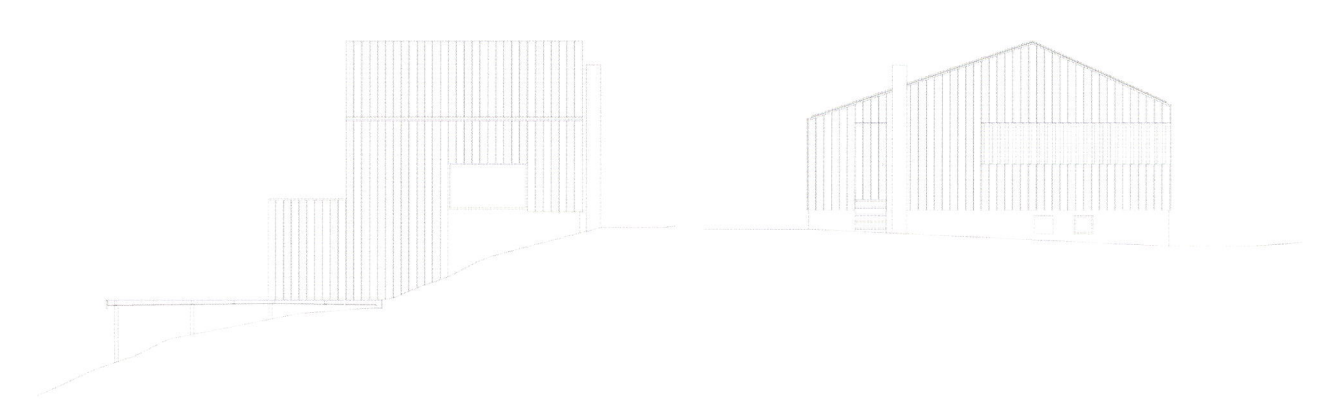

バジル邸 ウラジミール・ジュロヴィッチ・ランドスケープ・アーキテクチュア

無限のプール　INFINTE POOL

ファクラ―レバノン　撮影：ジェラルディン・ブルニール

　屋外でも華やかな社交パーティーを開くことができるように、この避暑地別荘の屋外庭園は住宅の導線をそのまま延長させる形で造られている。レバノン（セム語で白を意味する）の国名の由来である白い石灰岩のスラブが遠近法を強調するように大胆に配置され、ポーチのパーゴラにはレバノン杉の厚板が使われている。広いプールには縁がなく、そのまま雄大な風景に向かって無限大に広がっている。それはこの庭園に集う人々の心を解き放ち、温暖な気候をめいっぱい楽しむ気分にさせる。

The exterior of this summer residence follows the guidelines used for the house, to define areas where lively social events could be organized. To create these environments, a light colored stone was used and a porch was built from planks
of cedar wood. This space gives views
of the large swimming pool and the magnificent scenery that surrounds this home. The swimming pool is framed by the surrounding nature and provides a place to relax and enjoy the warm climate.

石灰岩の巨大なスラブはプール水面に浮かんでいるように見える。それはプールを渡る浮き橋となって、プールを分割している。長く突き出た1本のスラブの先、プールの先端部分はジャクジーになっている。

Large stone slabs, which appear to float over the water, divide the pool into two areas and create a walkway across it. One of the slabs gives access to the Jacuzzi, at one end of the pool.

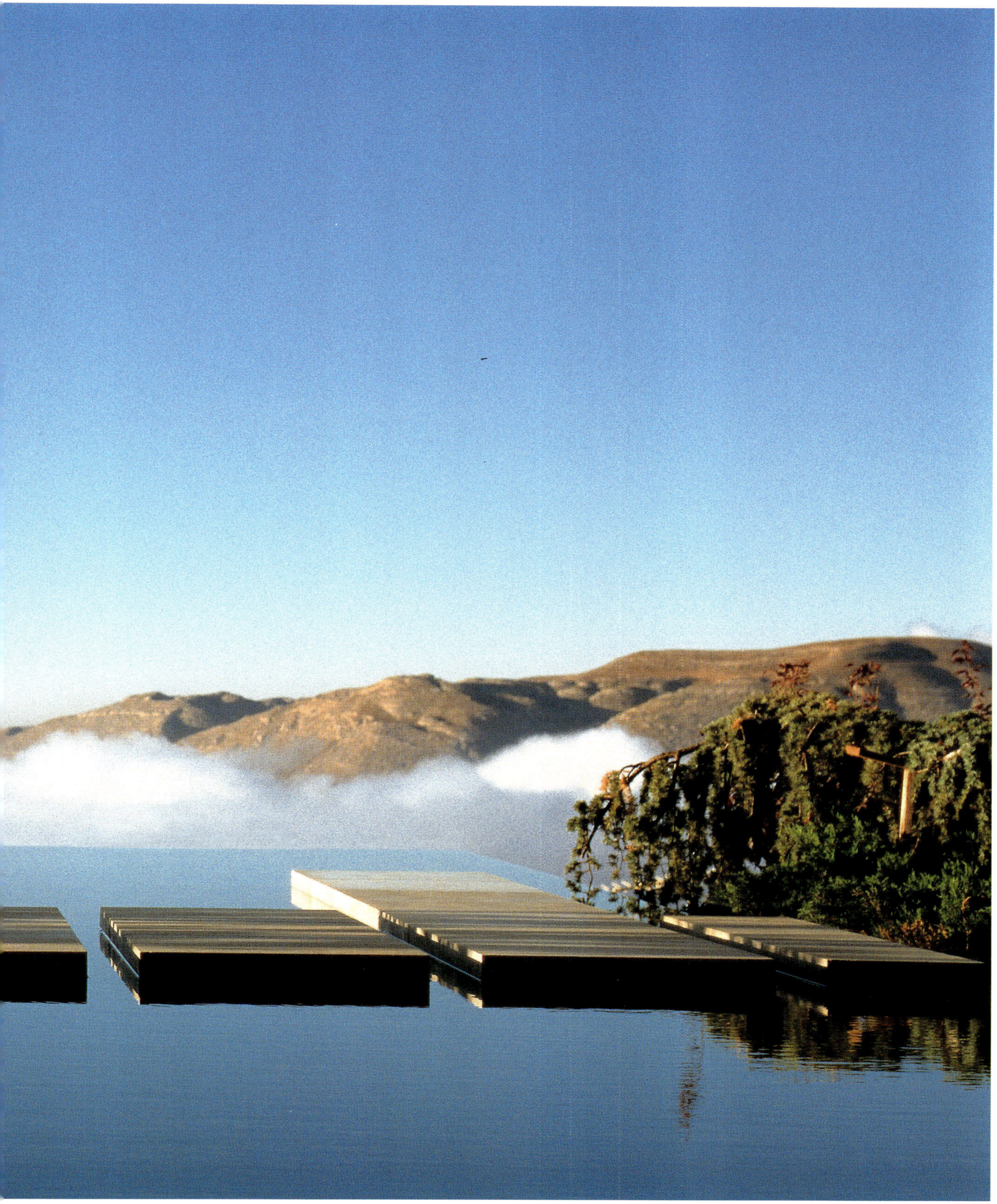

ハウス・ペイフェ クラエ & ジャメイン・ソシエ・アルシテクト

湖畔の隠れ家　LAKESIDE REFUGE

ザウアーブロート―ベルギー　撮影：ローラン・ブランダ

　豊かな緑に囲まれたこの湖畔の住宅は、伝統的な線使いと使用している材料のため完全に風景と統合している。住宅は木材を使うことによって高い断熱効果を確保し、この寒暖の差の激しい土地にうまく適合している。住宅はまたバイオ・コンストラクション構法によって環境との共生を図り、室内にはバイオ・ドモッティズム（植物を室内に多く配することによって空気清浄化と温度調整を行う）が導入されている。広々としたポーチの前方の柱が湖に足を浸けた格好になっており、その結果住宅が完全な対称図形となって湖面に映し出されている。設計者の独創性が遺憾なく発揮されている。

This chalet situated by a lake and surrounded by vegetation integrates perfectly in the surroundings thanks to its traditional lines and the materials used.
The utilization of wood allows for a heightened thermal insulation, which is very appropriate in this region of climatic extremes. Also bio-construction has been used and bio-domotism has been integrated
into the installations. A spacious porch enters the perimeter of the lake using pillars and creates a reflection in the water affording originality to the whole project.

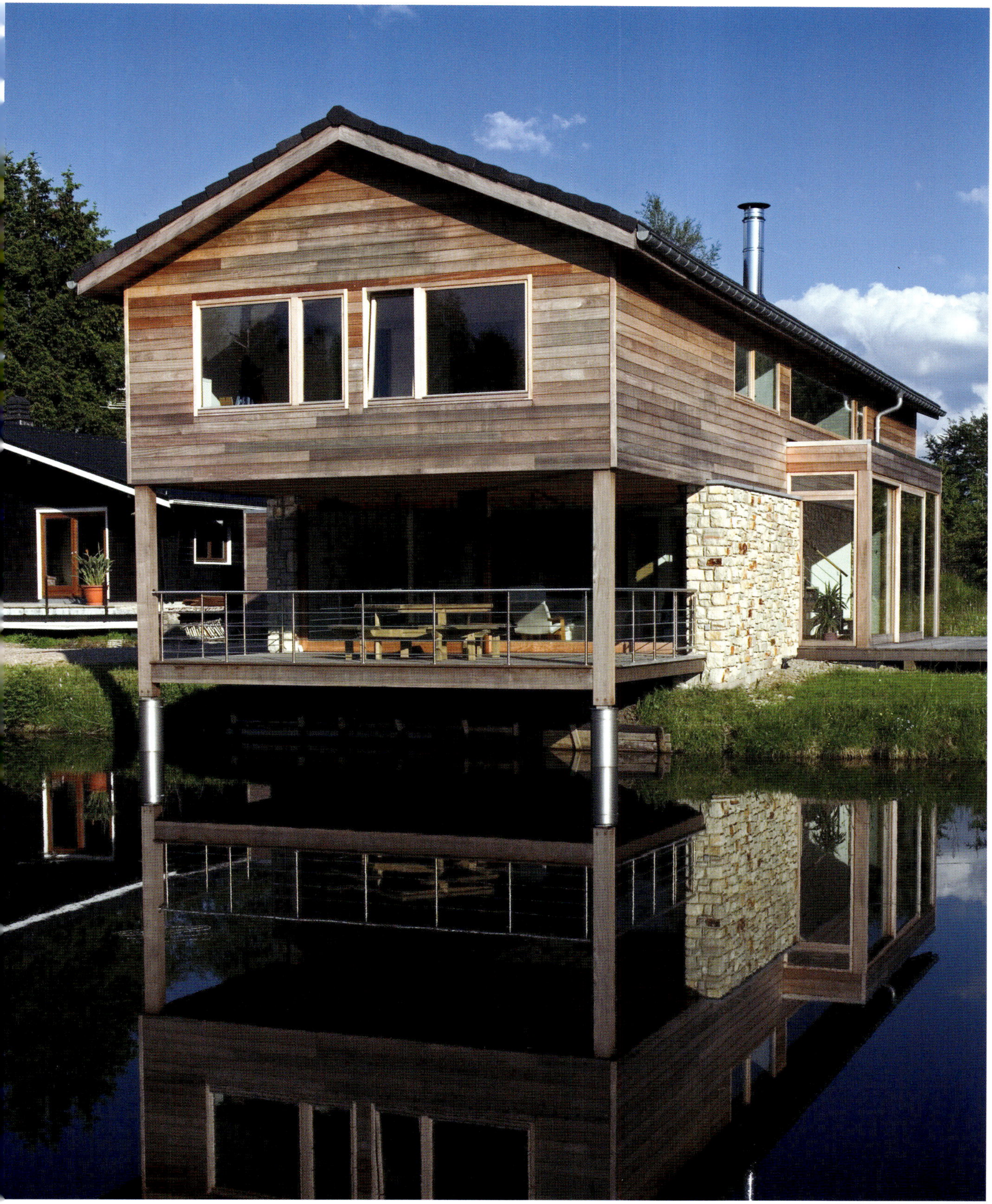

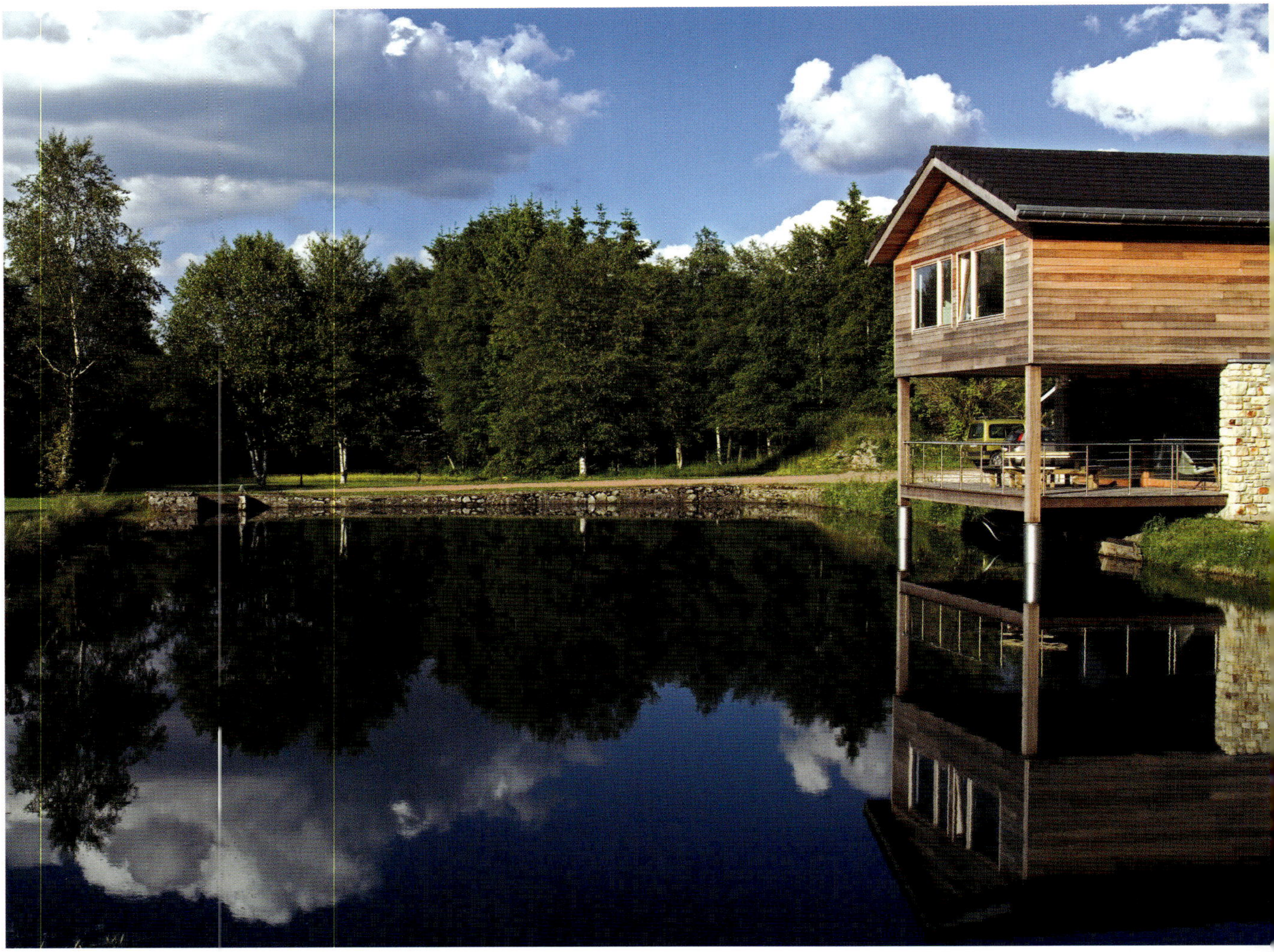

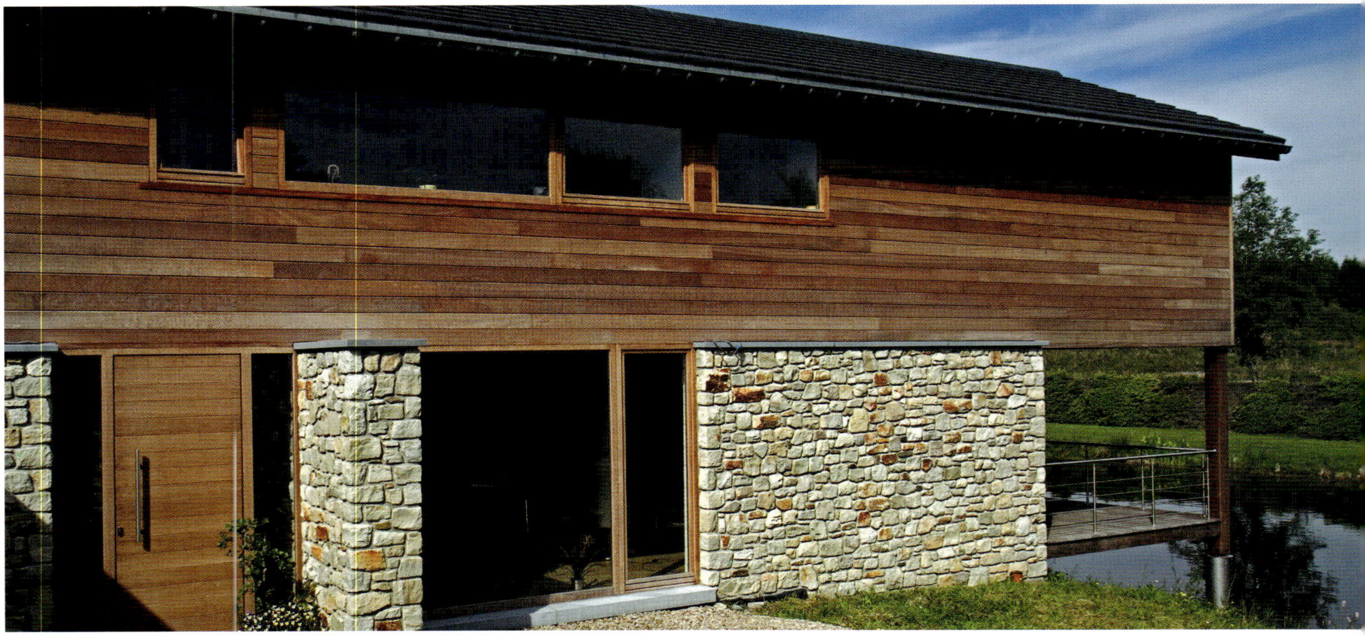

ハウス・ペイフェ | 41

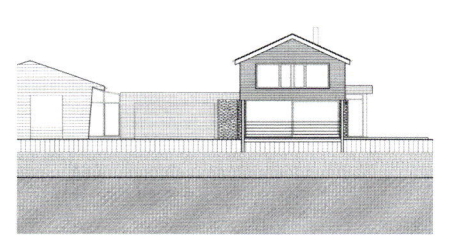

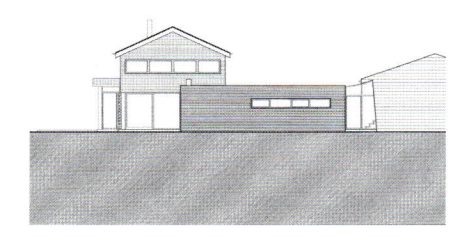

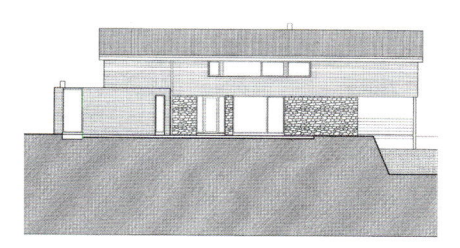

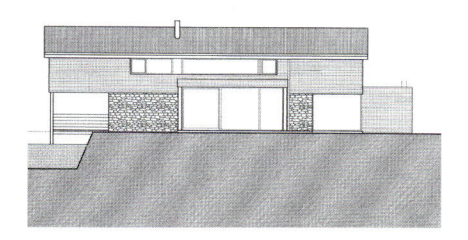

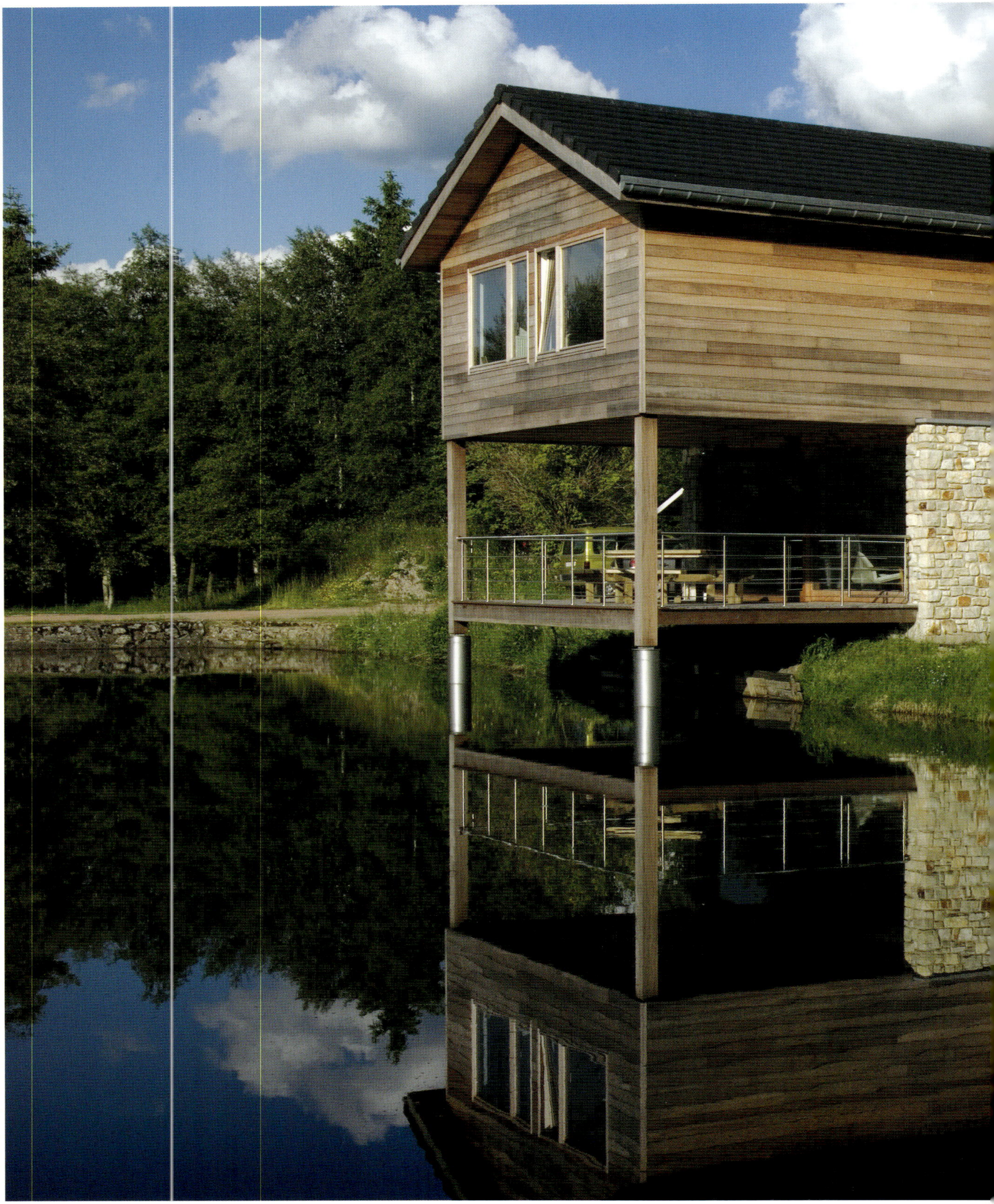

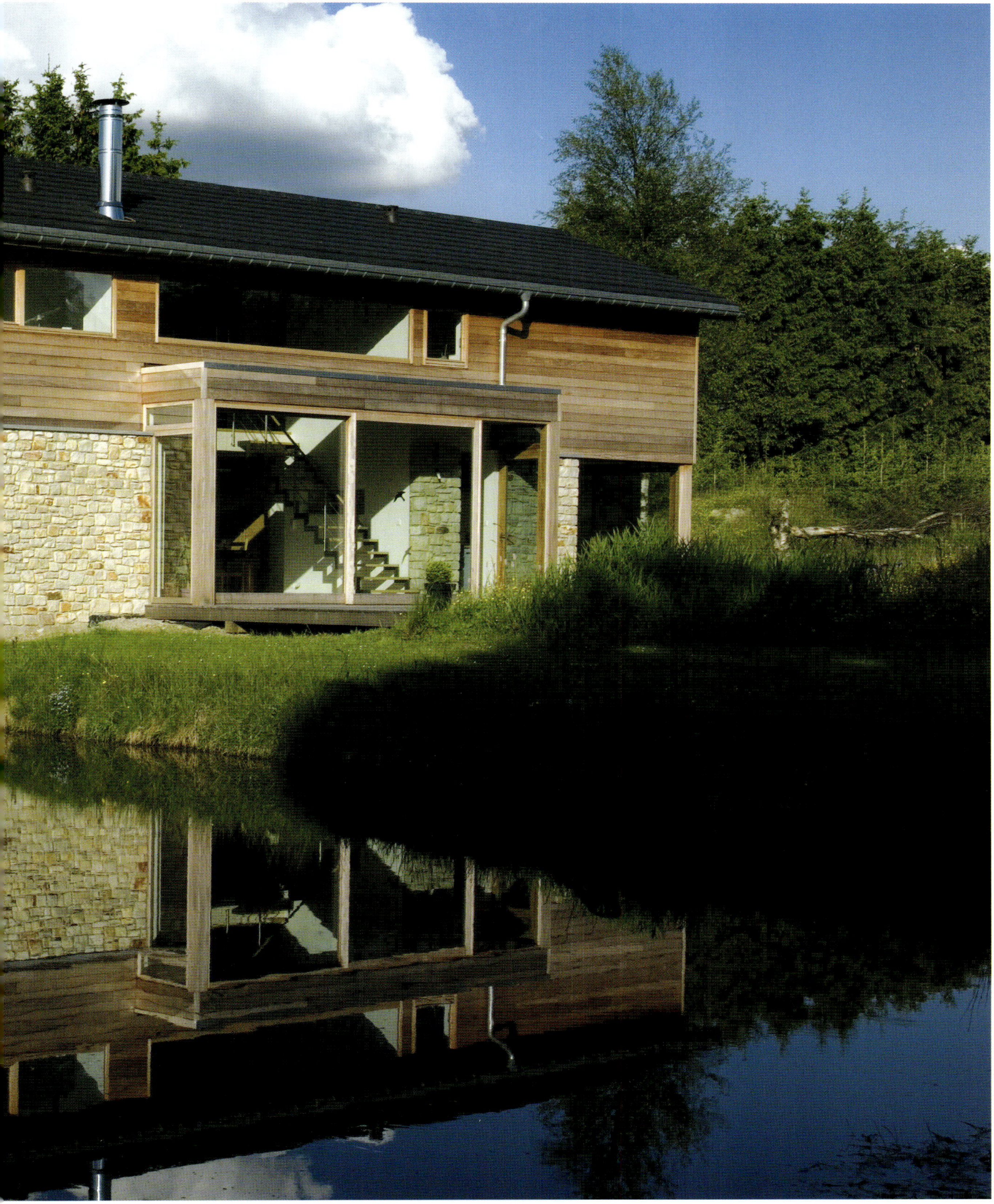

レイクサイド・レジデンス オーバーランド・パートナーズ

堤の上にて　*ON THE BANKS*

ホースシューベイ―テキサス州―アメリカ　撮影：ポール・バーディグジィー

　テキサス州出身の大統領リンドン・B・ジョンソンの名を冠した湖の堤に位置するこの住宅は、3つの主要なヴォリュームから構成されており、それぞれがポーチや中庭、湖面まで伸びたテラスなどのオープンスペースによって結ばれている。外壁に使われている石材やコンクリートが住宅に強く逞しい印象を付与しているが、それらの材料は住宅内部にも露出し、住宅の内と外との関連性を強調している。湖に開かれた大きな窓を通して、どの部屋からも湖の眺望を満喫することができる。

This home is located on the banks of lake LBJ, in Texas. There are three large volumes, which are connected through porches and open spaces such as the central courtyard or the terraces that stretch down to the banks of the lake. The exterior materials of the house, stone and concrete, give the house a robust appearance. These materials are also present inside the house to emphasize the relation between the interior and the exterior. Large windows afford views from the various rooms.

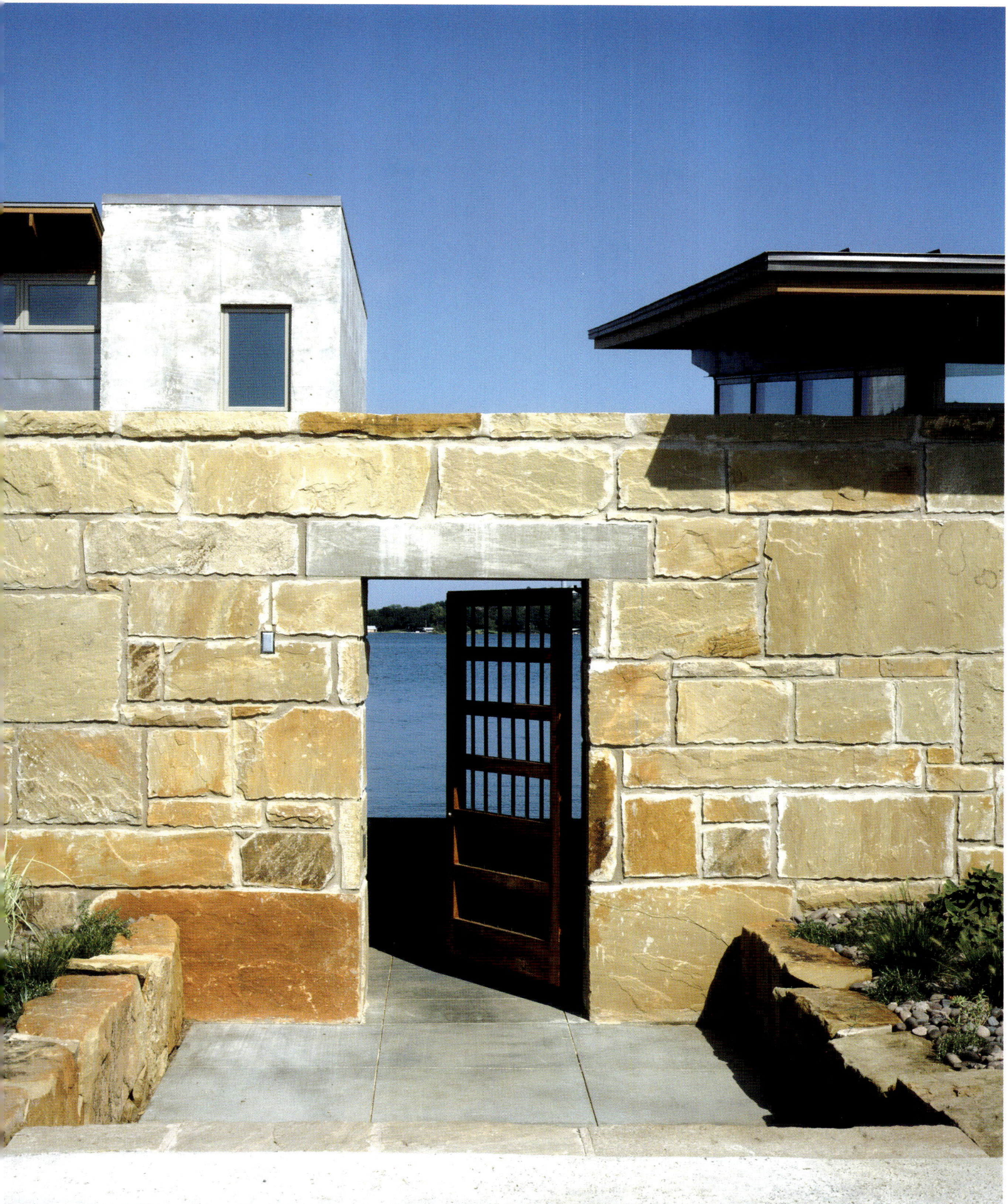

通りから見ると主宅は巨大な石造りの壁にしか見えないが、その背後には多様なブロックが隠されている。テラスが湖面に向かって低く横に伸びているので、ヴォリュームとヴォリュームの相関関係は湖の方向からはっきりと見ることができる。

From the street, the residence looks like a large stone wall, which hides various blocks. The interrelation between the volumes can be seen from the lake thanks to the terraces that reach down to the bank.

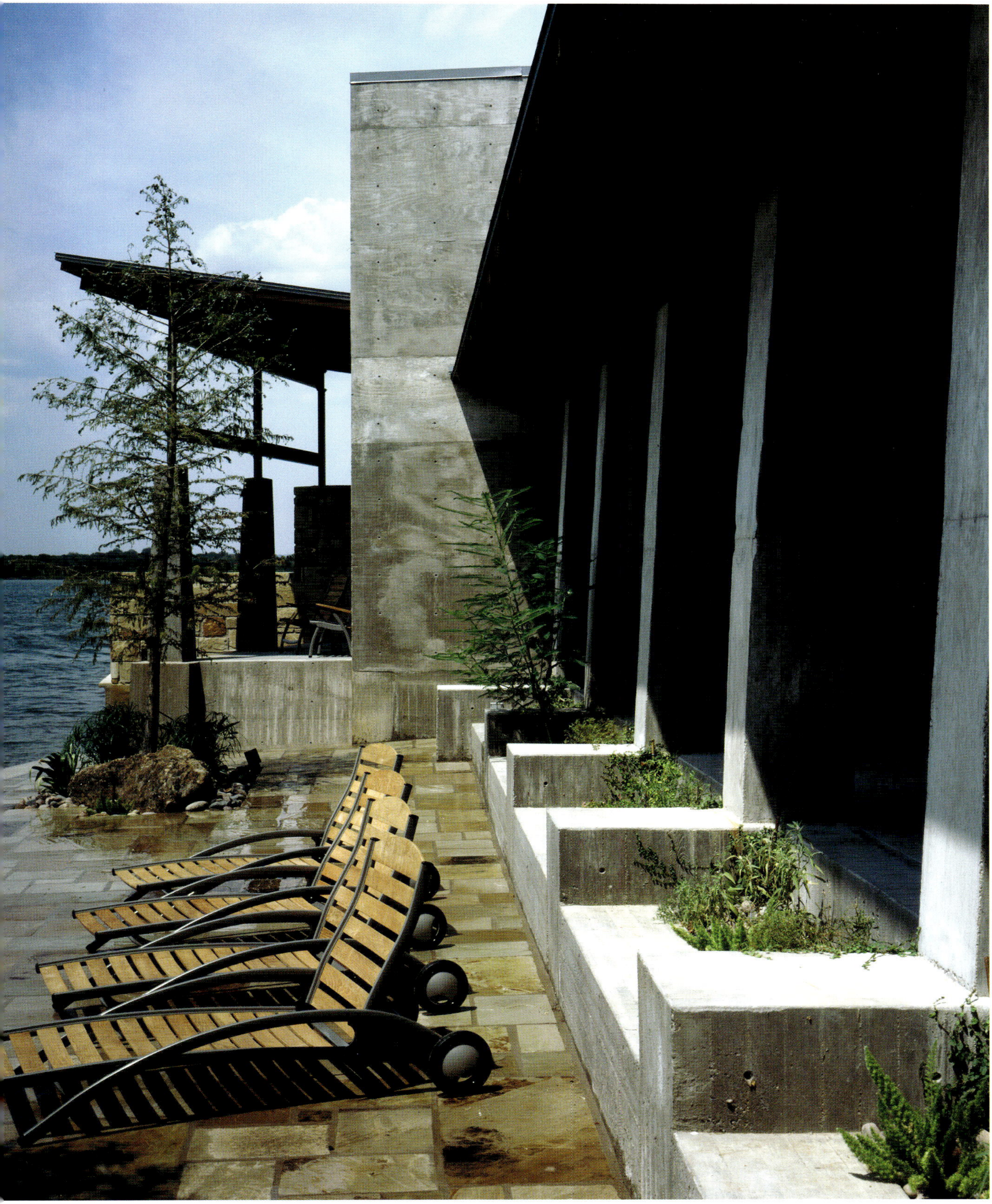

48 ｜ 視覚としての水 ｜ See it

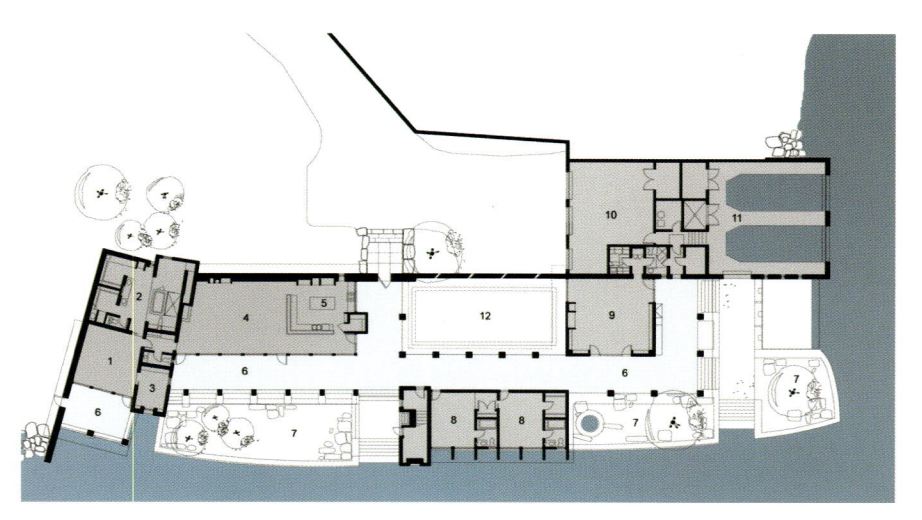

巨大なガラスウォールから明るい光がたっぷりと住宅に注ぎ込まれている。各部屋の前面にはポーチやバルコニーが配され、それらが補足的な屋外空間となって、なおさら人々の眼を風景へと向けさせる。

Large glass walls favor the entry of light into the house. In front of the rooms are the porches and balconies, which generate additional outdoor space and allow us to appreciate the scenery.

サマーハウス トット・サンダース＆トミー・ウィルヘルムセン

フィヨルドのなかの小屋　CABIN IN A FJORD

ハルダンゲル・フィヨルド―ノルウェー　撮影：ベント・レネ・シンバーグ

　数多くあるノルウェーのフィヨルドのなかでもかなり小さいものの1つ、その岸から約75m離れた場所にこの小さな別荘はある。建築家の意図したものは、周囲の景観と統合されてはいるが、ある種の視覚的コントラストを生み出す夏の別荘というものであった。木製のプラットホームはモジュールの基台としてだけでなく、テラスとしての役割も果たしている。フィヨルドの旁、深いノルウェーの森が少し開けた、周囲を小川に囲まれた空地にこの小さな別荘は座し、平穏と霊感に満ちた静寂の境地を開いている。

This small refuge in one of Norway's prettiest fjords is situated just 250 ft from the water. The aim of the architects was to build a refuge for the summer months that would integrate with the surroundings but create a certain visual contrast. A wooden platform acts as a base for the modules and as a terrace. The location of the refuge, in a clearing of a dense forest, by the fjord and surrounded by streams, creates a serene atmosphere, full of calm and spirituality.

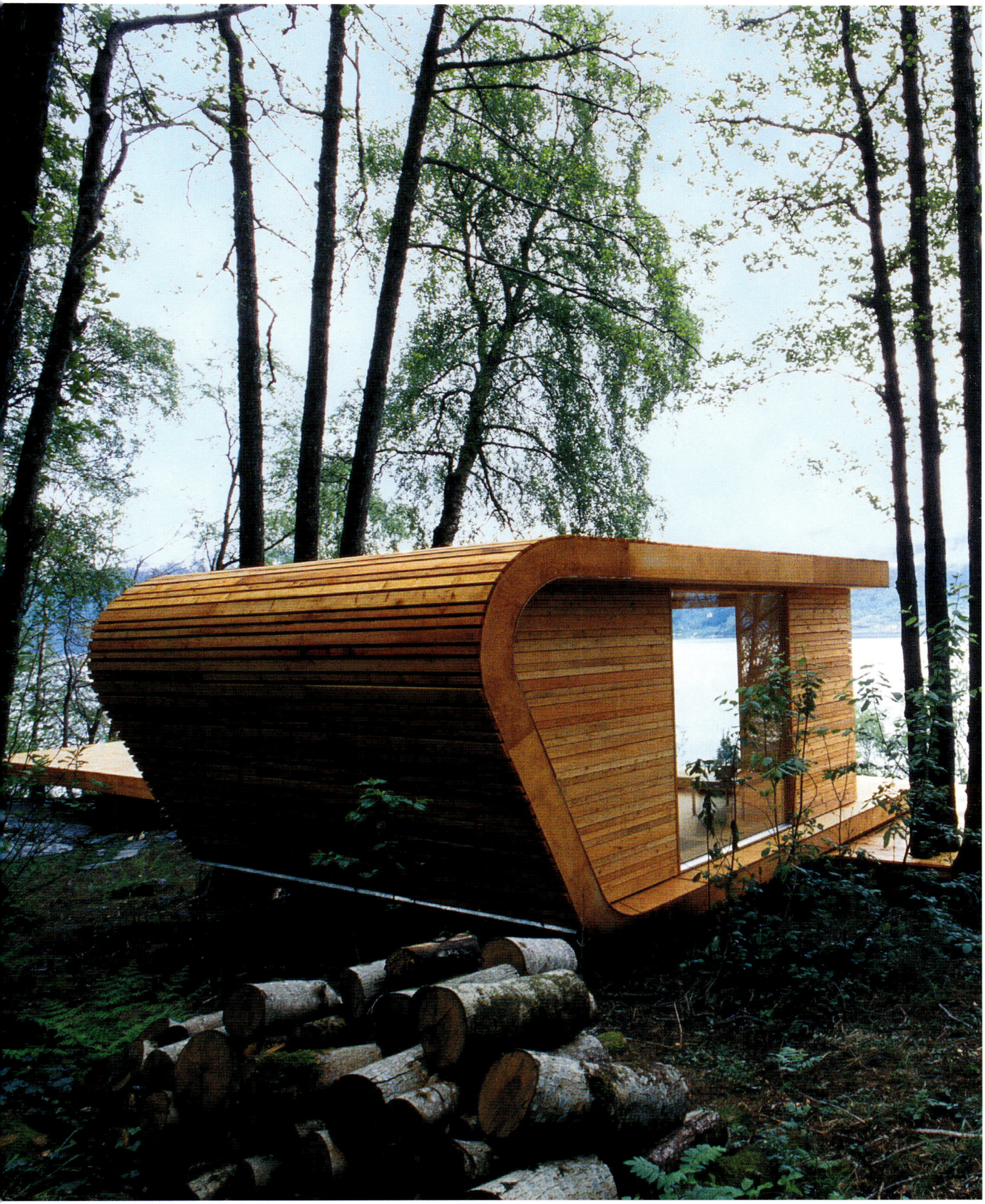

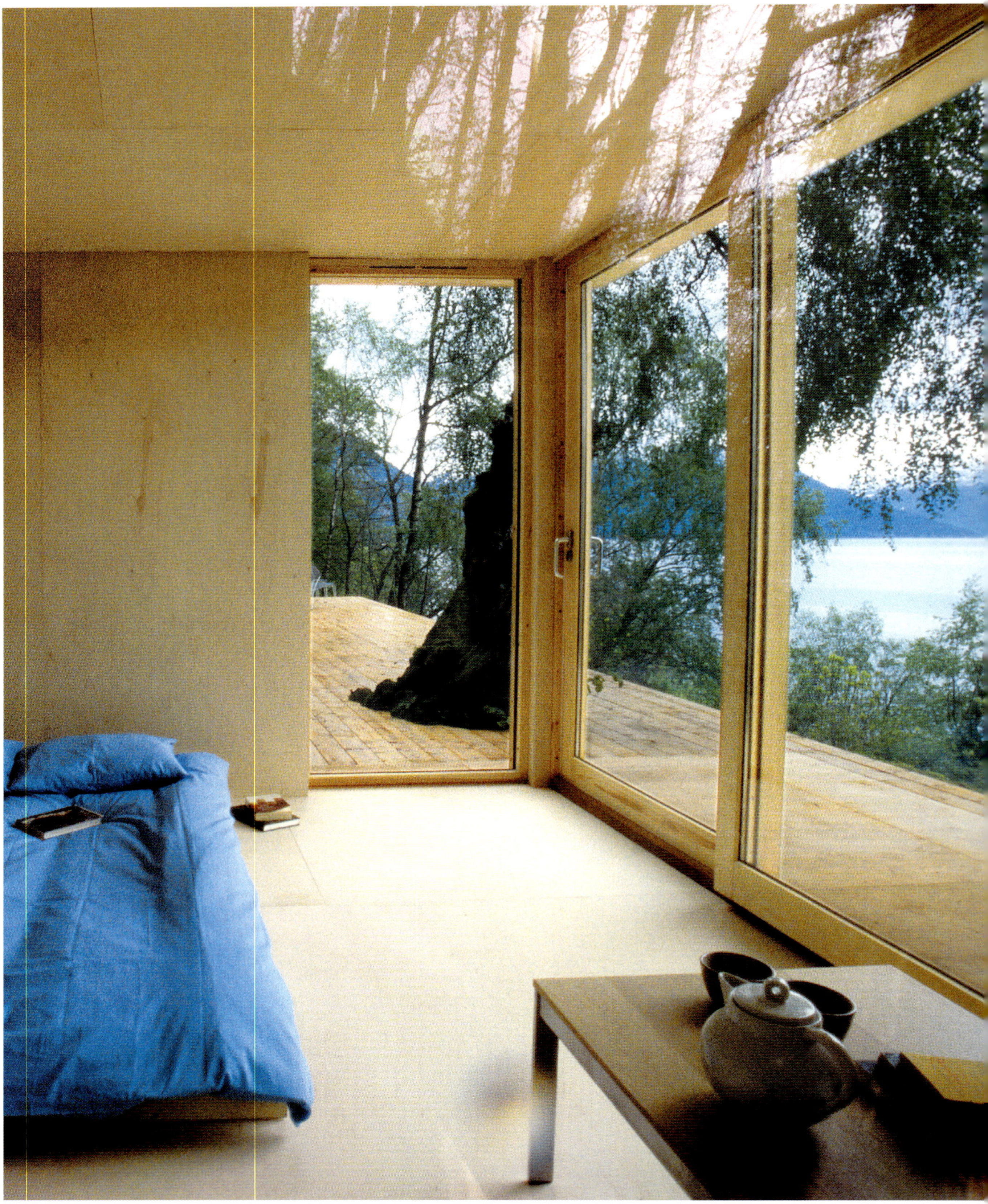

夏、ノルウェーの夜は短く、ほんの4時間ほど暗やむだけである。そのためこの大きな窓があれば他の照明は必要ない。

Since there are around four hours of darkness during Norway's summer, the large windows allow an adequate, constant lighting.

チキンポイント・キャビン　オルソン・サンドバーグ & クンディック・アレン・アーキテクツ
湖に眼を向けて　LOOKING TO THE LAKE

アイダホ州北部―アメリカ　撮影：アンディーヌ・プレール

　堅固な外観を示すコンクリート・ブロック組積造の独創的な湖畔の別荘。内部はそのコンクリート・ブロックと合板、そして大きな鉄製の暖炉を組み合わせた小ぢんまりとした仕上がりになっている。巨大なガラスウォールが軸を中心に縦に回転し湖とその対岸の森に向かって開かれると、自然と人との開けっぴろげな交流が始まる。石組みの階段を下りると小さな突堤が出ており、そこからボート遊びに出発する。

This unusual lakeside cabin presents a solid, concrete exterior structure. Inside, this material is mixed with plywood and a large steel chimney affording a cozy finish to the project. A large glass wall tilts on an axis allowing an opening towards the forest and lake opposite the house and shows the interaction the residence has with the surrounding nature.
The small jetty is used for the boats taken around the lake.

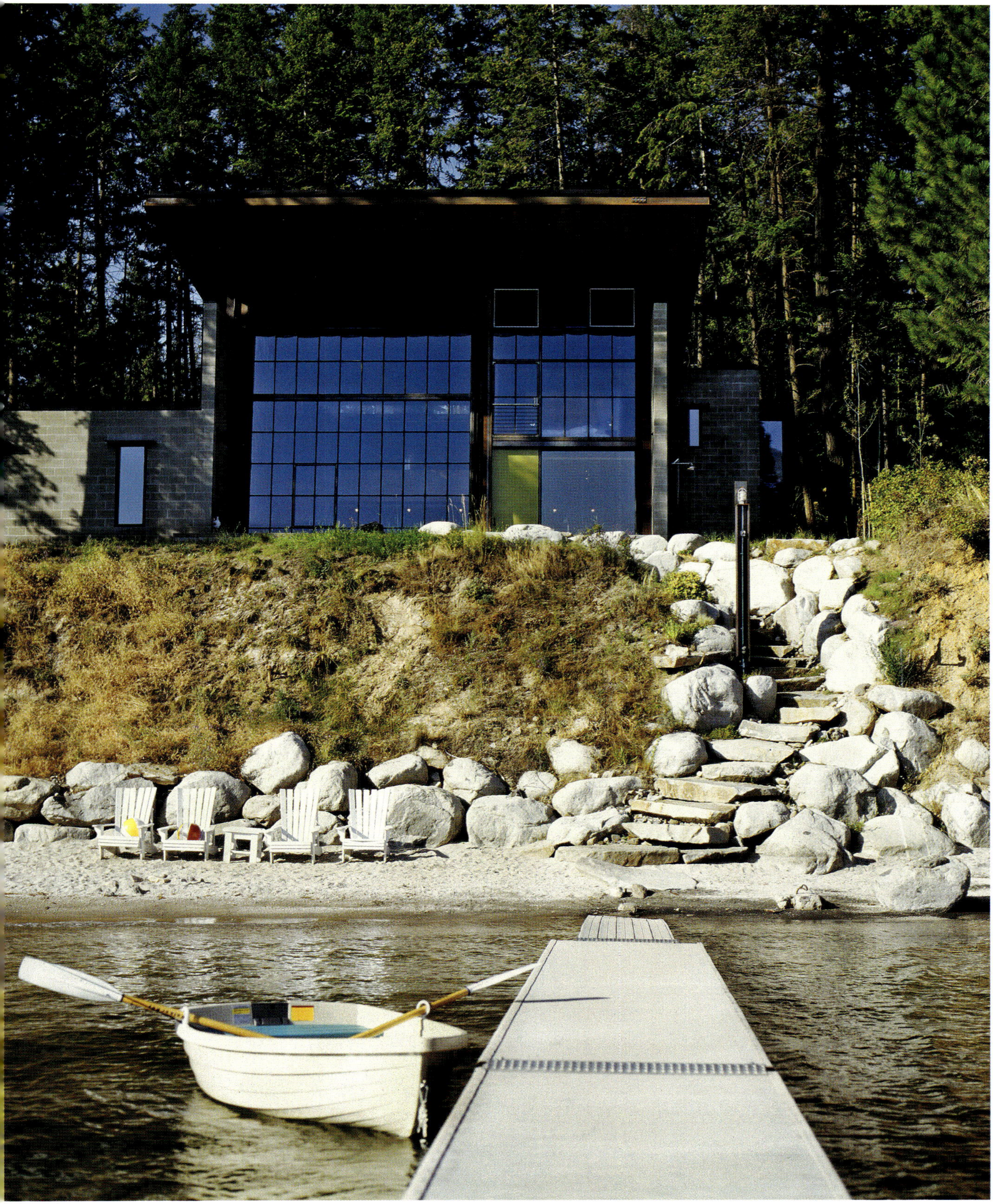

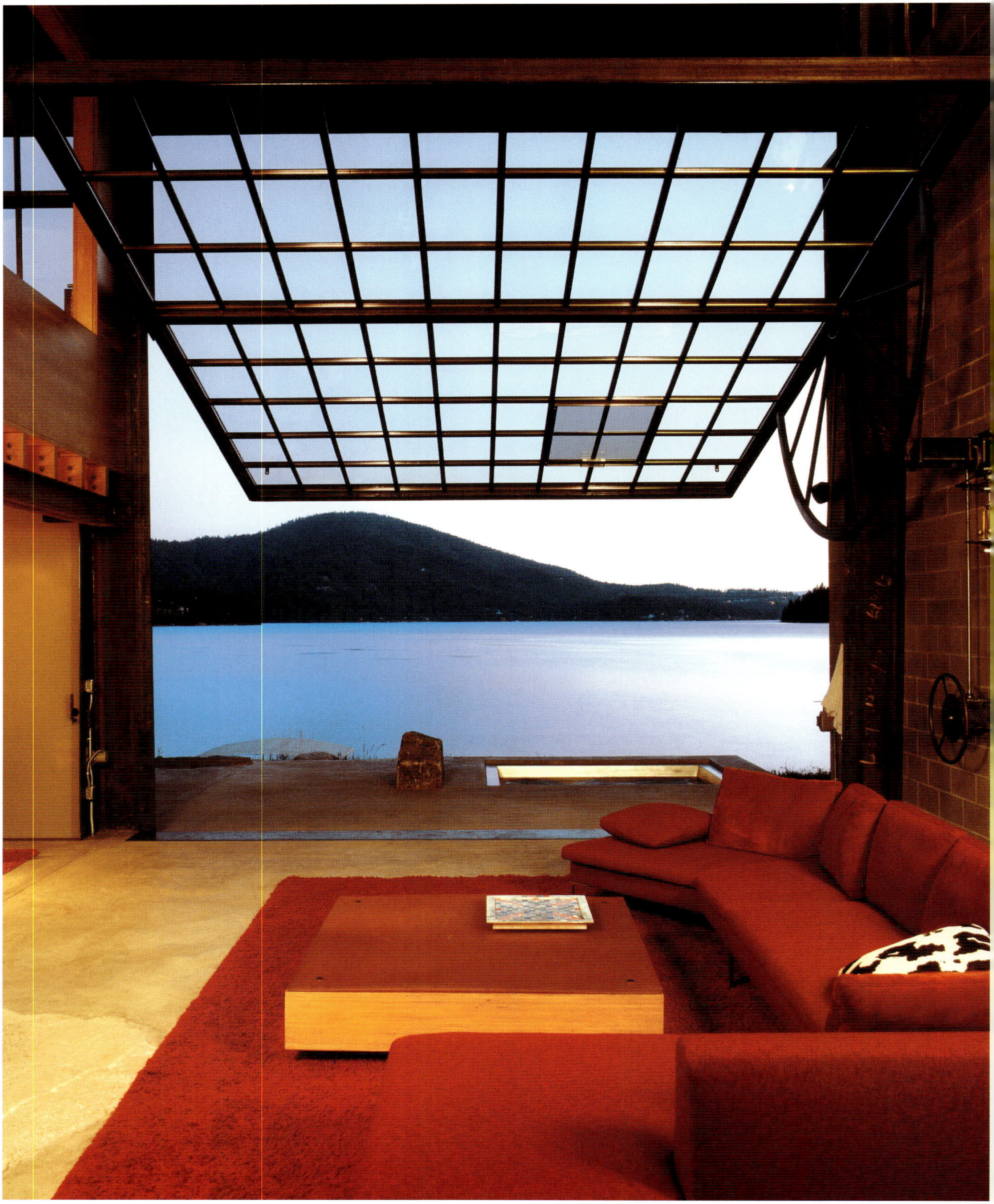

巨大なガラスウォールは雄大な景色をリビングルームに居ながらにして享受することを可能にし、自然の光を部屋の隅々まで届かせ、住人と環境との親密な関係を創造する。ガラスウォールは手動式になっており、小さな子供でも楽に操作できる。

The spectacular scenery can be admired from the living room; the large glass wall allows the light to enter and creates a closer relation with the environment. A manual system allows this wall to be easily opened and closed.

ボート・ドック ミロ・リベラ・アーキテクツ

湖畔の楽しみ　FUN BY THE LAKE

オースチン―テキサス州―アメリカ　撮影：パトリック・ウォン／アトリエ・ウォン

　湖面に浮かんでいるように軽やかで躍動的な構造、これがオースチン湖の岸辺に立つこの個人所有の突堤のコンセプト。自然環境への侵襲を避けるため、鉄の構造物は湖岸の湾曲部に据え、ボートは岸と平行に係留することとした。その結果構造物は、2艘のボートを係留するための突堤としてだけでなく、家族や友人が自然の真ん中で気ままな時間を過ごすことができる自由な空間となった。

The main aim of this private jetty's design in Lake Austin was to achieve a light and dynamic structure that appeared to float on the water. To avoid invading the natural environment the steel structure was placed on a bend in the bank and the moorings were arranged parallel to the water. The final result is a place that not only acts as a jetty with two moorings, but also a place to spend free time with family and friends whilst enjoying the natural environment.

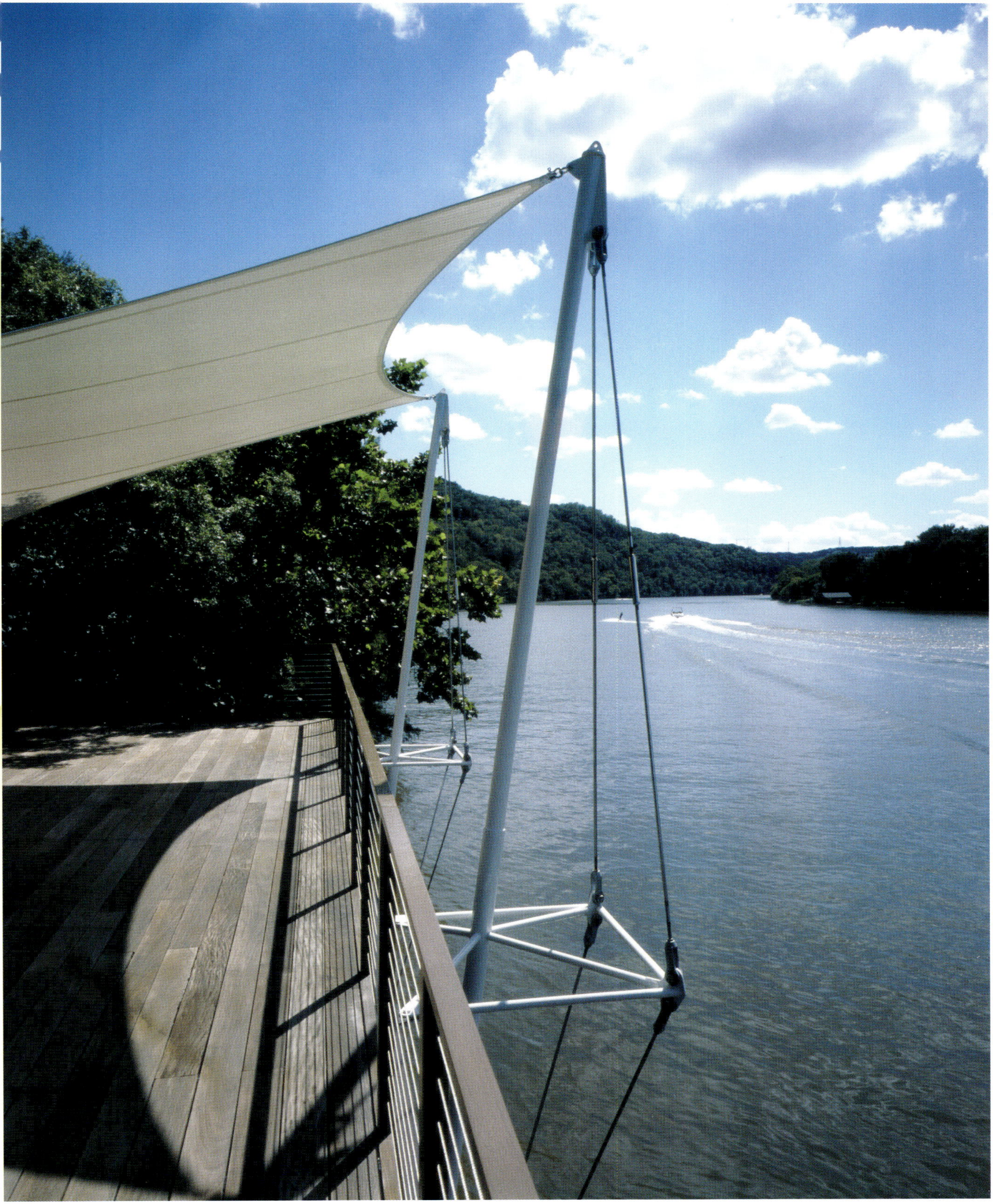

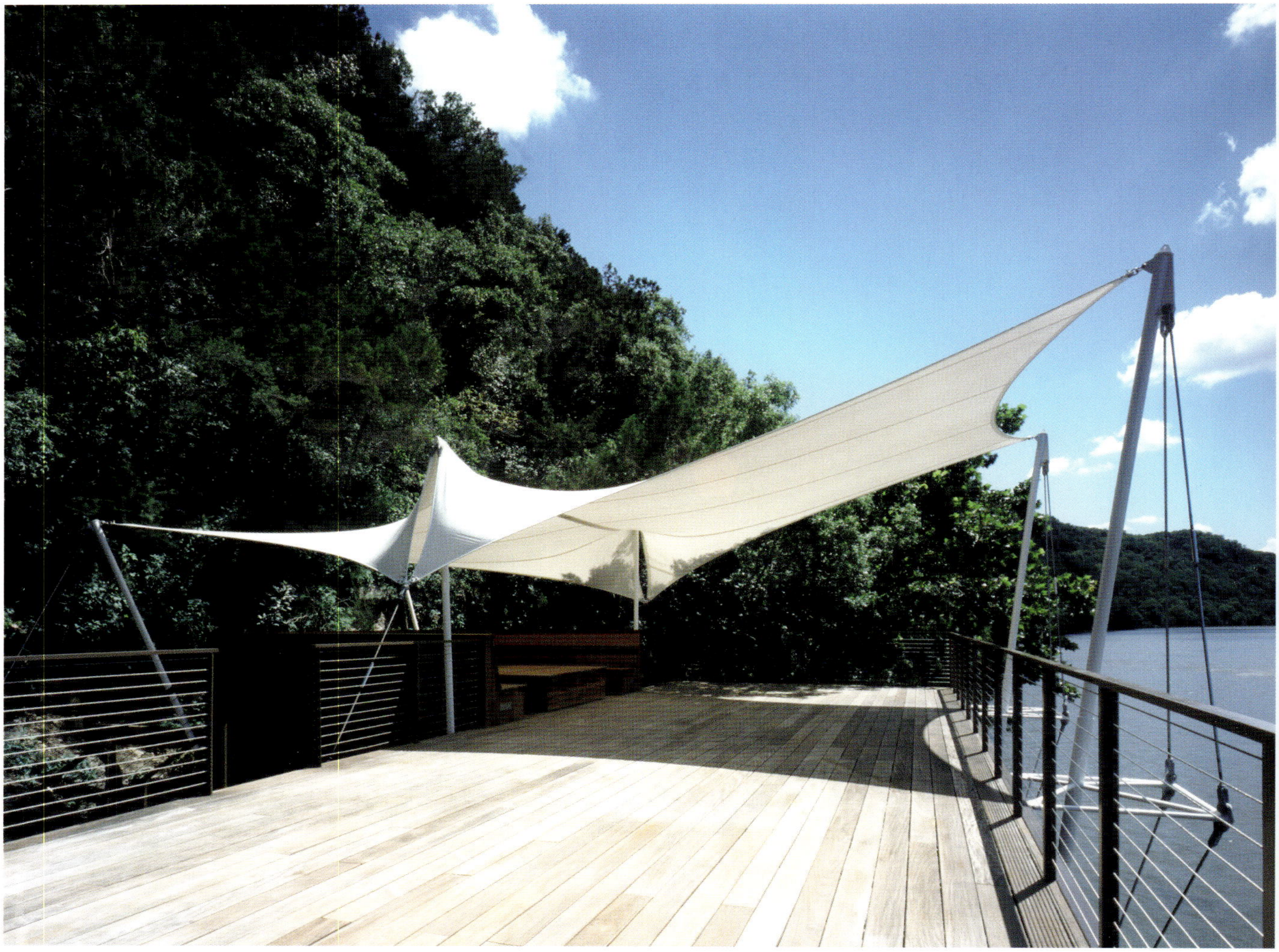
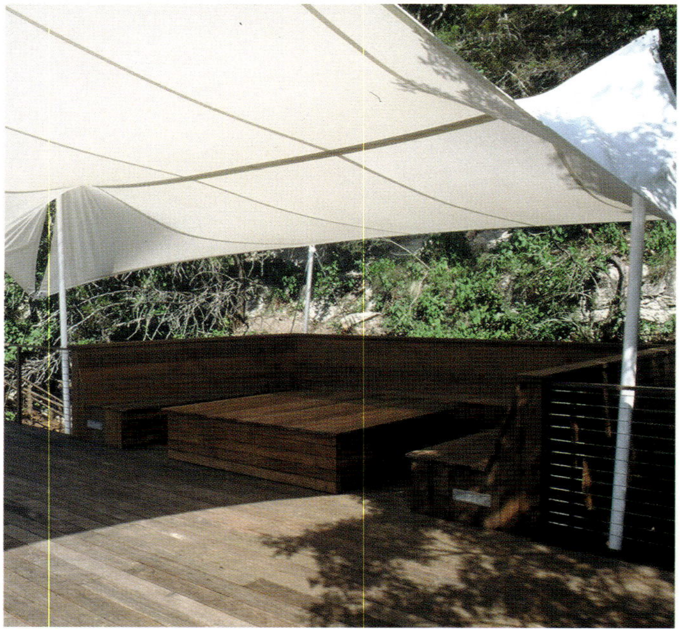
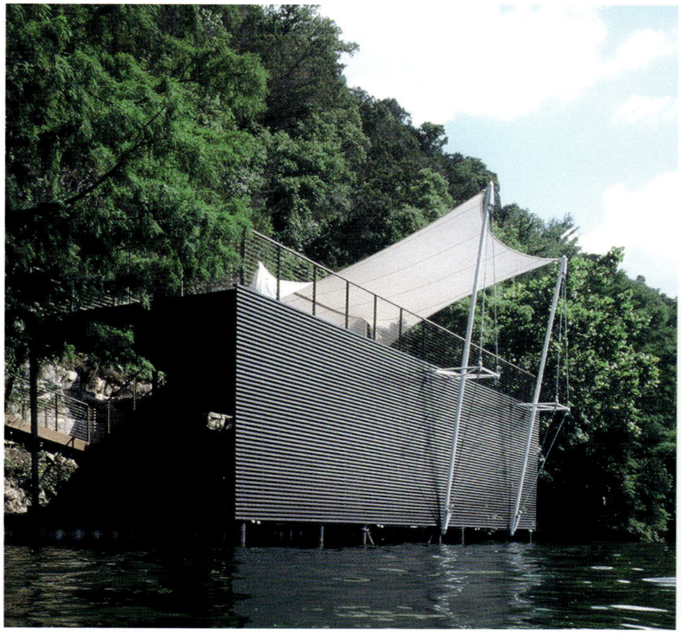

ボートを格納する構造物の上には、防水シートでできた簡易ルーフが白く輝き、存分にくつろぐための心地良い日陰を提供している。突堤から出ている厚板敷きの歩道を登ると、住宅へと続く小道に出る。

Apart from the structure that hides the moorings, the roof provides a space for playing and the tarpaulin roof offers pleasant shade.
A wooden walkway overcomes the changing level up until the path leading to the house.

ゲストハウス ミロ・リベラ・アーキテクツ

潟湖(せきこ)の真ん中で　　IN THE SALT MARSHES

オースチン―テキサス州―アメリカ　撮影：ポール・キンケル／ピストン・デザイン

　ほぼ全周をぐるりと水に囲まれたこのゲストハウスは、小さな半島のこのうえなく美しい風景のなかに立っている。環境に対する影響を最小限にとどめるため、敷地面積をできるだけ抑え、部屋は3つの階に分散することとした。ガラスの構造の中には、寝室とリビングルームが収められ、その外側を自由に開閉できるよろい戸が覆っている。よろい戸を開放した広い窓からは、潟湖の水面とそこに羽根を休める鳥たちの姿が楽しめる。鉄の表皮の構造物のなかには、バスルームと階段が収められている。

Located on a small peninsula, this guest residence is surrounded by scenery of exceptional beauty and almost entirely surrounded by water. To minimize the impact on the environment, the plan of the house has a small surface area and the rooms are spread throughout three floors. A glass structure contains the bedrooms and the living areas. This volume has large windows with views over the water of the salt marshes and the rest of the landscape. In the metal clad structure are the bathrooms and stairs.

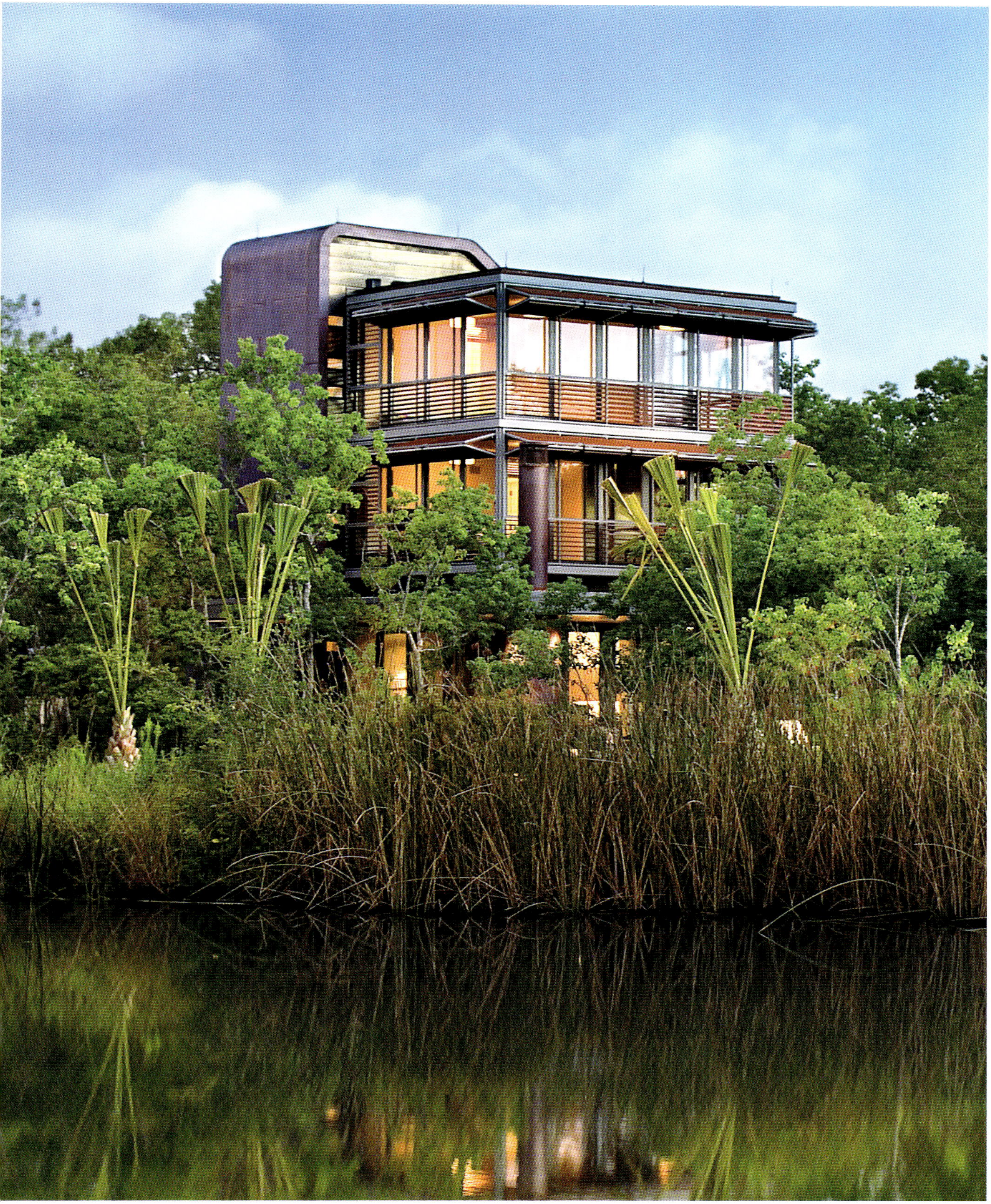

64 | 視覚としての水 | See it

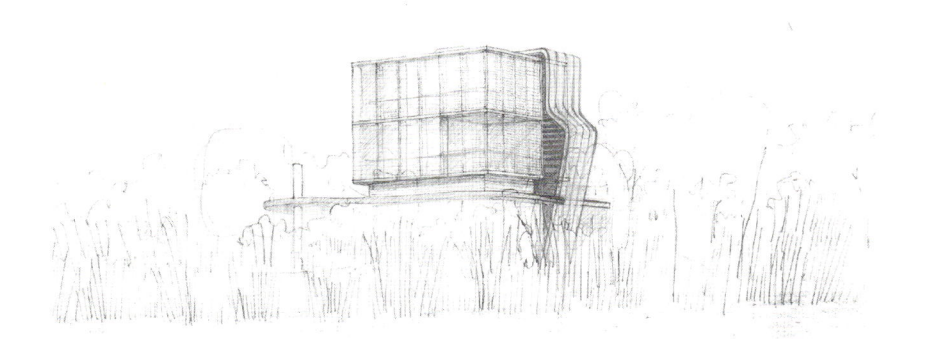

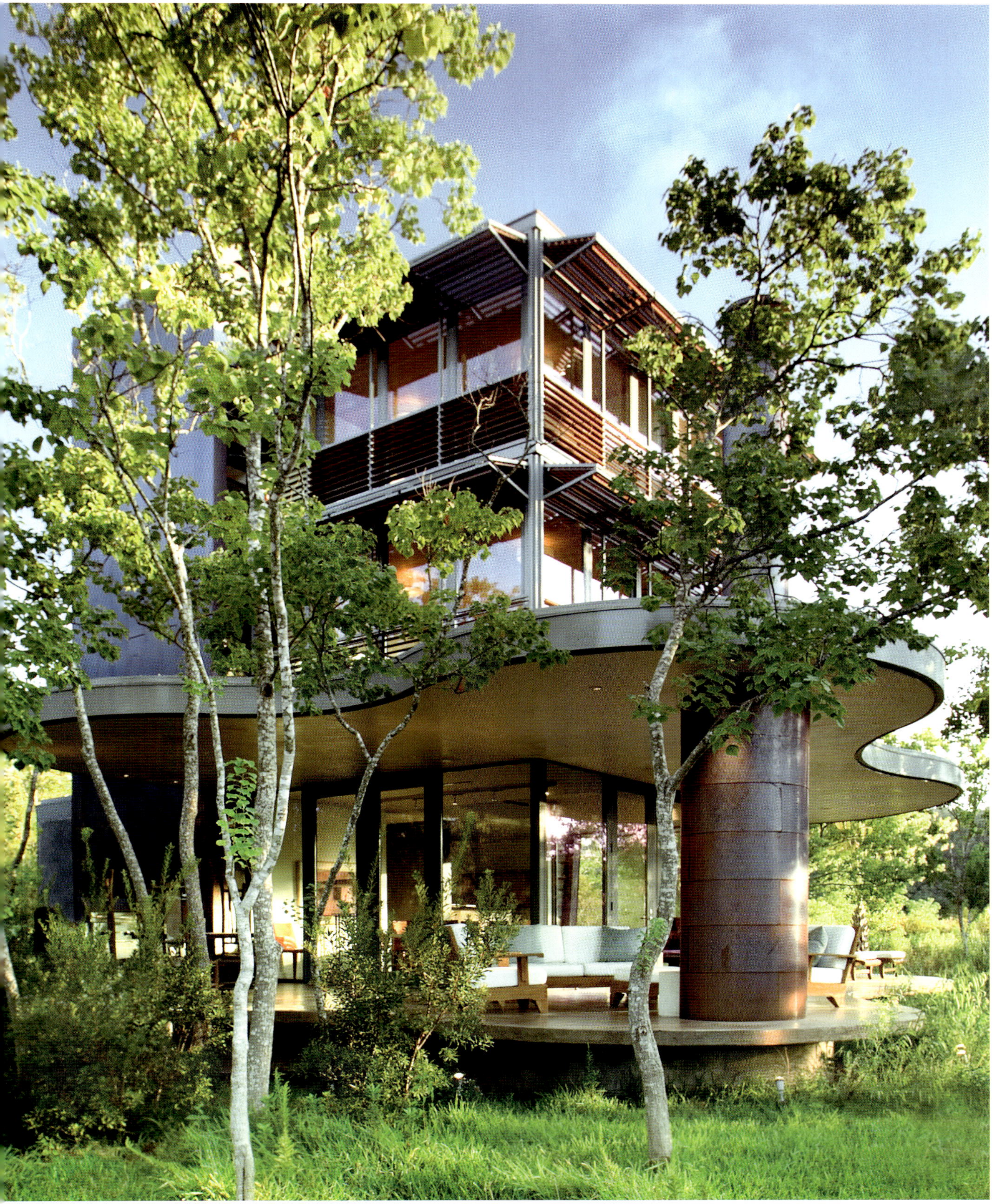

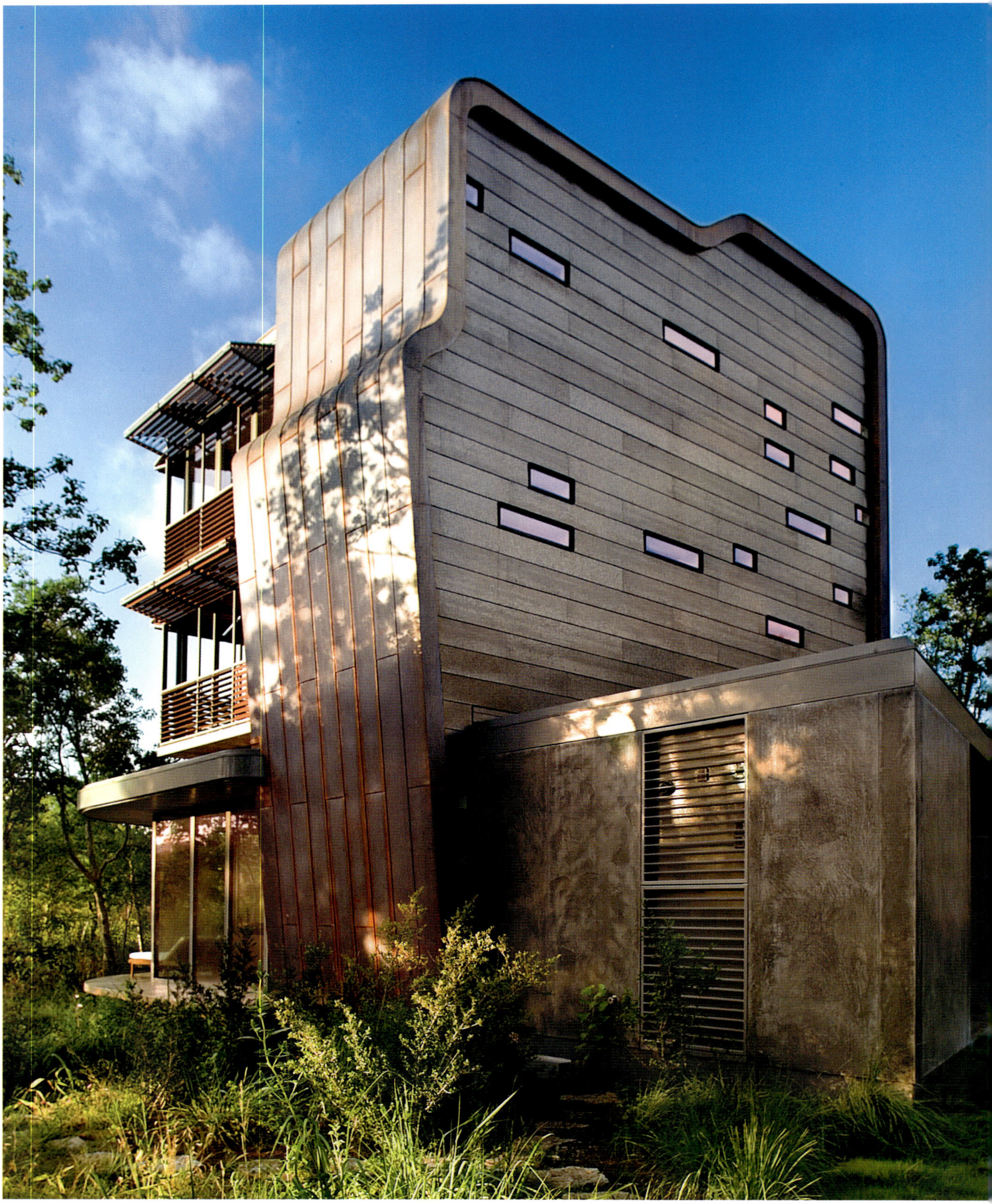

この潟湖は白鳥、ツル、シラサギなどの渡り鳥たちの休息地となっている。この地区の植生を再生させ、建物の影響を最小限に抑えるための研究が今も行われている。

This marshland acts as a rest point for migrating swans, cranes and egrets. An investigation has been made to recover the local vegetation and minimize the architecture's impact on this space.

ザ・スフィンクス ノイトリング・リーダイク・アーキテクツ

湖辺の静けさ　CALM BY THE LAKE

ホイゼン—オランダ　撮影：ジェローン・ムッシュ

　湖を見張っている5頭のスフィンクスの姿が、鏡のような湖面に写っている。周囲を水で囲まれたこれらのアパート群には、歩道とそれよりも一段低い車道からなる橋を通って進入する。南面のテラスは日照を最大限享受し、北面の大きな窓からは1日中光が差し込む。このような場所にアパート群を建てるという発想はまったく独創的だ。さざなみひとつない湖面が、静けさにみちた平穏な環境を創造している。

The five sphinxes look towards the water of the lake, where they are reflected as if in a mirror. These apartment buildings surrounded by water have a pedestrian point of access via the walkways over the water and via accesses for cars situated on a lower level. The south facing terraces maximize the sunlight and the large windows of the opposite façade provide light throughout the whole day. The location of the sphinxes is truly original and the stillness of the water creates a tranquil environment full of calm.

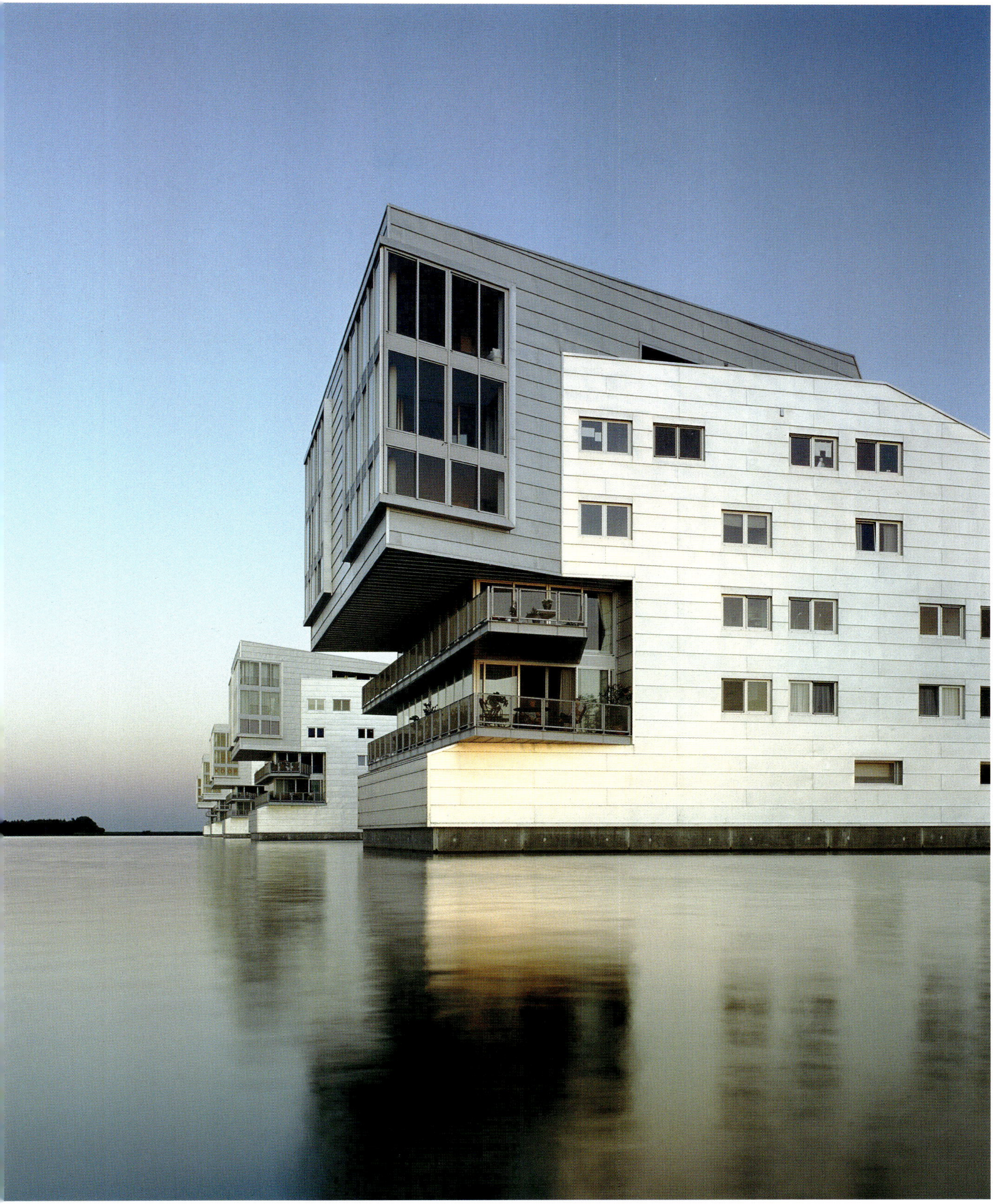

70 | 視覚としての水 | See it

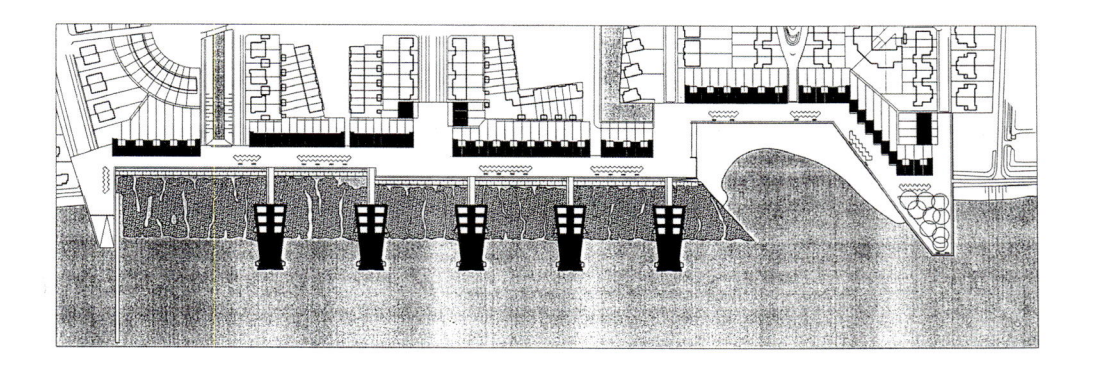

スフィンクスの構造は一部湖の浅瀬に立っている。石と葦が湖水を濾過し、湖岸と建物の間の移行をなだらかなものにしている。

The structure of the sphinxes is partially stood on a shallow area of water. Stones and reeds help to filter the water and soften the transition between the bank and buildings.

建物は14戸からなっているが、日照を最大限取り入れるため各住居の間取りはどれも違っている。高くなるにつれて各階の戸数を減らし、それによって独特のスフィンクス型形状が生まれた。

Each building contains 14 apartments, organized differently to take full advantage of the sunlight. There are fewer apartments as the building rises, which creates the characteristic sphinx shape.

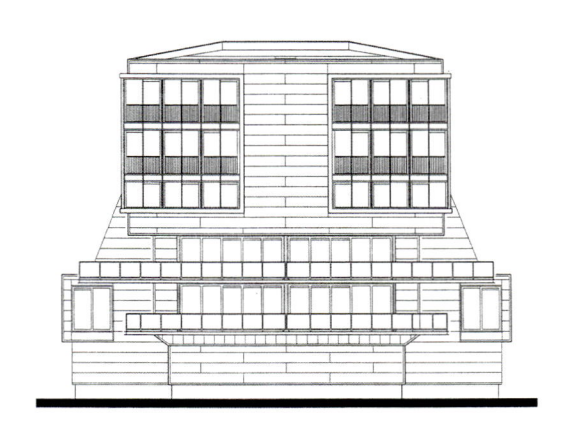

ザ・スフィンクス | 73

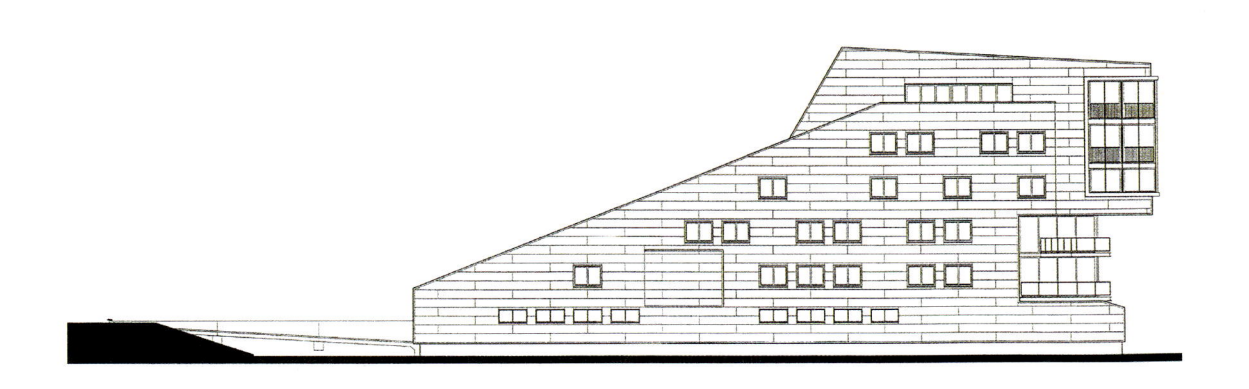

桟橋の家 オニキス

水上の幾何学　GEOMETRY ON THE WATER

ホーヘフェーン―オランダ　撮影：ペーター・ド・カン

　この町を縦横に流れる無数の運河、その1つの運河の周辺地区再開発でこの14戸の住宅は建てられた。ここでは住宅と水は濃密な関係を結んでいる。住宅は共同中庭を取り囲む形で建てられているが、そのうちの何戸かは運河に張り出した水上階段や、水上テラスで水と戯れている。住宅は北側正面で水と接しているが、住宅を被う木の表皮と水とのコントラストは鮮烈で、視覚的な感動を呼び起こす。

The restructuring of an area of the city required the construction of fourteen houses, situated next to one of the town's numerous canals. The interaction of the residential estate with the water is a strong one. Although the houses have been located around a communal courtyard, some of the houses have stairs over the water or small terraces that end in the canal. The north façade faces the water, which together with the wooden cladding of the volumes creates a strong contrast and an impressive visual effect.

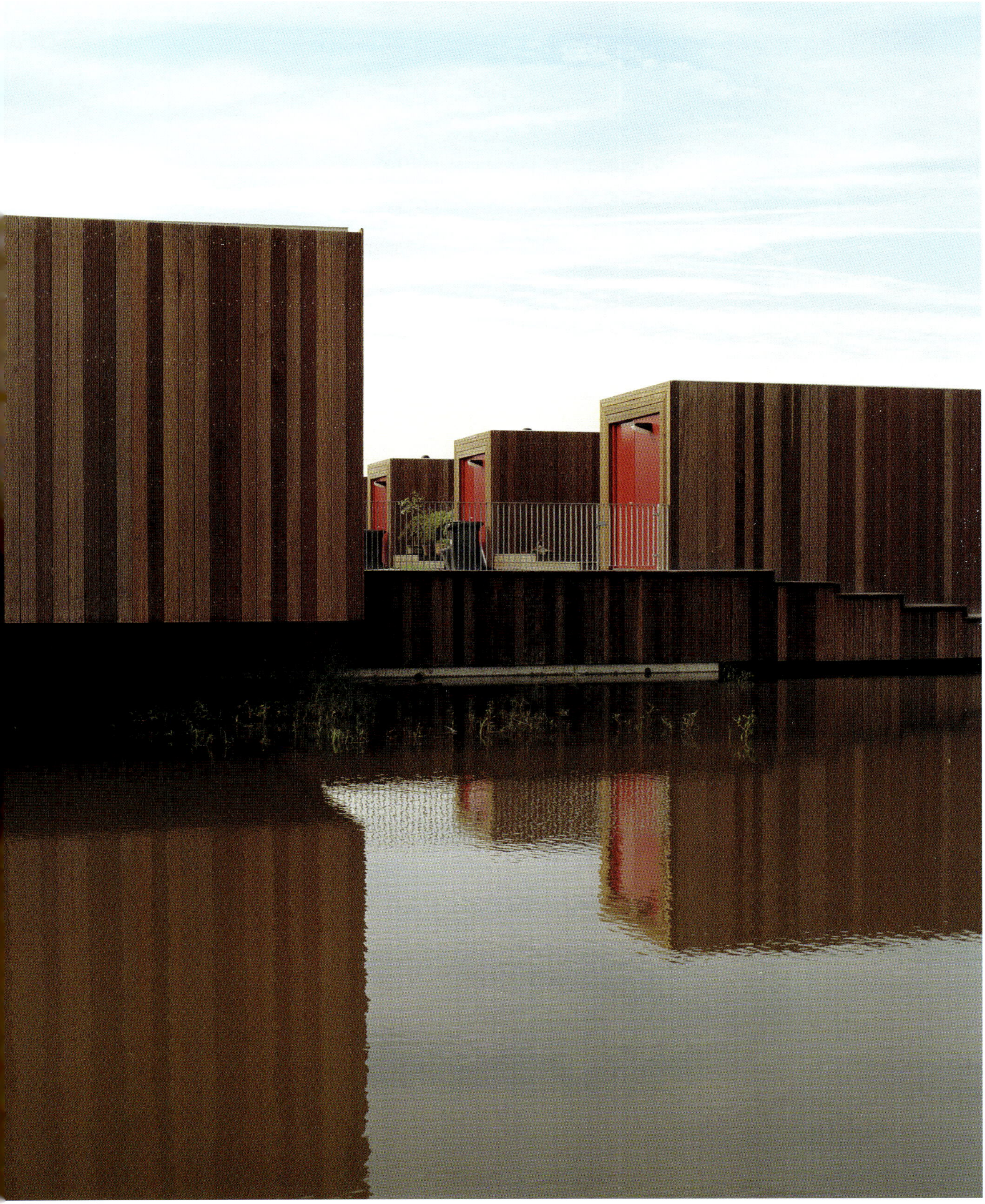

| 76 | 視覚としての水 | See it

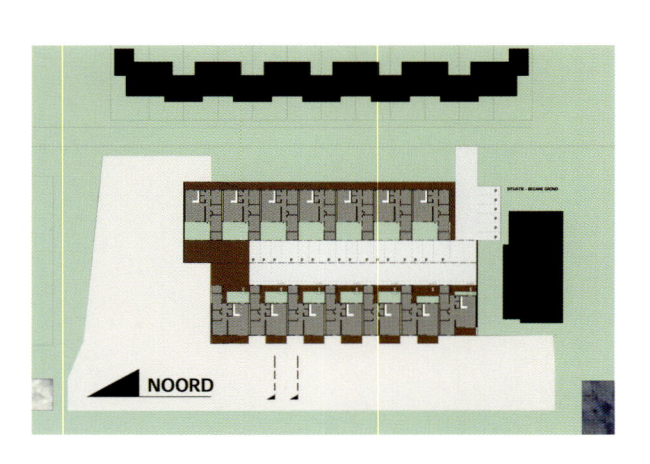

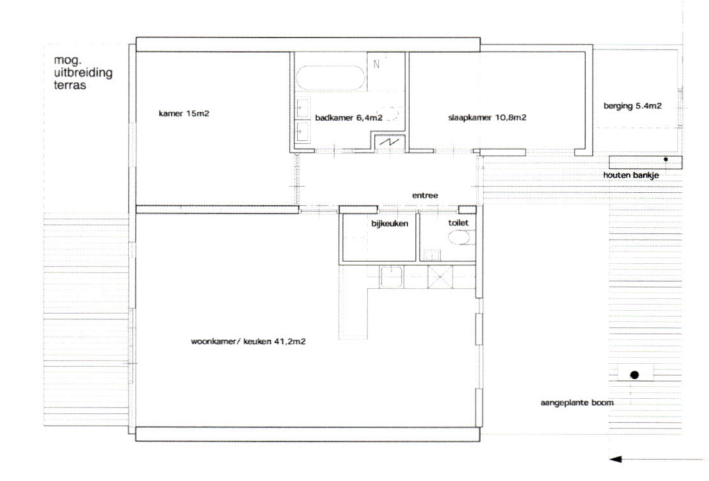

共有内部空間には集会場と共同中庭があり、そこからは各戸の玄関や裏庭へ続く入り口、屋根付駐車場、そして静かに水をたたえた運河が眺められる。

The public interior area is a mix of communal zone and courtyard. The accesses to the houses and their backyards, a covered parking and a view of the tranquil waters of the canals can be found here.

缶詰工場ロフト ターナーヘクト・アーキテクチュア

運河沿いのロフト　CANALSIDE LOFTS

ニューポートビーチ―カリフォルニア州―アメリカ
撮影：デイビッド・ヘクト, ブランダン・ダニガン, トビー・ポネイ

　ニューポートビーチのなかでも指折りの魅力的な地区であるライネ運河沿いにこの22戸の集合住宅は位置している。溢れんばかりの光と空気を浴びているロフトからは、運河の眺めが手にとるように楽しめ、ボートもすぐ乗れるように目の前に係留されている。プロジェクトのコンセプトは、エネルギーの充満した躍動的な飛び地、インディペンデント系の若い活動家が働き生活するロフトのある、歩行者天国の商業ゾーンというものであった。完成されたロフトは、現代的な建築を古くからある建築といかに融合させるかという課題を難なく乗り越えている。

This group of 22 houses is situated next to the Rhine canal, one of the most attractive places in Newport Beach. These lofts receive ample light and air, with good views and access to the canal. The aim of the project was to create a dynamic, active enclave, a pedestrian commercial zone with lofts where independent professionals could live or work. The result shows how modern day constructions can be perfectly adapted to already established neighborhoods.

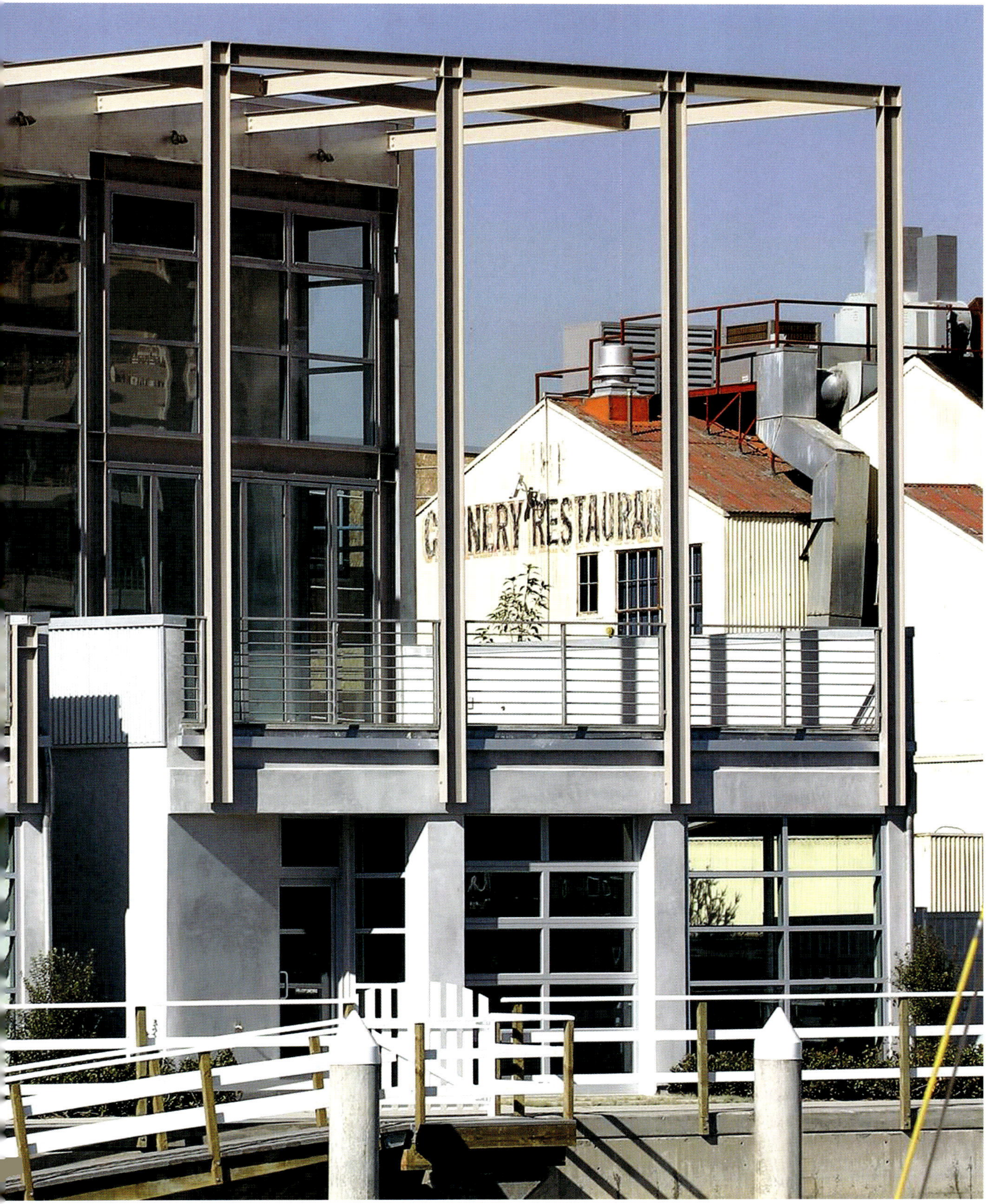
C NERY RESTAURAN

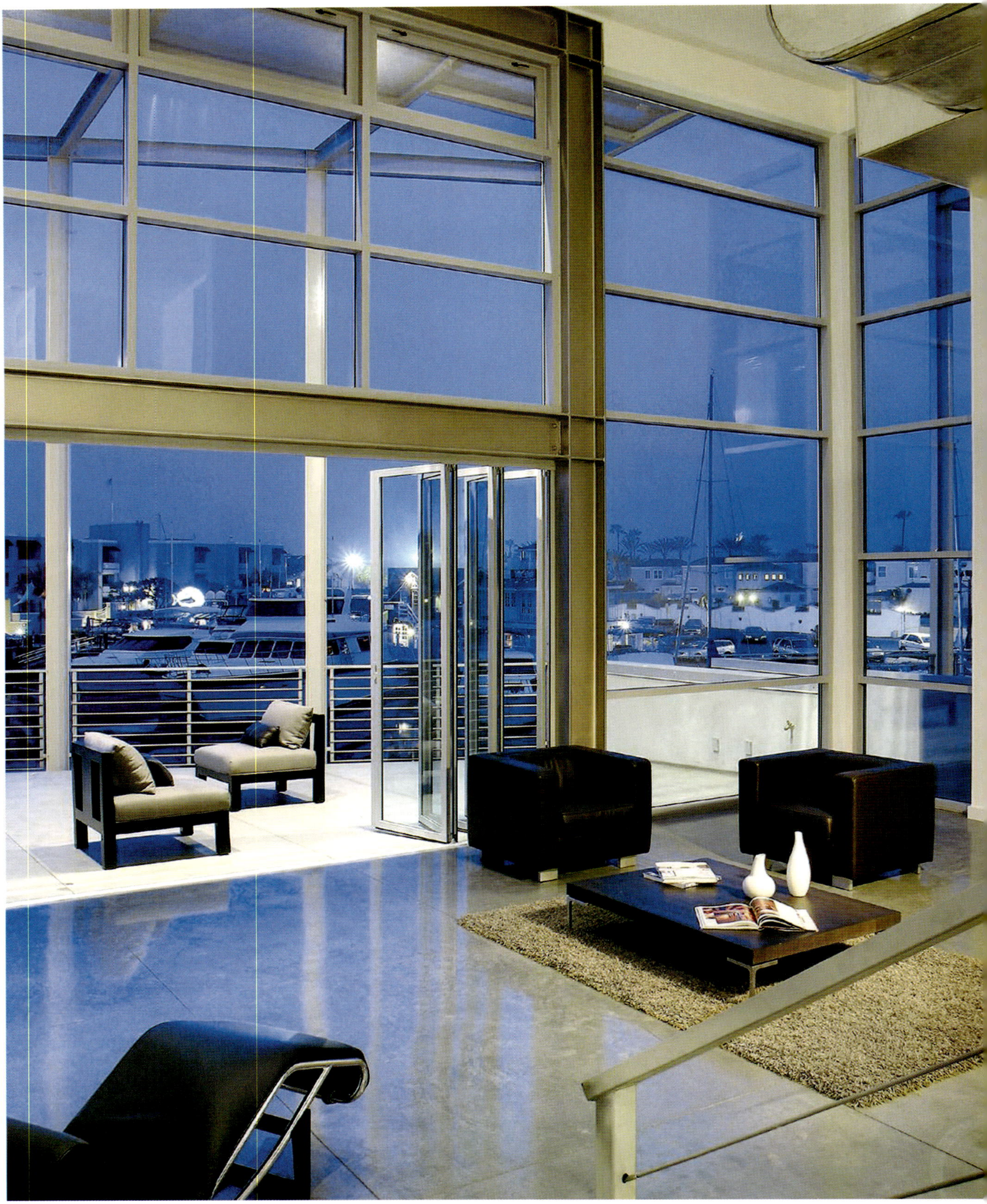

潤沢な光が大きな窓とガラスウォールから入り込んでいる。運河に錨泊しているボートやヨットがリビングルームやテラスから見え、それを眺める者も水上にいるようなゆったりとした気分になる。

The large windows and the glass walls allow abundant light to enter the apartments. The boats and yachts anchored in the canal can be seen from the inside of the living rooms and the terraces.

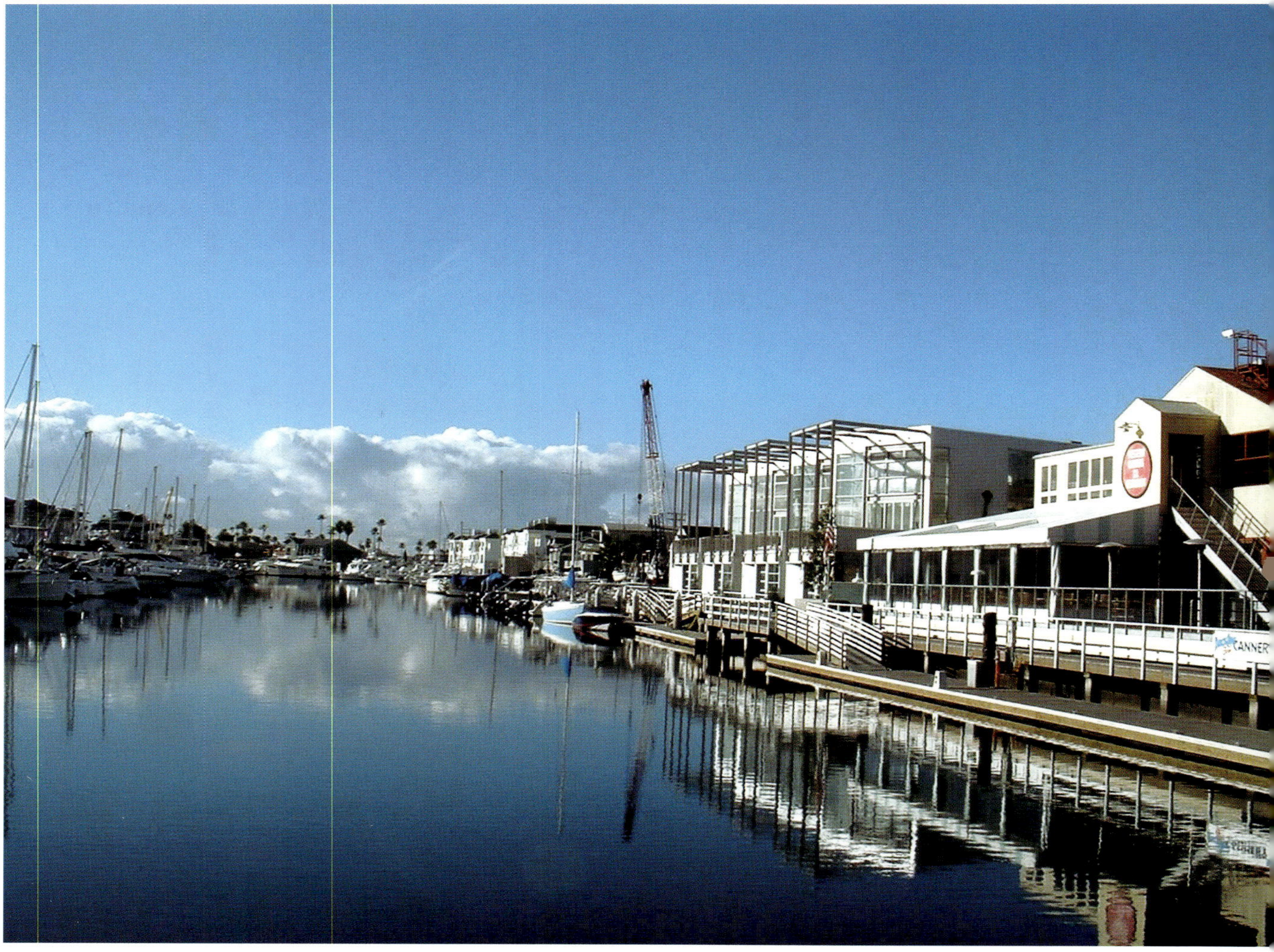

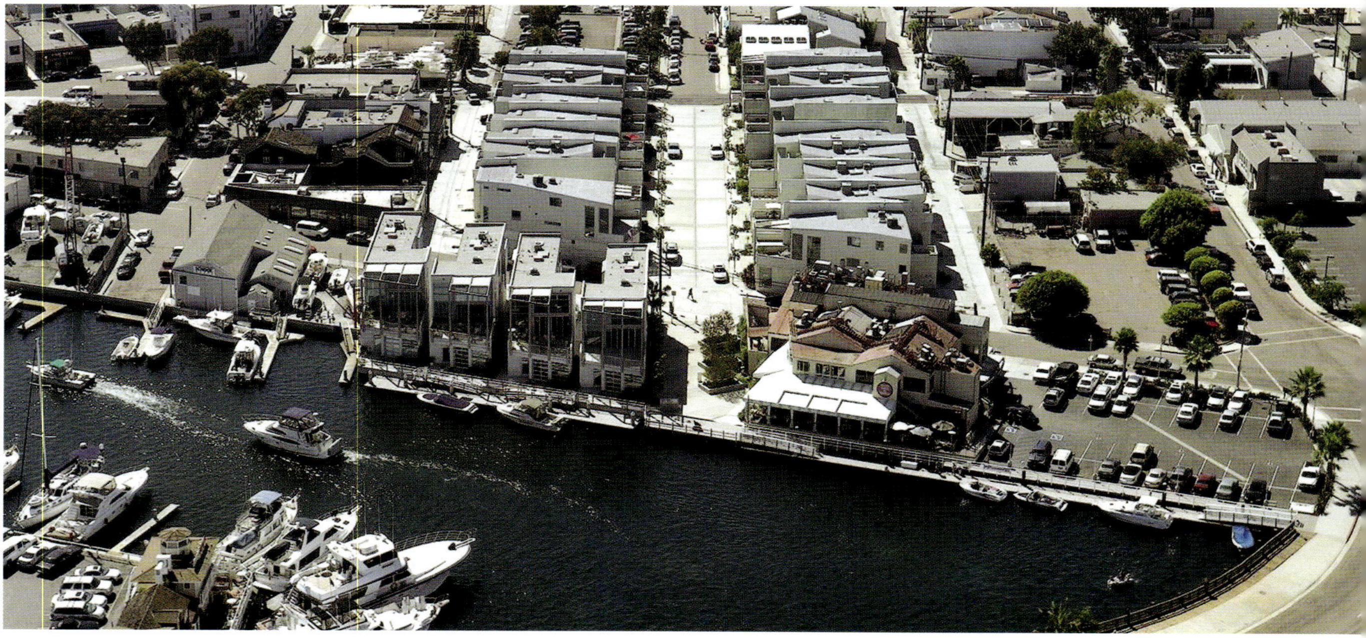

缶詰工場ロフト | 83

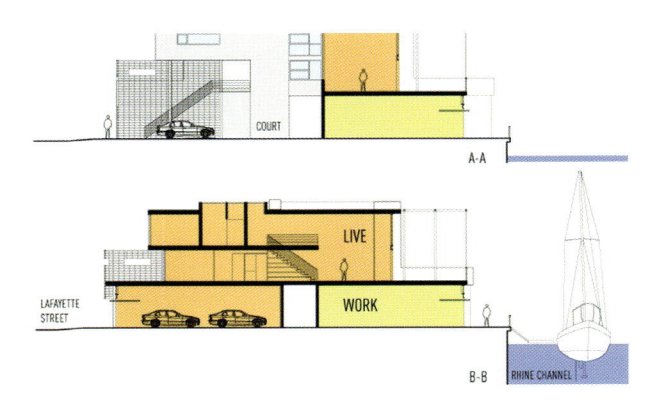

X氏邸 バークレイ & クラウス・アーキテクチュア
空と海との間に　BETWEEN THE SKY AND SEA

カニェーテ—ペルー　撮影：バークレイ & クラウス

　ペルー太平洋岸に位置するこの住宅は自然との統合をめざして建てられた。外壁の黄土色(オークル)が風景と住宅を融け合わせ、構造が生みだすヴォリュームと空隙の絶妙なバランスが空と海の関係を深めている。砂浜の延長として構想されたテラスと大きな透明のプールは、海に向かって開かれ水平線に溶解している。可動式のリビングルームのパネルと屋根を開くと、広々としたテラスが出現する。

Situated on the Peruvian coastline, this residence was designed to integrate with its surroundings. The ochre of the façades integrates the house with the scenery.
The volumes and empty areas that the structure creates allow the spaces to be arranged to increase the relationship between the sky and the ocean. Conceived as an extension of the beach, the terrace and a large transparent swimming pool open to the sea and fuse with the horizon. The living room's movable panels and roof open to form a large terrace.

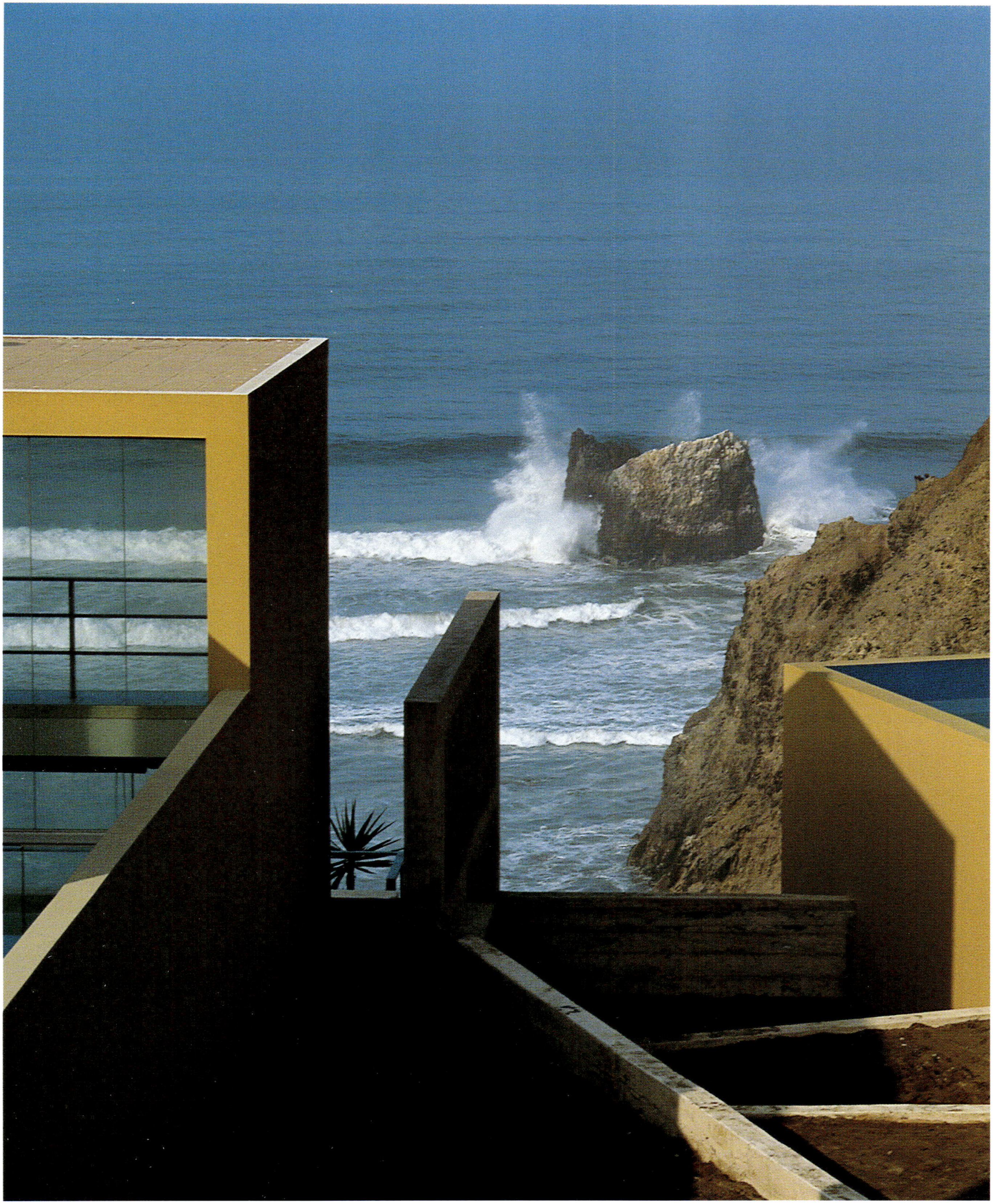

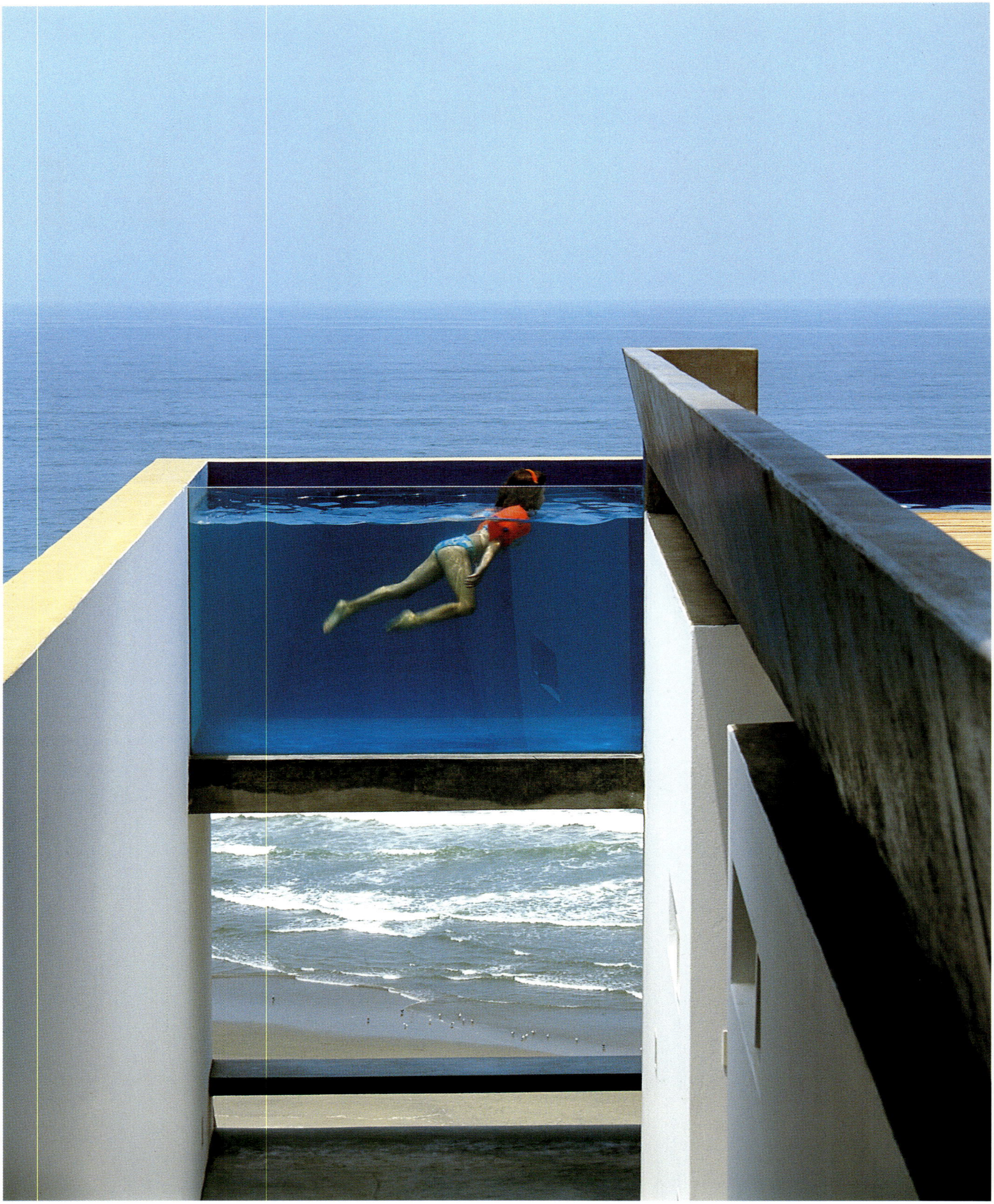

テラスの甲板は擬似砂浜であり、プールの縁は太平洋へと融けだしている。水平線を取り込んだすっきりとした直線ばかりで構成されたデザインが、調和のとれた安定感のある雰囲気を作り出している。その秩序を乱すのは太平洋の波だけだ。

On the terrace the wooden planks simulate sand and the limits of the pool merge with the ocean. This display of straight, clean lines creates a balanced atmosphere broken only by the force of the ocean waves.

ヴィラ＋ ハイメ・サナウーハ・アソシアードス

海辺の展望台　*A LOOKOUT BY THE SEA*

オロペサ―カステヨン―スペイン　撮影：ホセ・ルイス・オスマン

　海岸沿いの白い邸宅、そのプールの端にあるこの小さなあずまやはリラクゼーションと休息の場。構造は住居と屋外空間の様式を踏襲し、厚板の屋根が直射日光を防ぎ、白いカーテンが風を和らげてくれる。同じように白いクッションが、眩しすぎる陽光を避けながら地中海を眺めることのできる、可愛らしい小さなくつろぎの空間を創りだしている。

This small kiosk situated at the end of a coastal residence swimming pool is a space used for relaxation and rest. The structure follows the same style as the architecture of the house and outdoor spaces. The roof is formed by wooden planks and provides protection from the sun. The white curtains act as a windbreak and the cushions, also white, create a small and delicate chill-out area protected from the sun's rays and with views of the Mediterranean.

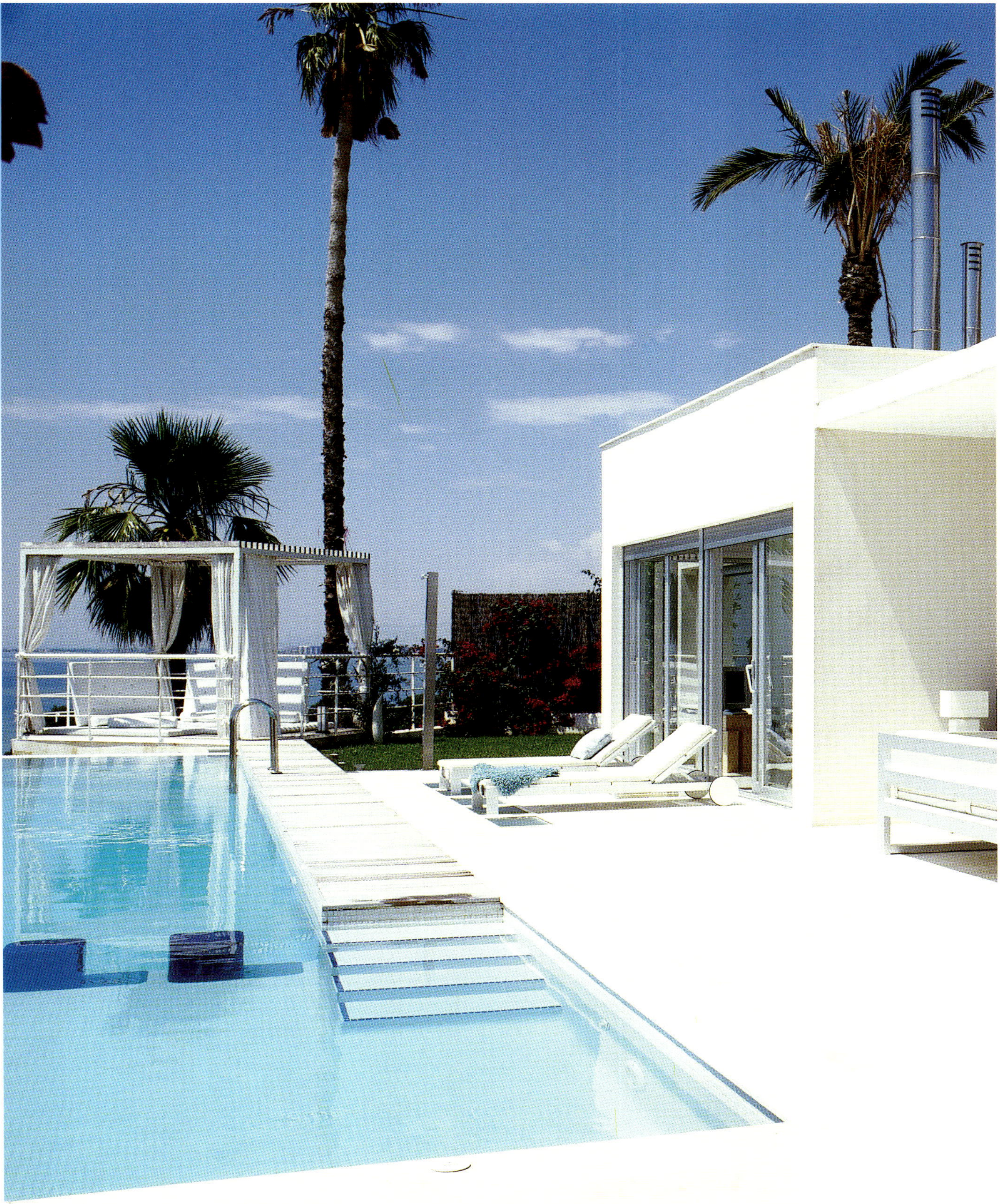

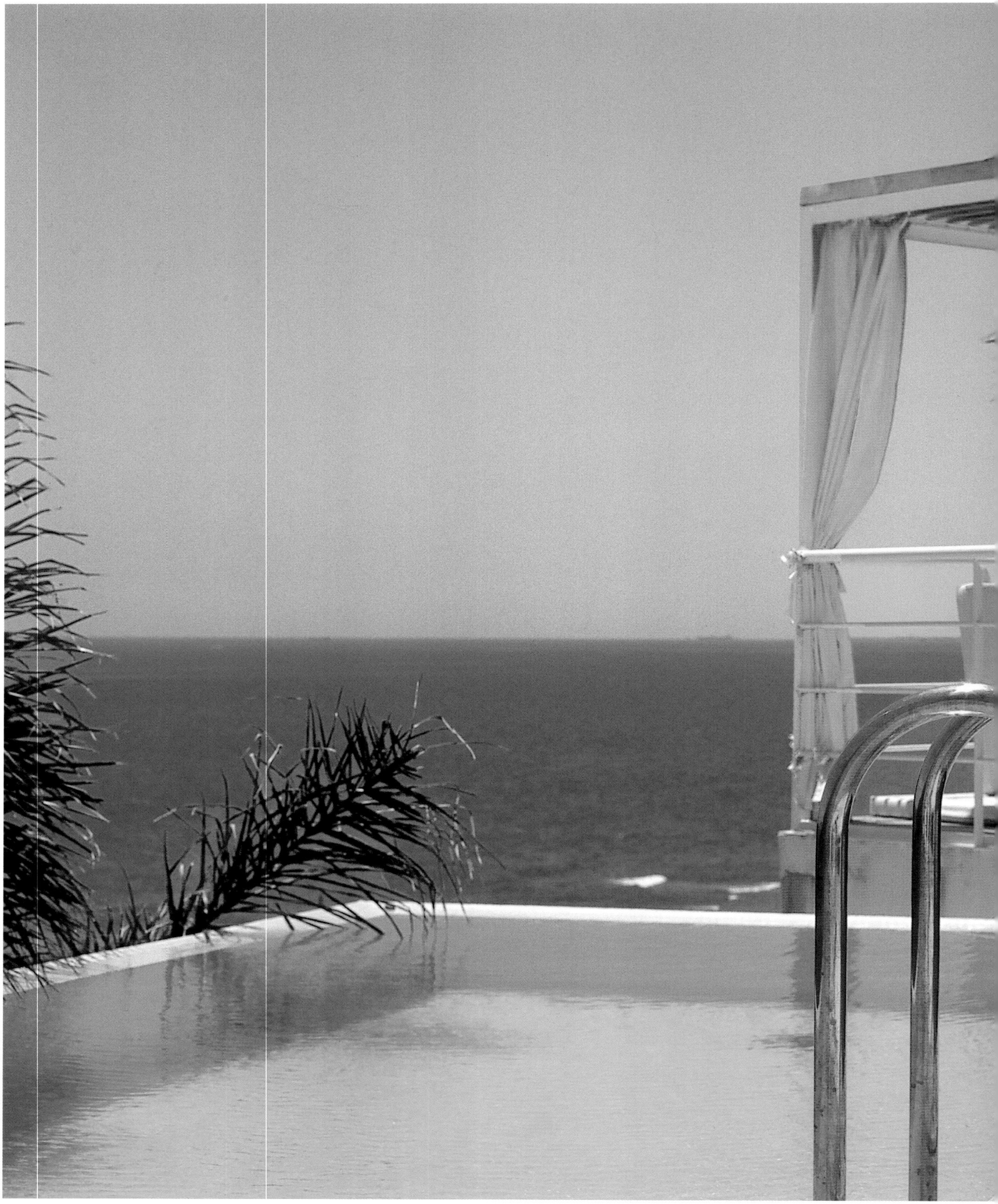

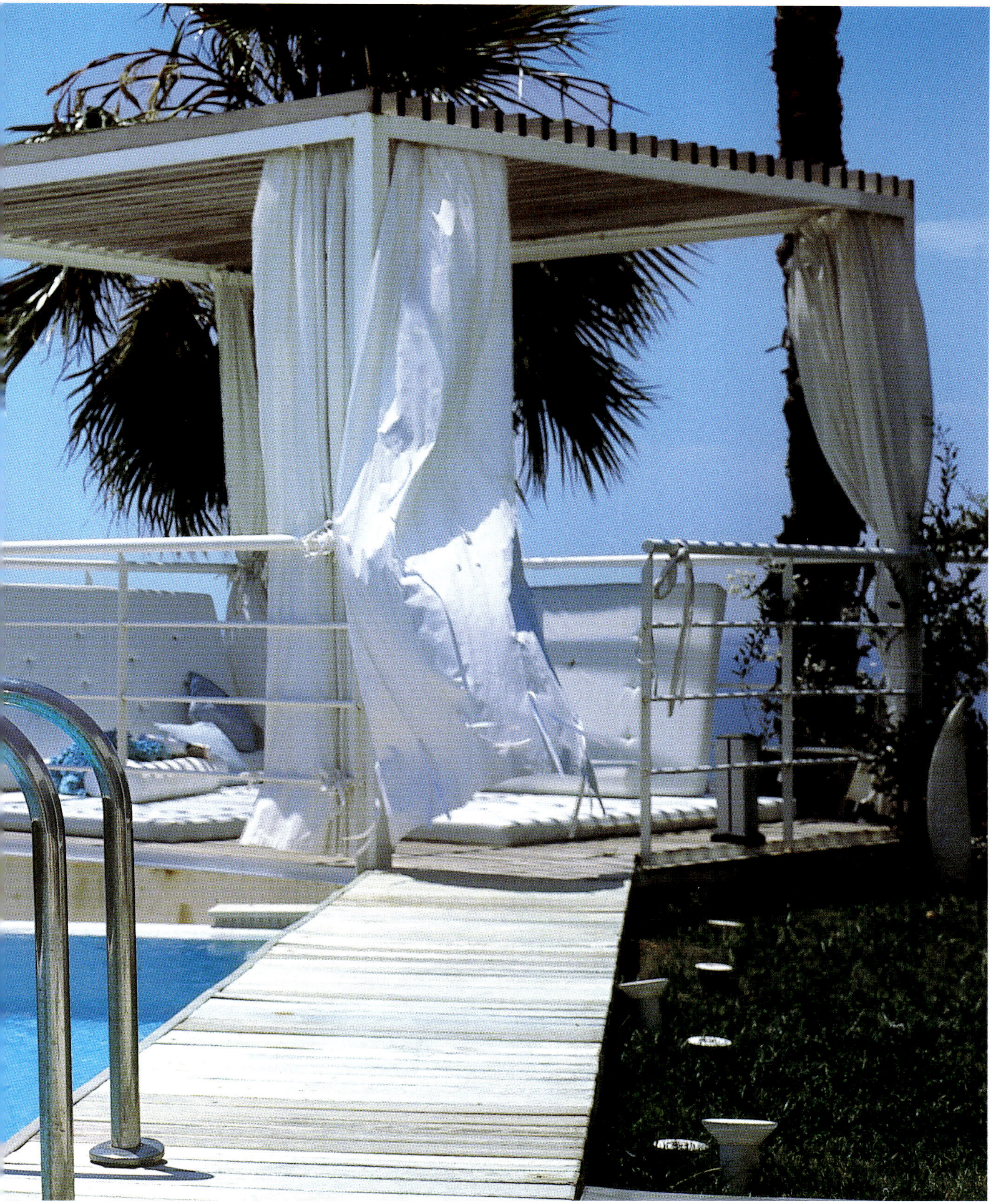

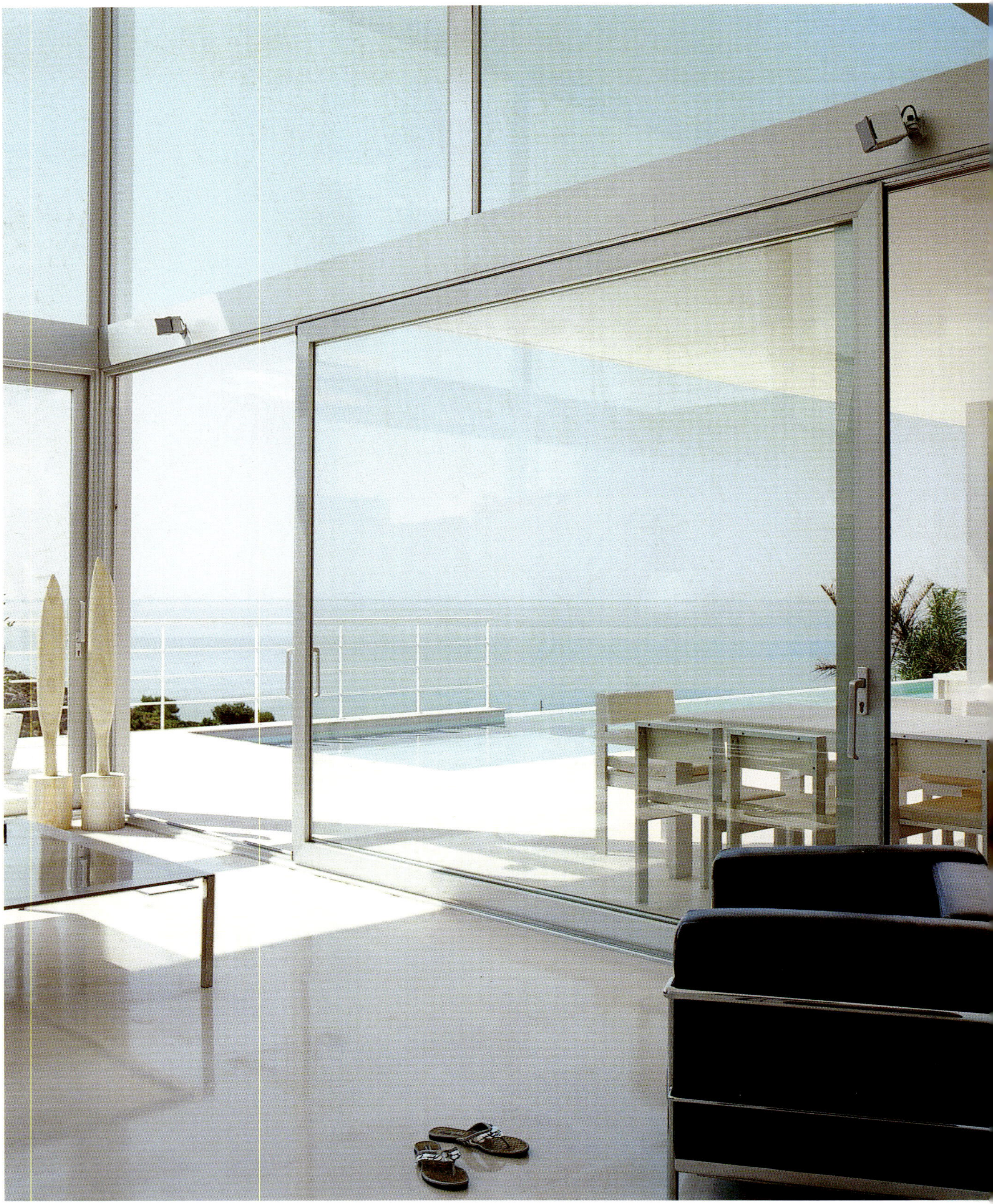

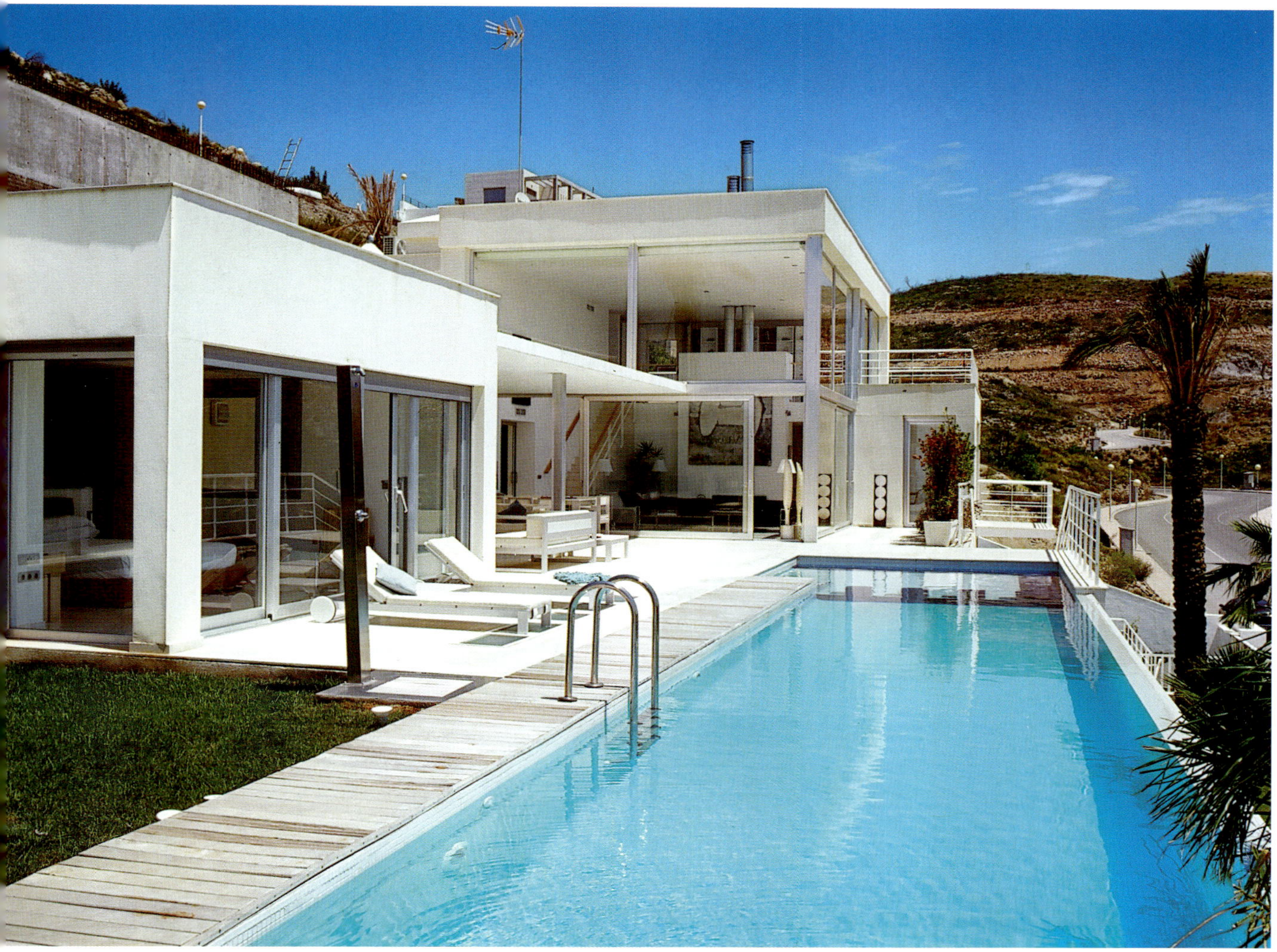

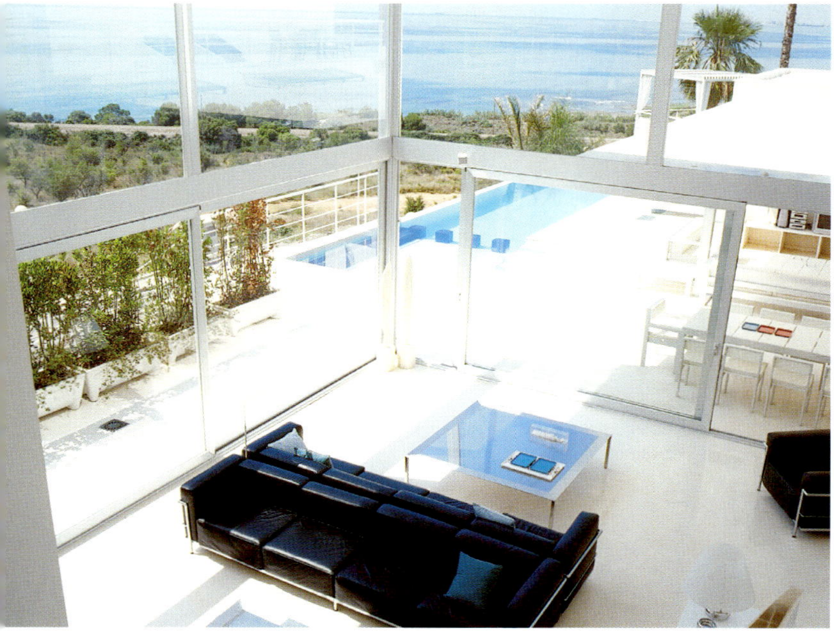

クロナキルティーの家 ナイアル・マクラフリン・アーキテクツ
光をつかまえて　CAPTURING THE LIGHT

クロナキルティー―コーク―アイルランド　撮影：ニック・ケイン

　古い別荘の修復にあたっては、地質調査だけでなく、日照時間の調査も行われた。日照を最大限捕捉するため、住宅の方向性に特別の注意が払われ、窓は最大限に拡張された。結果、独特の美しいフォルムができあがった。住宅は岩盤の上、潮の干満の影響を受けない場所に立てられている。どこにいても海を望むことができるが、空間の配置は水平線への旅というコンセプトで決められている。増築によってアイルランドの厳しい気候から保護された中庭が作られた。

The restoration of this old cottage was done after studying the land and the hours of sunlight. In order to maximize the light, special attention was paid to the orientation of the house and large windows were put in place, which give impressive results. It was built in a rocky area where it would not be affected by the tide. The ocean can be discovered through the house, and the layout of the spaces has been designed as a journey towards the horizon. The extension created a courtyard, which is protected from the harsh climate.

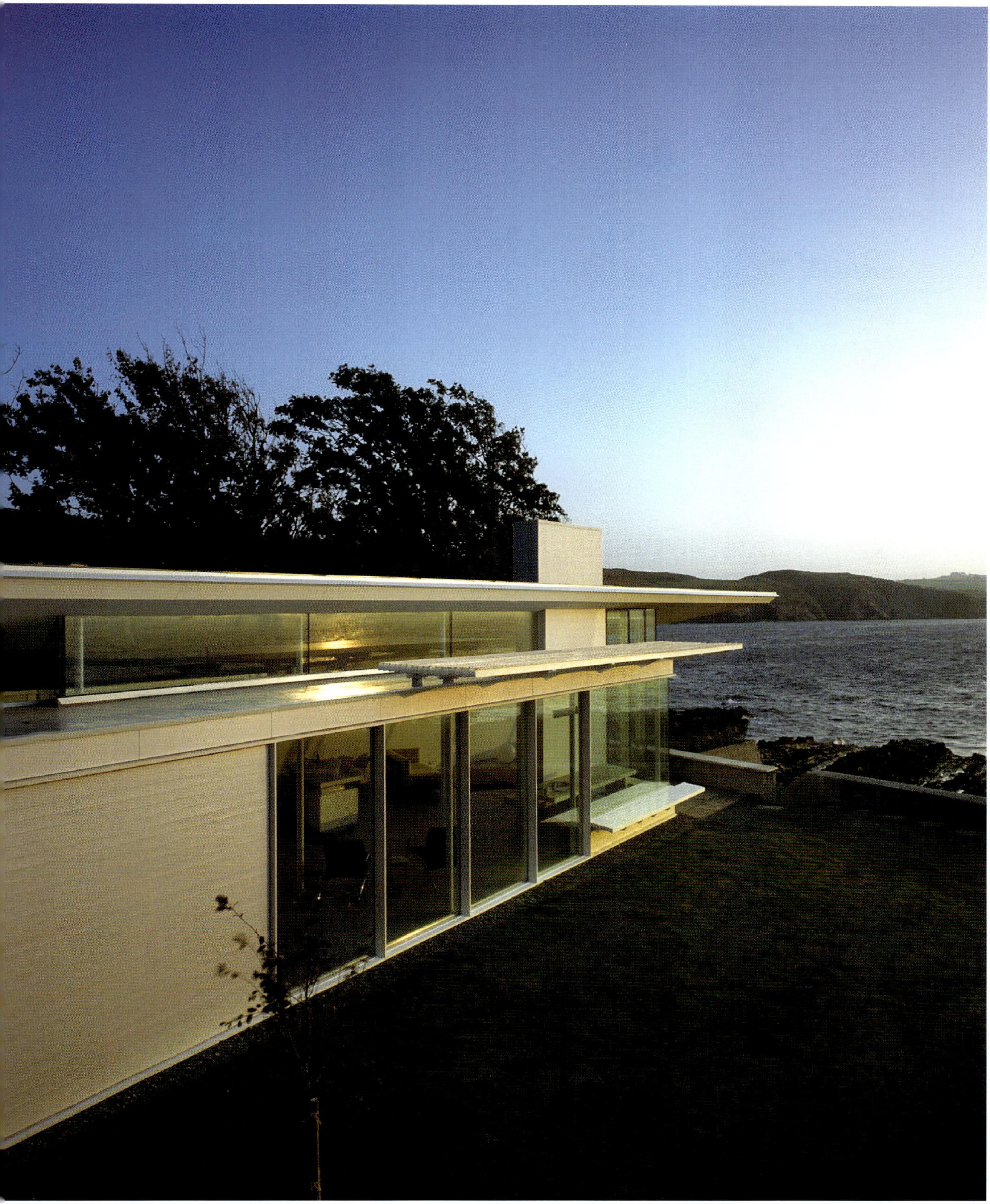

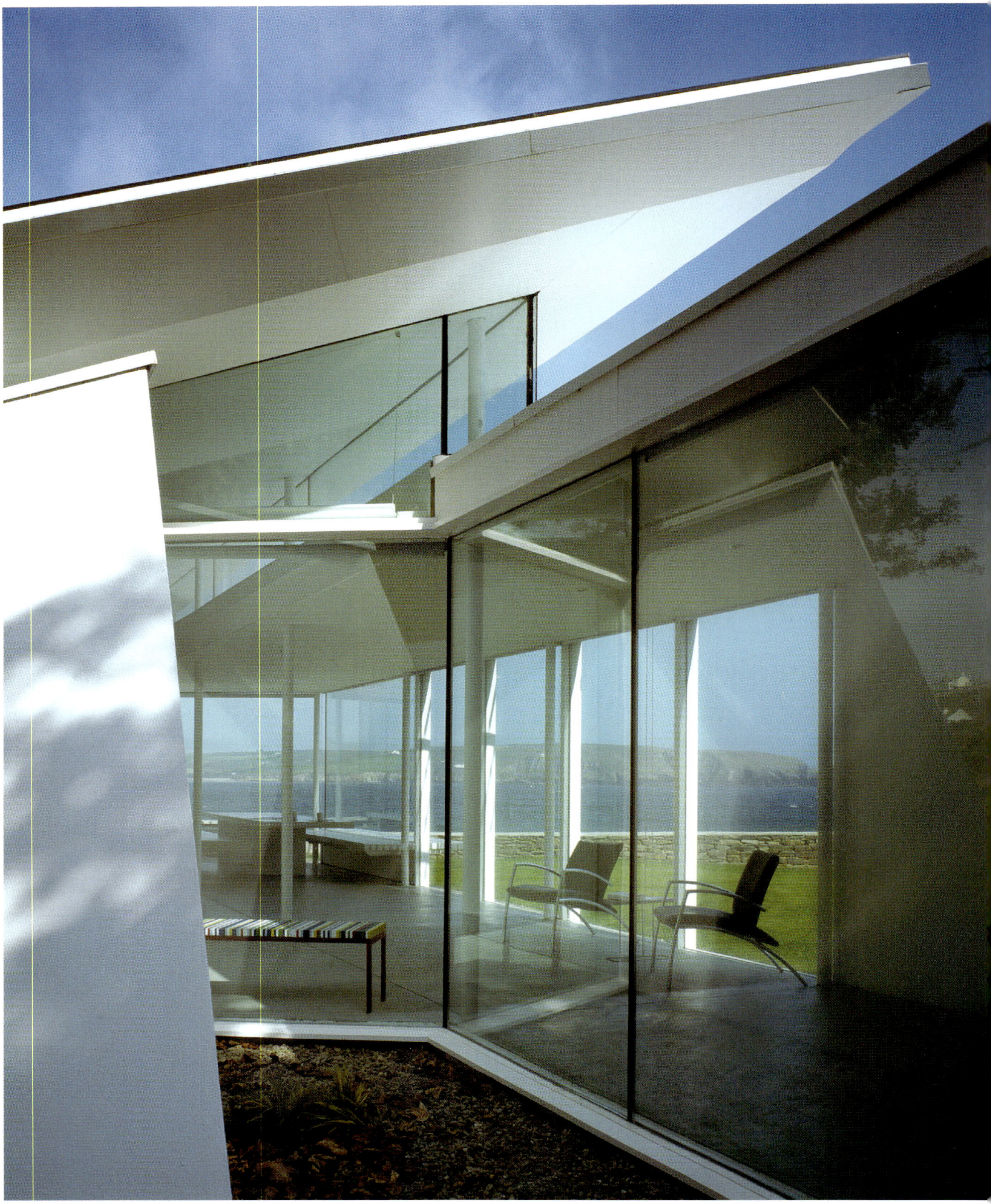

ガラスウォールで囲まれた広い回廊を進むと、ダイニングルームへと導かれる。このヴォリュームには他に2つの部屋があるが、それらの部屋も光をつかまえることができる透明なガラスウォールで囲まれている。1つは窓いっぱいに大西洋が広がるリビングルームで、もう1つは南向きの部屋。

A wide corridor with glass walls leads to the dining area. There are two more rooms here, also with transparent walls that capture the light: one living room with views over the ocean and another, which faces south.

ポルタス・ノヴァス　ファン・ロカ／アクアート, ヴィクトール・カニャス

海に浮かぶ家　FLOATING ON WATER

オコタルビーチ―コスタリカ　撮影：ジョルディ・ミラーレス

　この住宅は、海岸から180メートルほどしか離れていない小高い山の頂上という特権的地位を与えられている。そのため360度の視界が得られ、隣国ニカラグアの海岸までも見晴らすことができる。プールから溢れ出す水が常に住宅を取り囲み、水上に浮かぶ家というイメージを創りだしている。プールのミラー効果が構造のミニマリスト的フォルムを強調している。空と、海と、プールの青が混合され、魔法のような景観が生み出されている。

The residence is situated on top of a mountain, barely 600 ft from the sea.
This privileged lookout post offers 360° views, which even include the Nicaraguan coastline. The design of the house includes an overflow swimming pool that surrounds the house giving it the impression
of floating home. The mirror effect
of the swimming pool complements
the minimalist shapes of the construction.
The mix of blues from the sky, the ocean and the swimming pool water creates
a magical environment.

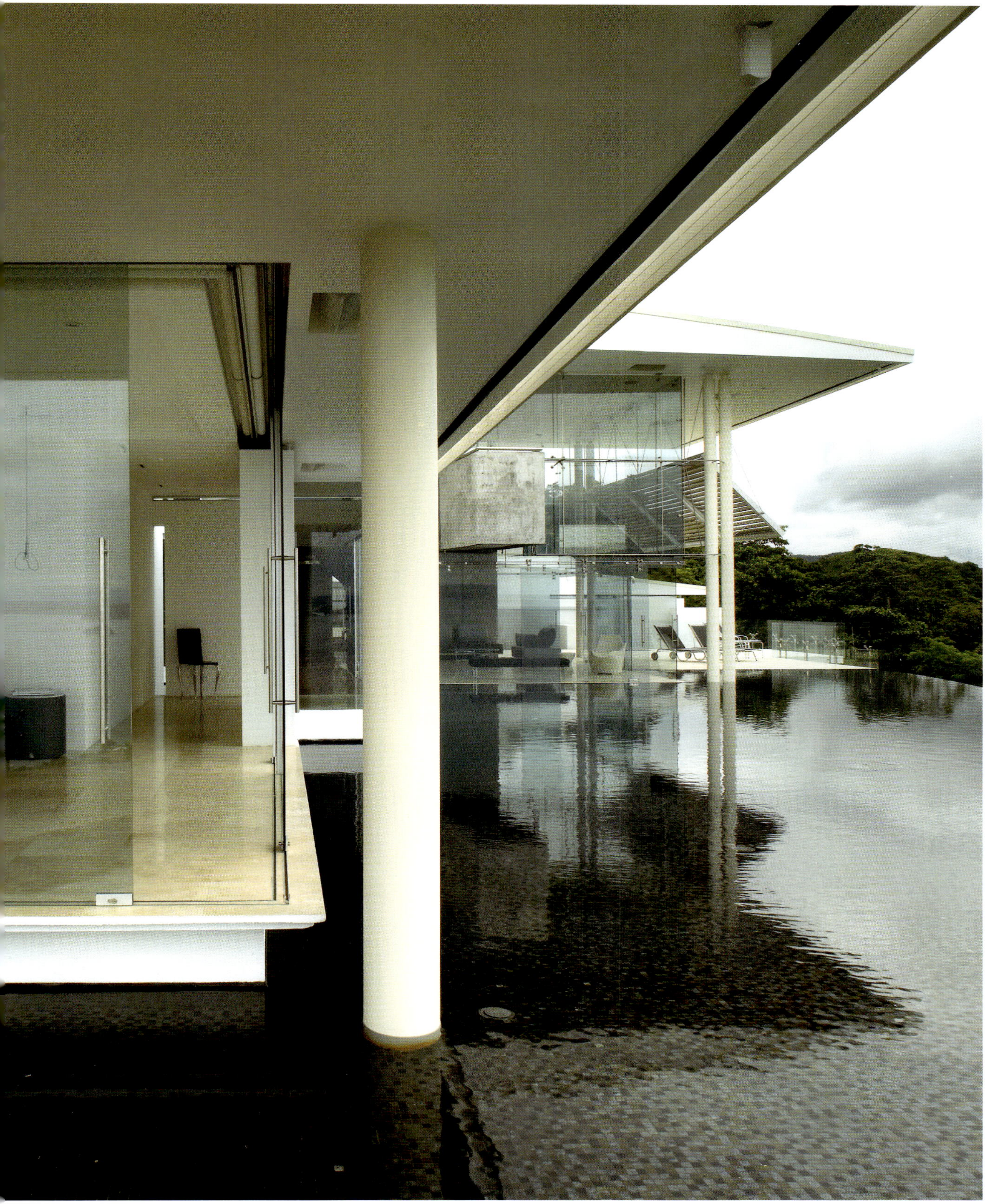

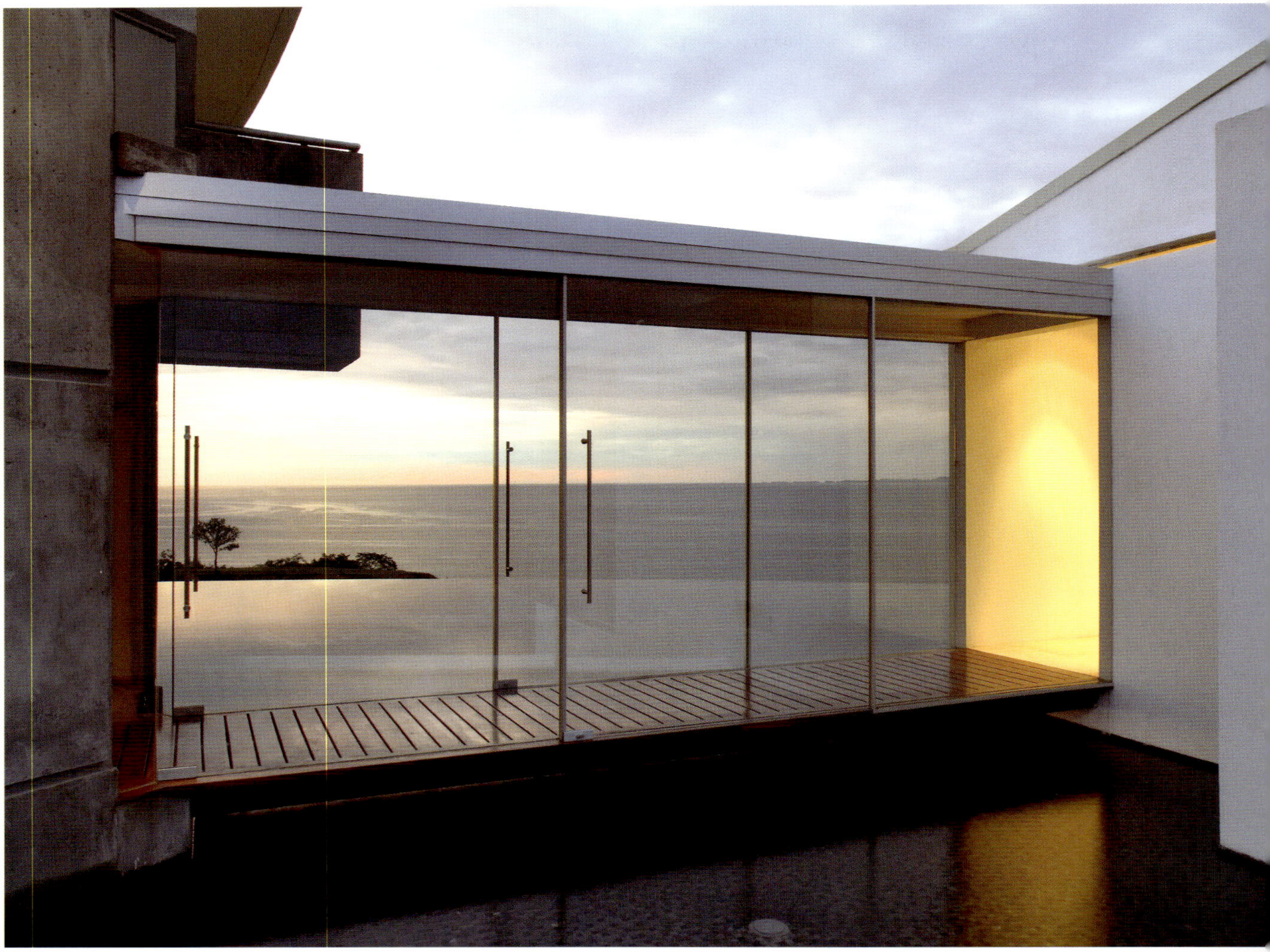

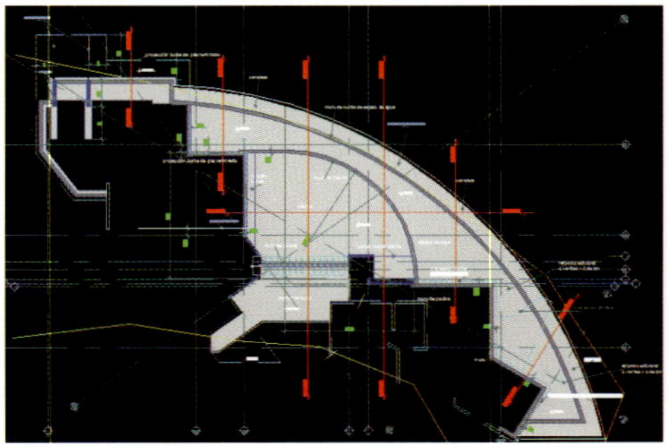

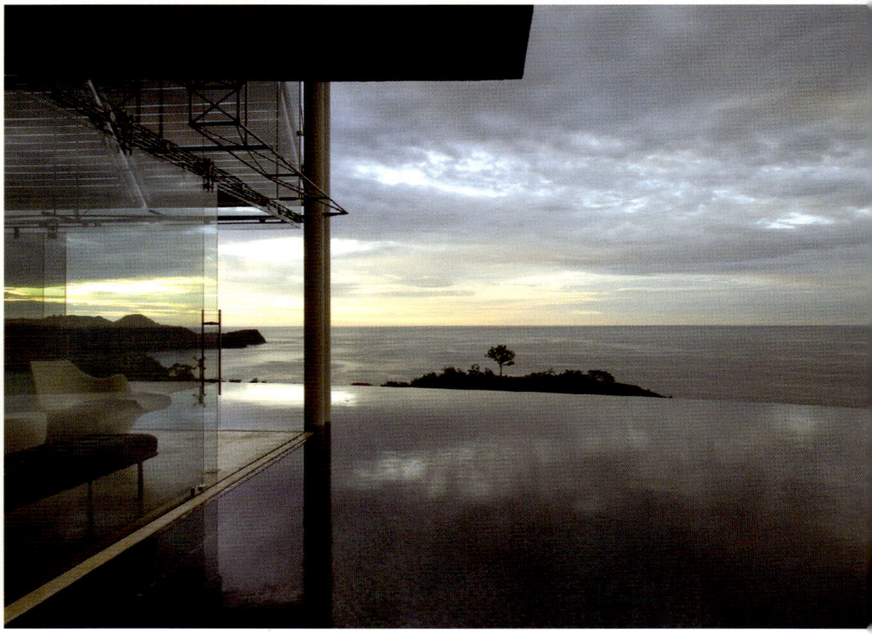

テラスとリビングルームには同じ大理石が使われ、そのクリーム色が内部空間へ、屋外空間へと拡散している。主寝室にはチーク材を張った専用のテラスがあり、それはまるで海に浮遊しているようだ。

The terrace and the living room use the same marble; the color cream fuses the interior and exterior spaces. The main bedroom has a private teak terrace that seems to float gently over the water.

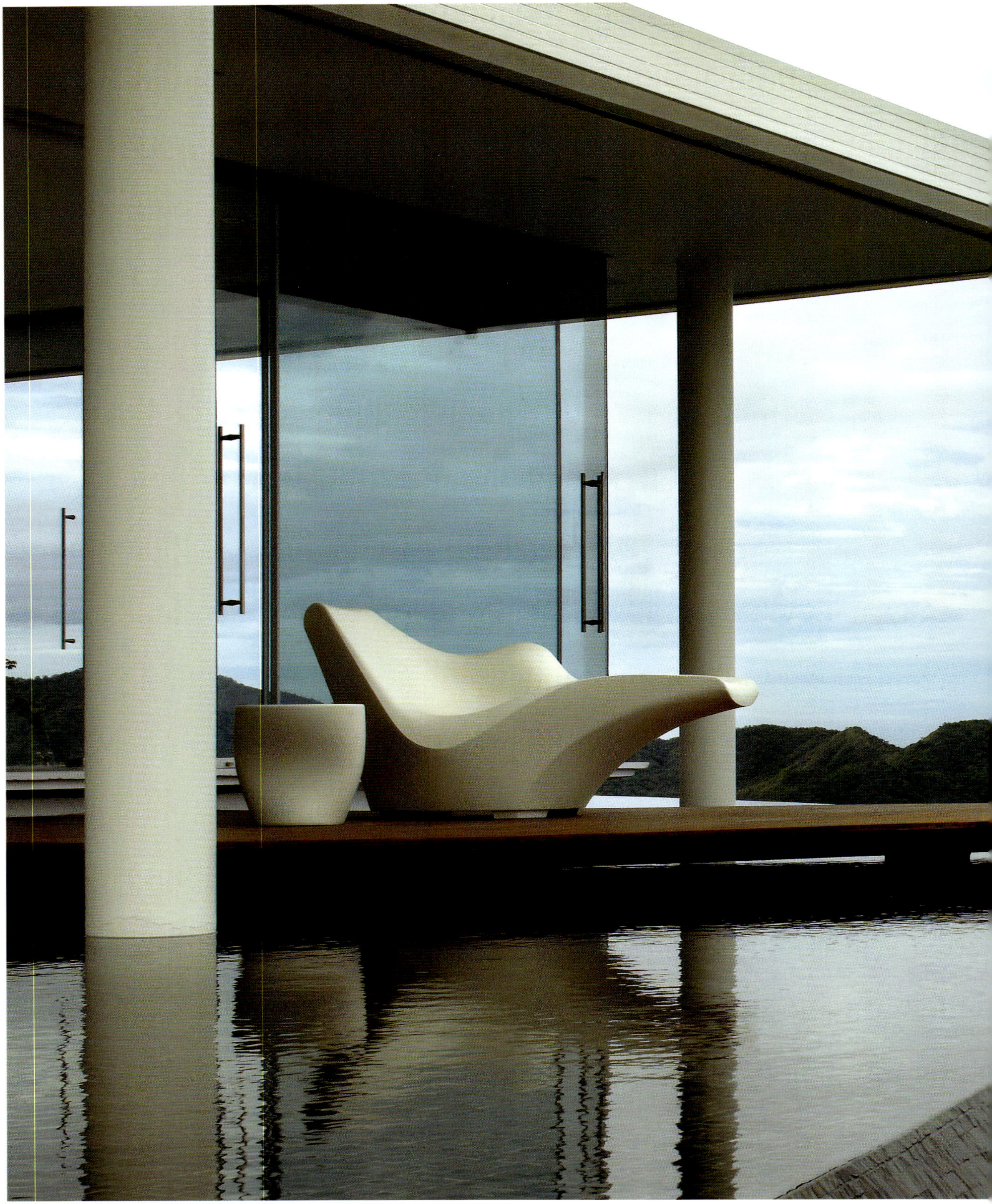

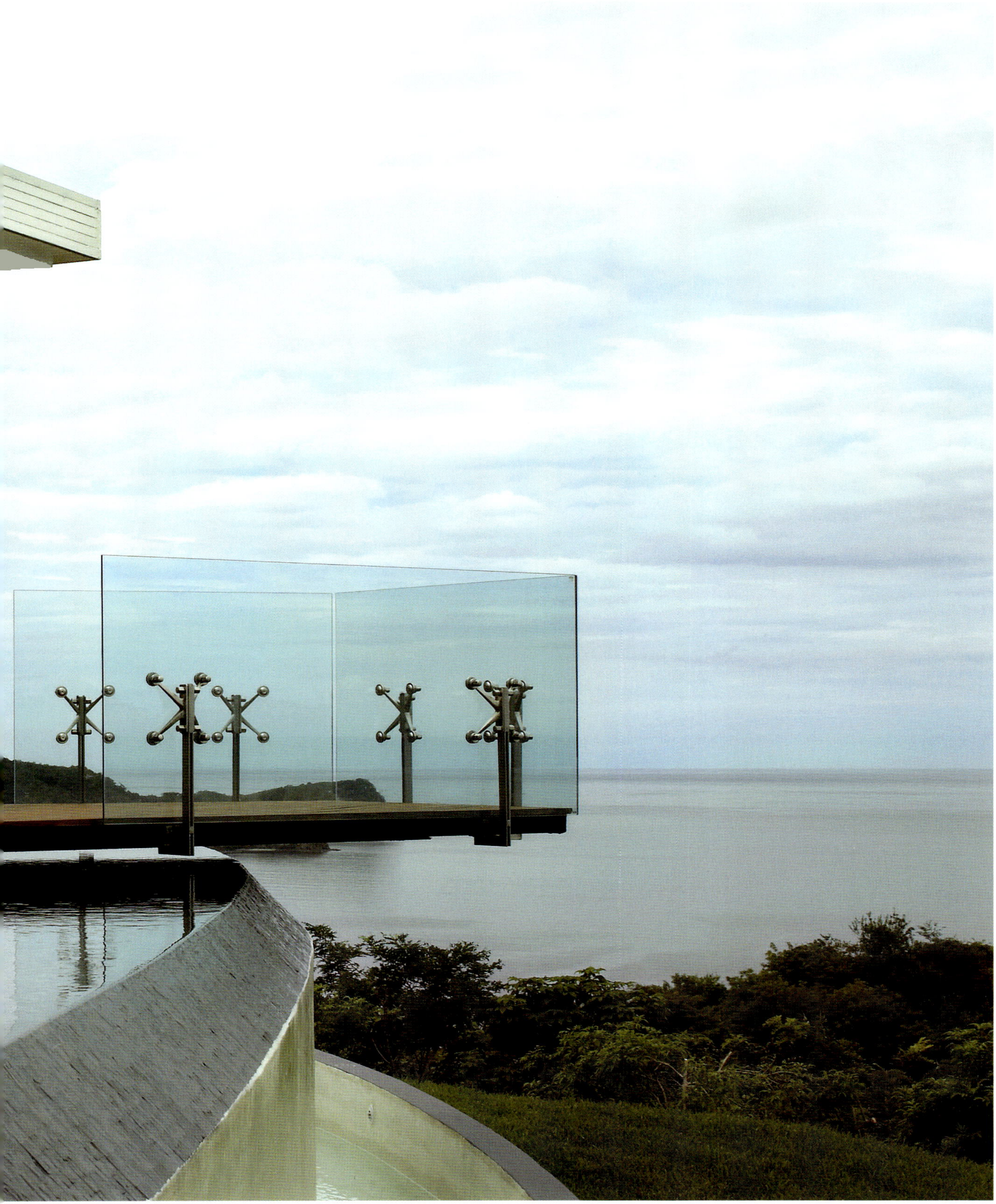

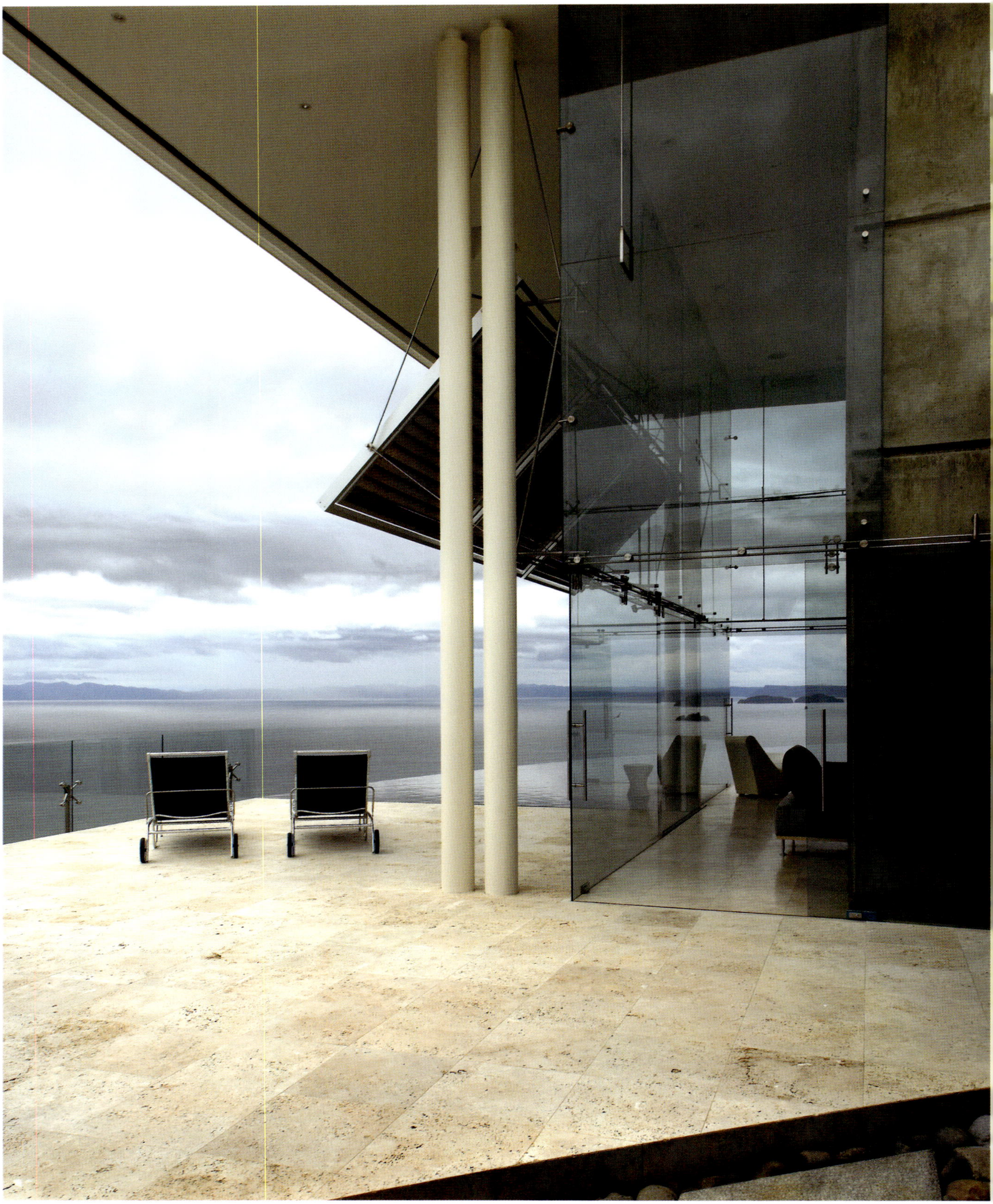

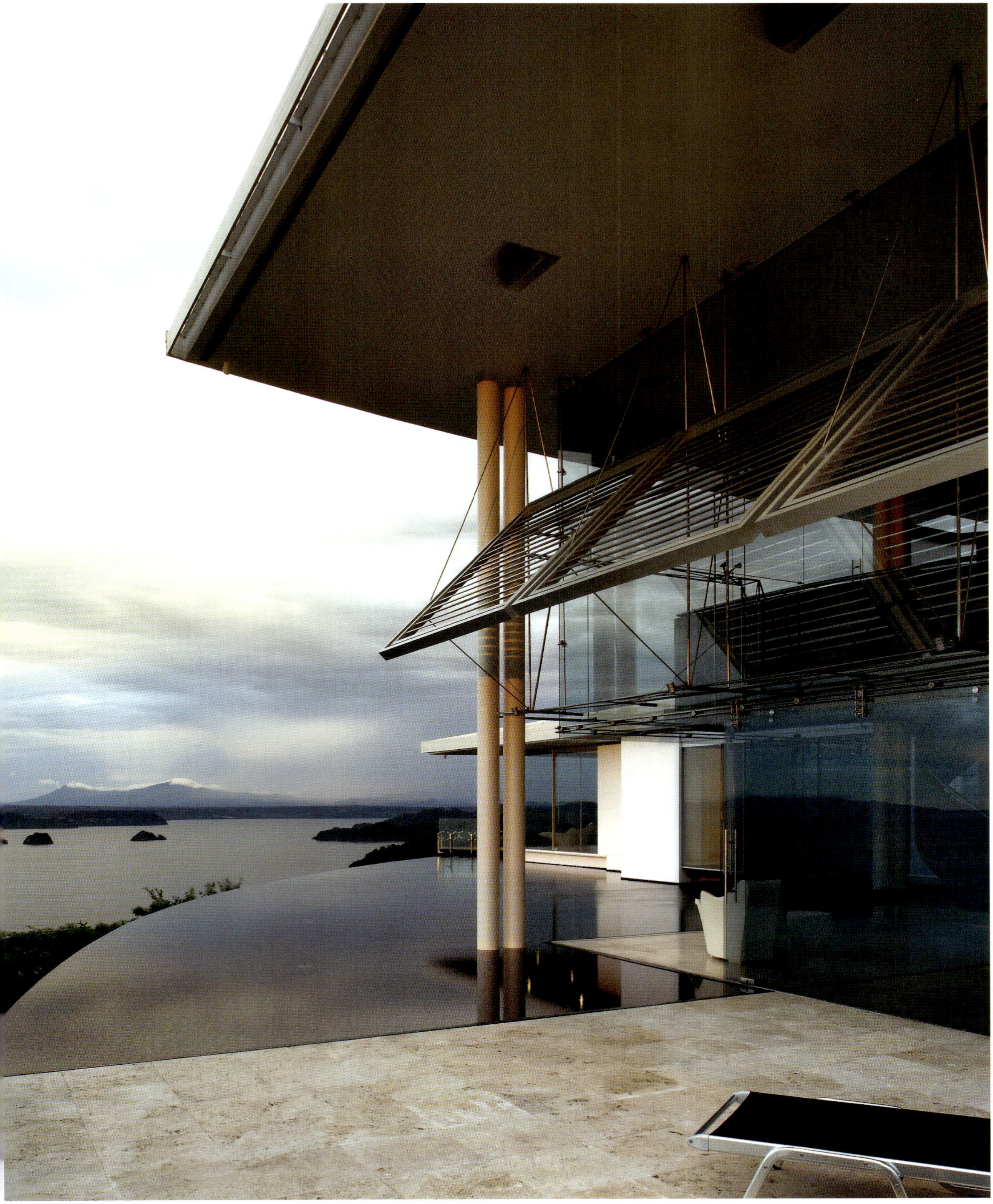

水平線の家 小川 晋一　都市建築設計事務所

無限の広がり　WITHOUT LIMITS

熱海―静岡県―日本　撮影：ナカサアンドパートナーズ

　熱海湾を一望に見渡せるなだらかな斜面に立つこの住宅のコンセプトは、自然との全面的な交流であった。水、光、風、そして太陽。

　そのためすべての部屋から湾が望めるようにし、2階のリビングルームは完全に屋外空間へと開け放たれた。仕切りのない大きな窓はそのままテラスにつながり、水平線へと拡散していく独創的な空間が創りだされた。アルミニウムのブラインドが風や雨から部屋を守り、また違った印象を部屋にもたらす。

This house sits on a slope with magnificent views of the ocean. The aim of the design was to achieve total interaction with nature: water, light, wind and sun.
To do this all rooms have views of the sea and the living room on the second floor opens completely to the outside. The large windows open onto the terrace creating a unique space, which fuses with the horizon. Aluminum blinds offer protection from the wind and rain and come together to change the appearance of the room.

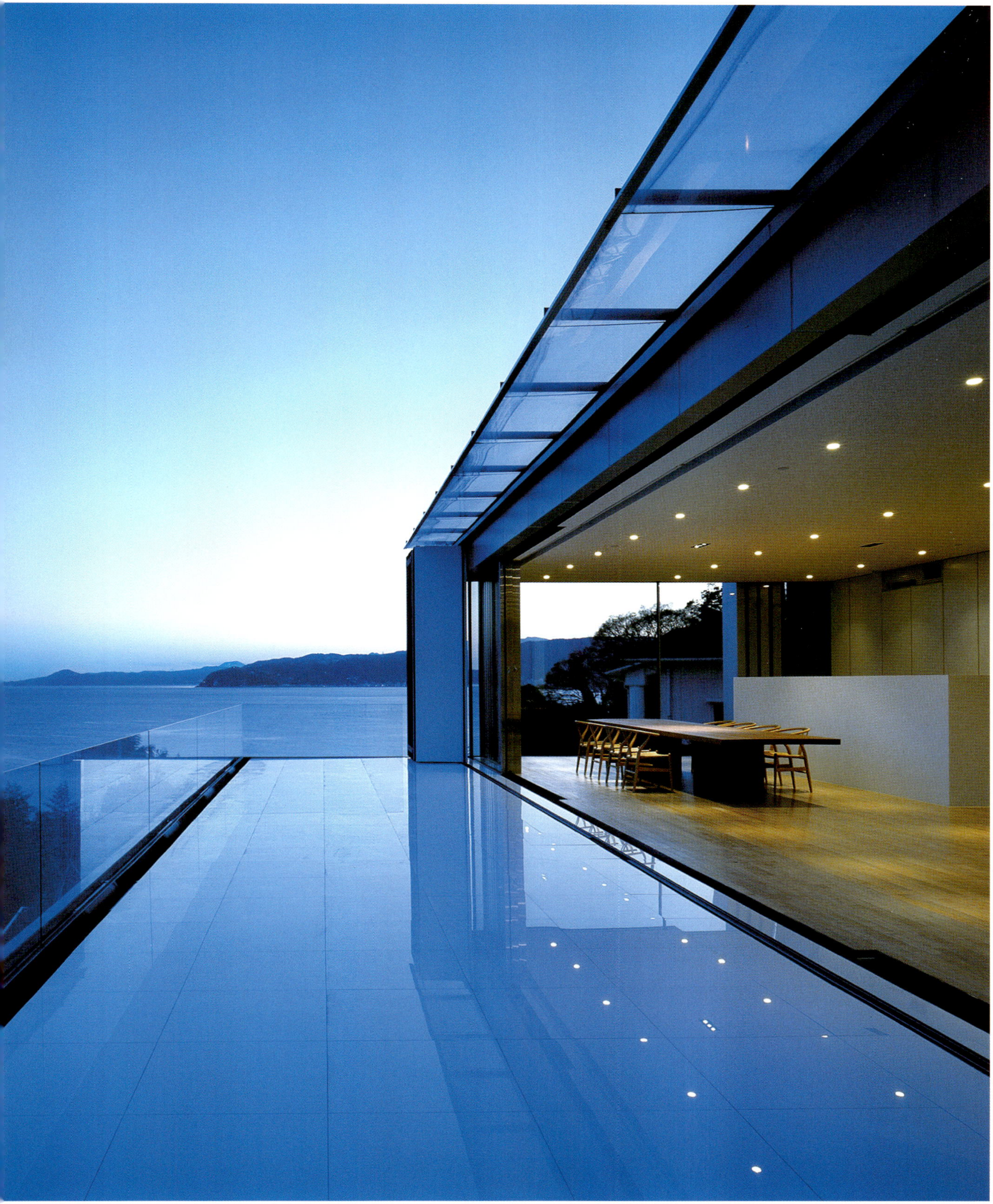

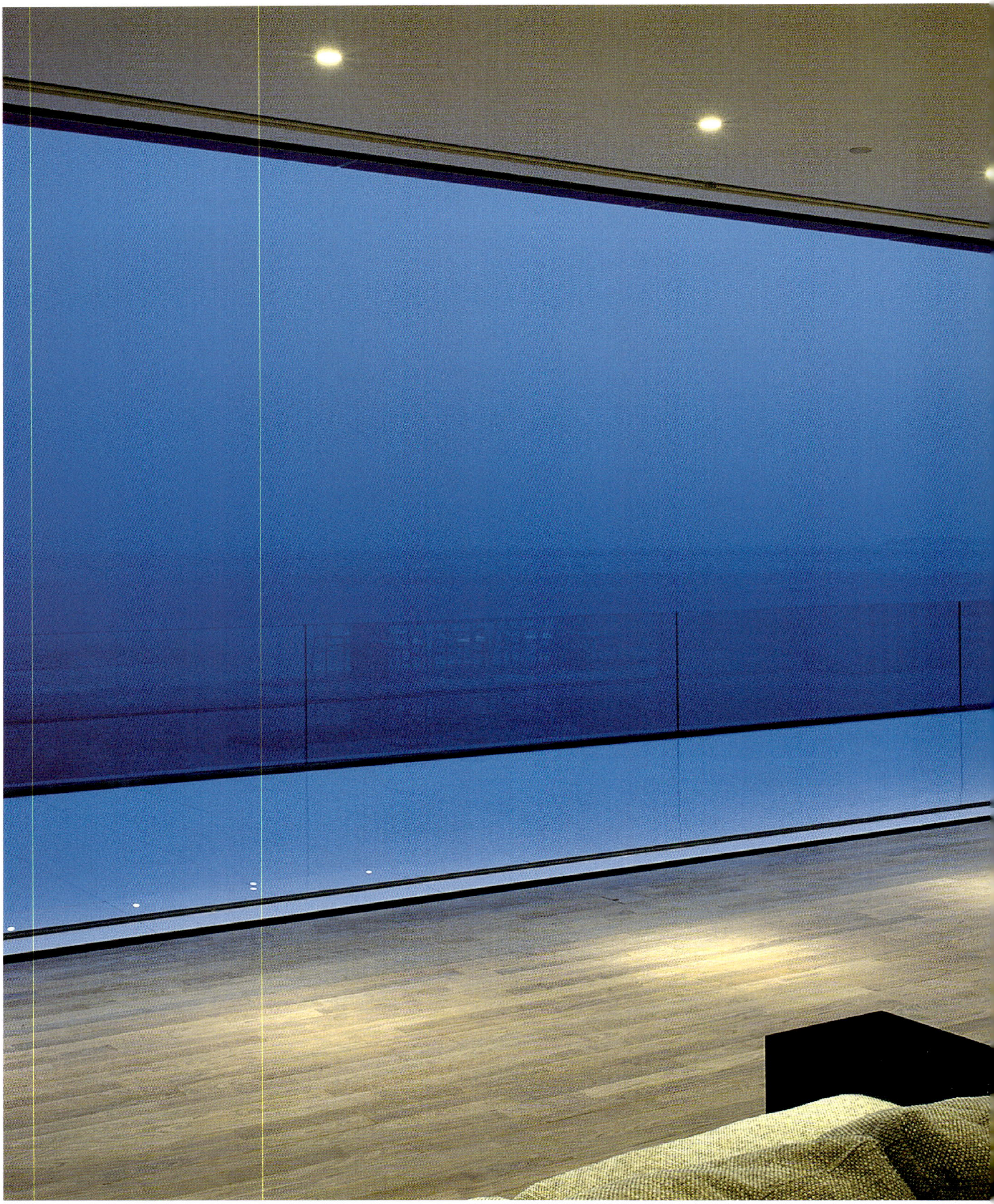

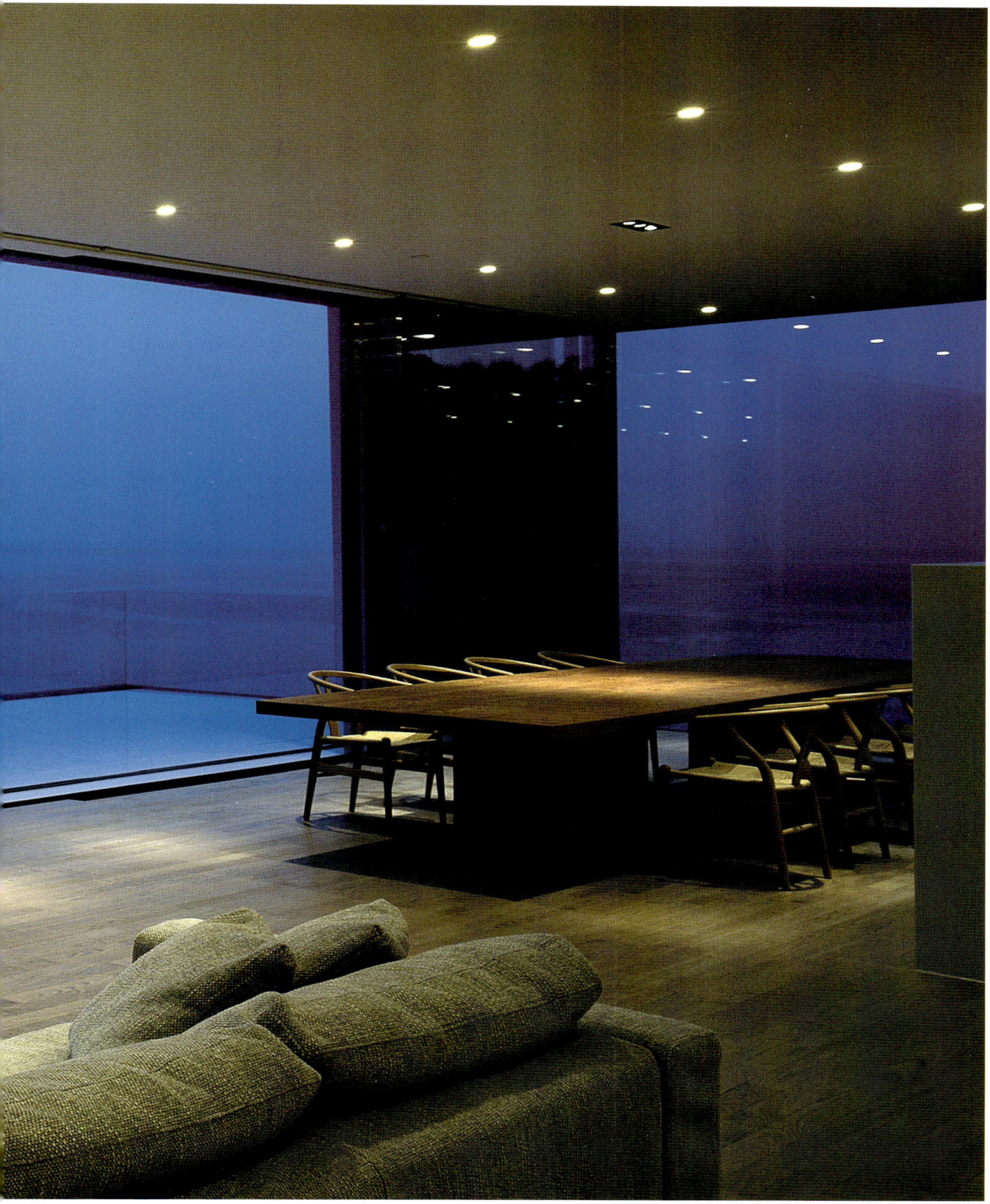

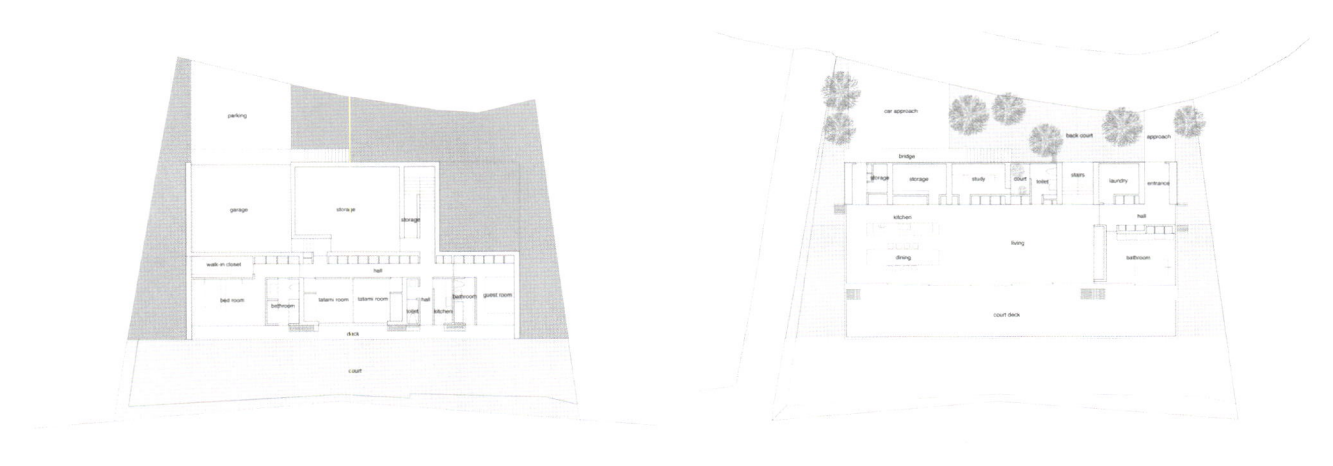

110 | 視覚としての水 | See it

大きな窓とガラスの手すりが、仕切りのない空間という視覚的な感覚を生みだす。透明ガラスを通して住宅のほとんどすべての位置から湾が望め、心は海で満たされる。

The large windows and glass railings create the visual sensation of a space without limits. The transparency of the glass allows us to enjoy the impressive ocean views from almost every point of the house.

サ・リエラ　アルフォンソ・モラレス

海の傍の純粋　PURENESS BY THE SEA

バレアリック島―スペイン　撮影：ホセ・ルイス・オスマン

　プールは心を落ち着かせるリラクゼーションの場であり、身体をリフレッシュさせ、子供を水遊びさせる活動的な場でもある。バレアリック島の住宅にあるこのプールはそれほど大きなプールではないが、その軽い線と建物の形の明快さのため、広がりのある軽やかな屋外空間を創りだしている。海の眺めと構造の純粋さを妨げる過剰な装飾はすべて削ぎ落とされ、傍に伸びている木々の梢が住宅を風から守りながら、終わりのない風景の広がりを演出している。

A swimming pool can be a place for tranquility and relaxation or an active place to refresh yourself and play games in the water. This residence's pool in the Balearic Islands is not very large, but the lightness of its lines and the simplicity of the adjacent construction create a light, spacious outdoor area. There are no superfluous details that distract you from the pureness of the scenery and the sea views. The trees growing next to the house protect it from the wind and allow for unlimited views of the panorama.

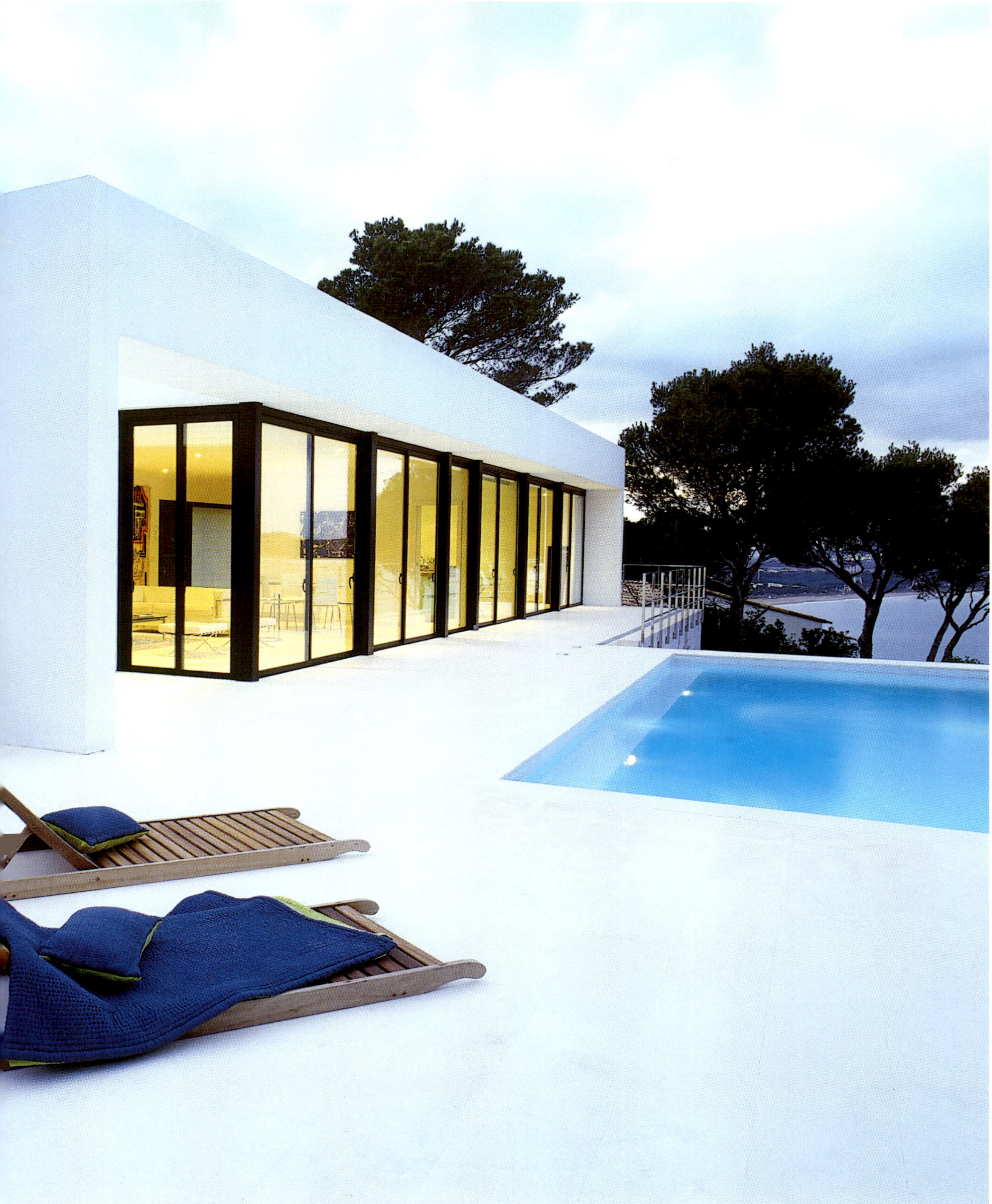

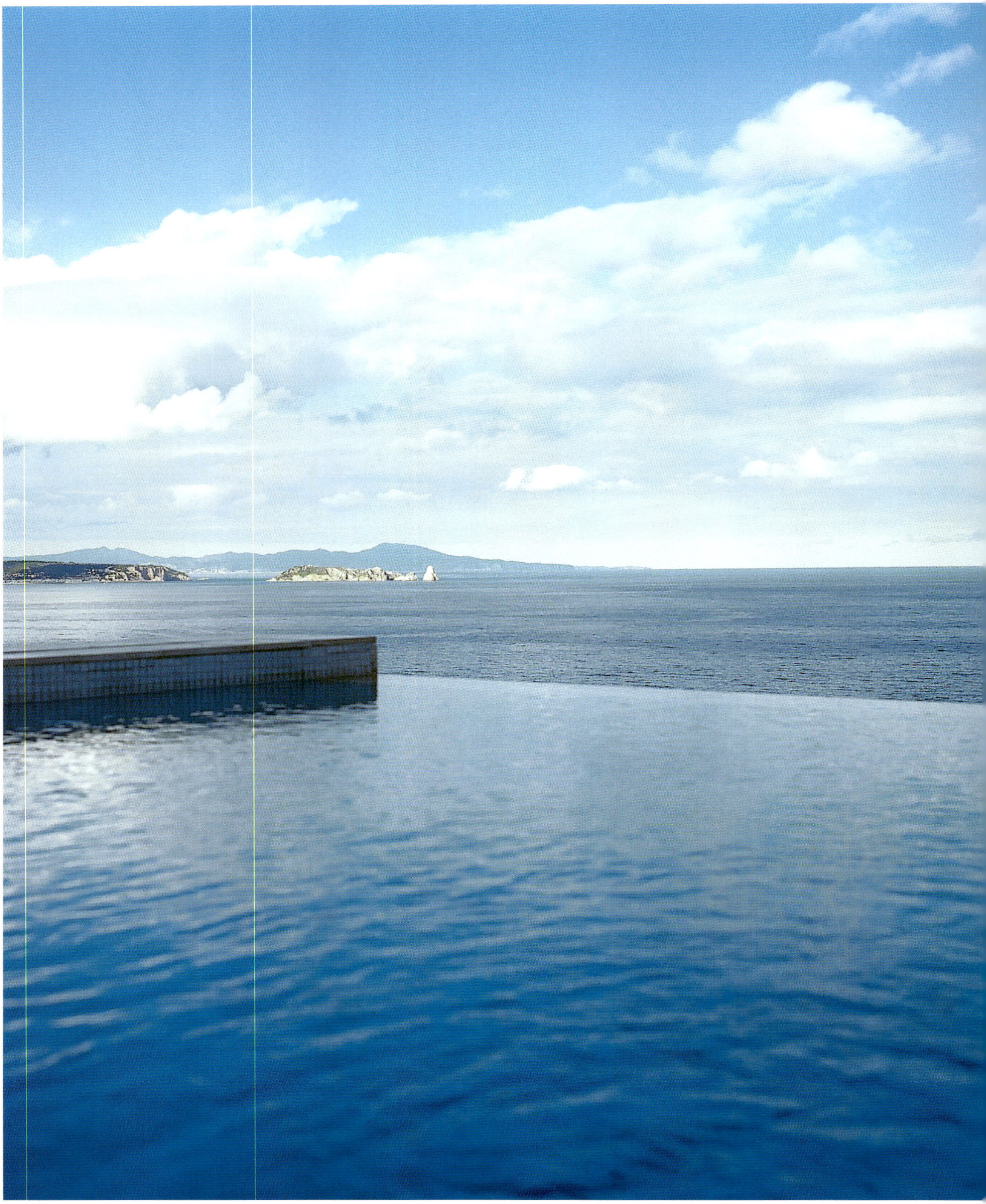

プールは海と対面しており、常に溢れでている水が海水と淡水の境界をぼかしている。金属製の手すりは転落防止のためだけでなく、視線を下に向けさせないためのもの。

The overflow swimming pool faces the sea and blurs the limits between fresh and salt water. Metal railings protect the exterior terraces from the changing level of the plot.

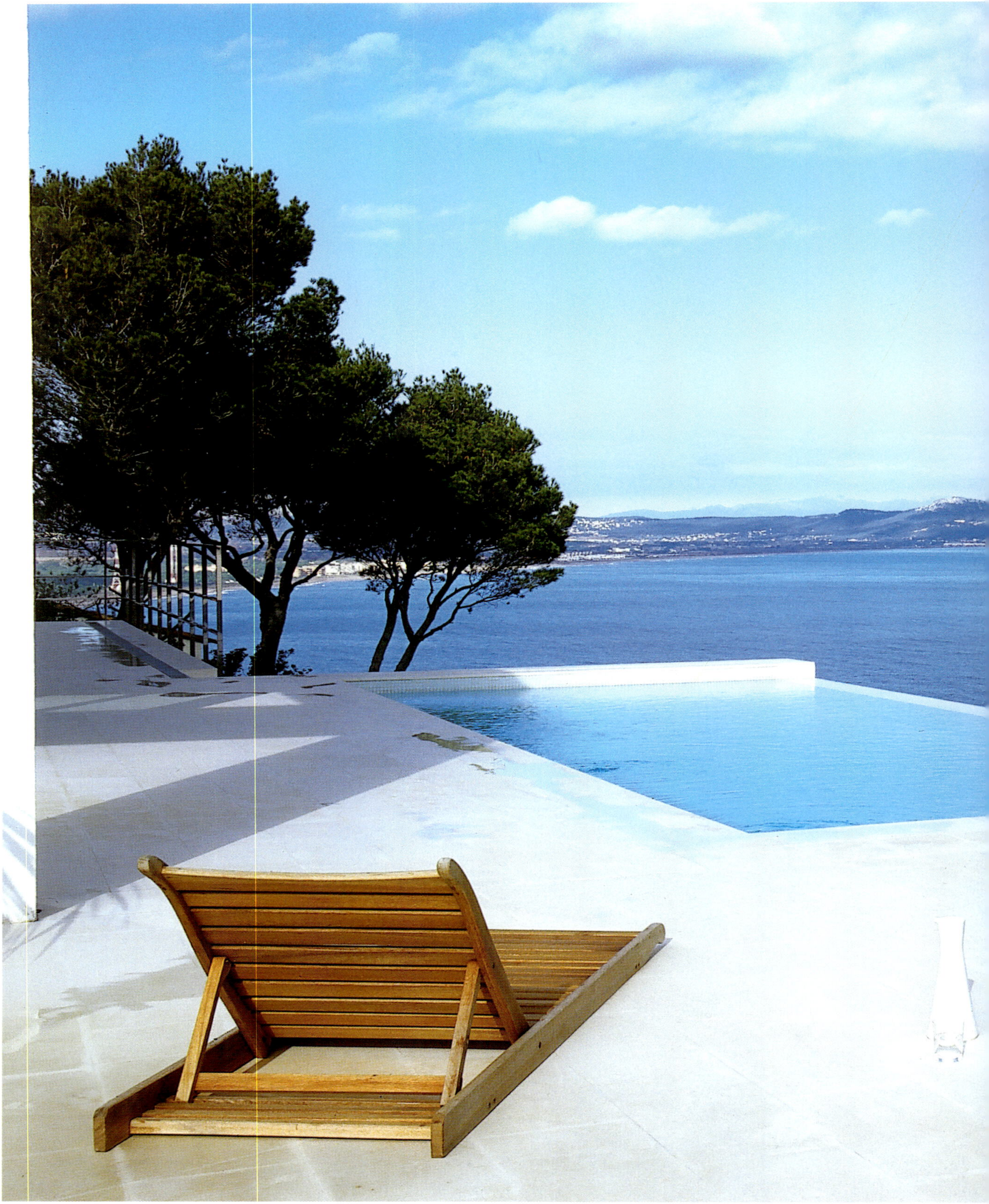

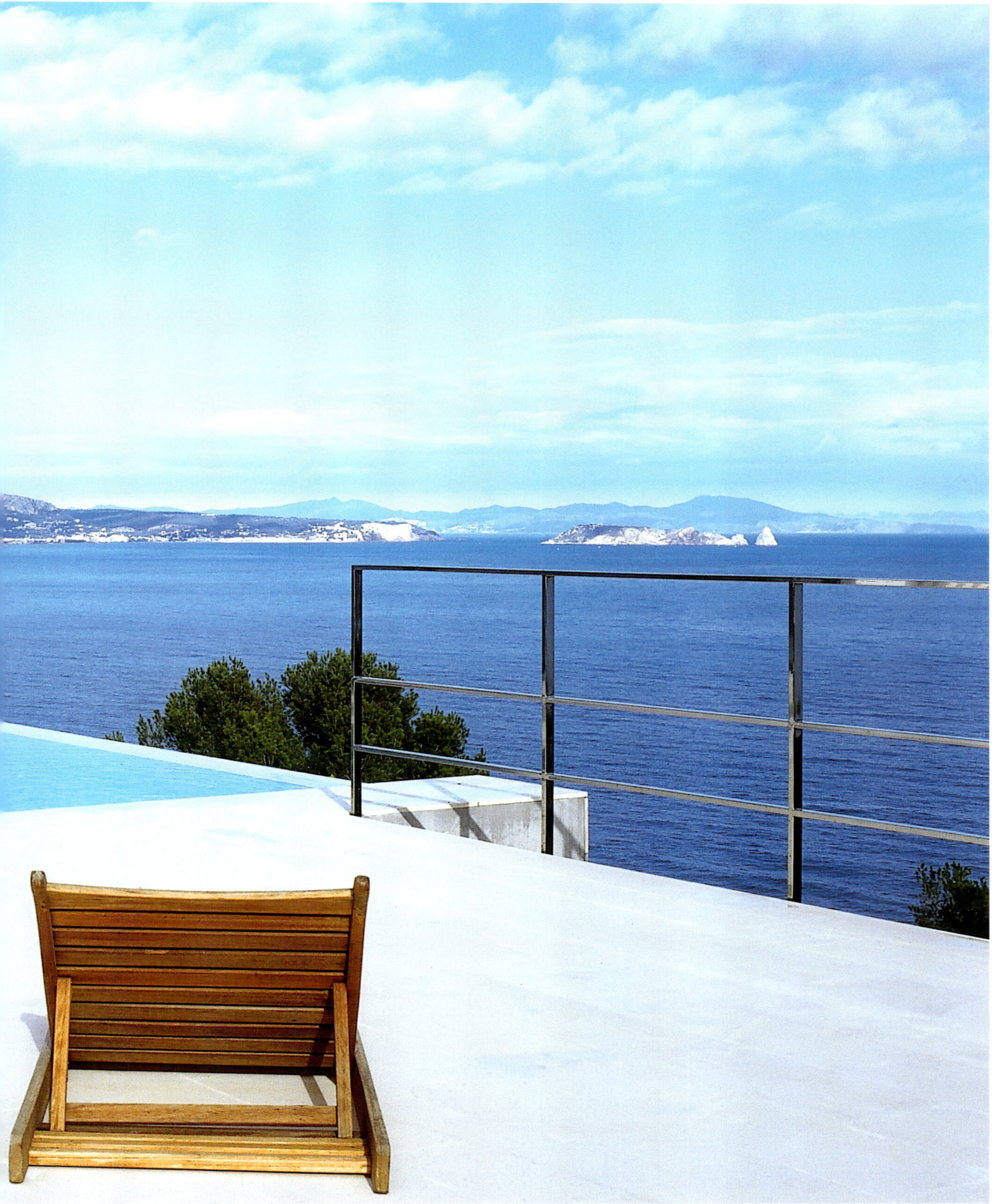

ナムリー通りの家 ベドマール & シー

森と水と石に囲まれて AMONG TREES, WATER AND STONE

シンガポール　撮影：ベドマール & シー

　プールのある中庭を中心に、住宅はU字型に組織されている。庭の木々とプールを囲む石の壁が、純粋で魅惑的な空間を生みだしている。並んで立っている本石のブロックは5体の石仏のように風景のなかに融けこみ、住人を見守っている。プールと庭と住宅は渾然一体となっている。

This residence is organized in a U-shape, around a courtyard where the swimming pool is located. The trees in the garden and the stone of the wall that protects the pool create an attractive, simple space. The nature mixes with blocks that act as sculptures in this outdoor space. The swimming pool is integrated with the house and not separated from it.

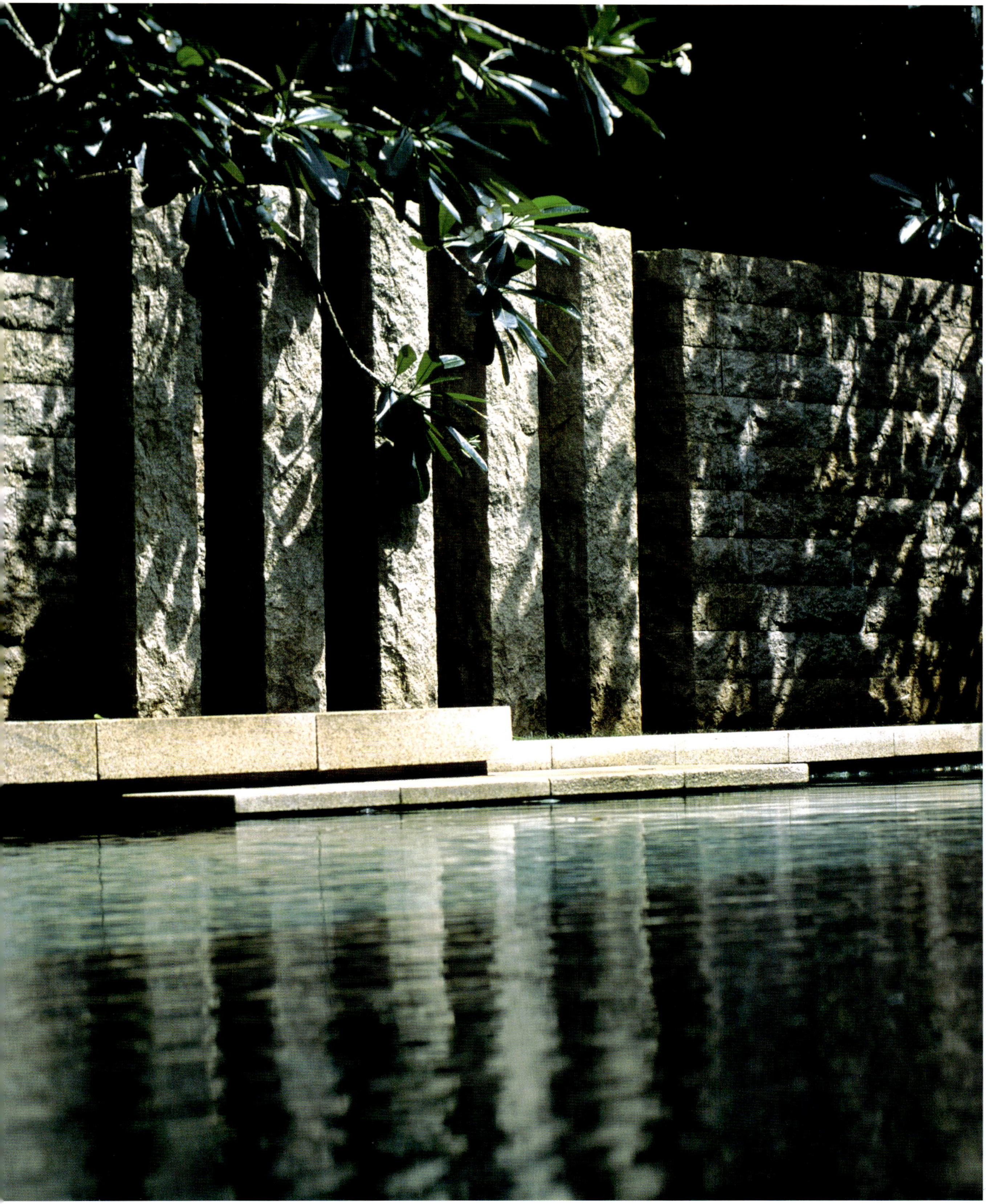

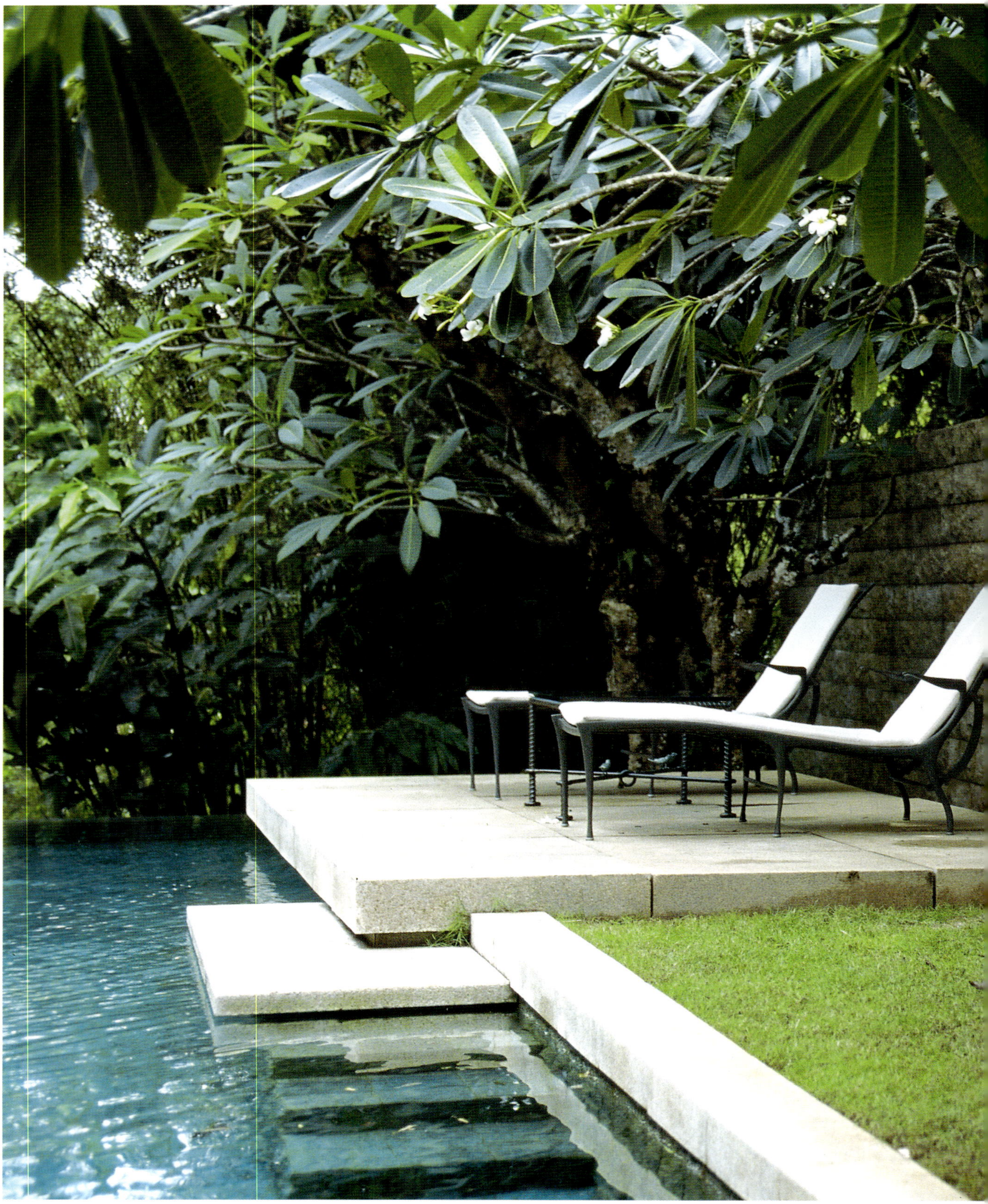

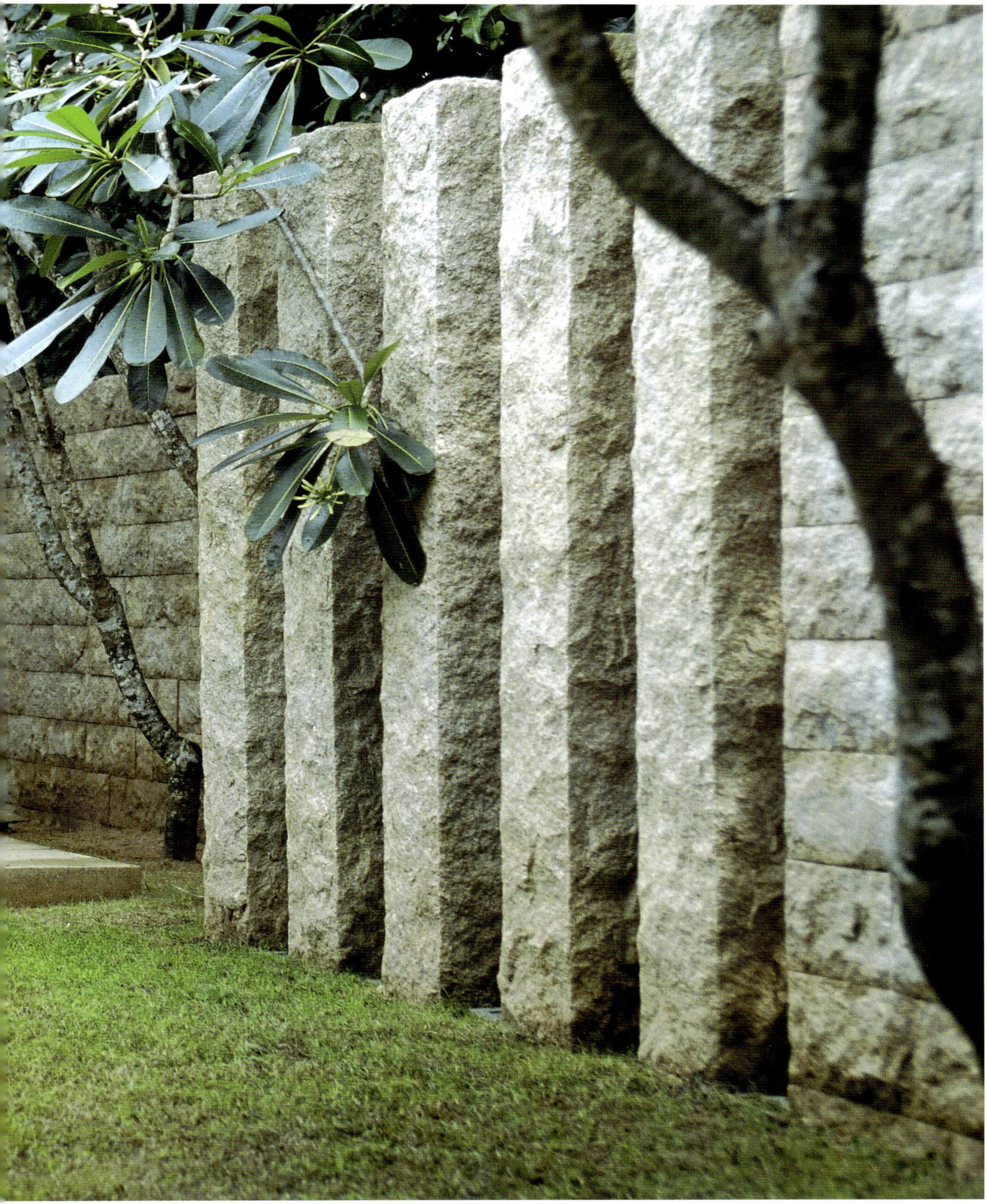

アイランド・モダン ジャングルズ・ランドスケープ・アーキテクチュア

プールと滝と庭　SWIMMING POOL NEXT TO GARDEN

キーウェスト―フロリダ―アメリカ　撮影：レニー・プロボ

　建築と自然を巧みに融合させ、屋外空間の魅力を最大限建築に生かすランドスケープ・アーキテクチュアの手腕が見事に証明された住宅。住宅北側、プールに面した壁には滝があり、水が陽光を浴びながら勢いよく流れ落ちている。フロリダ原産の熱帯植物が自然のスクリーンを作り、場を完結させている。こうしてプライバシーがしっかりと守られた小さな庭の中にフロリダの自然が再現された。プールの横には日光浴とリラクゼーションのためのさまざまな形のラウンジチェアが点在している。

The construction of this residence is an example of the skills used by a landscape architect to fuse architecture with nature and use the exterior space in the best way possible. A swimming pool is situated in a north-facing space with a waterfall emerging from the wall. Tropical plants from Florida complete the area forming a screen of vegetation. These bring a greater level of privacy while forming a small garden. Next to the swimming pool are various sun loungers for sunbathing and relaxing.

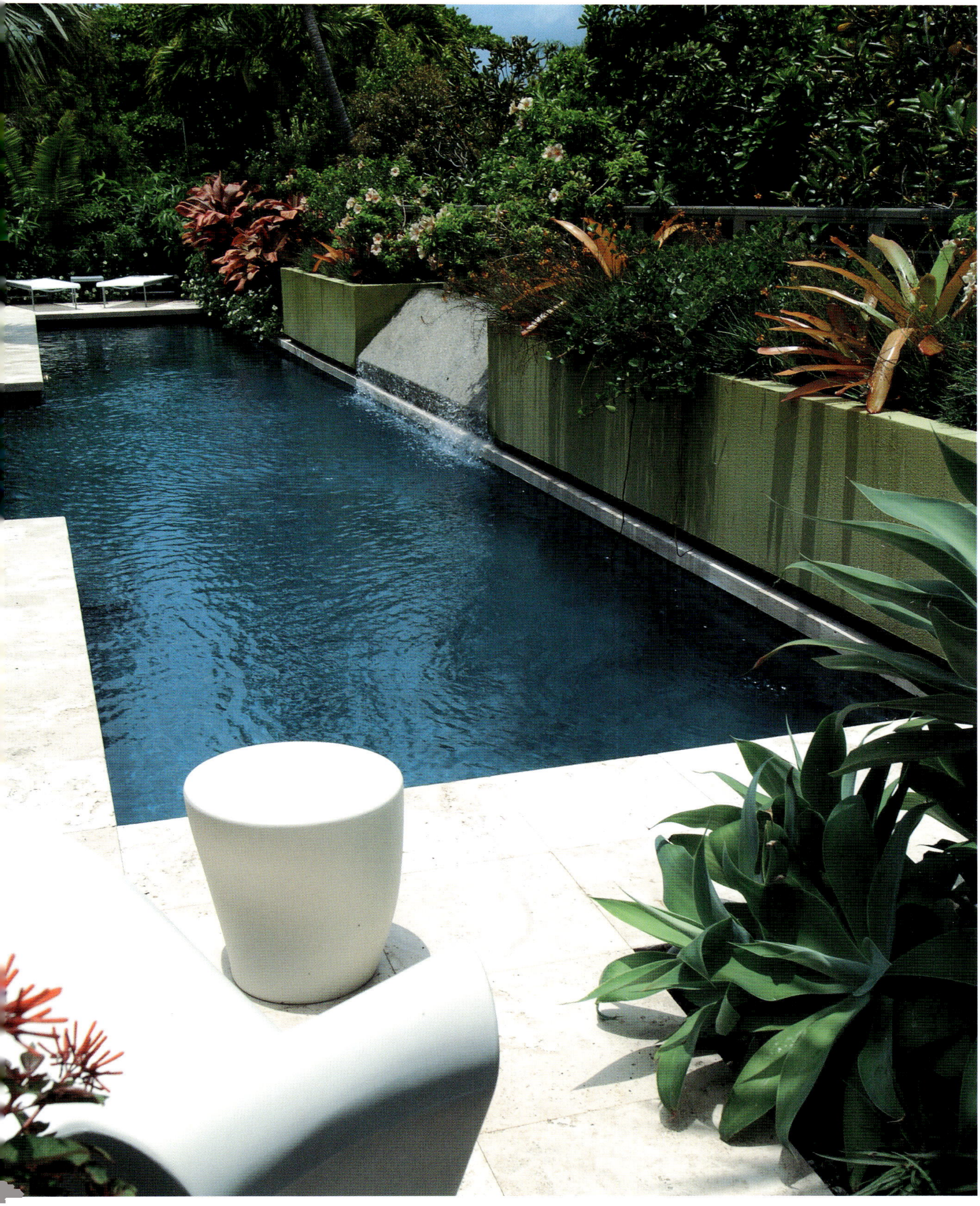

カサ・マルドナド アルベルト・ブルクハルト

山懐に抱かれて　SURROUNDED BY NATURE

アナポイマ—コロンビア　撮影：ジャン・マルク・ブルシュレーガー

　共用部分と集いの場を2階に集め、ポーチには屋外リビングルームを設置し、その前に幅4m長さ20mのプールを置いた。そうすることによって雄大な山々の風景が近づき、住宅は自然の一部となった。自然と建築の調和というこのプロジェクトの目標にとって、プールは最重要の意味を持つ。プールを前景とすることによって、それはそのまま樹冠を越えて景観へと伸展し、湖へ、山頂へと拡がっていく。

The public and social area of this residence is found on the middle floor. This is where the 65 x 13 ft swimming pool can be found along with a porch with an outdoor living room. This place affords views of the impressive mountain scenery and makes the house seem like part of the environment. The project attempts to find harmony between nature and architecture, which is why the swimming pool is located in the foreground. It seems to stretch out into the landscape through the treetops and towards the lake and mountains.

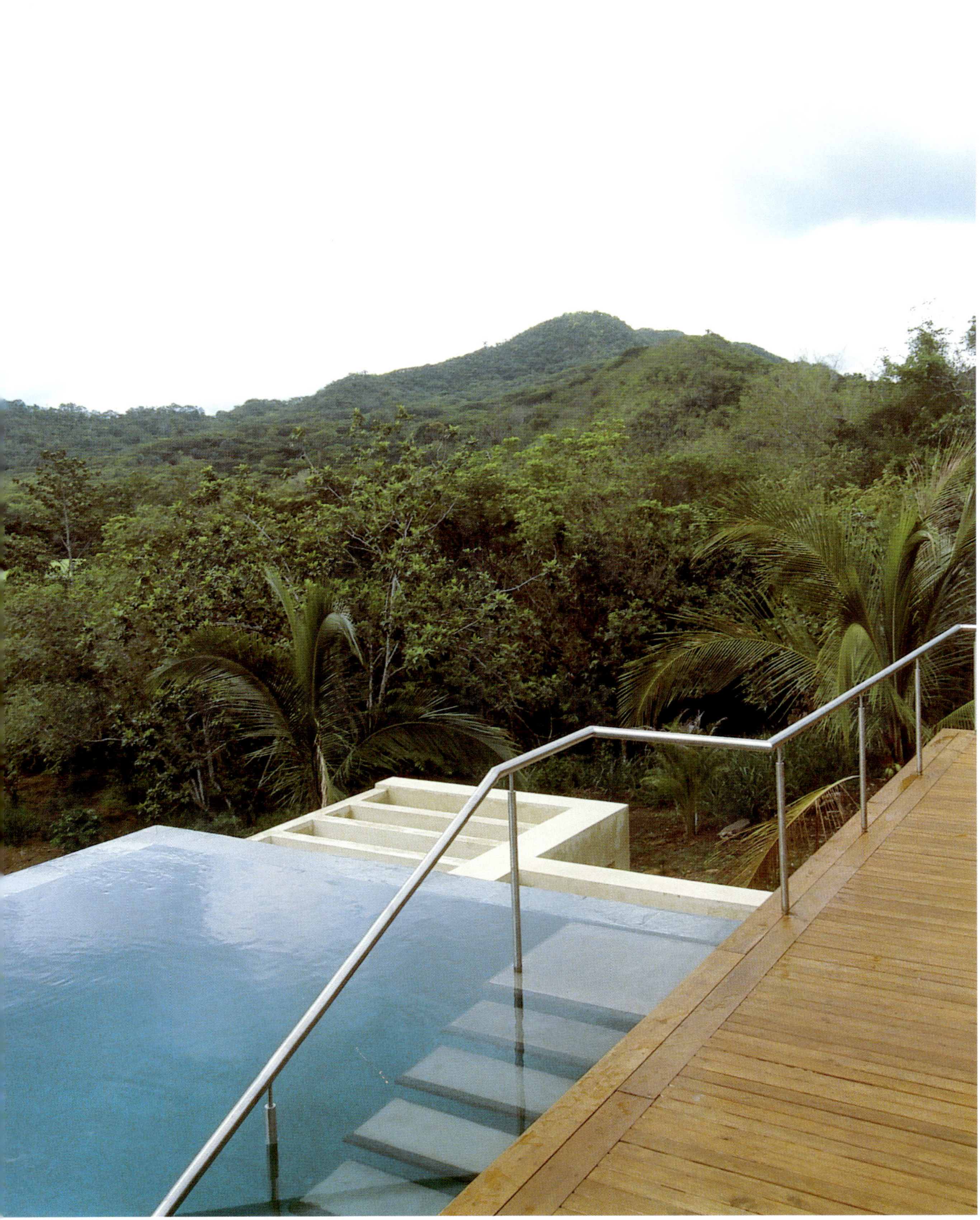

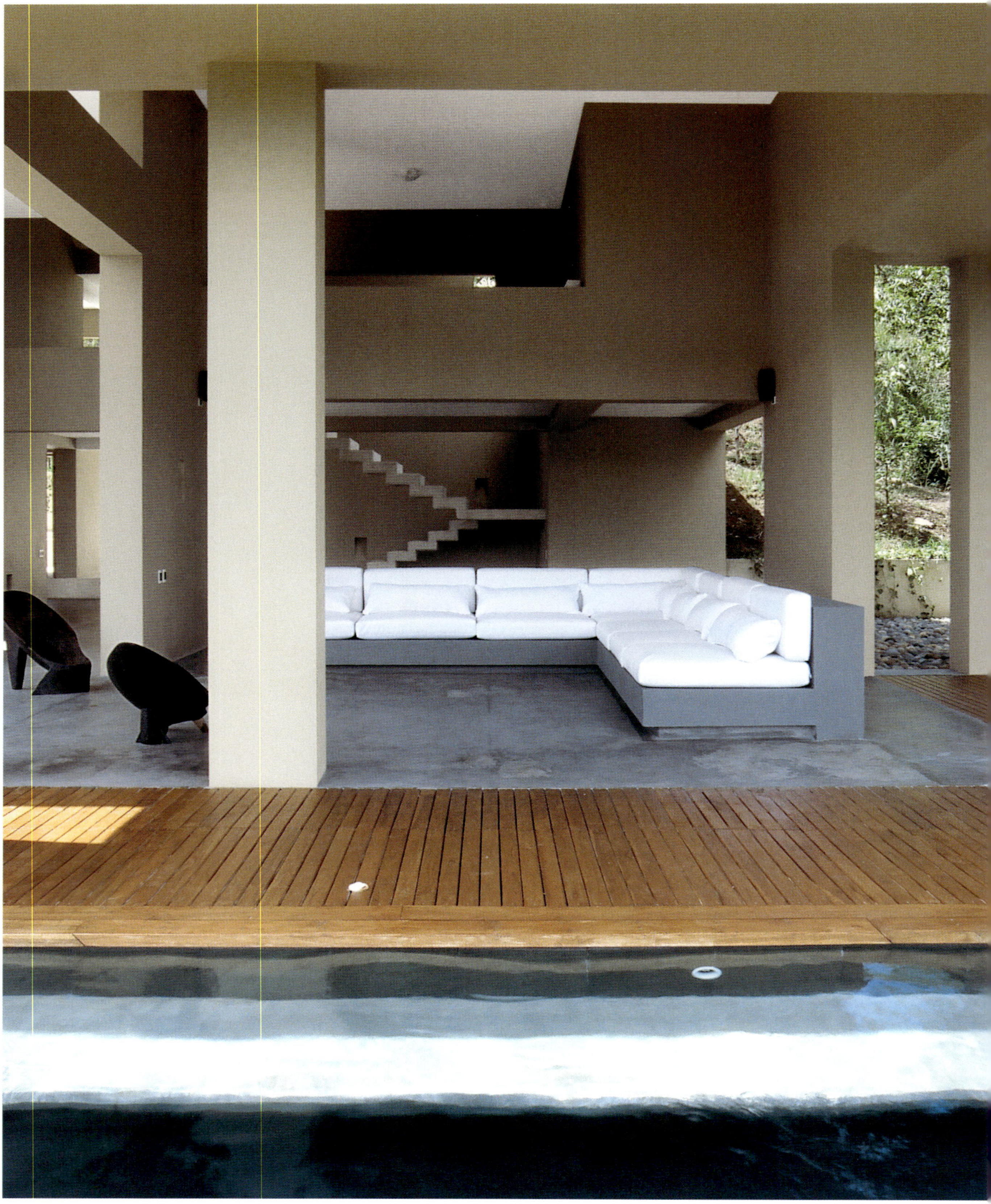

ポーチを2階吹き抜けとしているため、住宅内部を爽やかな空気が循環する。構造的な調和は軒やアーチの形にも貫かれており、それらが太陽や雨からリビングルームを防護する。

The double-heighted porch allows the circulation of a draught through the interior of the house. The harmony of the construction is reflected in the eaves and arches that offer protection both from the sun and the rains.

カブリー邸 ハビエル・プラナス／プラナス―トーレス建築設計事務所

平和の楽園、イビザ　*A HAVEN OF PEACE IN IBIZA*

イビザ―バレアリック島―スペイン　撮影：ルルド・グリヴェ

　個人邸のプールは屋外空間の一部を構成すると同時に、特に夏場には実際に遊泳できるものでなくてはならない。建築家ハビエル・プラナスはこの2つの条件を、スペイン独特の建築様式を尊重した明快な線を用いることによって統一した。田舎の風景を彷彿とさせる木とパイプのポーチは、住宅の主要部から眺めることができる。プール入り口に張られた縁甲板は、水平線のかなたへ航海するための桟橋のようだ。

Swimming pools in single-family residences are usually outdoor and are for playing in, especially in summer. This project from architect Javiar Planas unites these two characteristics using clean lines, which respect the local architecture. A wooden and pipes porch that evokes a rural environment can be seen from the house's main volume. Wood has also been used to create an entrance into the pool like a jetty from where we can sail into the horizon.

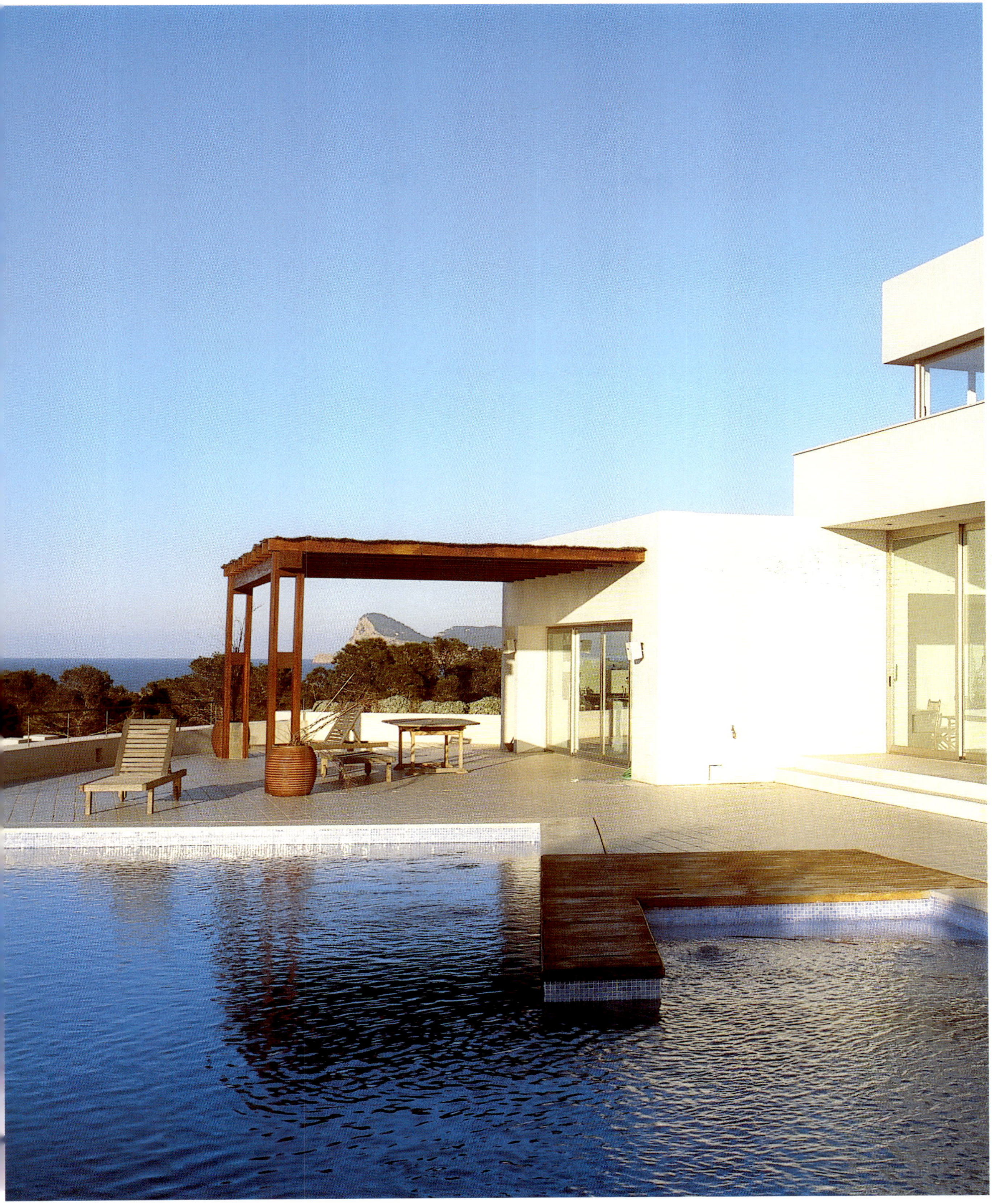

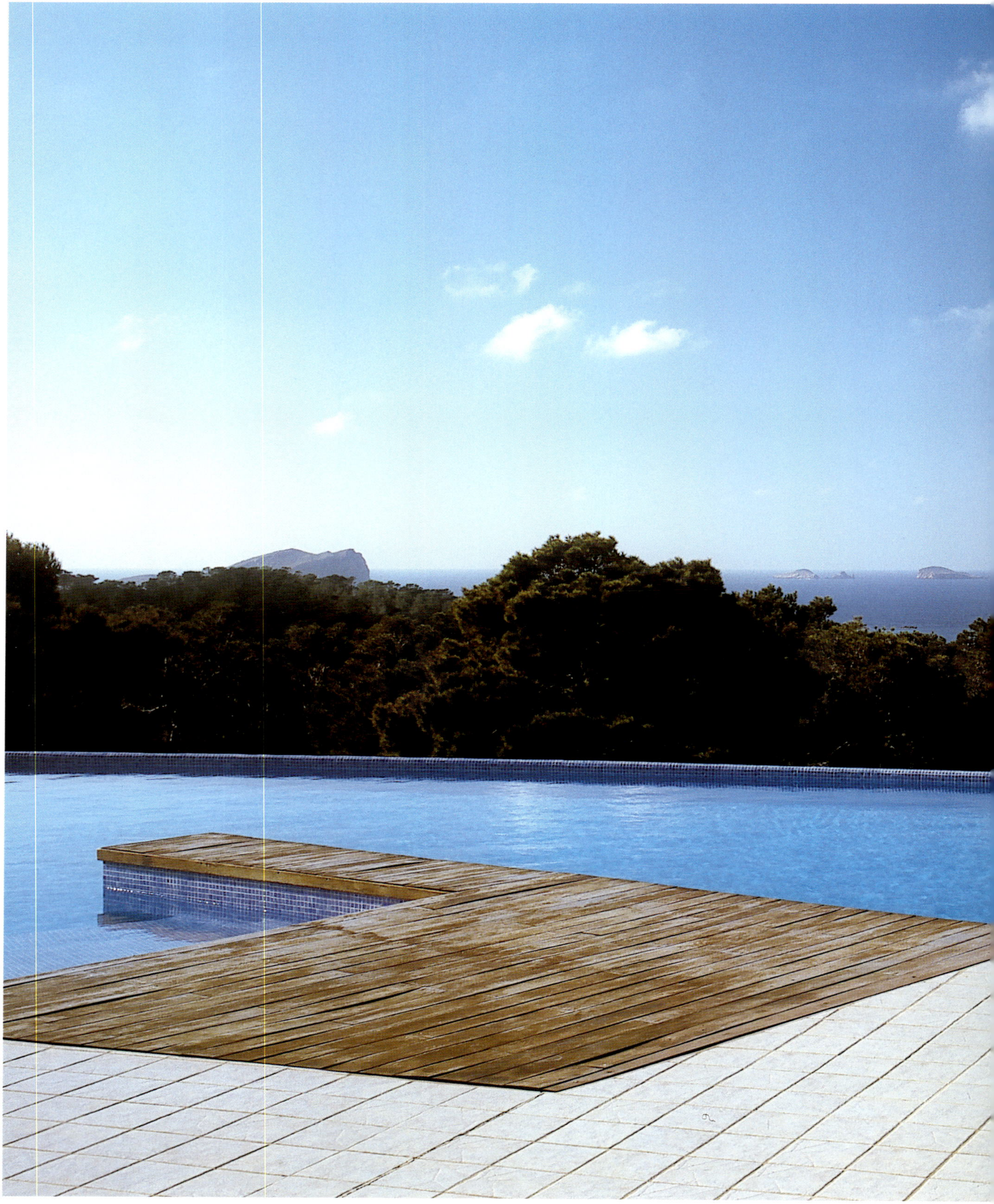

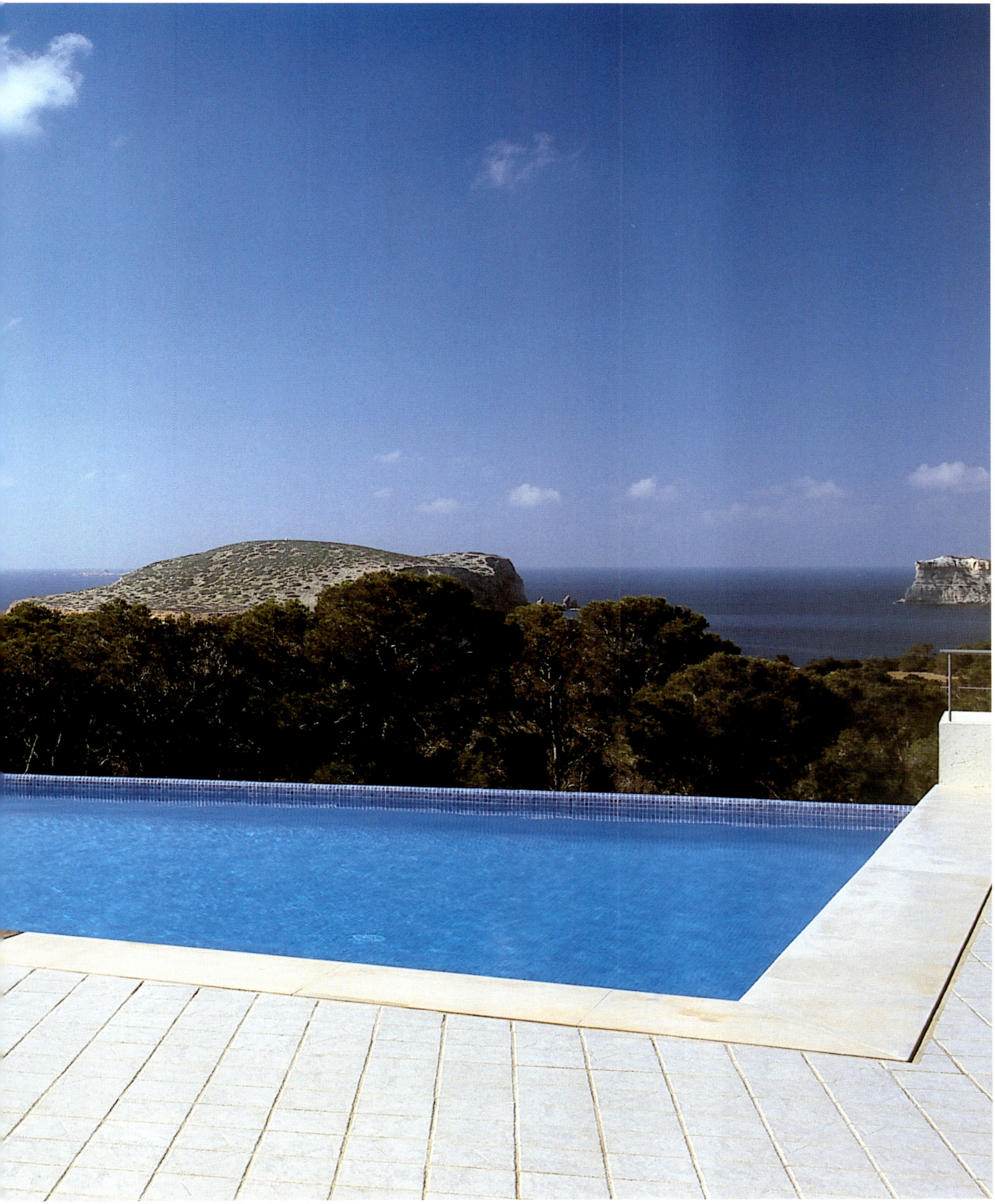

ピエリーノ邸 アルベルト・ブルクハルト

天然の茂み　*NATURAL LUSHNESS*

バル—コロンビア　撮影：アントニオ・カスタネダ

　バルの海岸沿い、カリブ海の群青色と温暖な気候が育んだ豊かな植生がこの邸宅のフォルム、線の組み合わせ、指向性を定義している。海の景色が設計に組み込まれているのはいうまでもないが、屋内空間には水や植物といったコロンビアの特色である自然的要素も大胆に取り入れられている。住宅のさまざまな要素が結合する場所となっているプールは、異なった質感を持つ種々のテラスによって囲まれている。その上を木の茂みが蔽い、新鮮な空気を住宅全体に降り注いでいる。

This residence is situated in the coastal region of Baru, and its location next to the sea and natural surroundings defines its shapes, line composition and orientation. The ocean view has been exploited but also the interior spaces have been designed taking into consideration natural elements such as water or vegetation.

The swimming pool is found at a point joining various parts of the house and is surrounded by a terrace of different textures and the lush nature, which provides freshness.

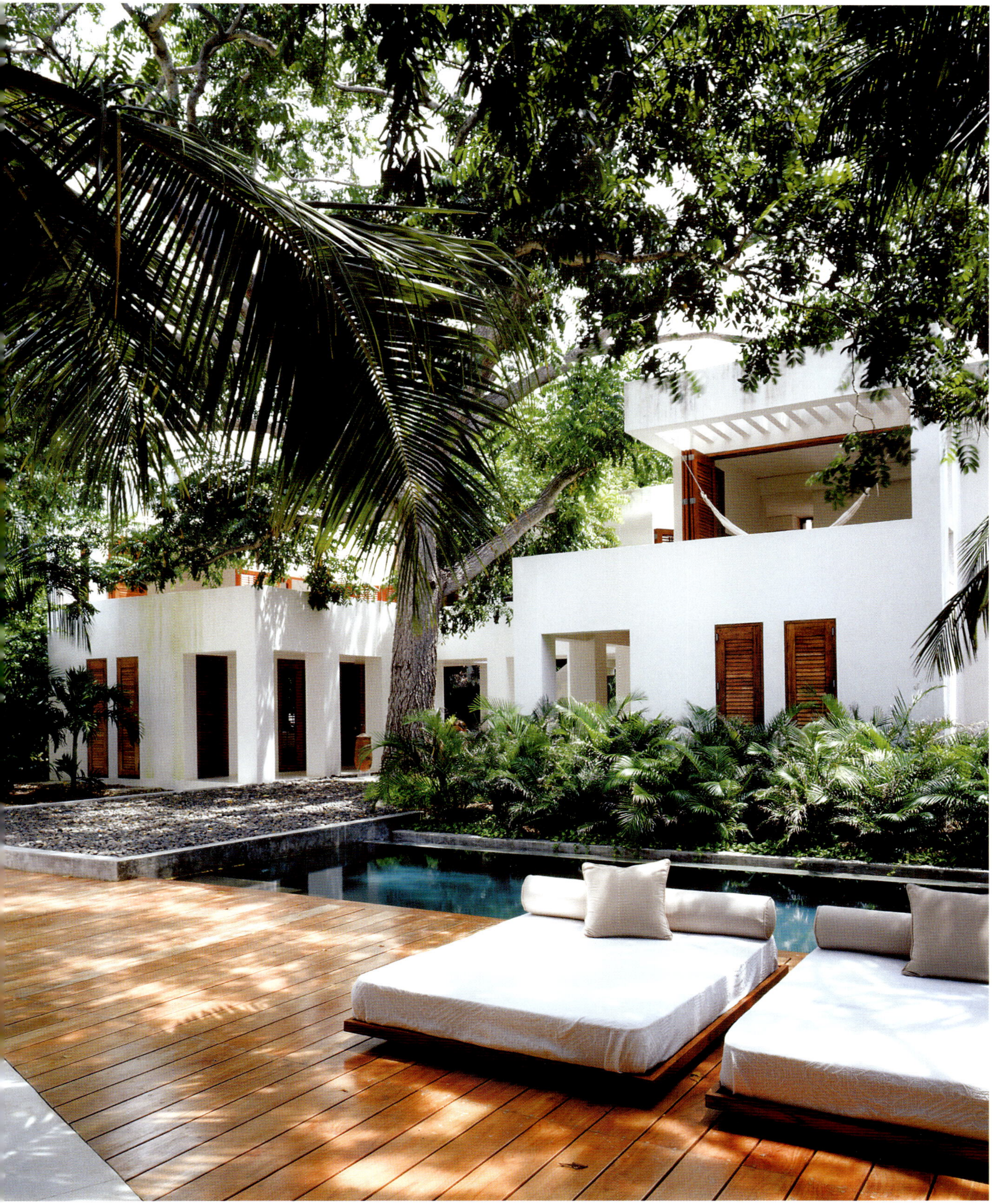

134 | 視覚としての水 | See it

住宅の各ヴォリュームはそこから派生するテラスによって結ばれている。海を眺めるテラスは真っ白で、純潔。そしてプールの周りのテラスは、この住宅を定義する材料と形のサンプル集になっている。

The house has many terraces situated between the volumes it is formed from. One has views of the ocean and is white and immaculate. Another, around the pool, combines materials and shapes to define its style.

エリー・サーブ邸　ウラジミール・ジュロヴィッチ・ランドスケープ・アーキテクチュア

山間の優雅な憩い　REST BETWEEN MOUNTAINS

ファクラ―レバノン　撮影：ジェラルディン・ブルニール

　庭園は普段は住人のリラクゼーションの場であるが、時に豪華なパーティー会場となる。プールのラインはあくまでも純粋で歪みがなく、その水面は空が自分の顔を映す巨大な鏡のようだ。手前のテラスにはテーブルと椅子が置かれ、夜になると傍の2基の炉床の火がそこに集う人々に暖かさと安息をもたらす。人々はかつて砂漠でそうしたように、星を眺めながら明日の平和を祈る。

The garden of this residence is a space designed both to hold social events and for relaxation. The swimming pool has impeccable, clean lines, and the water appears as a large mirror, where the sky looks down at itself. Next to the pool is a terrace with seats and a small tables.
This space is flanked by two fireplaces, which provide heat and comfort at night, whether during nocturnal parties or nights spent peacefully staring up at the stars.

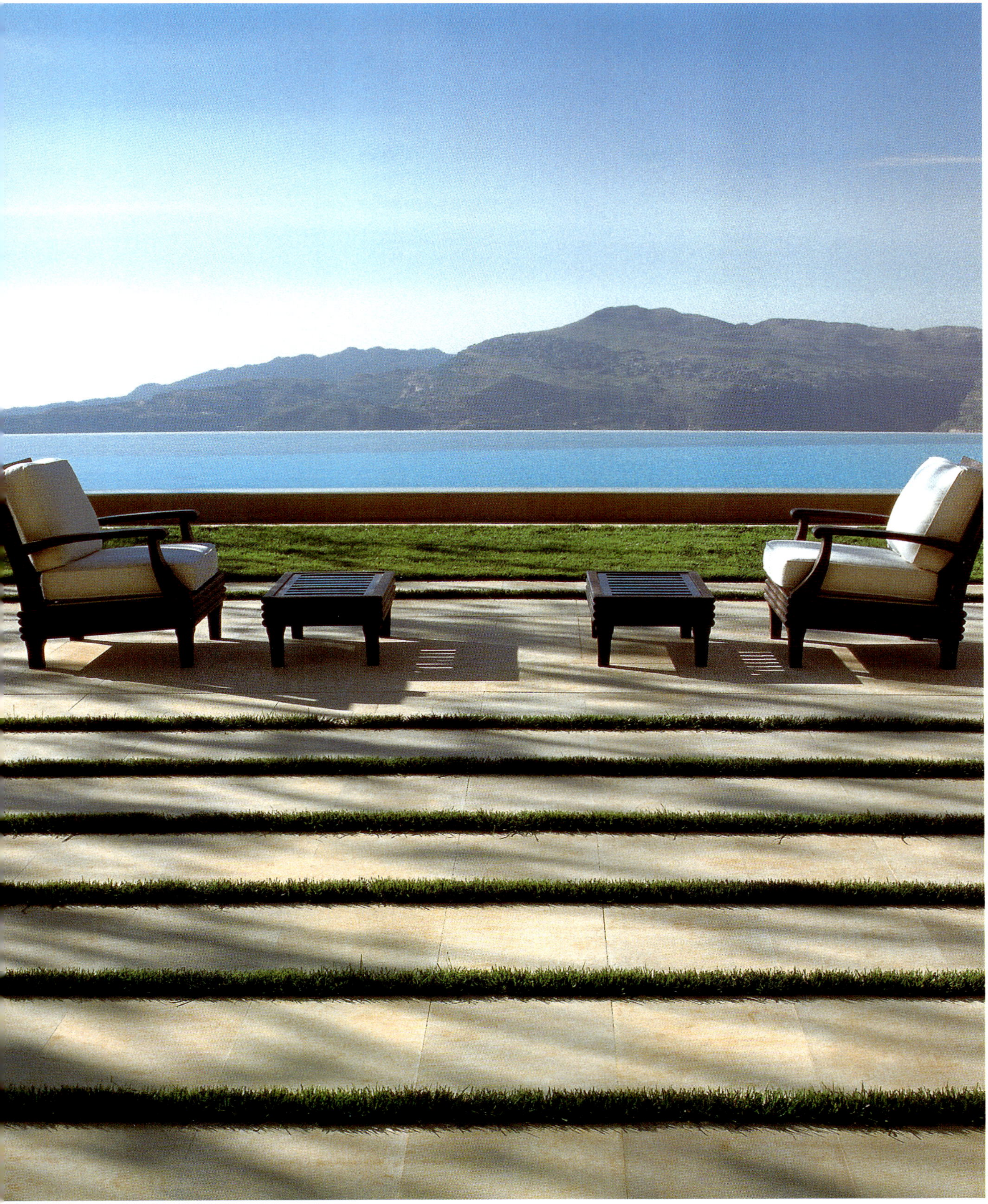

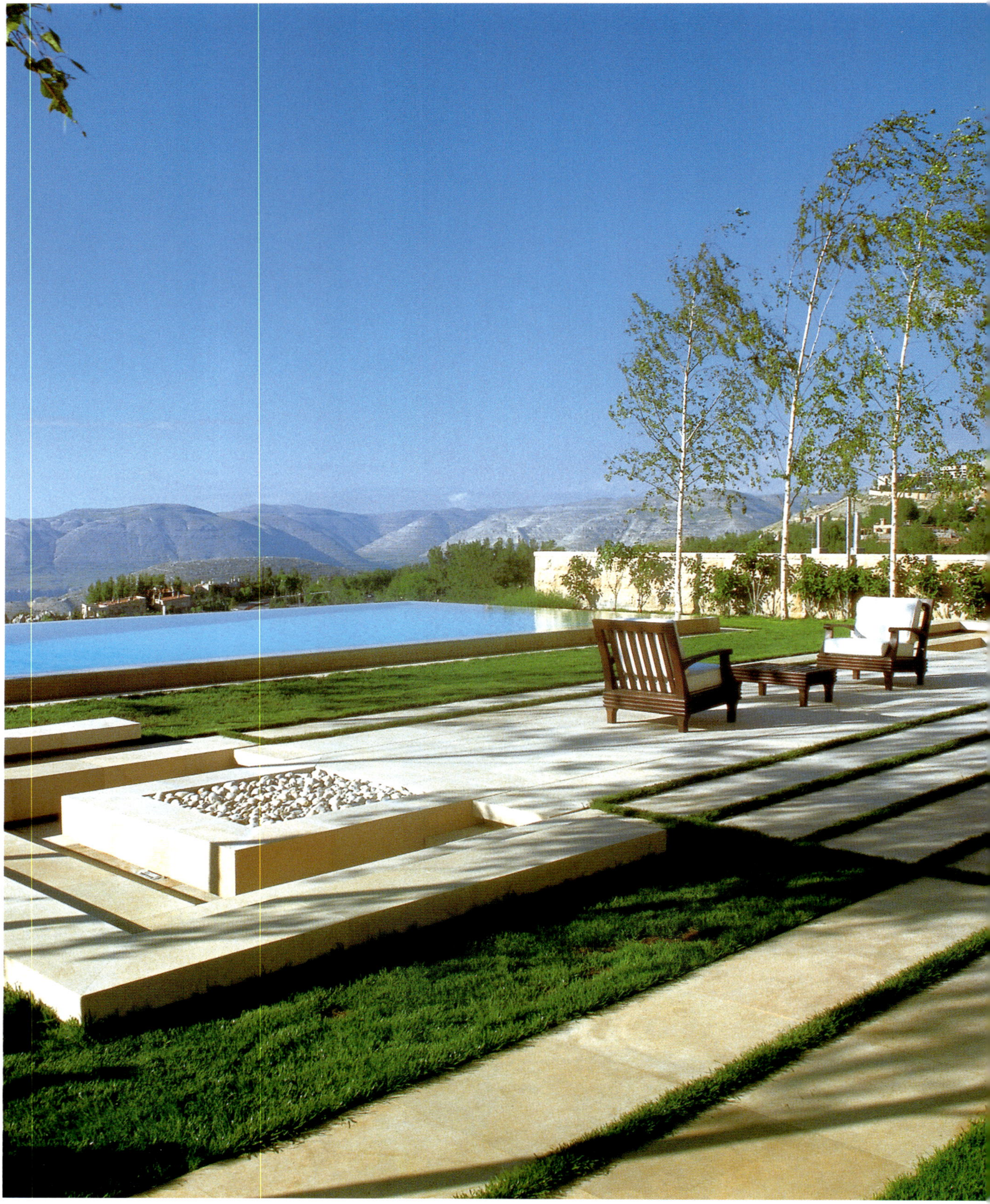

日が沈む頃、住宅を優しく包む山々の稜線とプールやテラスの水平な線が美しいコントラストを描き出す。自然と建築が創造した詩的世界が広がる。

At nightfall, the horizontal lines that mark the terrace and the swimming pool form a strong contrast with the scenery that surrounds the house. The nature and tranquility make this an idyllic place.

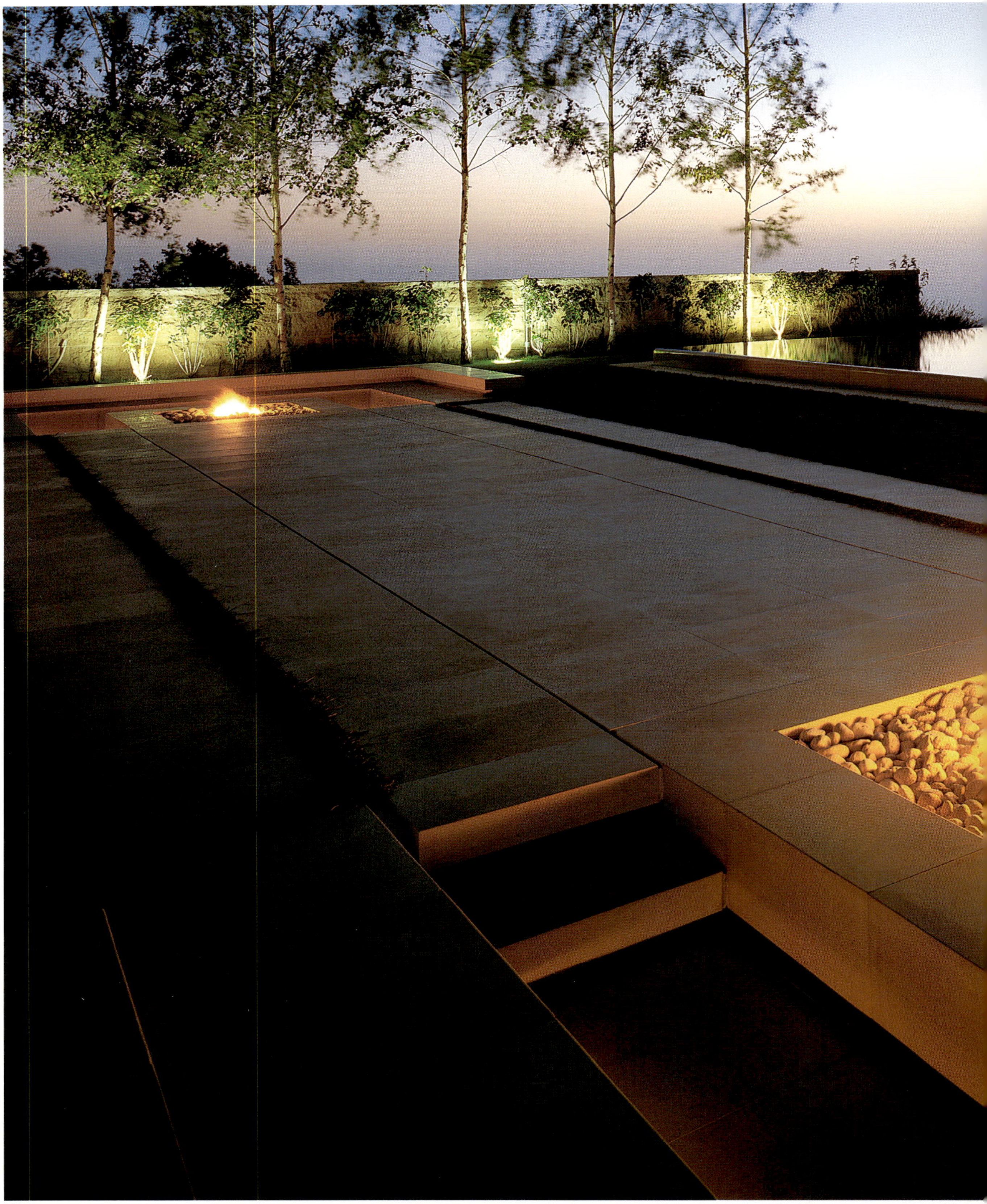

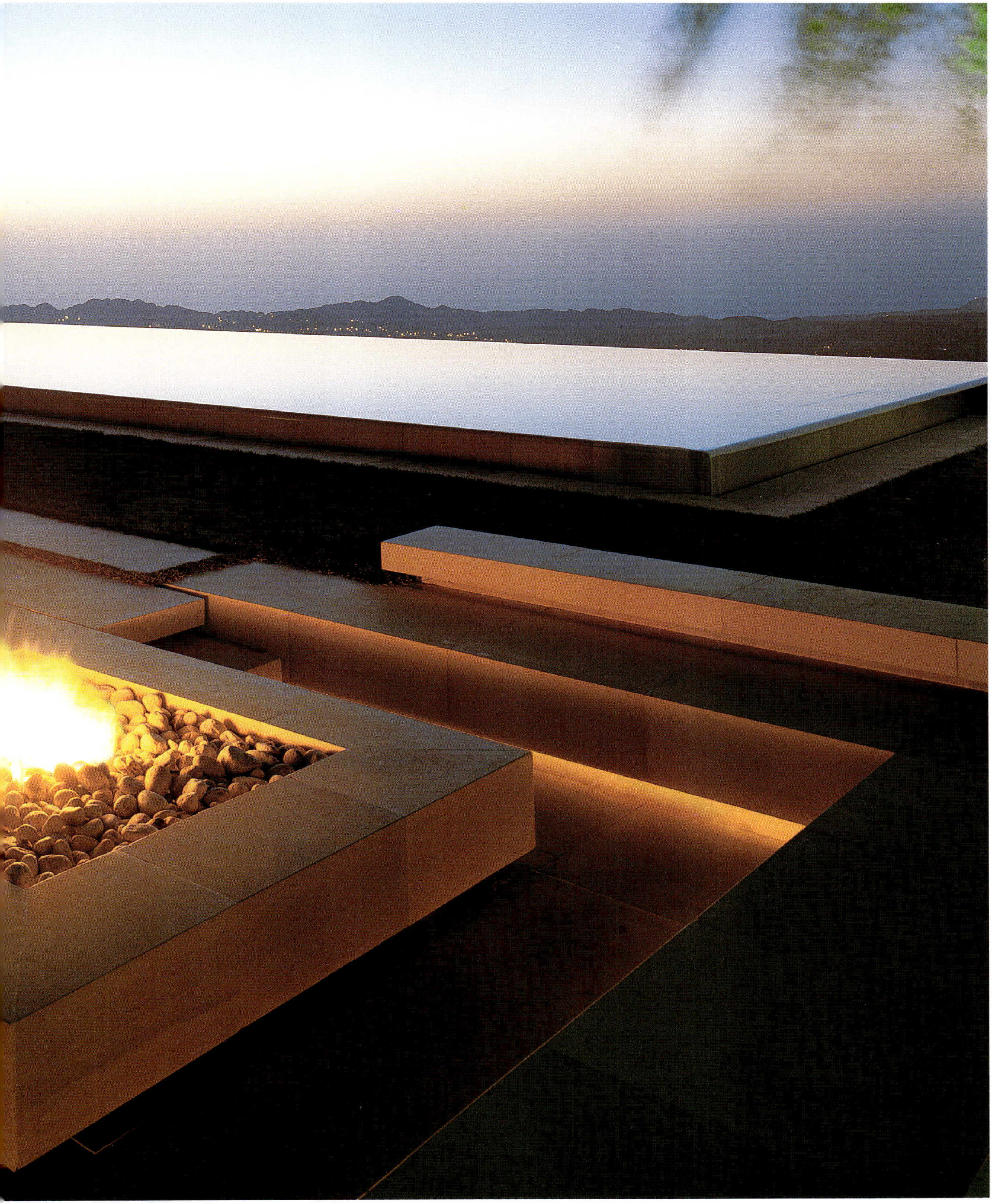

カルデラ湖のある家 GADアーキテクチュア

歴史の十字路にて　IN AN HISTORIC PLACE

ボドルム—トルコ　撮影：アリ・ベックマン

　3000年以上もの昔に開けたトルコの港湾都市ボドルムの背後に広がる山地に、この住宅は立つ。地区の建築規制により75㎡以上の建物を建てることが許されなかったため、3つのヴォリュームをポーチで結ぶこととしたが、それが逆にダイナミックな構造を生んだ。開放型平面にすることによって、気温の高い季節に欠くことのできない柔らかい風が誘い込まれ、屋外プールが極暑の夏にリラクゼーションの場を提供する。

This residence is located in Borum, a rural region of Turkey with over three thousand years of history. The architectural restrictions on the area have determined the design of this house. Three 800 ft^2 volumes, the maximum permitted, are joined by porches and have generated a construction full of dynamism. The open plan guarantees the breeze, which is essential in hotter seasons. Outside, a swimming pool provides a place for relaxation during the extreme heat of the summer.

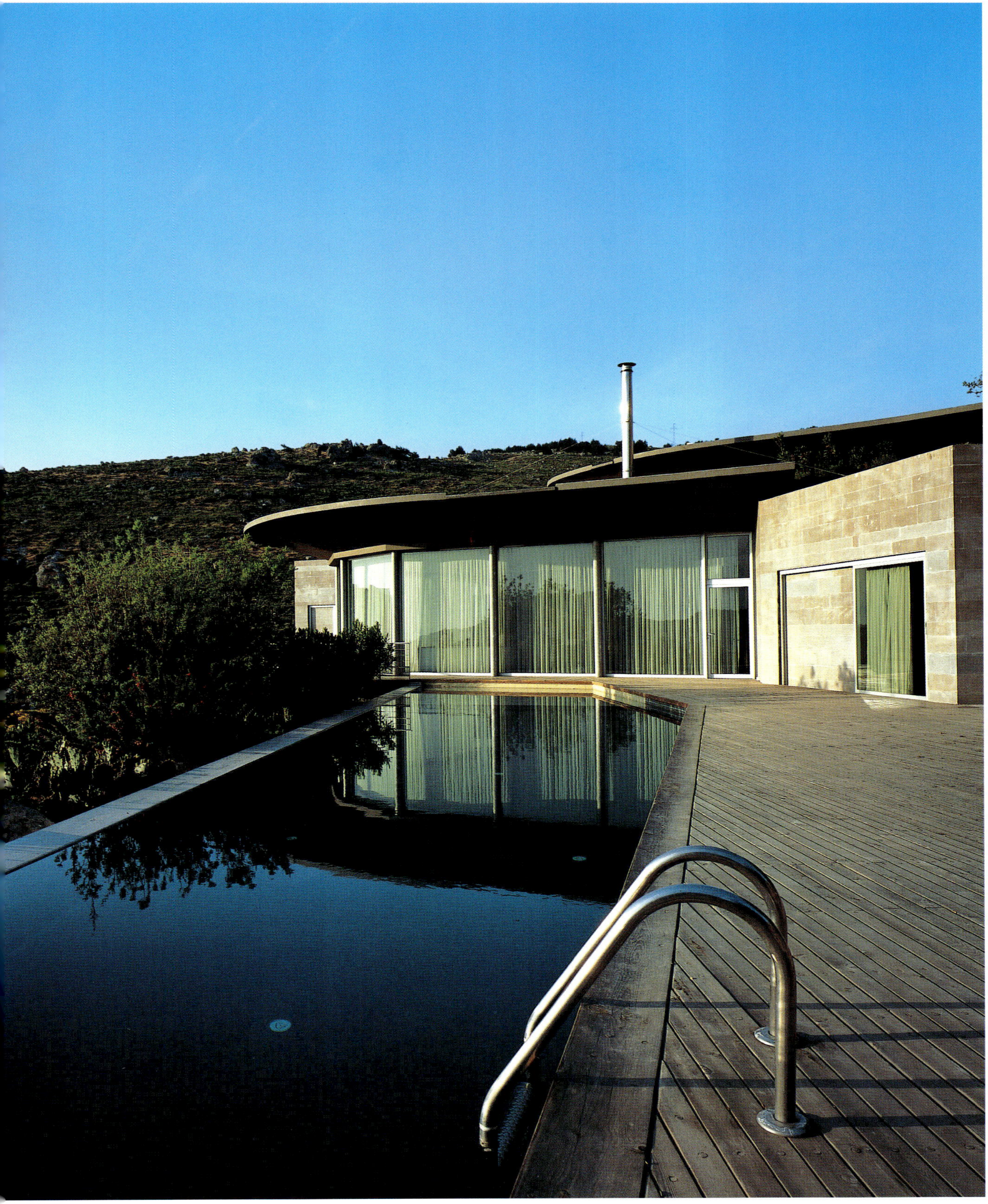

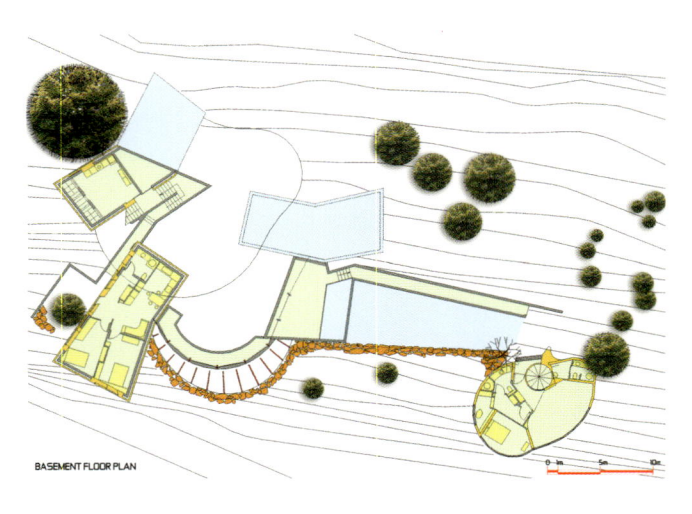

BASEMENT FLOOR PLAN

GROUND FLOOR PLAN

屋根が雨水を溜める浅いプールになっており、1つのプールから次のプールへと流れ落ちていく滝が水の循環を作り出し、天然の冷房システムとなって住宅を冷やす。

Shallow pools that gather rainwater form two of the roofs. This natural cooling system is achieved thanks to the circulation of water, which flows through waterfalls from one pool to the next.

カサ・トーロ アルヴァロ・レイト・シザ・ヴィエイラ
流れ落ちる住宅　A HOUSE ON A SLOPE

アルヴィテ―ポルトガル　撮影：フェルナンド・グエッラ／FG＋SG

　建築家にとっては困難ではあるが挑戦しがいのあるプロジェクトだった。現場の地形はある種の標準的形状の住宅を建てることを拒んでいたが、南向きの斜面が日照をふんだんに供給してくれるため、住宅を景観と同一方向に開くという発想が生まれた。ヴォリュームは斜面のさまざまなレベルに配置され、それらを屋外庭園が結ぶ形ができあがった。それは住宅へと続く日当たりの良い小道となった。プールは景観に統一され、段差を利用してシャワー、小さな落水、テラスが作られた。

The project for this residence was a real challenge for the architect. The layout of the plot made certain standard forms difficult, but its orientation towards the south favored the lighting and the orientation of the house towards the scenery. Various levels were designed to locate the volumes, which connect with outdoor courtyards and allow a path to reach the house from south. A swimming pool integrates with the landscape and the changing level is used to install a shower, a small waterfall and a terrace.

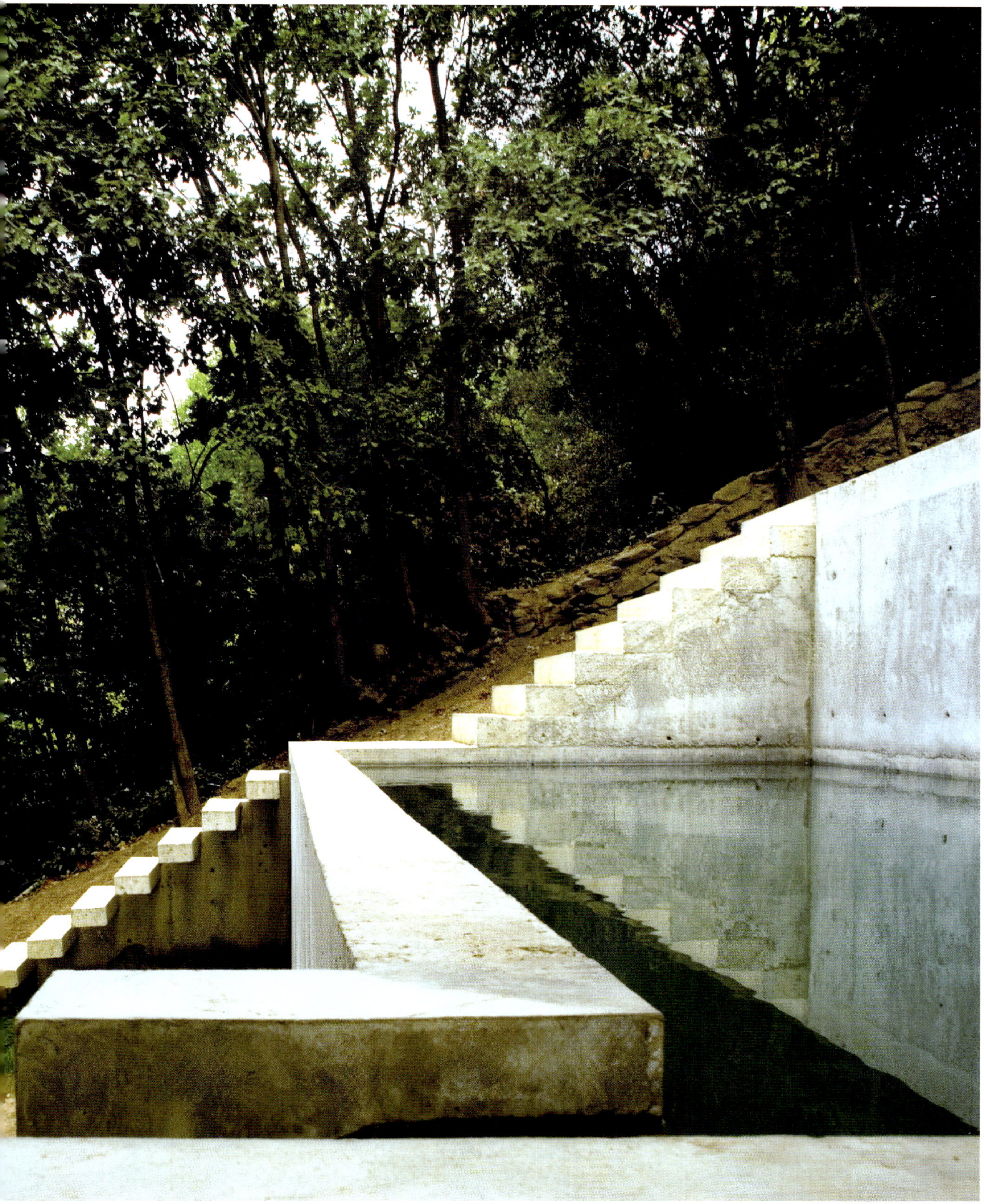

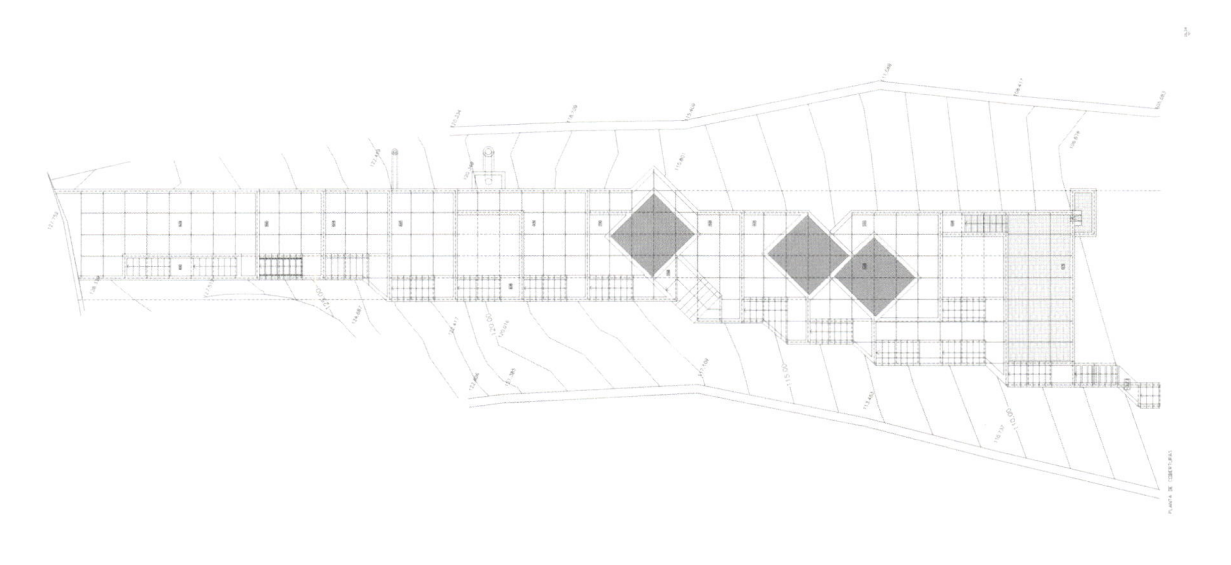

148 ｜視覚としての水 ｜See it

流れ落ちる住宅の最下段にあるプールにはテラスとシャワーがついており、余分な水は崖から湧出するわき水のように排水される。まわりを森に囲まれた平和な空間。

The swimming pool situated on the lower levels includes a terrace with shower and a small drainage point where excess water overflows. The forested landscape surrounds the area creating a peaceful space.

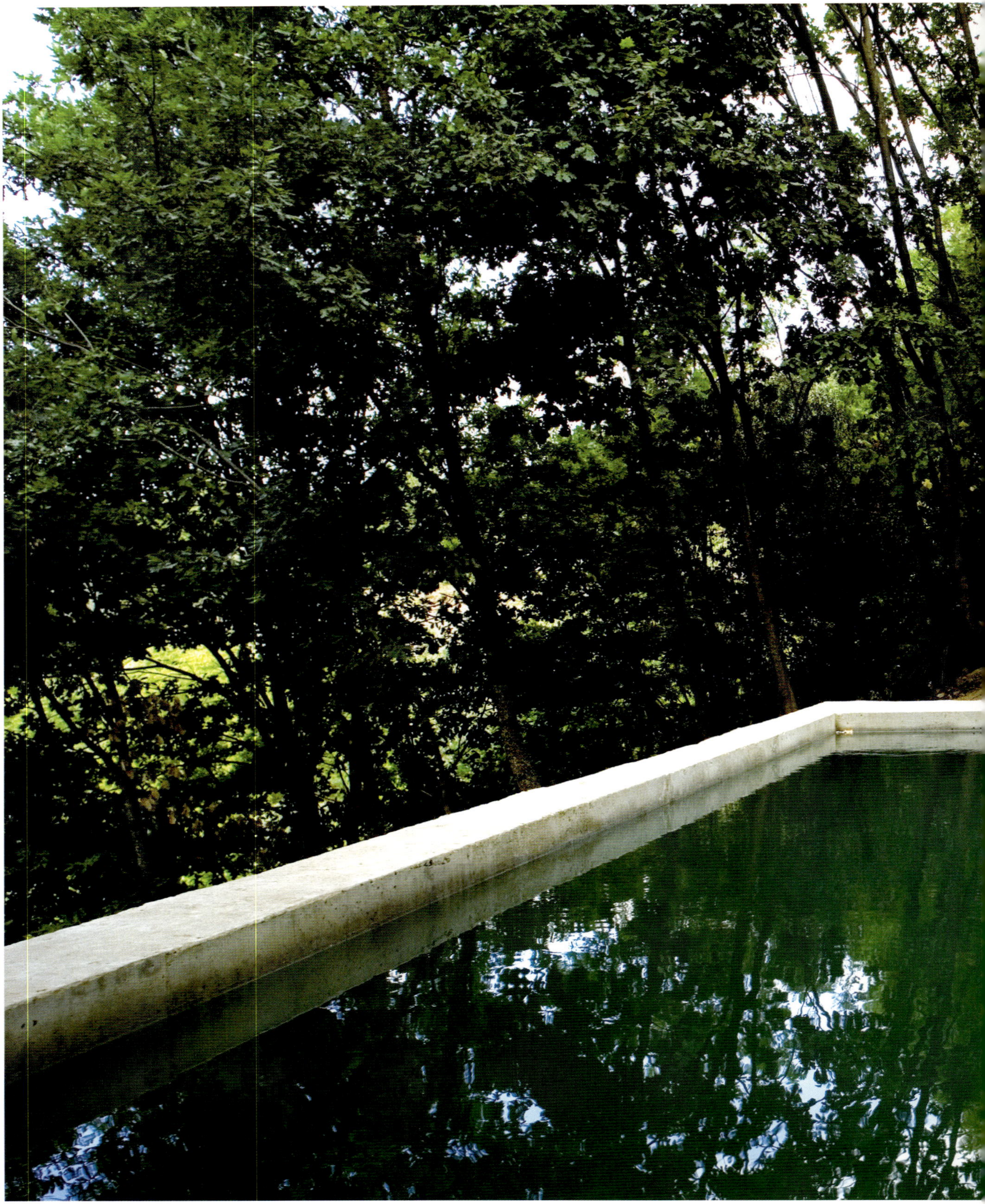

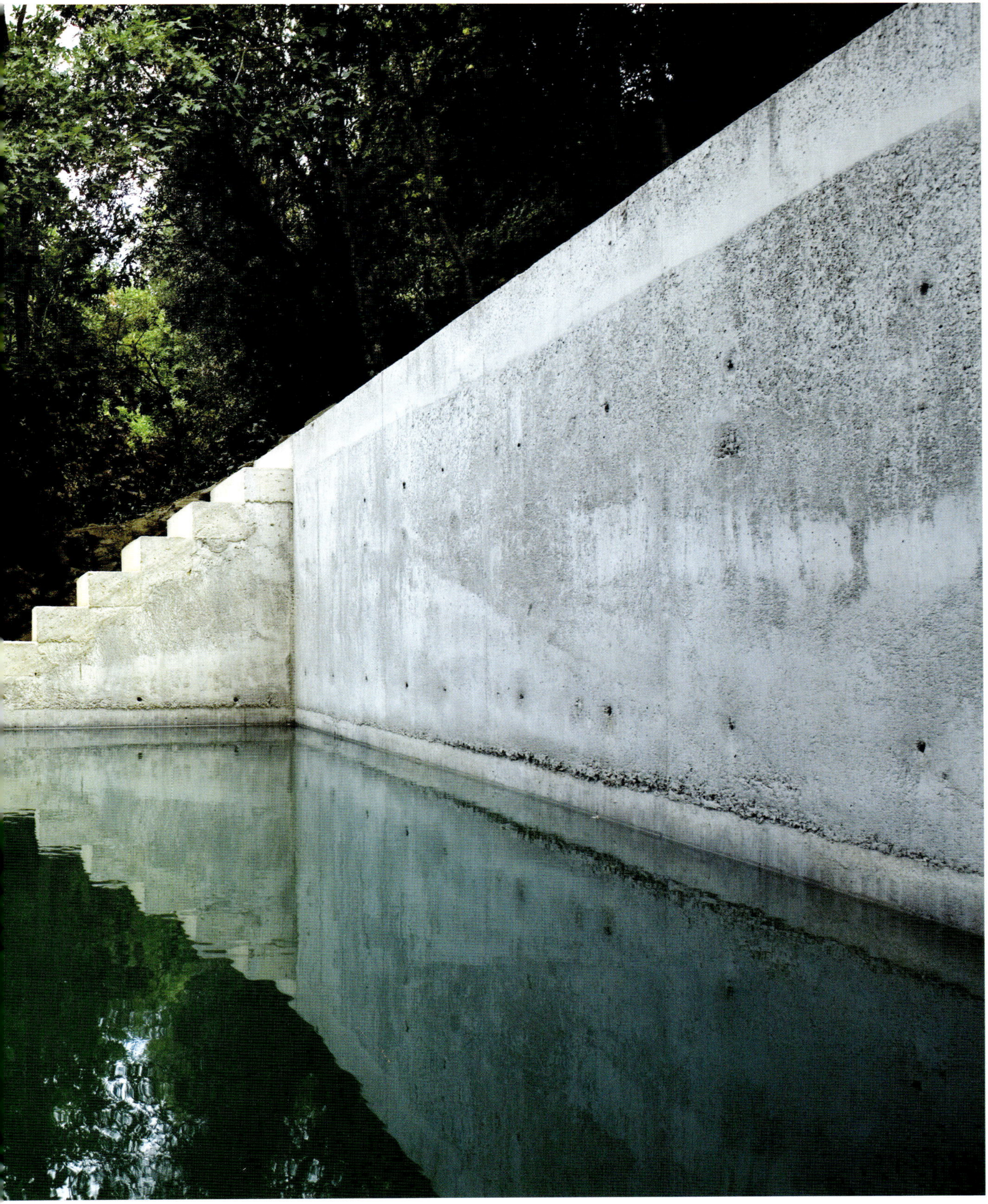

ウッドサイド・レジデンス ラツコー建築設計事務所

水の小道　THE PATH OF WATER

ウッドサイド―カリフォルニア―アメリカ　撮影：ニコラ・ブラウン

　ラツコー建築設計事務所は、水の持つ実験的性質と空間を創造し分界する能力を最大限生かし、泉から湧き出る水の流れの庭園を作りだした。この広がりのある空間の中心にあるのは、小川からの水で満たされた池だ。玄関のすぐ横、ドアへと向かう石畳の脇にある5本の筒口を持つ泉が源流となり、そこから流れ出た水は勢いを得、石畳の向こう側で小川へと注ぎ、最後に池に到達する。

Lutsko Associates have taken full advantage of the experimental qualities of water and its ability to create spaces and limits, by constructing a garden that makes use of a spring stream. The central element of this spacious area is a pond that fills with water from a small channel. The flow of water begins next to the entrance to the house: a fountain with five jets that marks the entrance walkway. On the other side the water gains strength, falls into the channel and finally arrives at the pond.

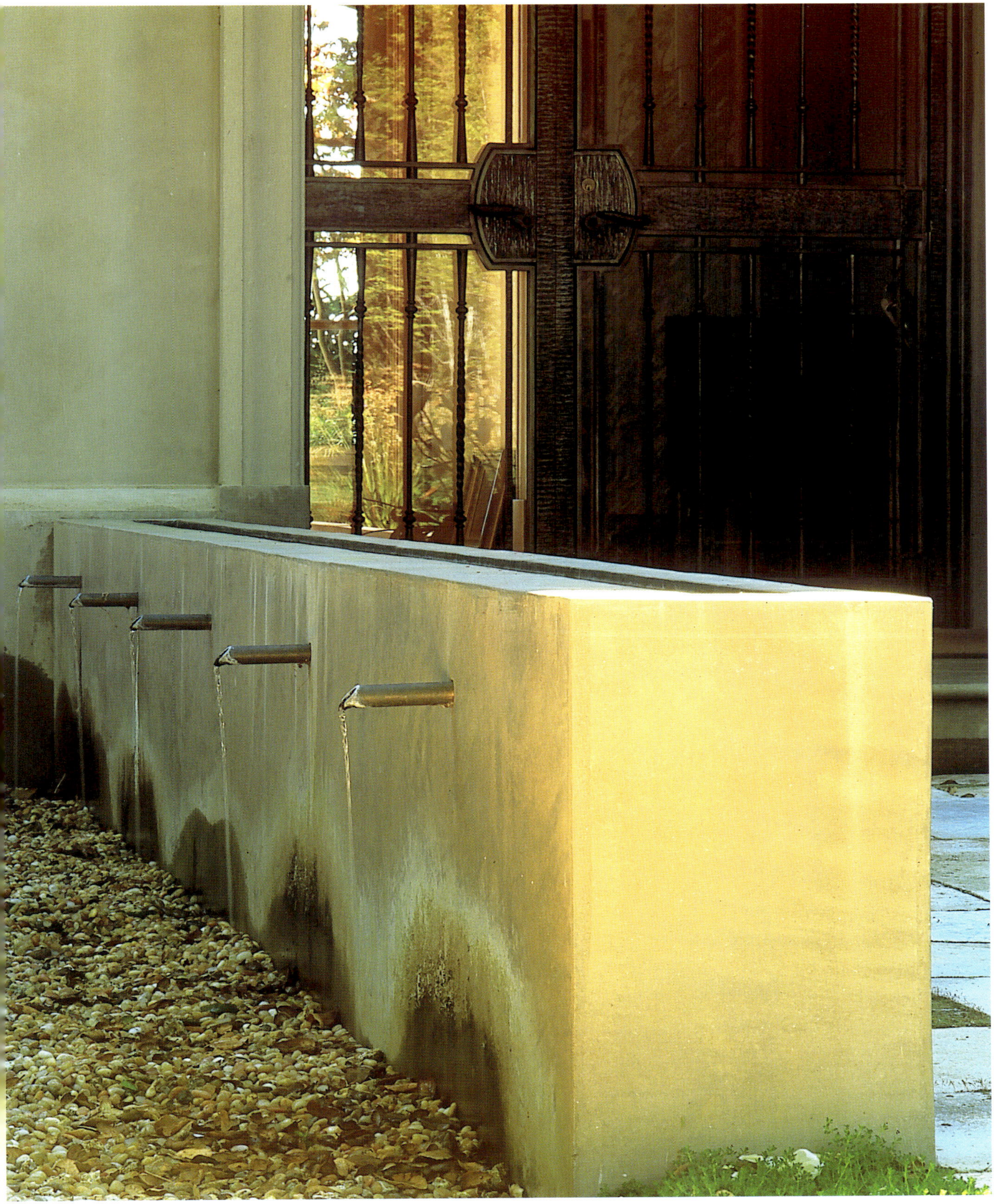

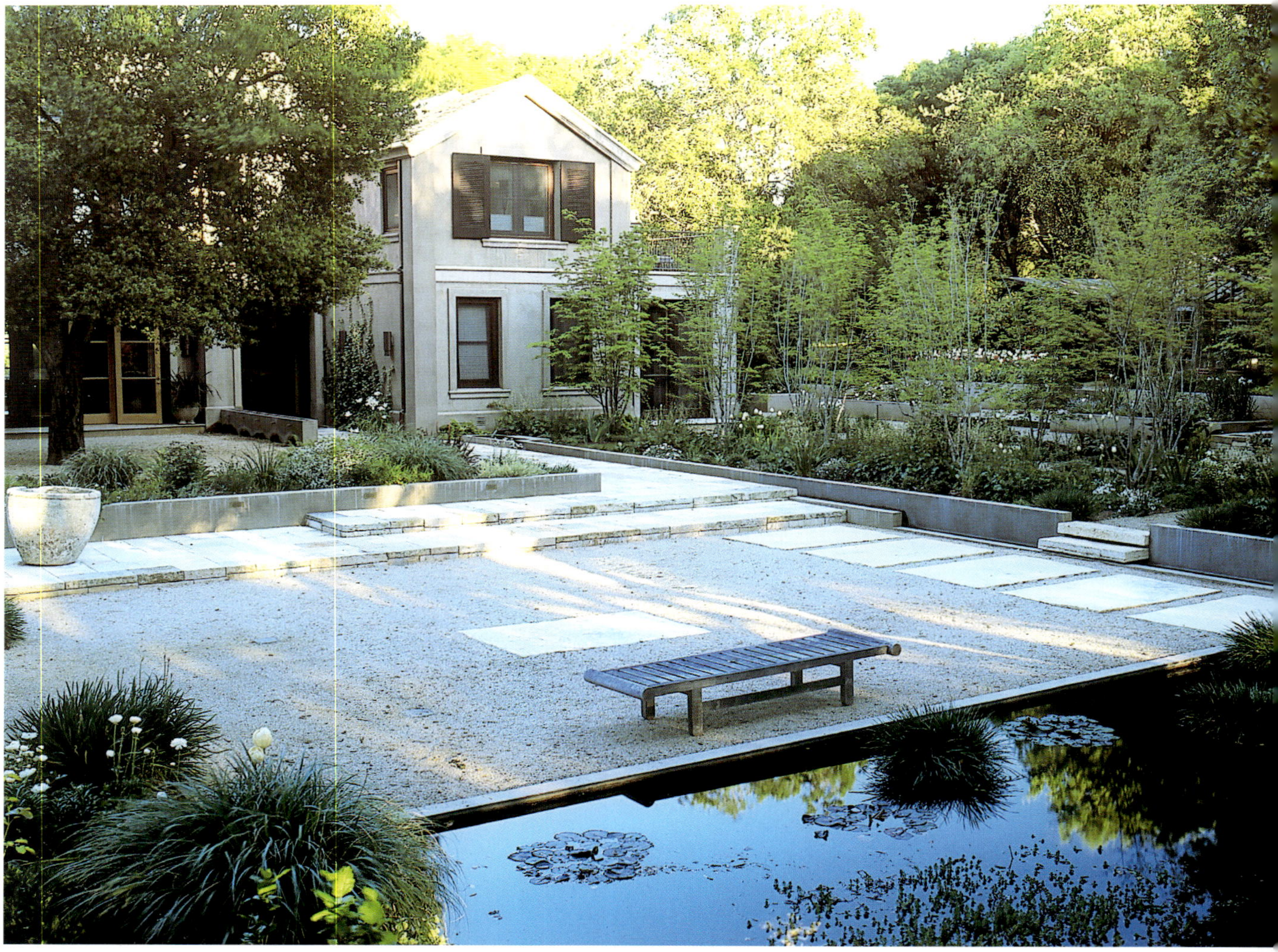

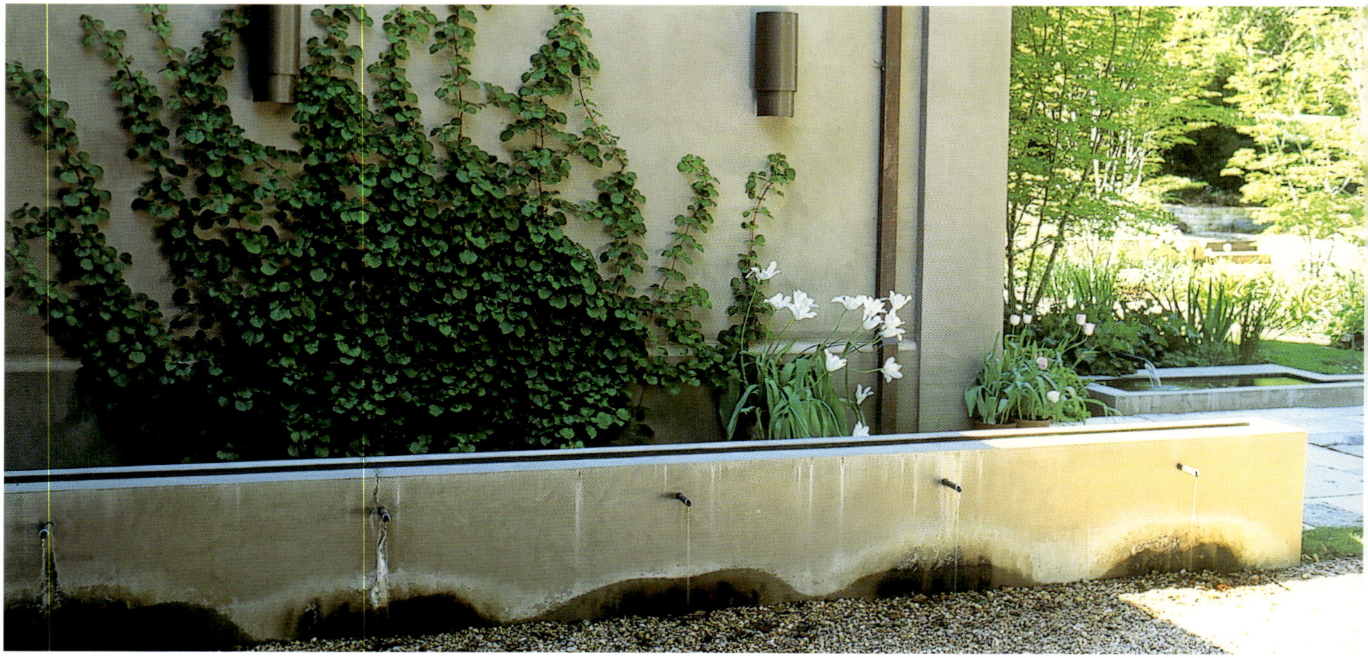

筒口からほとばしる水は小さな溜まりに注ぎ、そこから小川のせせらぎとなって流れ出す。段差のある場所では2つの小さな滝となって流れ落ち、最後に池を満たす。小川は青々と繁った植物で縁取られている。

The water spurts from the jets and fills a small pool. It flows down a channel and creates two small waterfalls when the level changes, before reaching the pond. The vegetation lines the flow of water with nature.

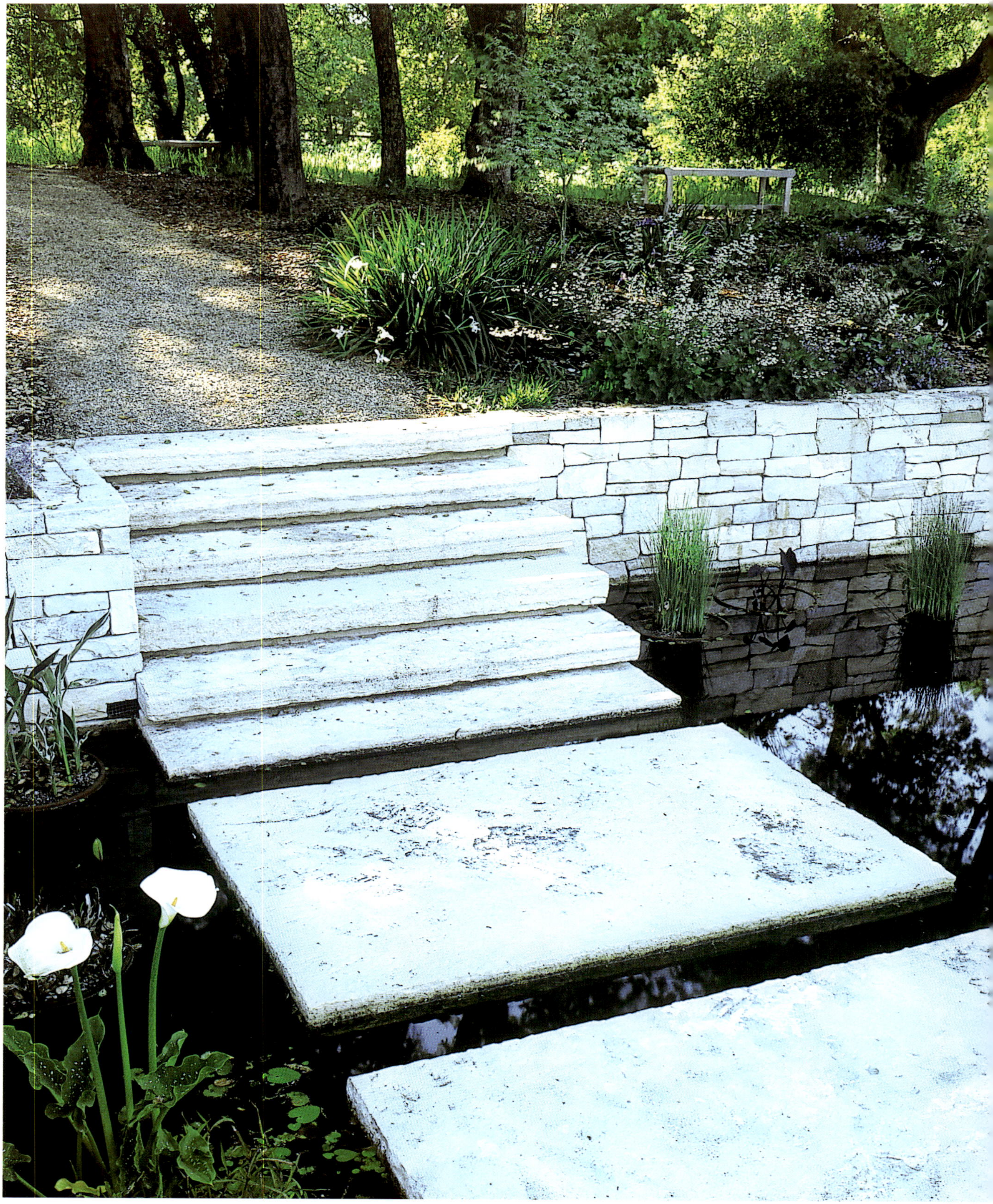

石灰岩のスラブの飛び石を踏みながら池を横切り、数段石の階段を昇ると、そこには地中海性気候によって育まれた豊かな植生が広がる。中心の池はこの豊かな空間を散策する数本の小道の始まりでもあり、終わりでもある。

The limestone slabs form the walkway that crosses the pond. The stairs lead to the garden where Mediterranean vegetation has been planted. The central pond is the beginning and end of several paths around the space.

リューティ　ドナルド・ヤコブ／ヤコブ・ラントシャフツアルヒテクテン

分界する水　CREATE A LIMIT

リューティリンク―リーヘン―スイス　撮影：ドナルド・ヤコブ

　住宅とバーゼル市街地の景観との間に広がる空間に家族がゆっくりとくつろぐことのできるプライベートな環境を創造すること、これがこの庭園に与えられた使命だった。この庭の主要エレメントは立方体の石の泉。その泉から湧き出た水は、ファサードと平行に走る水路を通り、池に注ぐ。水路は庭園を、緑の芝生の部分と住宅の前の砂利や玉石の部分とに分界する役割を果たしている。その形とレイアウトは、庭園の異なった領域にそれぞれの使命を与え、異なった空間にそれぞれの用途を付与している。

The design of this garden had to create a family environment integrated into a space between the house and the views of Basel. A cubic stone fountain is the main element. The water springs from the fountain and enters a channel that runs parallel to one of the façades of the house, finishing in a pond. This channel separates the green area of the garden from the stone and gravel area in front of the house. These shapes and their layout give order to the different areas of the garden and delimit the uses of the different spaces.

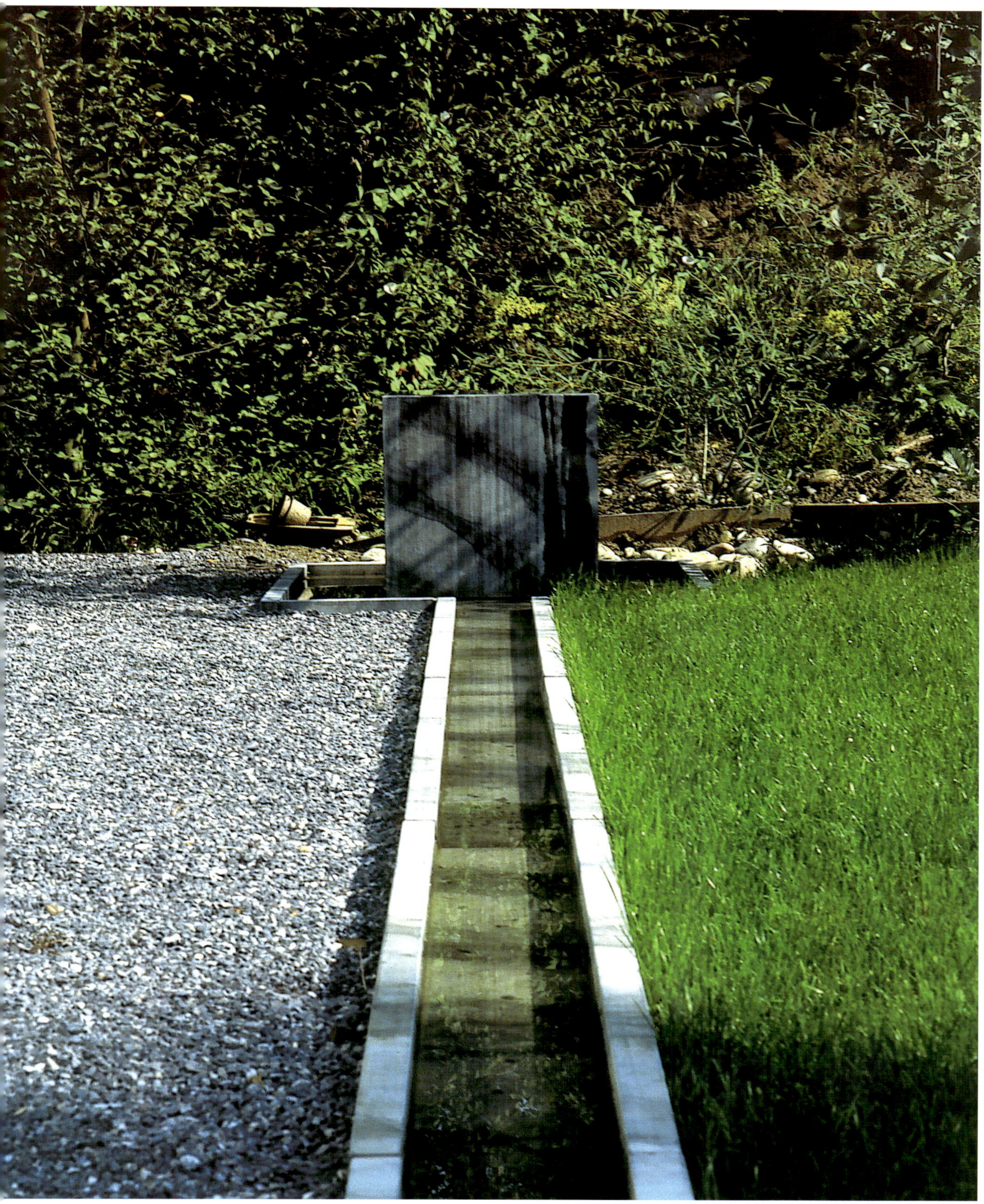

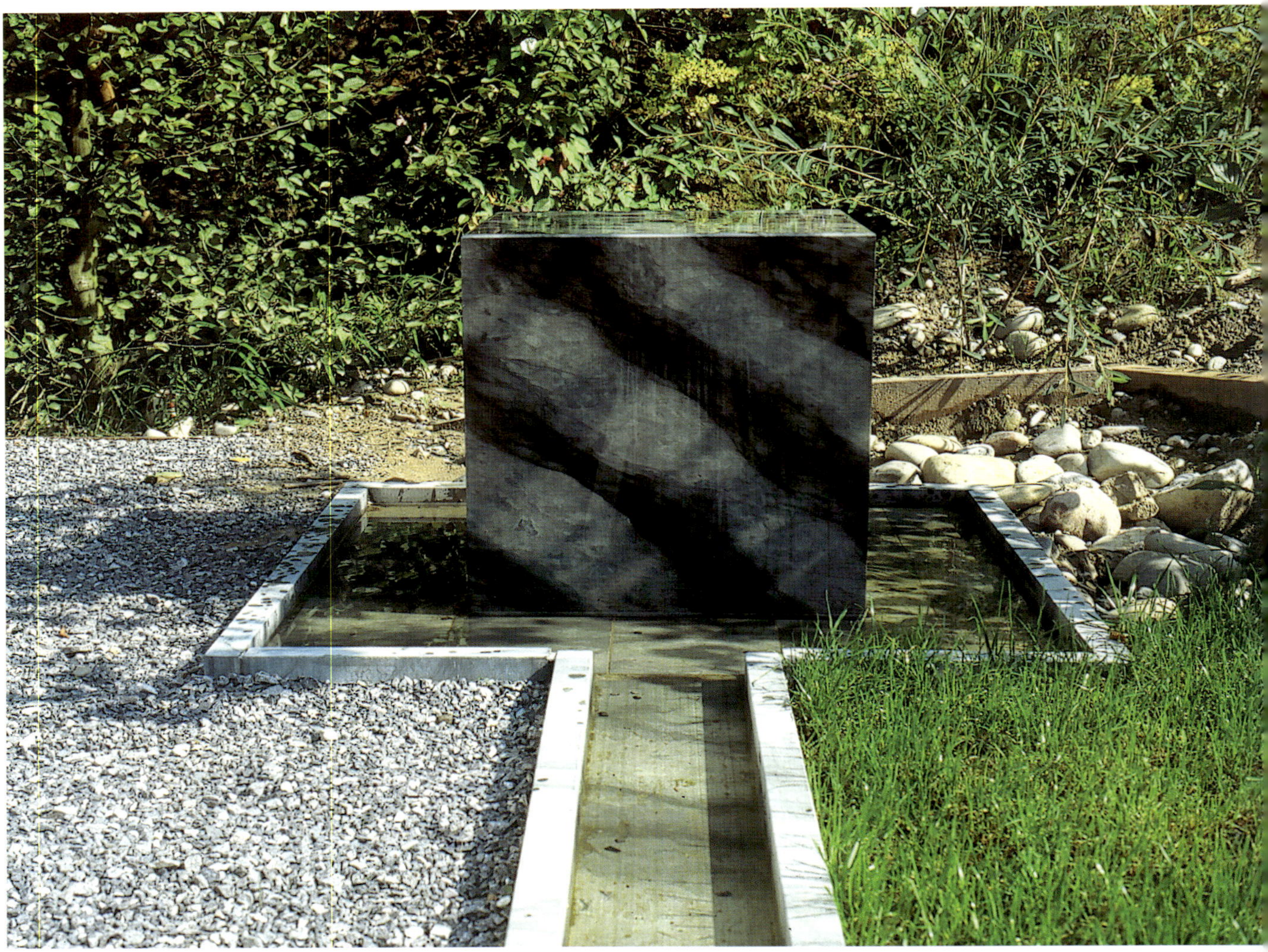

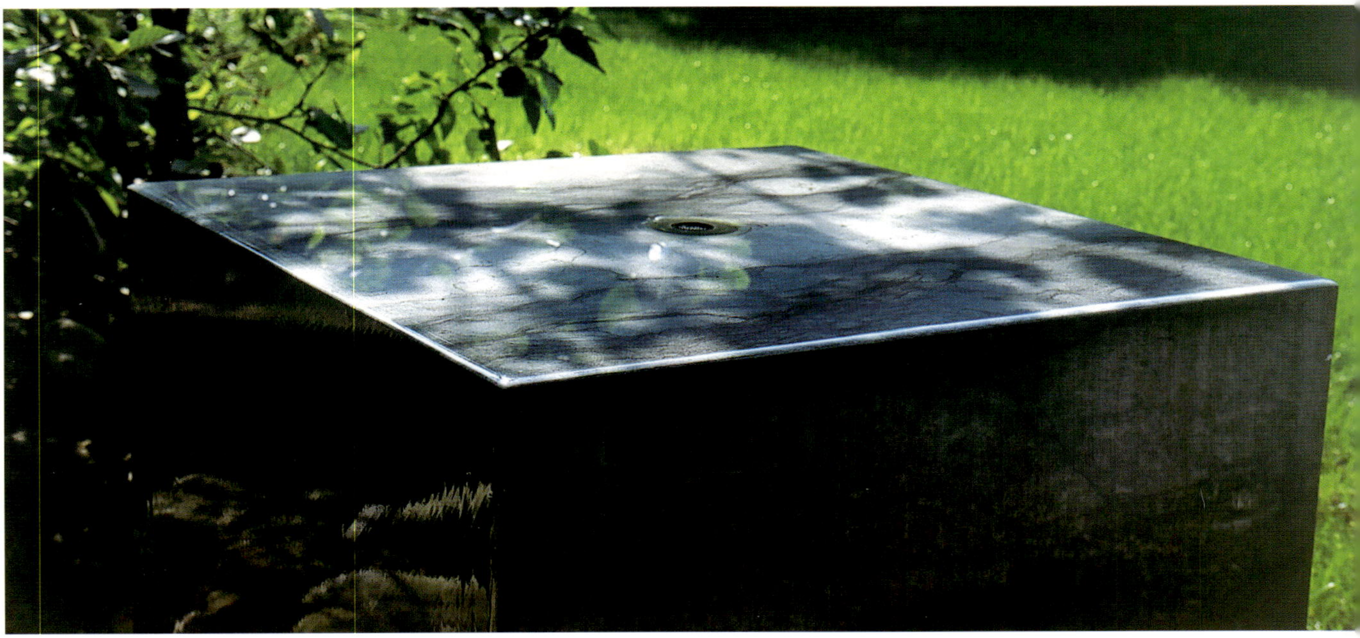

泉と水路の垂直、平行な線が庭園に均衡をもたらしている。細いコンクリートの水路は2つの空間を仕切る境界となり、立方体の泉は彫像的要素としての役割も果たしている。

The straight, clean lines of the fountain and channel give the garden balance. The small concrete channel acts as a border between the two spaces and the cubic fountain acts as a sculptural element.

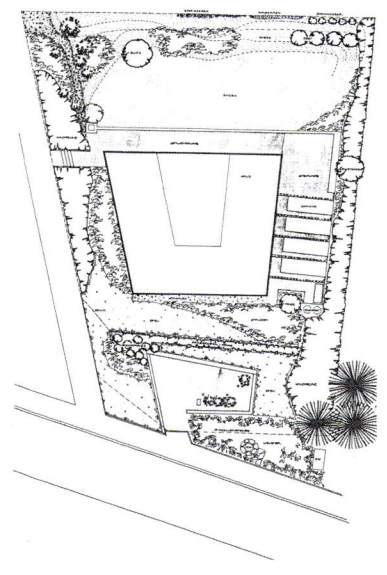

シューベルト邸 ホルガー・シューベルト

ガラスの泉　GLASS FOUNTAIN

ベニス―ロサンゼルス―アメリカ　撮影：ベニー・チャン／フォトワークス

　数年をかけた修復作業により、ミニマリスト的な採光の良い部屋が作られた。庭園にしつらえたガラスの泉と池は、生垣の向こうにベニス運河が流れていることを想起させる。低い壁の筒口から湧き出した水は、礫石の上に25個のゴム製のフェンダーで支えられたガラスの池に注ぐ。形は簡素で、線は清潔だ。透明なガラスと壁の白色が、この庭園に光と侘びの精神をもたらしている。

Throughout the years that this restoration lasted, some minimalist and well-lit rooms were created. In the garden is a glass fountain and pond that remind us that behind the hedge are the canal of Venice. The water springs from behind a small wall and falls in the glass pond, which rests on stones. Twenty-five rubber fenders cushion the glass pond. The shapes are simple and the lines clean. Glass and the color white, generated the sought after simplicity and lighting.

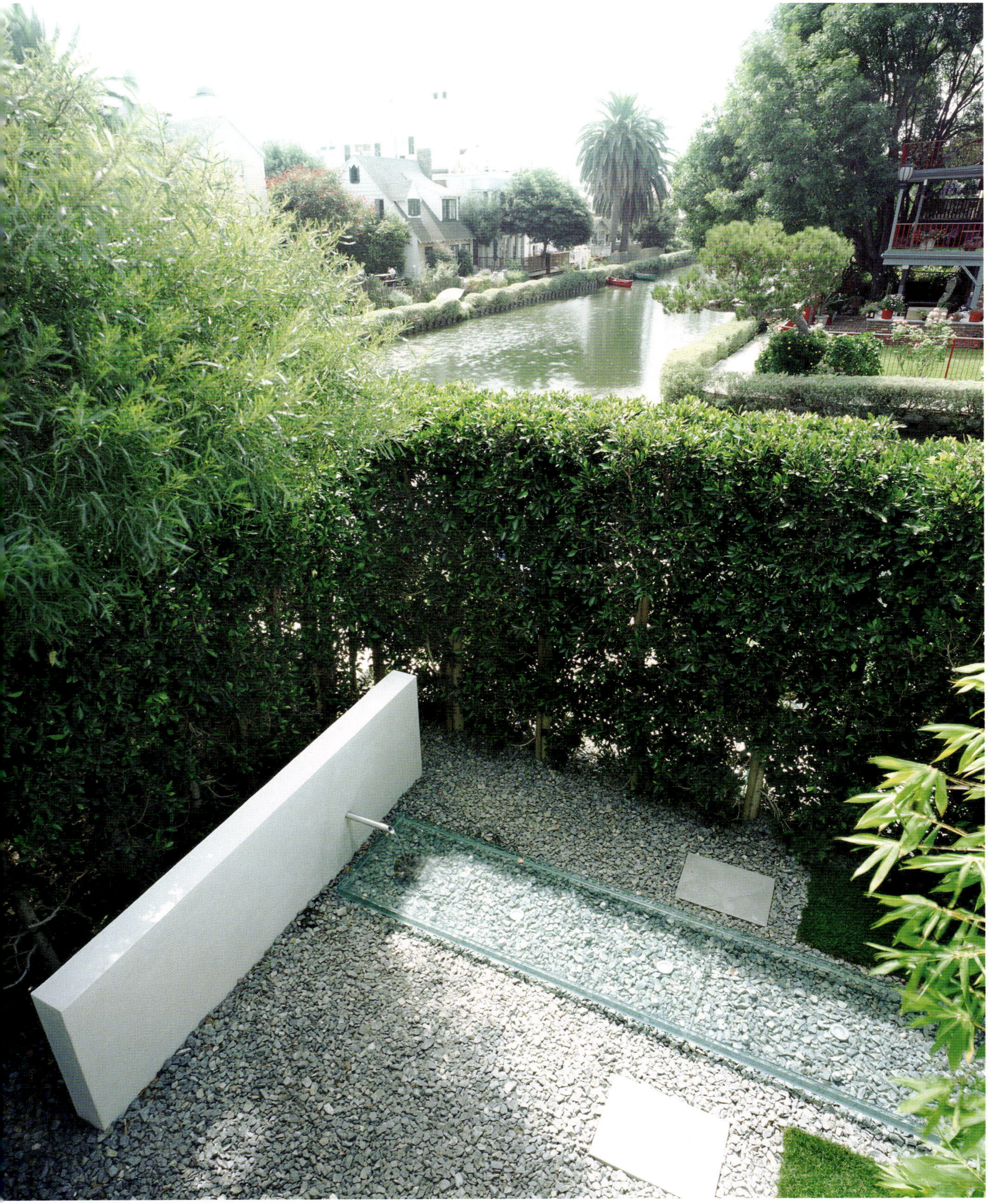

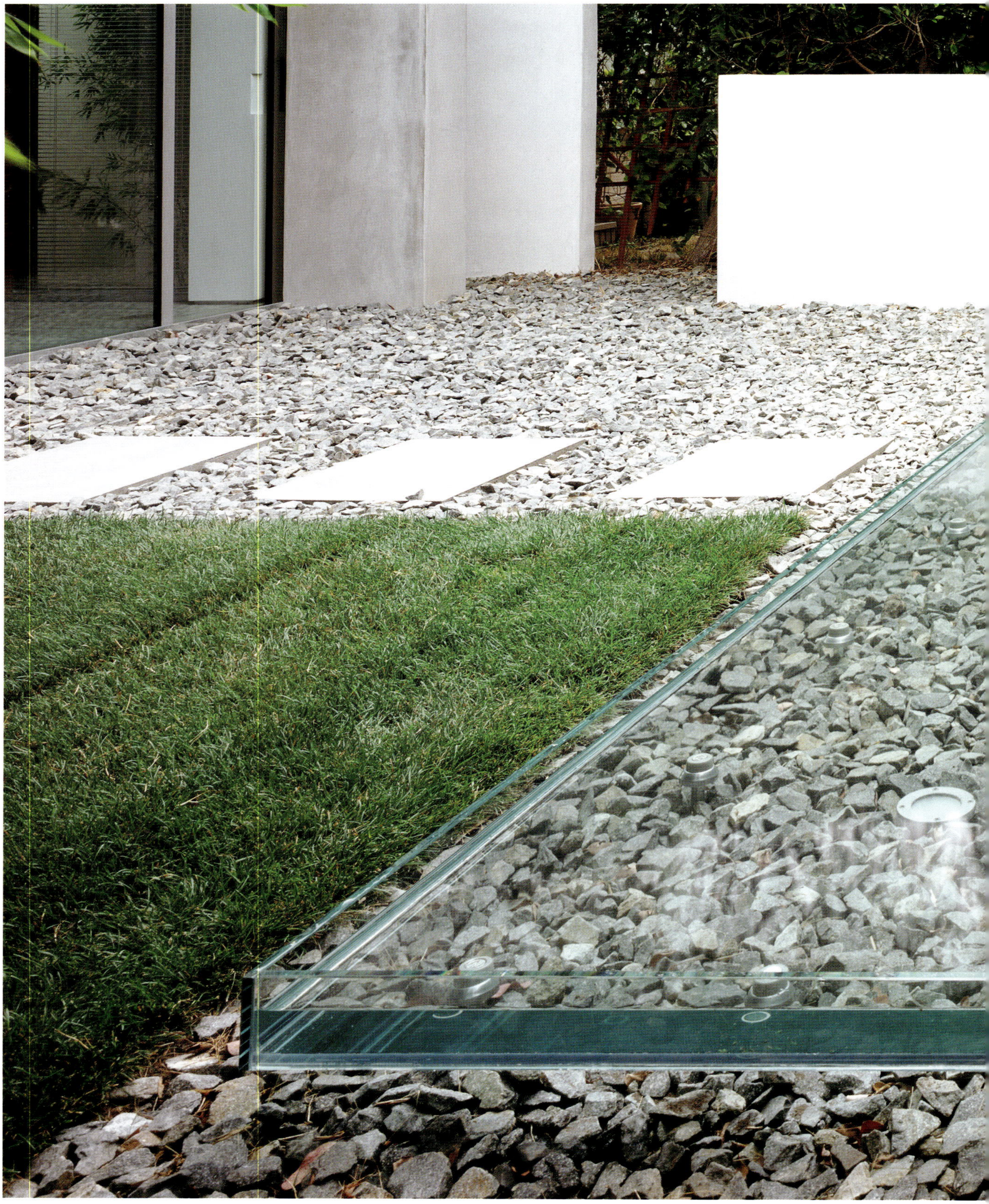

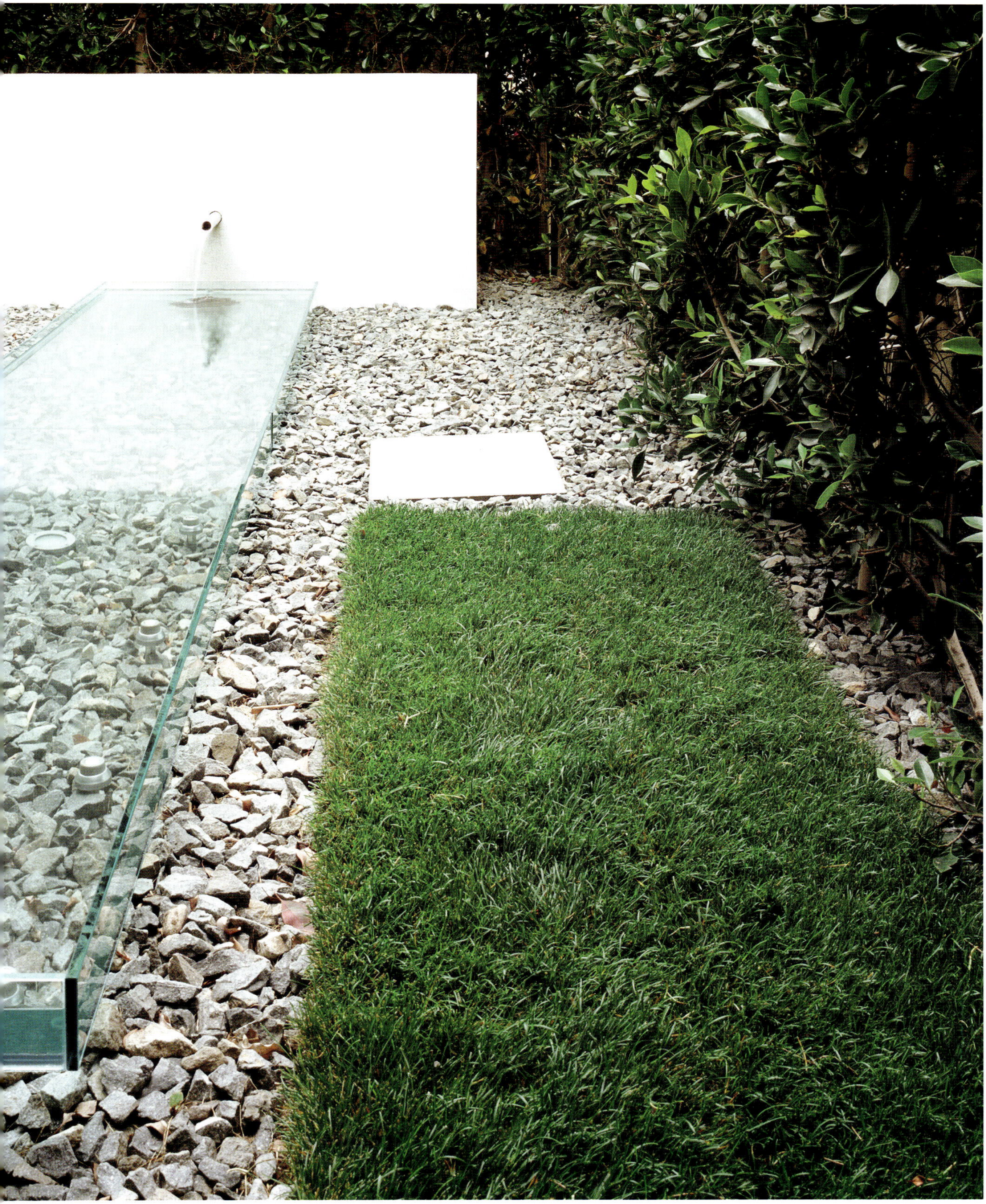

プライベート・レジデンス　ウラジミール・ジュロヴィッチ・ランドスケープ・アーキテクチュア

炎と水　FIRE AND WATER

ヤーファ―シリア　撮影：ジェラルディン・ブルニール

　ダマスカス郊外の豪華な邸宅の庭園、楕円形プールの真向かいにこの空間は形づくられている。この堅牢な空間の焦点となっているのは、意外にも屹立する2面の巨大な壁の一方から湧き出す小さな泉であり、それが空間を定義している。泉から湧き出す水は炉床を囲む水場を満たし、その炉床に炎が燃え上がるとき、炎と水は隣り合わせに存在しながら互いに打ち消しあうことなしに饗宴を繰り広げ、驚くべき光景を現出する。泉から流れ出す新鮮な水は大気を清浄化し、ポーチに集う人々の心を潤す。

These outdoor areas belong to a magnificent country house in Syria. This space is situated opposite an elliptic-shaped swimming pool. The focus, however, is on a fountain that emanates from one of the two walls that define the space. Water falls onto a surface that surrounds a brazier, which when lit creates a surprising scene in which both elements, fire and water, exist side by side without destroying one another. The fountain also freshens up the atmosphere and allows us to comfortably enjoy the porch and its surroundings.

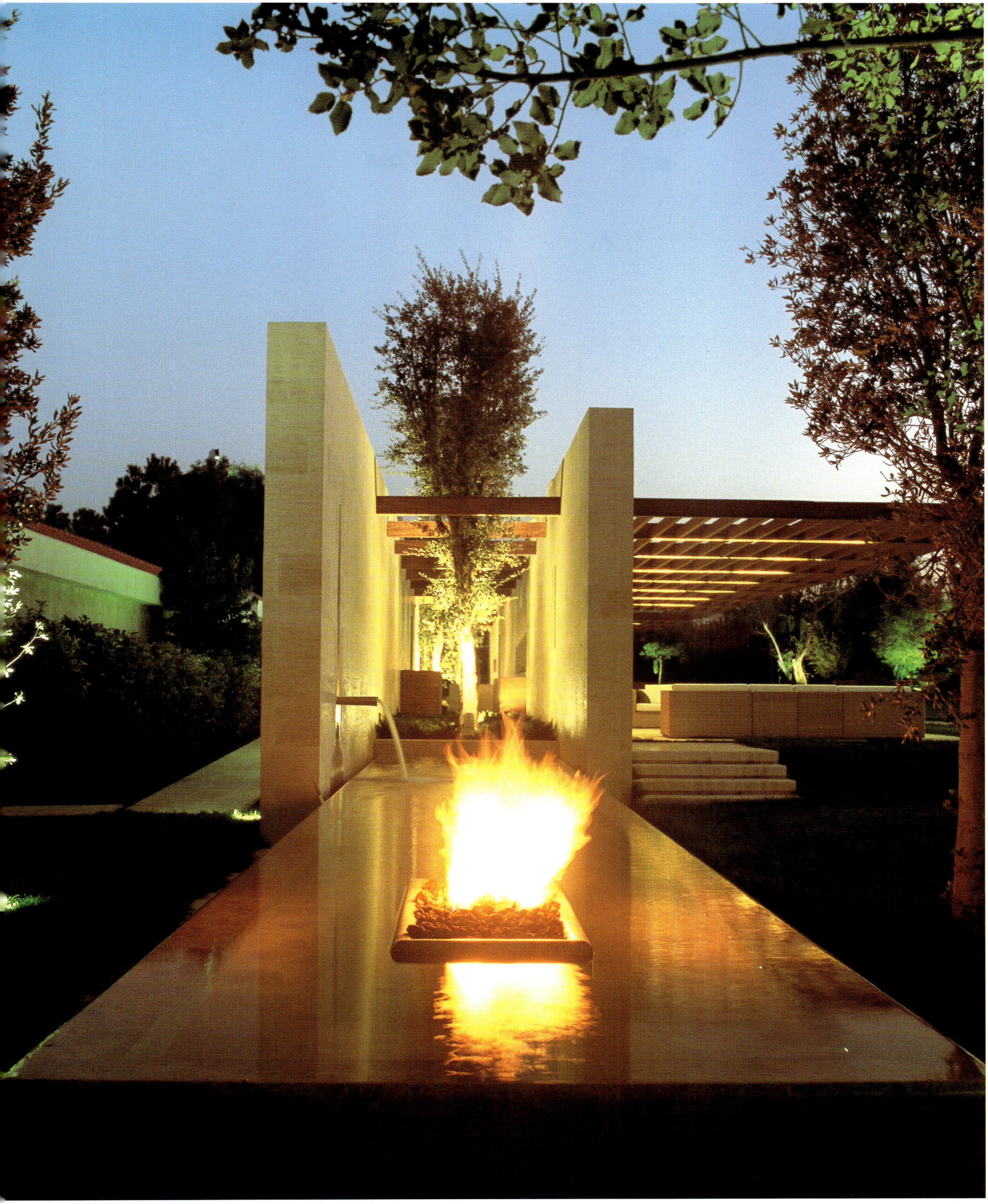

視覚としての水 | See it

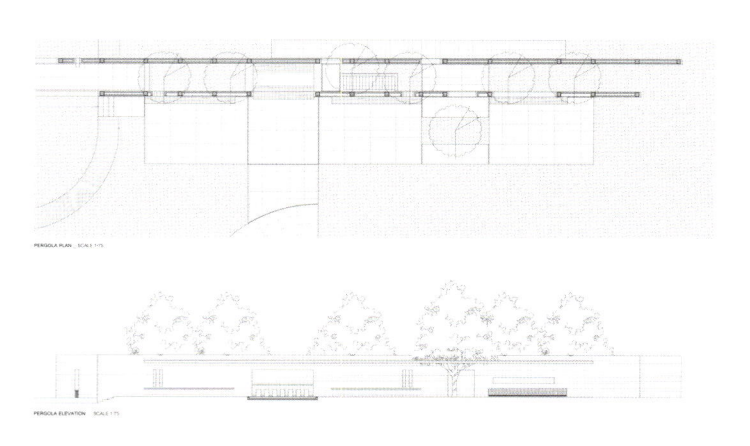

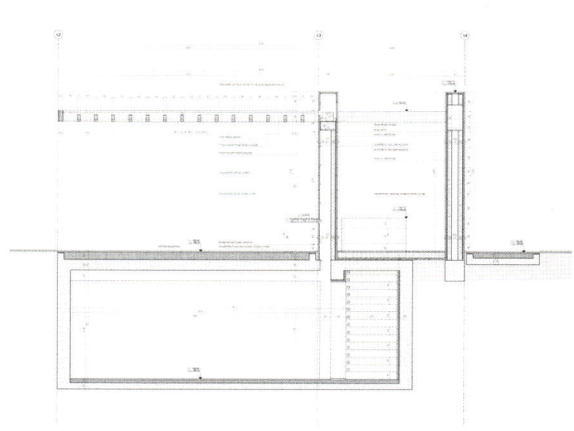

キッチン、シャワー、バスルームなどの設備は2面の巨大な壁に挟まれた空間に置かれているため、遮るもののない広いセンターステージが可能となった。片持ち状の梁がソファーに体を沈める人々に陰を差し出す。

Services are hidden between these two walls, such as a kitchen, showers, a bathroom, etc. that give center stage to this construction. The protruding beams offer some shade to the area where the sofas can be found.

チューリッヒの家 クリスチャン・ビュートリッヒ

2つの世界の間に　BETWEEN TWO WORLDS

チューリッヒ―スイス　撮影：アジ・シモエンス／ザパイメージズ

　池がこの住宅の中庭を支配している。池の周囲は甲板で縁取られ、それがそのまま広縁となって居間に続いている。広縁にはテーブルが置かれ、夏の宵にはそこで私的な宴が開かれる。すべてがリラクゼーションのための個性的な空間を演出するために捧げられ、組み立てられている。植木やプランターは気持良く手入れされ、その配置が空間を定義している。ランタンなどの小物類も暖かくなごみのある空間にするために一役買っている。この中庭は本物の豊かさと安寧に満ちた別世界へとわれわれを空間移動させる。

The pond occupies a space in the courtyard of this residence. It is bordered by a wooden platform next to which is an outdoor dining area used primarily in the summer. Everything is decorated and organized to create a unique environment for relaxation. The plants are well cared for and their arrangement defines the spaces. Decorative elements such as the candles lend warmth. This space transports us to another world full of luxury and peace.

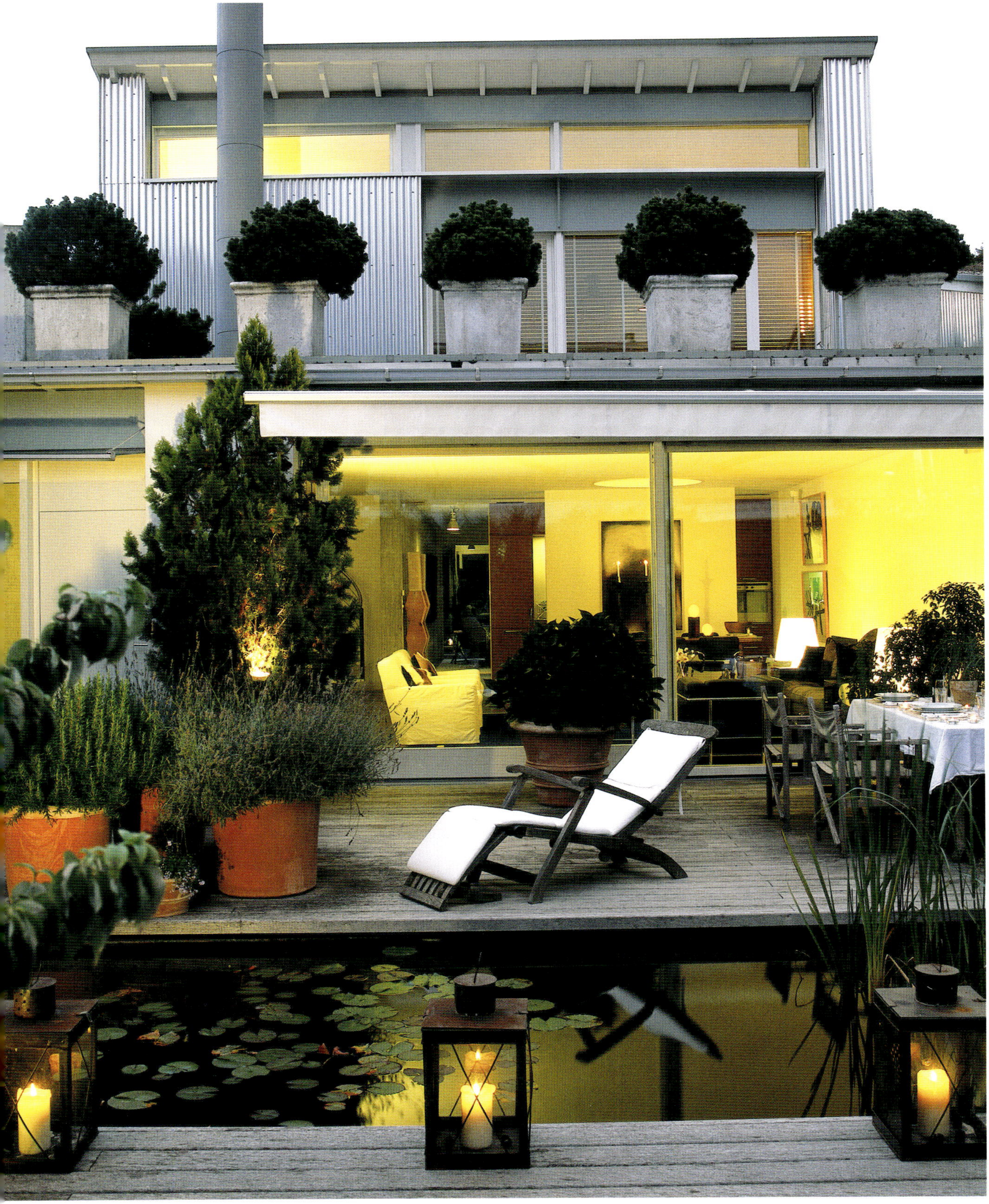

デザイナーの家 ブッジ・ラユグ／ブッジリビング・バンコク

密かなオアシス　*A PRIVATE POOL*

バンコク―タイ　撮影：アジ・シモエンス／ザパイメージズ

　家具デザイナー、ブッジ・ラユグはバンコクの私邸に密かなオアシスを創造した。大きな池には睡蓮が浮かびパピルスが伸びる。その周囲には青々と豊かに生育した熱帯植物が繁り、空間は静謐の気を充満させ、超俗的である。この庭に一歩足を踏み入れると、静寂と平和に包み込まれる。ハンモックに揺られながら心を休めるもよし、石のスラブを踏み渡りながら省察するもよし。宵やみに照明が灯されると、梢の影と、光を反射する葉裏がさらに空間を濃密なものにする。

The furniture designer Budji Layug has created a small oasis in his house in Bangkok. In the exterior courtyard he has designed a lush garden including a magnificent pool with water lilies and bamboo. This place exudes tranquility and is full of spirituality. It is possible to walk around the garden and feel peace and tranquility. One can rest in the hammocks or take a walk across the pool thanks to the stone slabs. At nightfall, the trees, plants and lighting create a more intimate atmosphere.

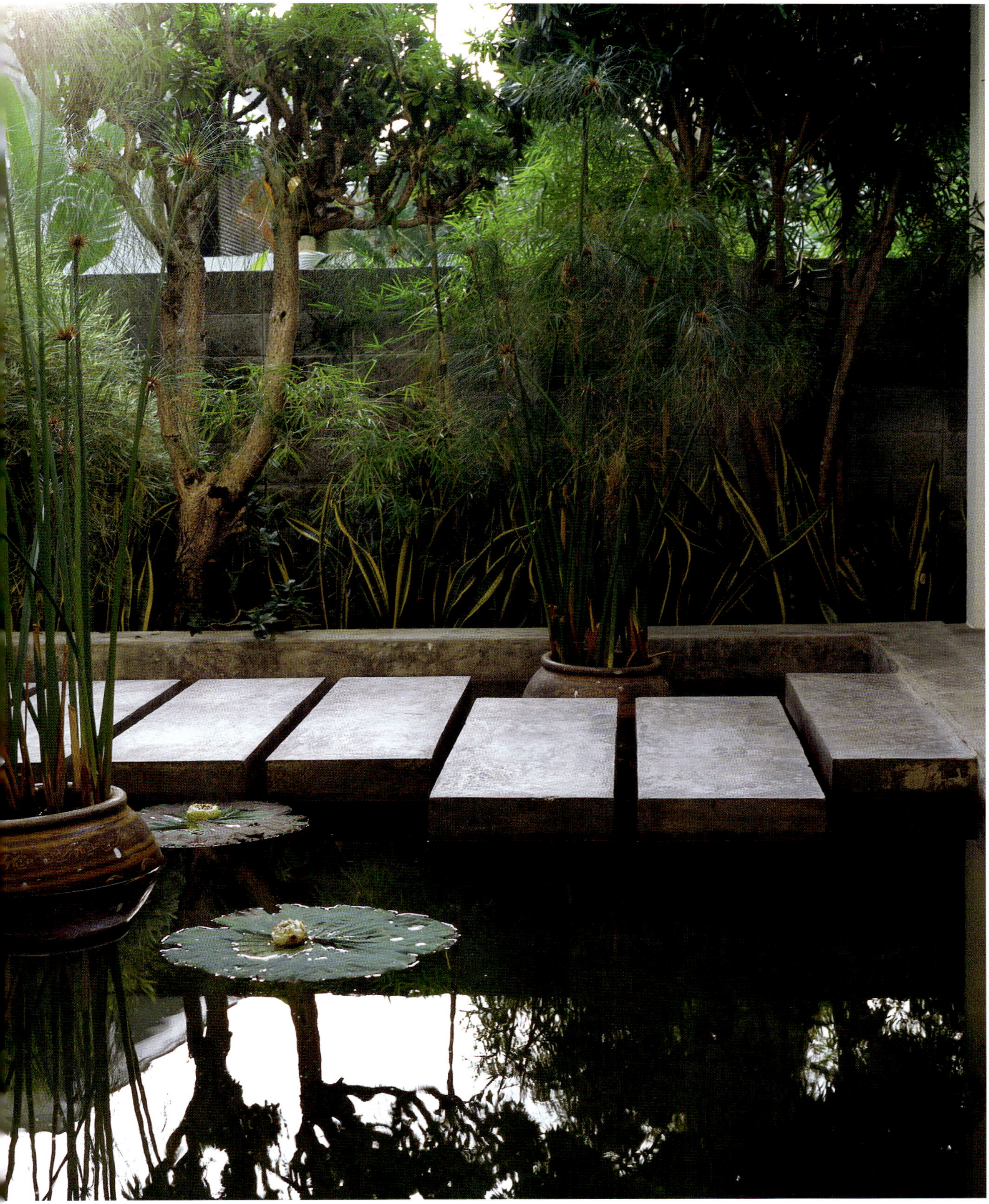

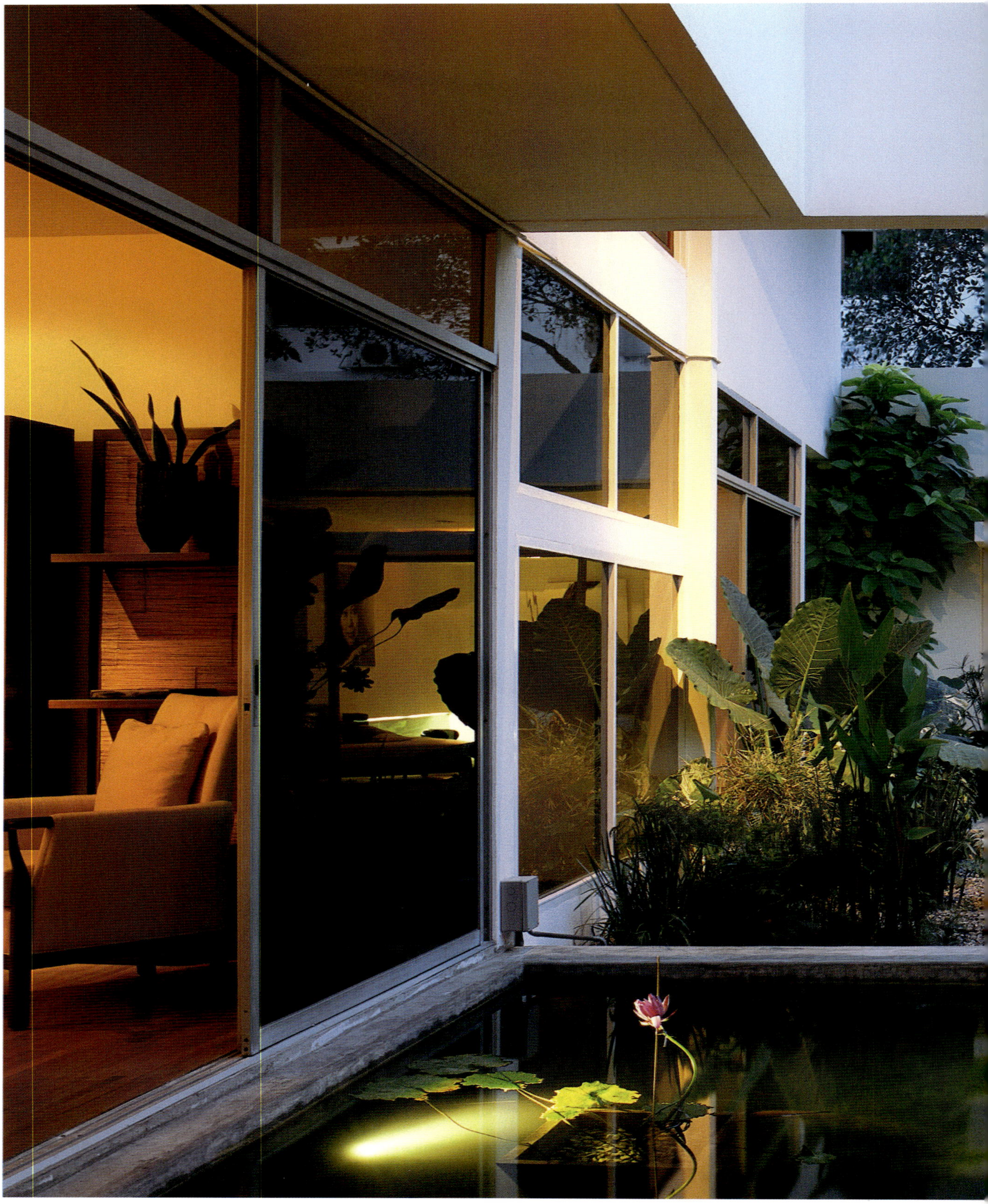

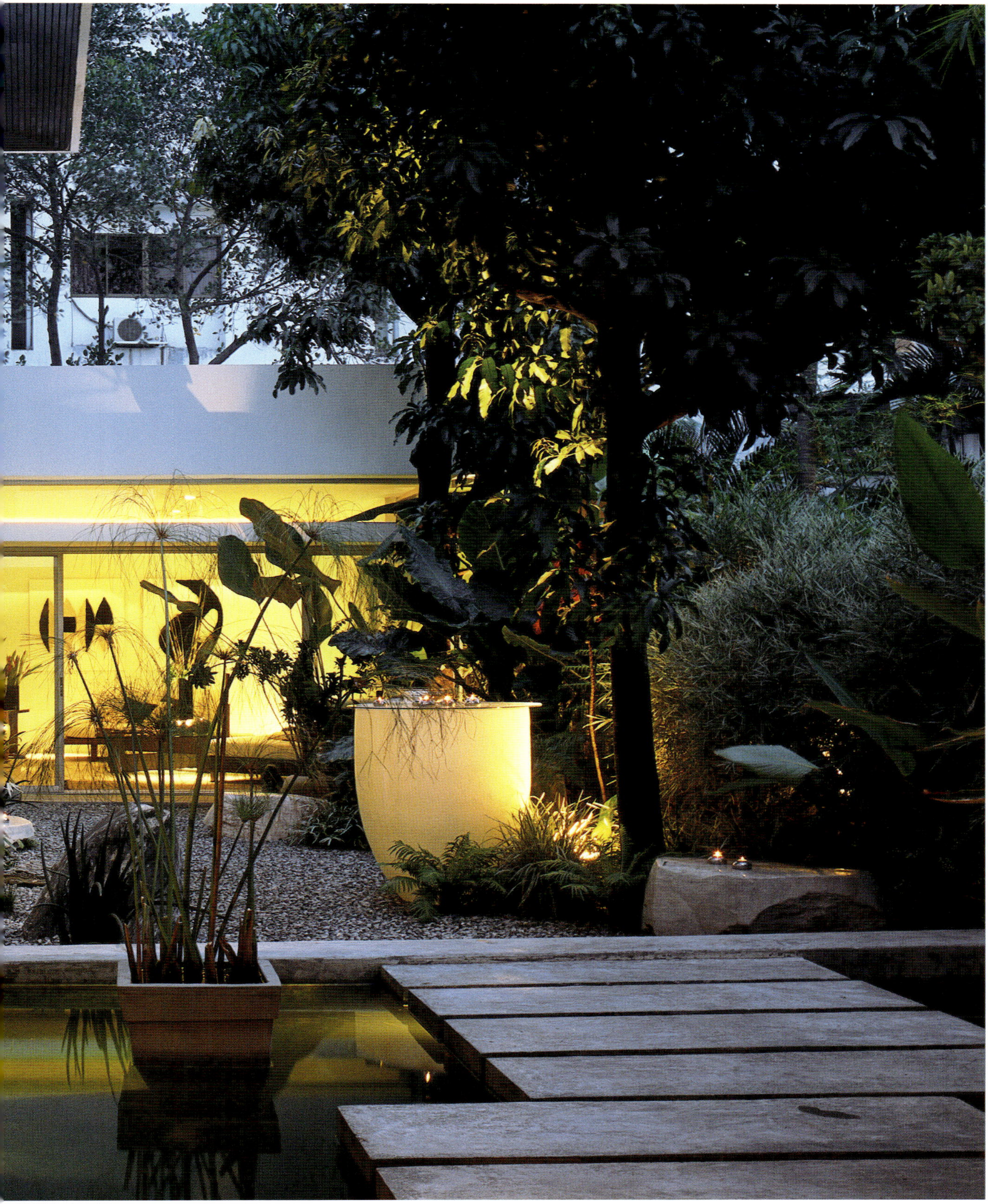

ナムリー通りの家 ベドマール & シー

タイ様式　THAI STYLE

シンガポール　撮影：ベドマール & シー

　住宅は3つのブロックがU字型に配置され、その両側の部分が境界の一部を画す水路上の渡殿、細いポーチになっている。ポーチの柱が水と接する部分は、浸蝕を防ぐための処理が施されている。

　ポーチの外側に植えられた竹垣がポーチにやわらかな影を投げかけている。熱帯特有の半開放型レイアウトにより邸内を風が吹き渡り、異国情緒に溢れた美しい空間が創造されている。

The three blocks that compose this house are laid out in a "U" shape. At the sides are small porches or walkways over the water that border part of the house. Due to their contact with the water the pillars must be protected to avoid them wearing.

A bamboo garden that encircles the porch provides shade. This semi-open layout of the spaces, typical of tropical architecture, helps the air to circulate and creates an exotic aesthetic.

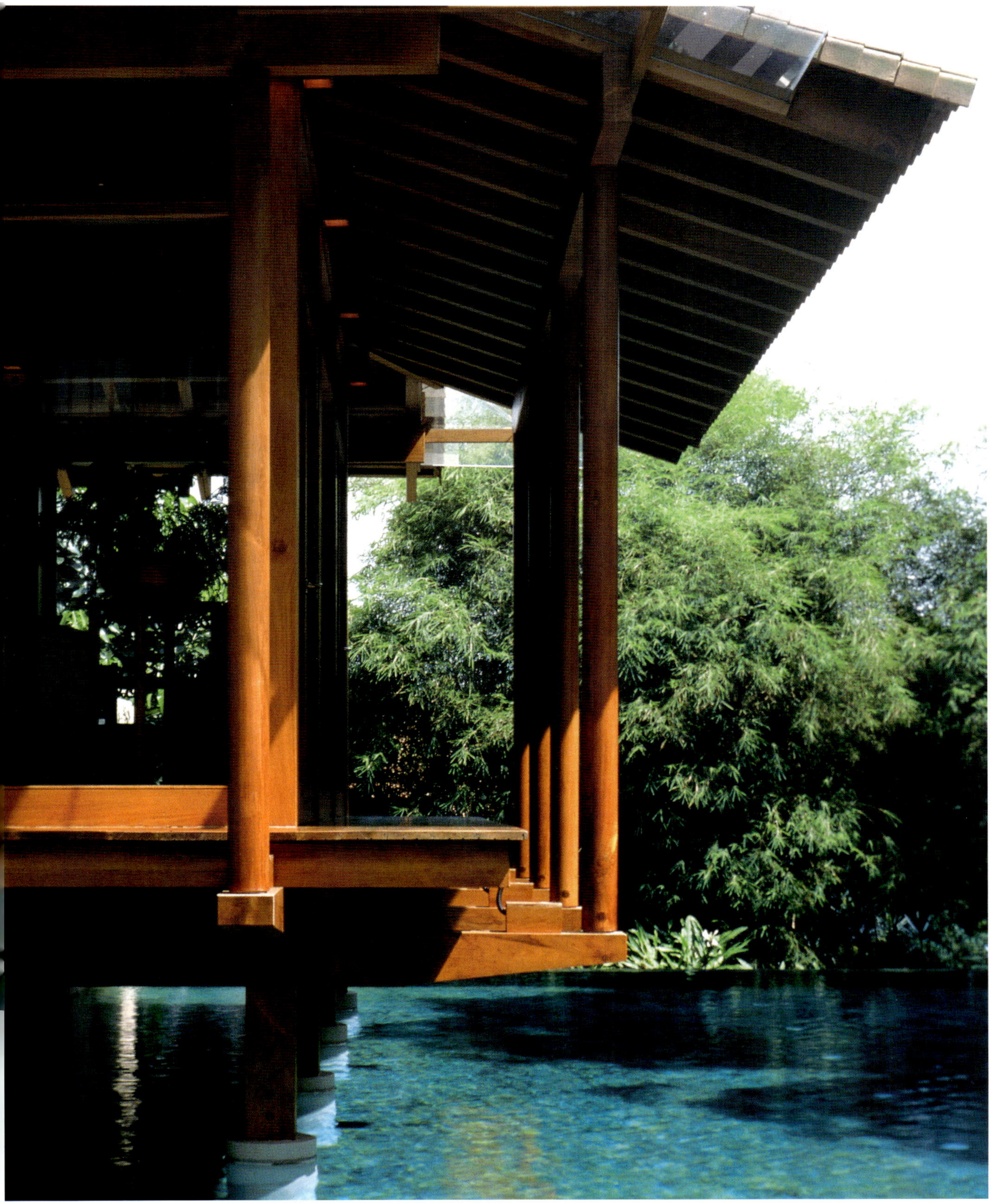

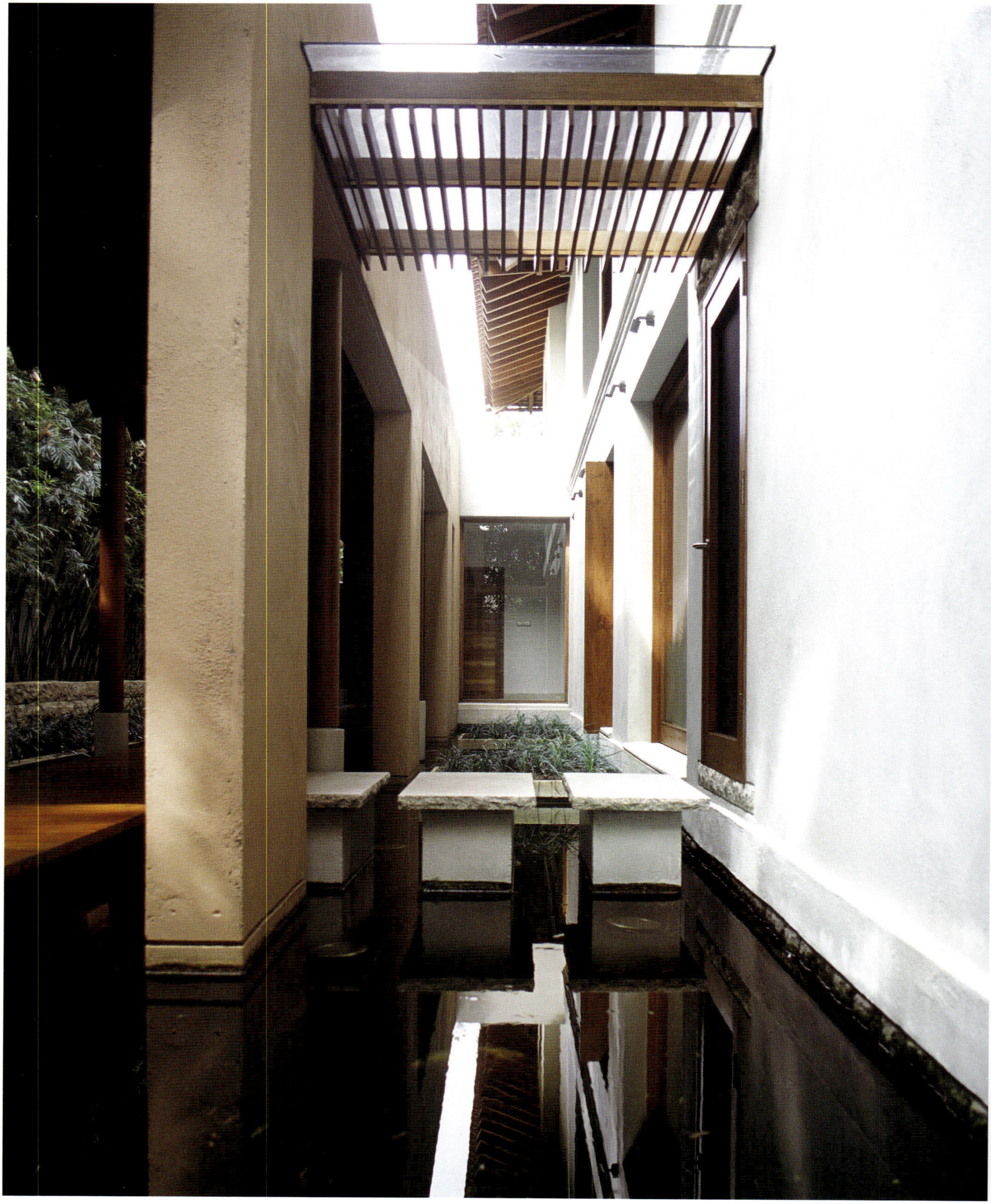

構造は、チーク材に石とコンクリートの要素を組み合わせたもので、常に水を視界にとどめながら、それと接することなくあずまやを渡ることができるようにという意図のもと、すべての要素が配置されている。

The structure combines teak wood with elements of stone and concrete. All the elements are laid out to allow for walking among the pavilions without coming into contact with water, but also never losing sight of it.

ブドウ畑の池 ラツコー建築設計事務所

水上の踊り場　　*PLATFORM ON THE WATER*

カリフォルニア―アメリカ　撮影：マリオン・ブレンナー

　ブドウ畑の所有者は、催し物会場ともなり、また訪れた家族が思い思いにランチを楽しめる場所ともなる空間を望んだ。さらに泳いだり水遊びのできる池も欲しいと言った。この要望に応えるため、計画の大部分が水平面上に配置され、水面との境界には低いコンクリートの壁が設けられた。最後に小さな木造の桟橋を水上に渡し、家族が水上で憩える場所とした。コンクリートと石の壁がレベルの変化をやわらげ、すべてを周囲の自然に完全に融けこませている。

The owners of the vineyard wanted a space for social events that would also serve for small family get-togethers. They also wanted a place with water for swimming, diving etc. To achieve this a large part of the plot was leveled off. The surface area of the water is defined thanks to concrete walls. Finally a small wooden jetty was positioned over the water for the small reunions. The concrete and stone walls help to soften the changing levels and integrate them into the natural surroundings.

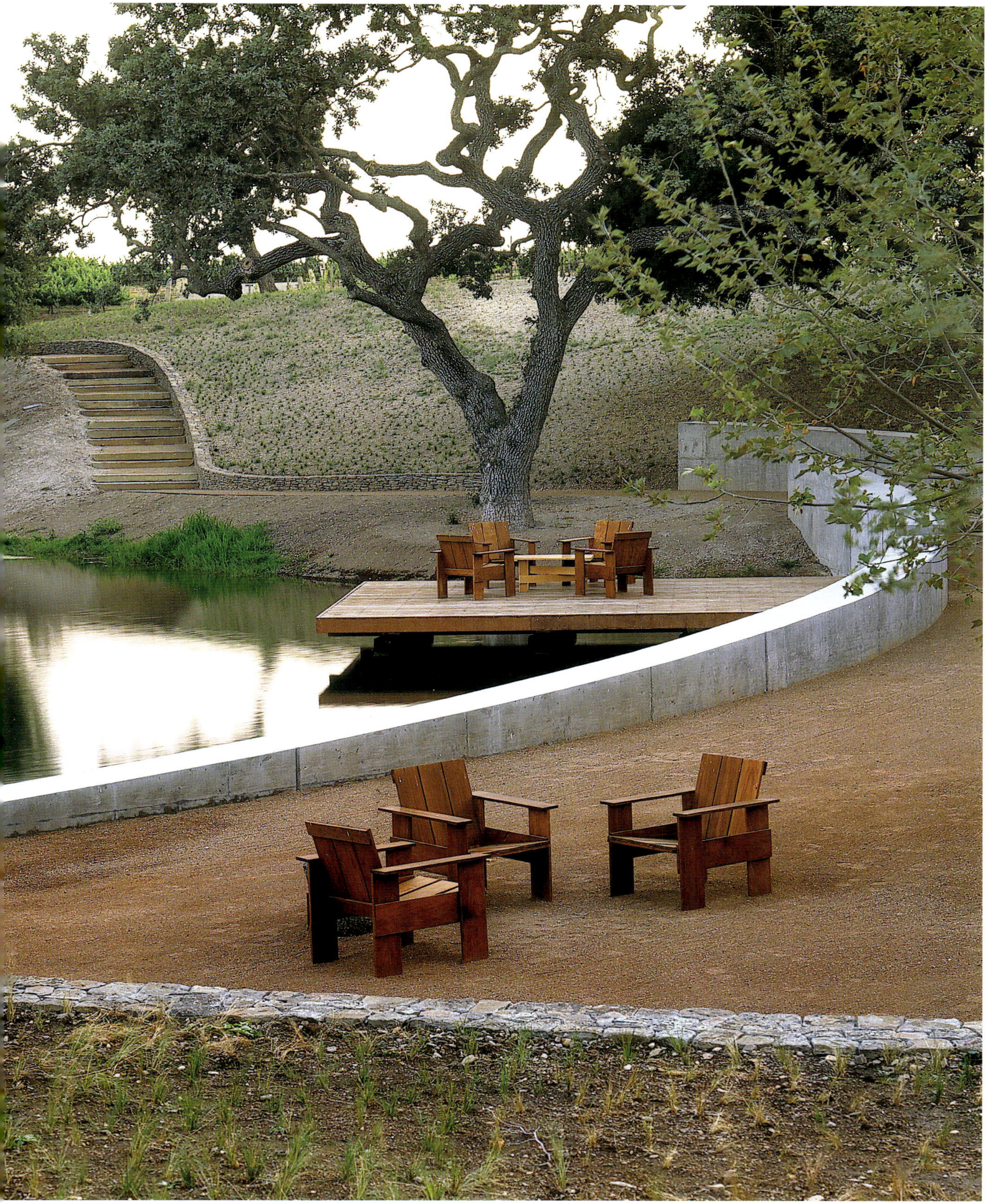

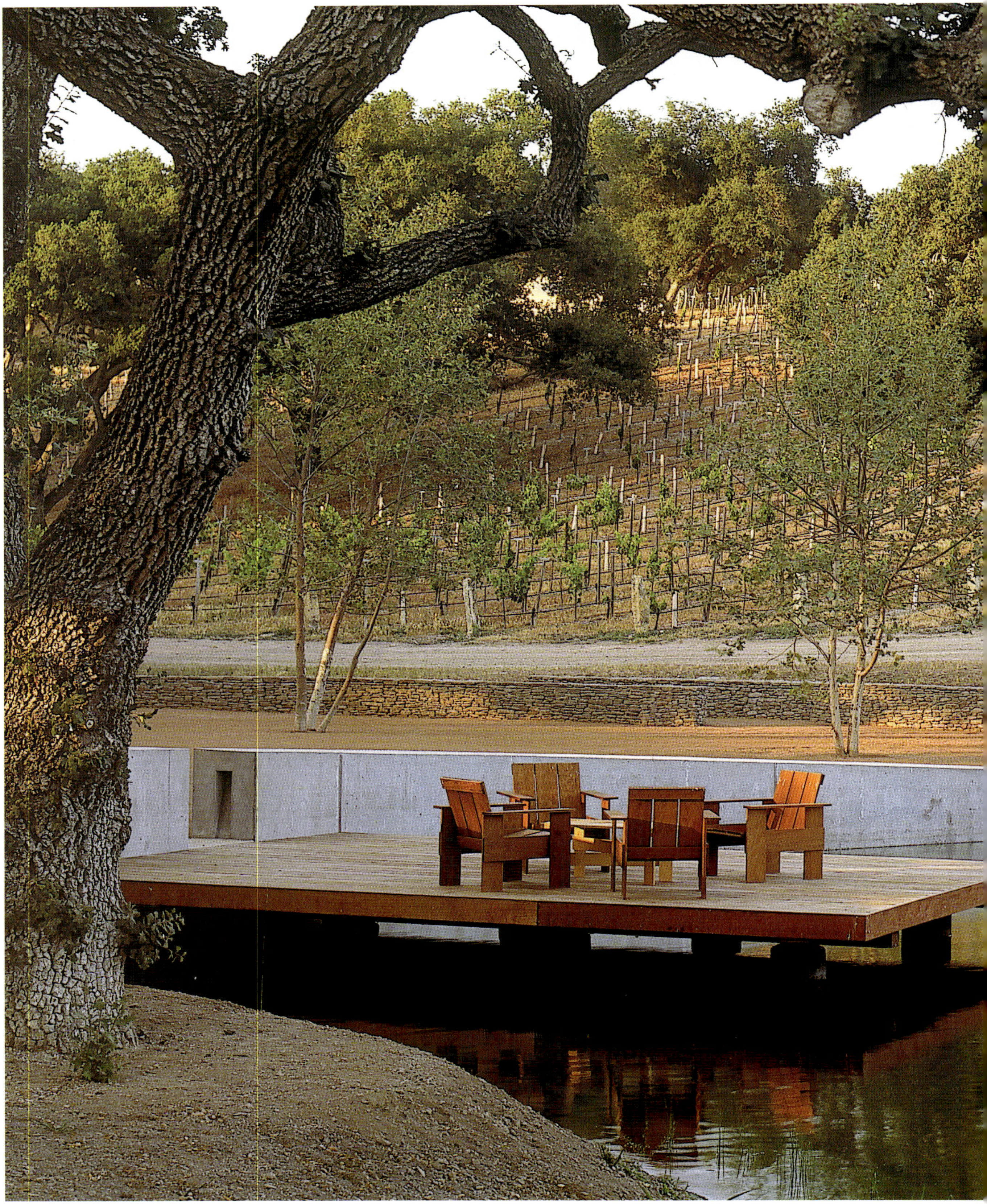

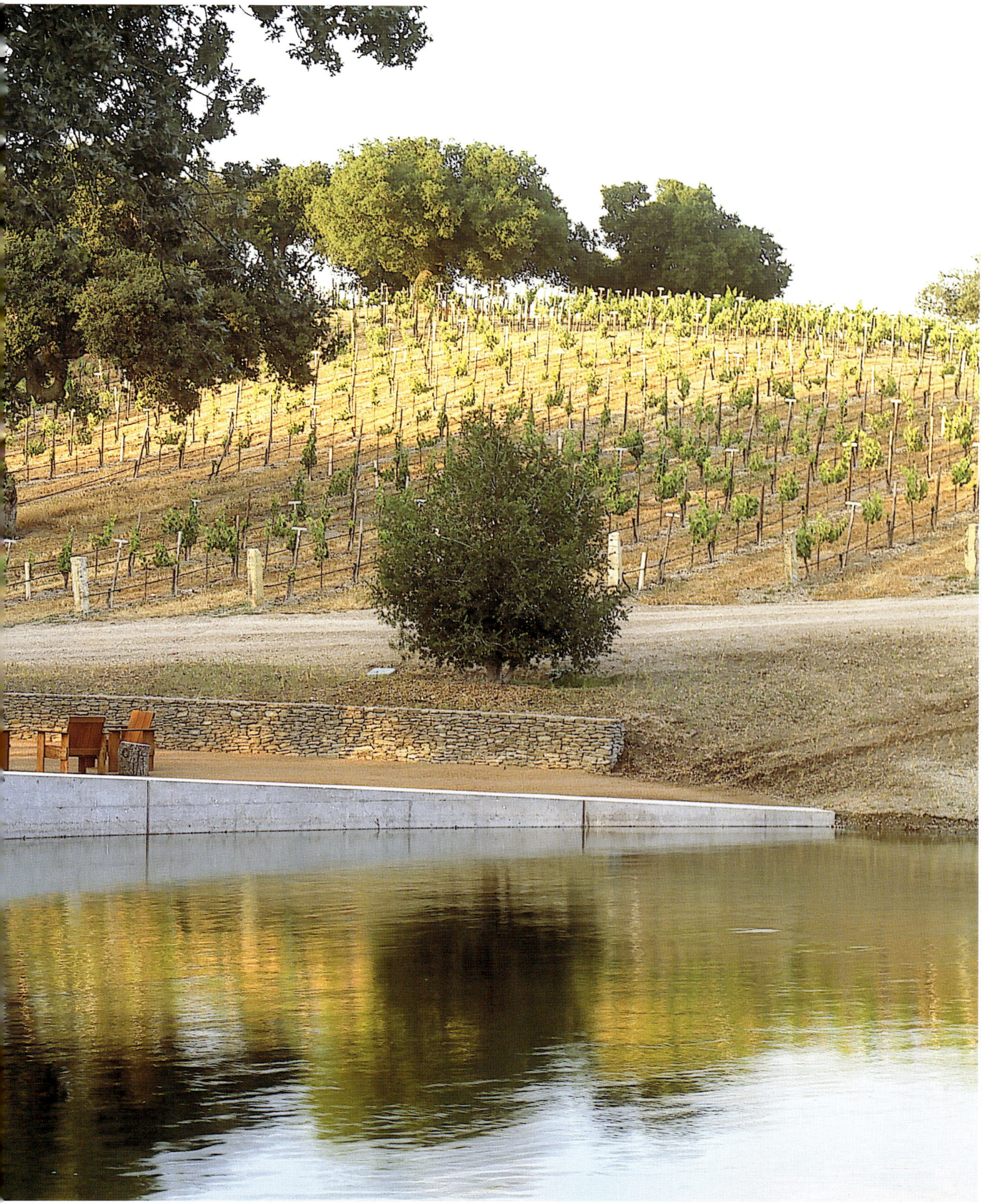

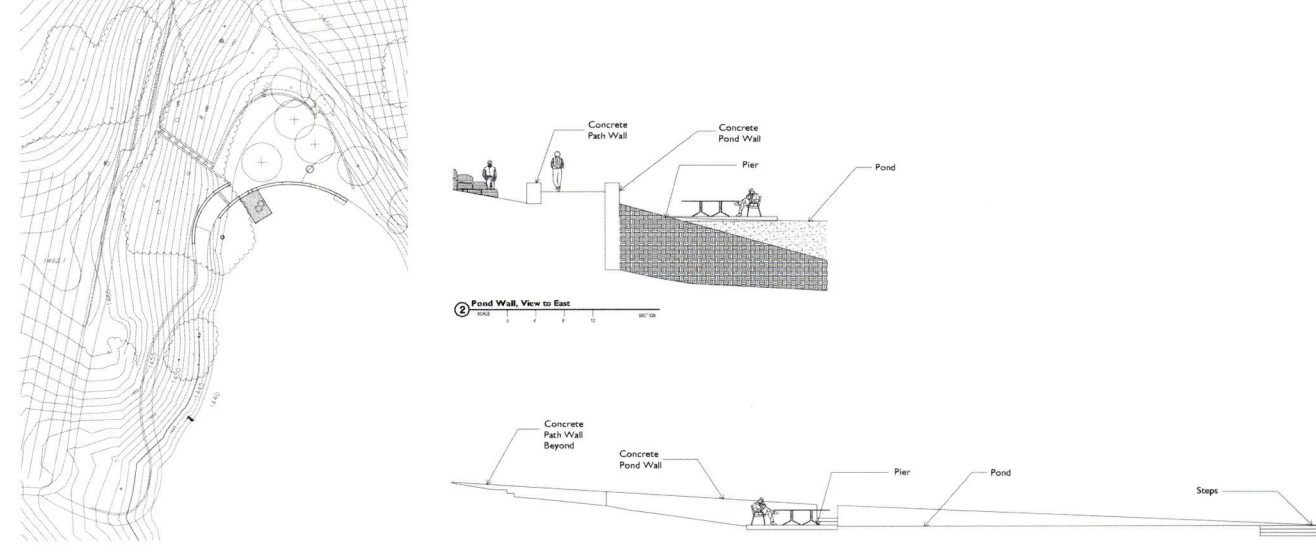

184 | 視覚としての水 | See it

ブドウの樹とオークの林は所有者がここに来る以前からこの場所に存在していた。この地域の植物を移植し、この地域の色彩を使うことによって、きわめて自然な景観が創りだされた。地元の植生がこの計画を完成させた。

The vines and the oak trees were already there when the owners arrived. Vegetation and colors from the area were used to achieve a natural environment. The aim was accomplished thanks to the local vegetation.

歩道橋 ミロ・リベラ・アーキテクツ

景観に統合されて INTEGRATED IN THE LANDSCAPE

オースティン―テキサス州―アメリカ　撮影：ポール・フィンケル／ピストンデザイン

　客人は、このオースティン湖にかかる30mの歩道橋を渡ってゲストハウスに向かう。ドローイングの線は、葦などこの地域特有の植物を描いた上に引かれた。太い鋼管で構造を支え、それに細い棒鋼がより合わされている。棒鋼は橋の底面と側面を構成した後、そのまま任意の長さで上に伸び、下に垂れ下がっている。それはまるで葦がそのまま橋を作ったかのように、違和感なく自然に融けこんでいる。このメンテナンスを必要としない歩道橋は、景観に統合されながらも、そこに出現した繊細な現代彫刻のようでもある。

This 100 ft long footbridge, on Lake Austin, connects a main residence with a guest house. The design draws on the rushes and other typical plants of the region. Robust steel tubes form the structure, around which other thinner ones intertwine. The bars form the base and the sides of the bridge merge with the surroundings thanks to its similarity with the rushes. The bridge, which does not require maintenance, integrates with the scenery, from which it seems to emerge like a delicate sculpture.

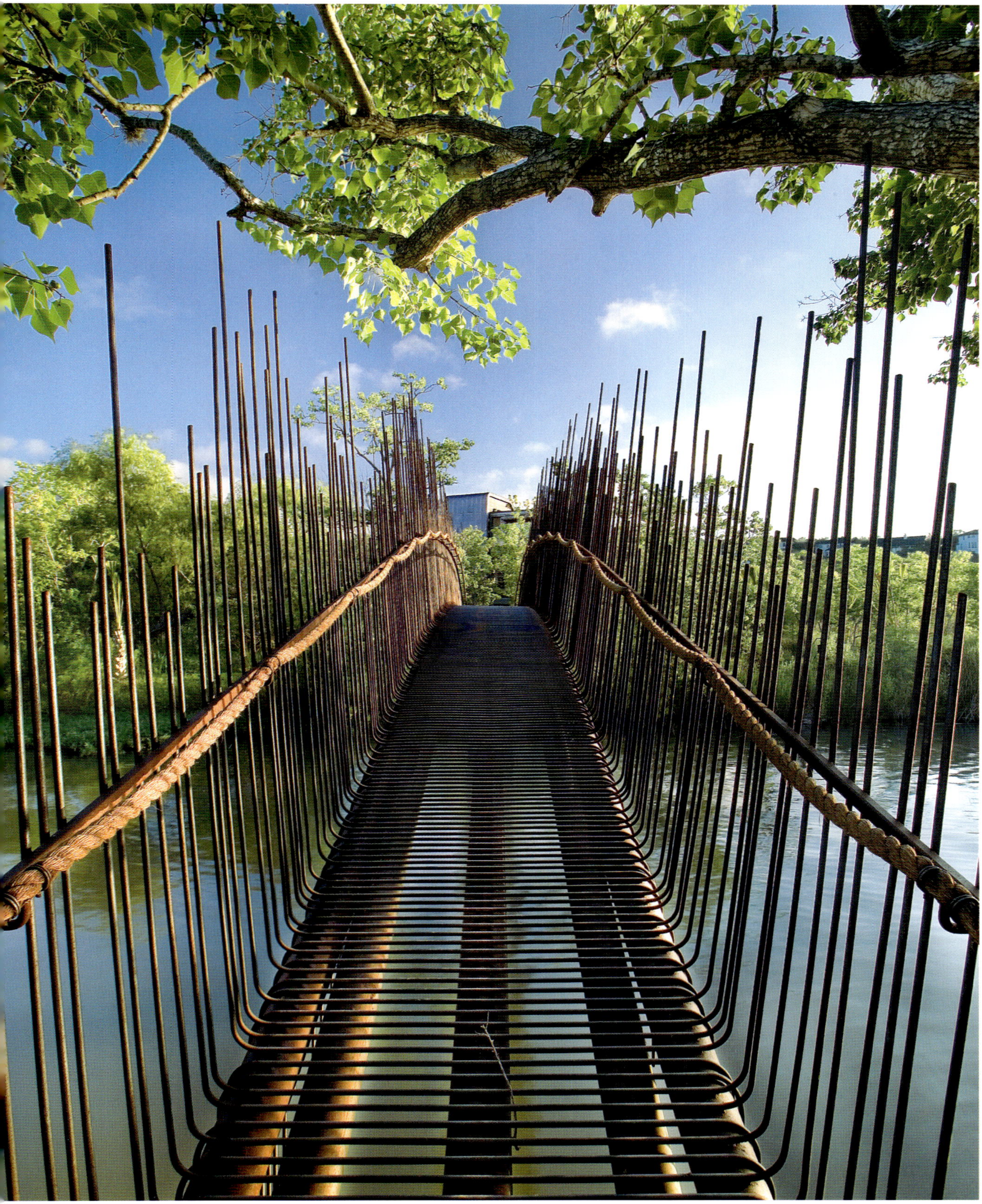

視覚としての水 | See it

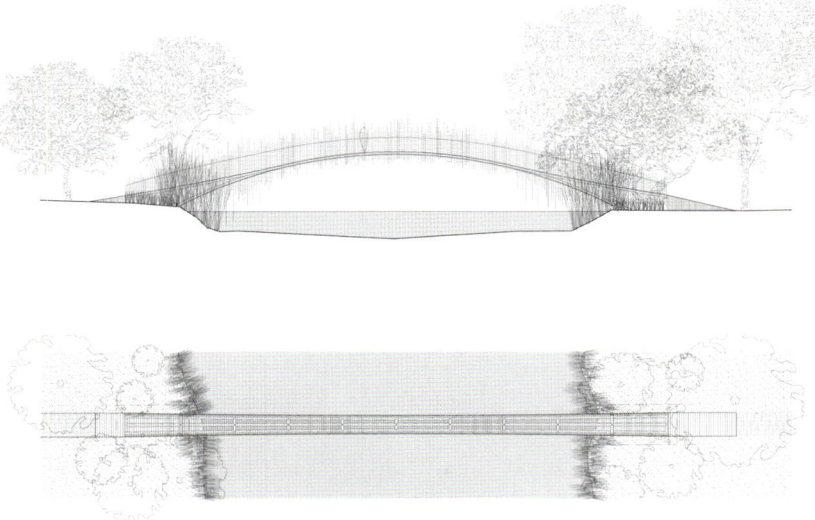

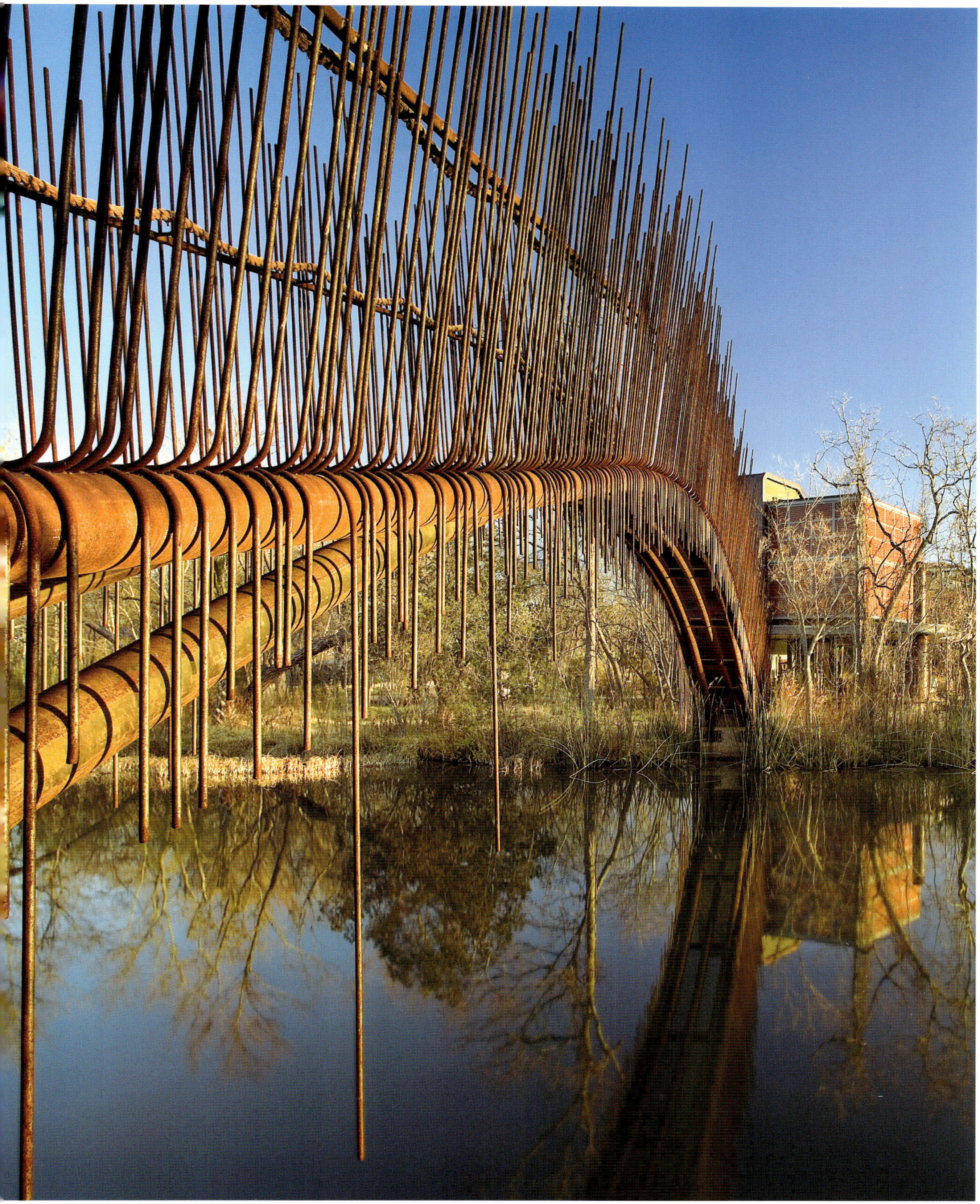

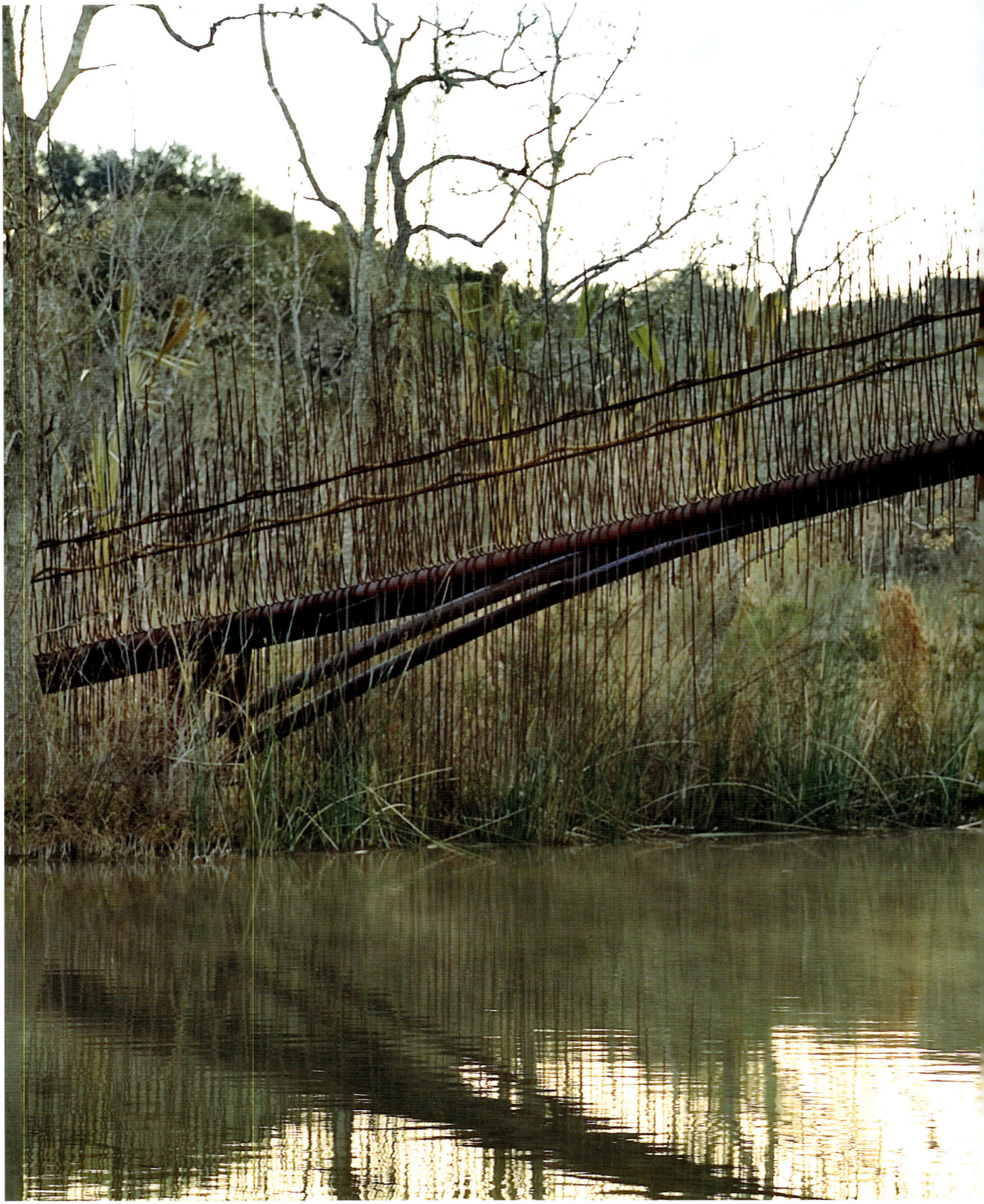

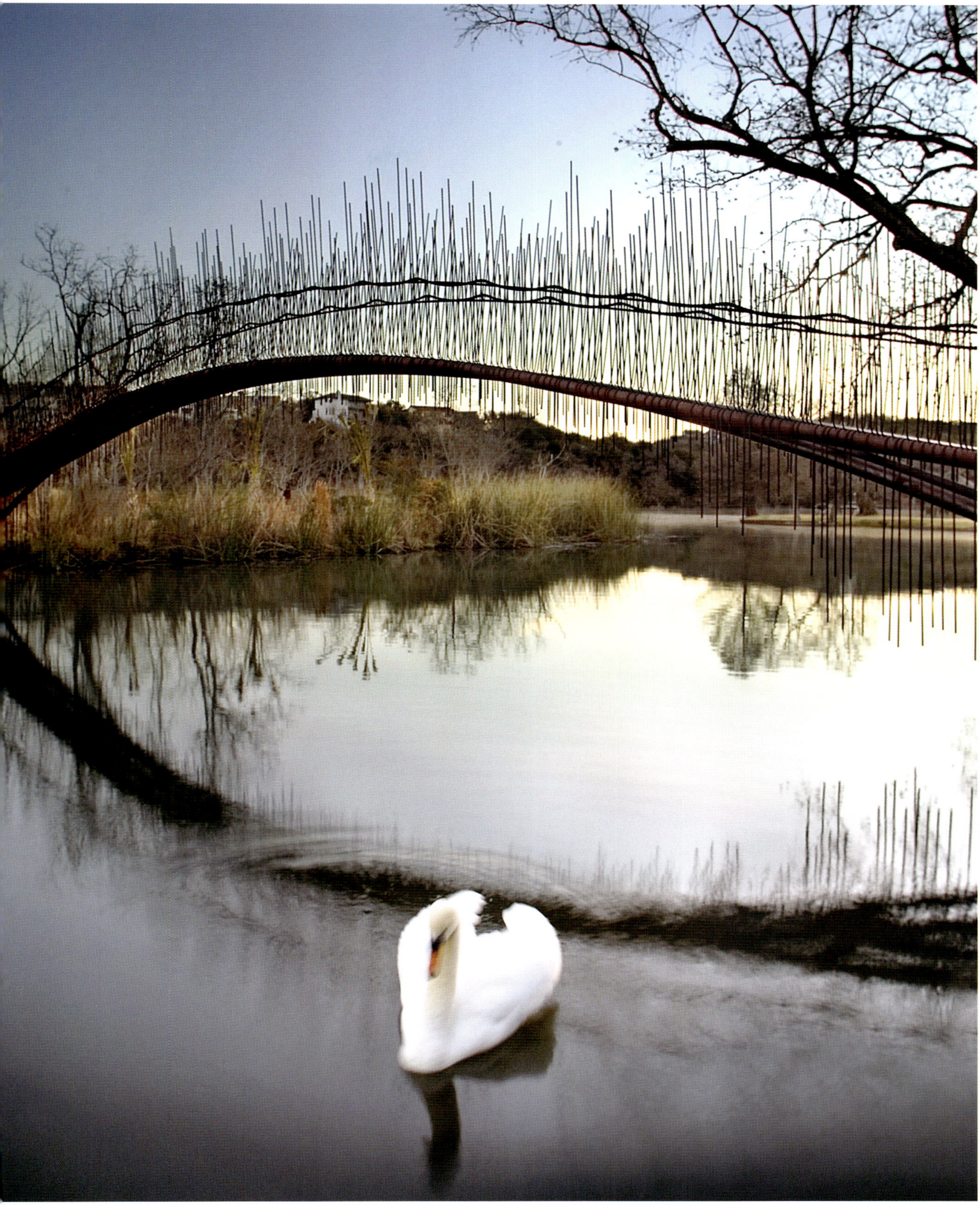

これから紹介するプロジェクトは、すべて水と特別な契約を結んでいる。水は不可欠な要素として、意外な場所、空間に登場する。リラクゼーションのための小さなプールは、住宅に詩的な空気をもたらし、巨大なアクアリウムは観察者を大洋へと誘う。スパも忘れてはならない。また日本式のお風呂は、心と身体の両方が満たされる感覚とはどういうものかを教えてくれる。

The following projects establish a special relationship with water,
an indispensable element present in the most different environments and spaces, from relaxing pools, which form idyllic corners, to magnificent aquariums, which capture the attention of the observer. Spas deserve special mention; small bathing pools offering a longed for physical and mental well-being.

体感としての水

グラスハウス

GLASS HOUSE

　住宅の周囲に張られた水は床と同一平面にまで達するが、側溝を通って排水され室内に浸入することはない。この巧妙なシステムにより、インドアとアウトドアは同一平面上に並び、境界は消え去り、2つの空間のまったく新しい関係が構築された。水面から反射する光がリビングルームに柔らかな光を投げかけ、落ち着きのある雰囲気をかもし出している。コンクリートの壁面とガラスパネルが今までにない景観を出現させ、建築と水との新たな関係を強調している。

The water that surrounds the residence reaches the level of the flooring and overflows via a groove that prevents it from entering the house. This sophisticated system creates an invisible border between indoor and outdoor, which being at the same level, underlines the interrelation between the two spaces. The swimming pool's reflection in the water creates a relaxing atmosphere, which can be appreciated from inside the living room. The walls and glass panels reveal incredible views and accentuate the relationship between architecture and water.

ポルタス・ノヴァス

ファン・ロカ／アクアート，
ヴィクトール・カニャス

オコタルビーチ—コスタリカ
撮影：ジョルディ・ミラーレス

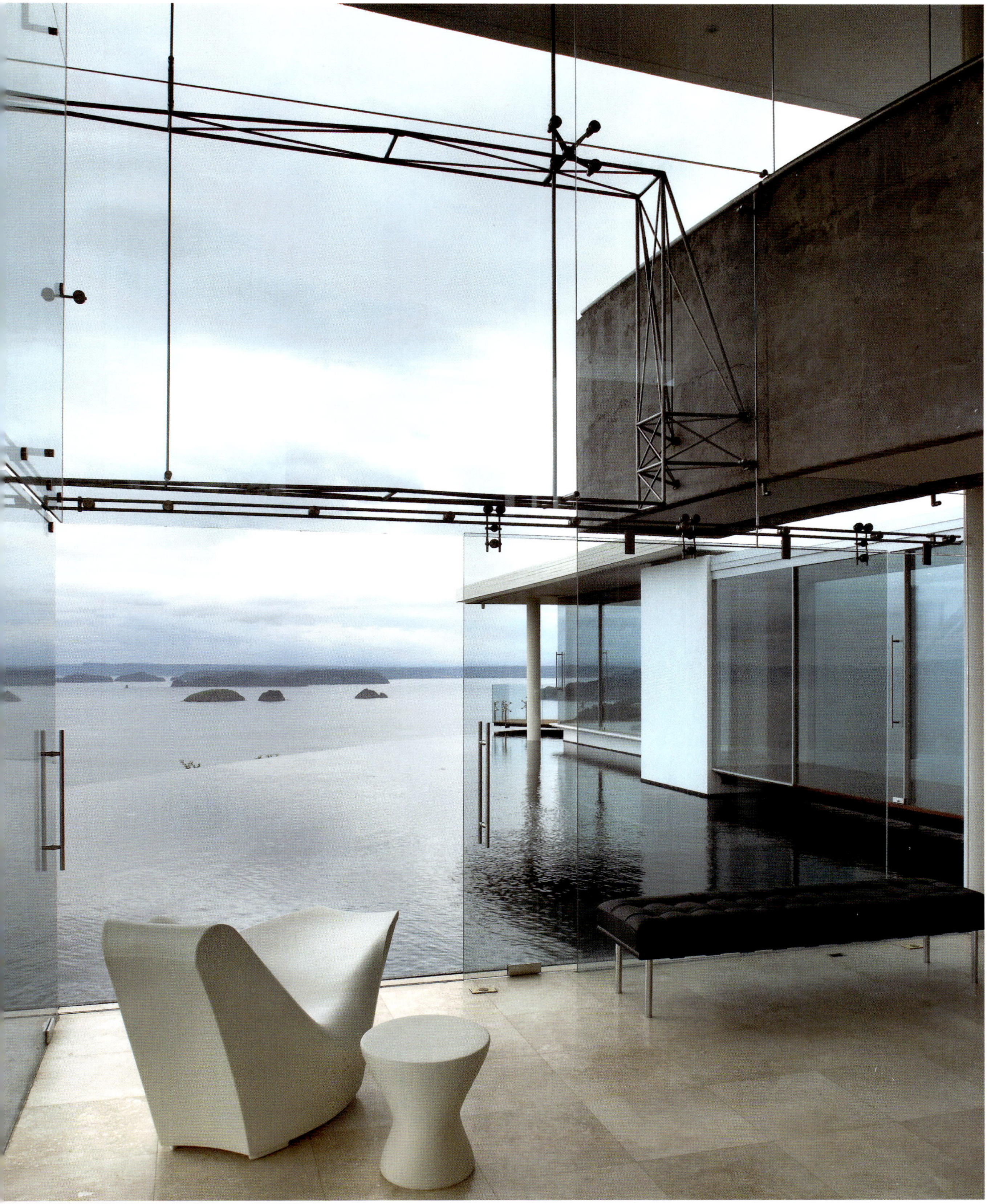

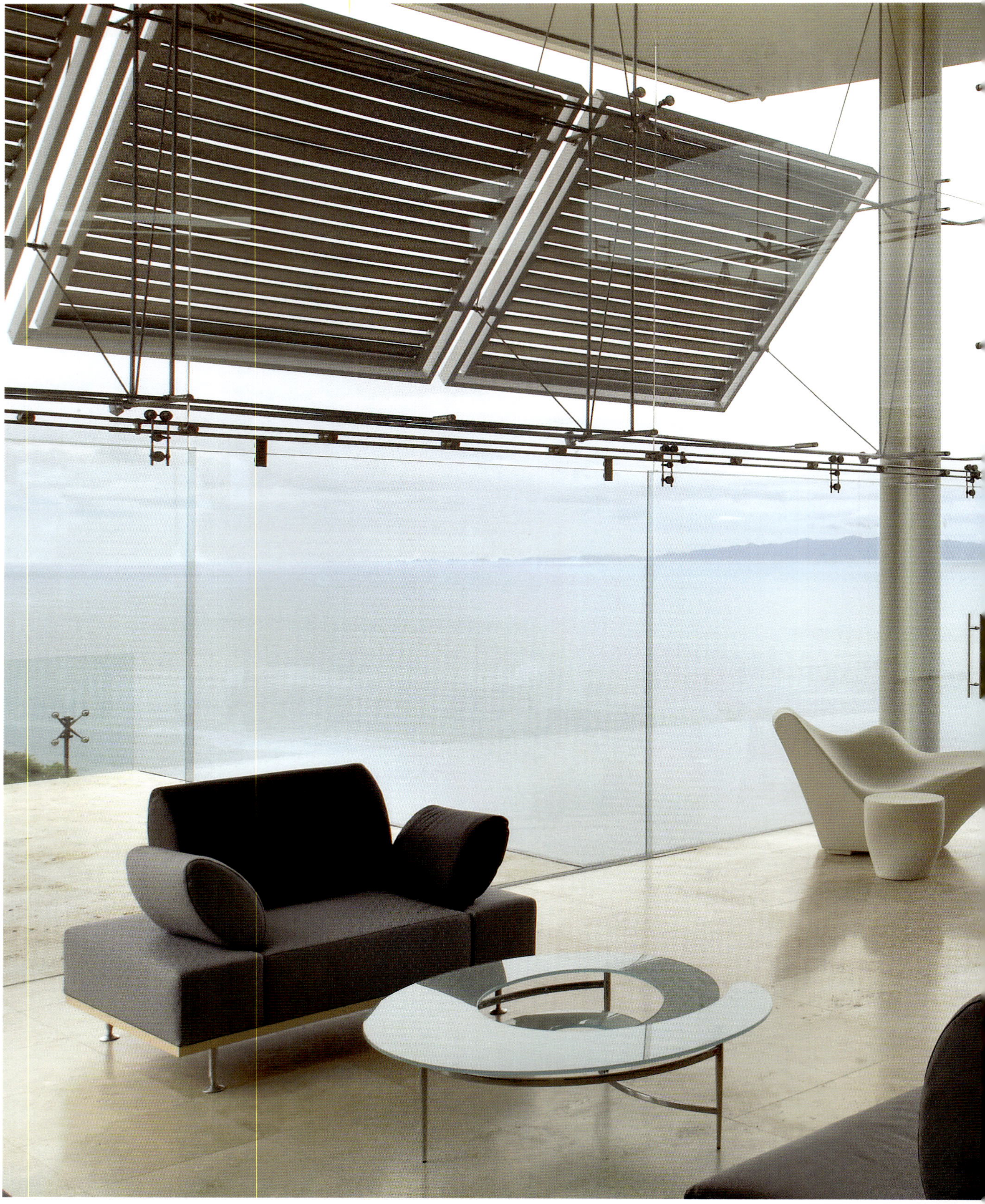

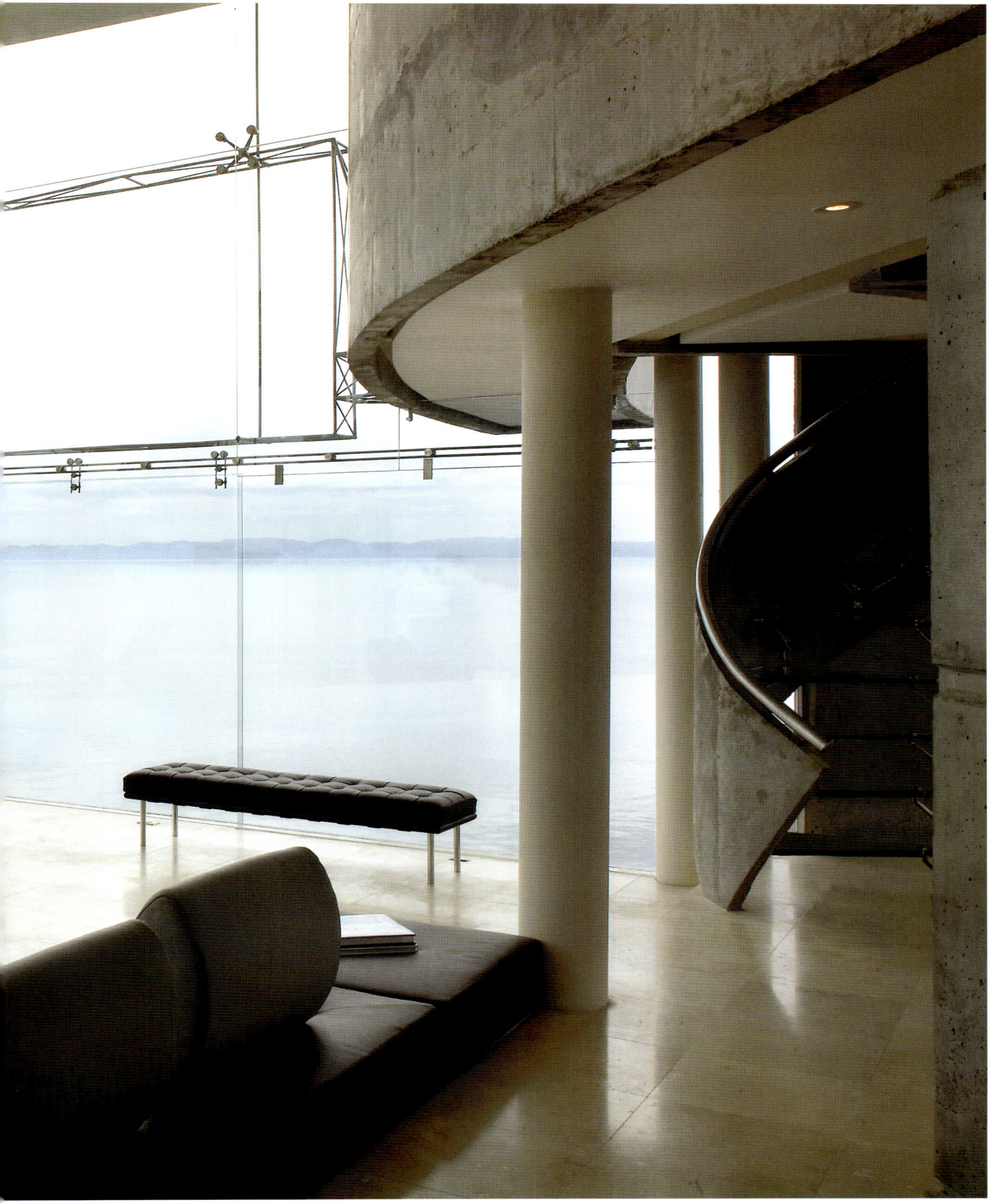

風景のあるラウンジ
LOUNGE WITH A VIEW

　活気に満ちたアングルシーの海岸沿いの町、その目抜き通りにこの住宅はある。優美で洗練された直線の美しいこの住宅の特徴は、リビングルームからダイニングルームへと住宅を囲むように造られた広いデッキスペース。それと室内を仕切るフロートガラスの全面ガラスウォールはバス海峡の雄大な眺めをもたらし、居室と屋外空間の境界線を消滅させる。同じことはガラスの手すりについてもいえる。デッキスペースには風と寒さを避ける覆いのある空間もあれば、直射日光を楽しむテラスもある。

This house is located in one of the most central streets of the lively coastal town of Anglesea. The house, of elegant, refined lines, has a porch that surrounds an area encompassing the living room and the dining room. The glass walls that enclose this space offer magnificent views of the ocean and break the limits between the house and the exterior, as do the railings. One of the areas is a porch that offers protection from the cold and wind. On the opposite side, the terrace enjoys direct sunlight.

アングルシーの家
デイヴィット・ラック・アーキテクチュア

ビクトリア州―オーストラリア
撮影：シャナイア・シェゲディン

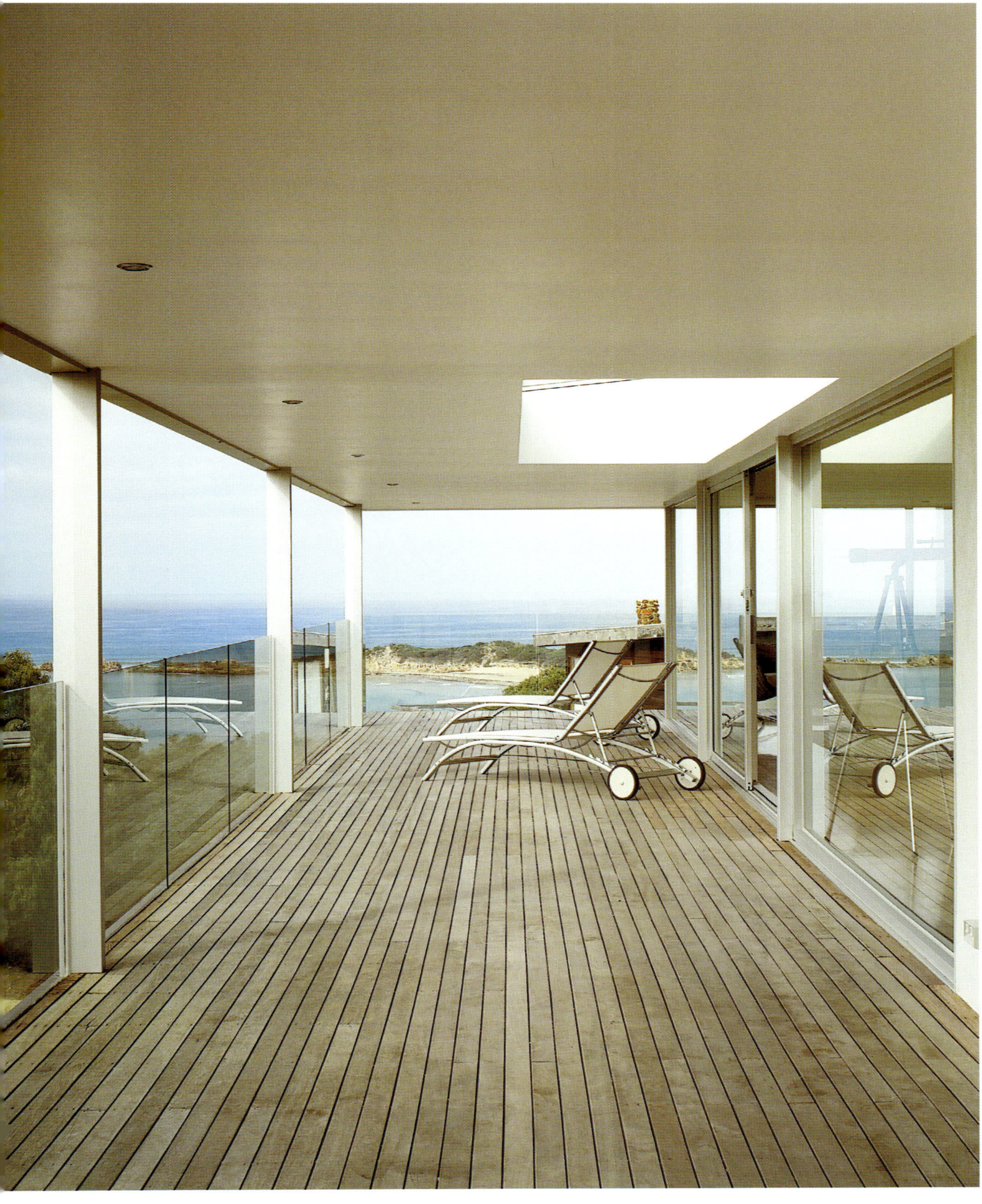

風景のあるバスルーム
BATHROOM WITH A VIEW

　この住宅は観念的にではなく実質的に環境と統合されている。設計の段階から、バスルームはリラクゼーションの空間としてだけでなく、瞑想のための空間としても考えられ、その重要性からこの特権的な場所を与えられた。開閉式のガラスパネルを開くと、バスルームとテラスの間をさえぎるものはなく、室内空間と屋外空間が完全に統合される。床と同一平面にあるお風呂は、黒潮を全身で感じることができる瞑想の場だ。

This residence practically entirely integrates with the environment.
The bathroom was designed as a space
for relaxation and meditation.
Its privileged position in the house reflects the importance given to this room.
The glass panels can be moved opening the bathroom to the terrace, with no divisions between indoor and outdoor.
The bath, positioned at floor level, is a refuge with a view of the ocean.

水平線の家

小川　晋一
都市建築設計事務所

熱海—静岡県—日本
撮影：ナカサアンドパートナーズ

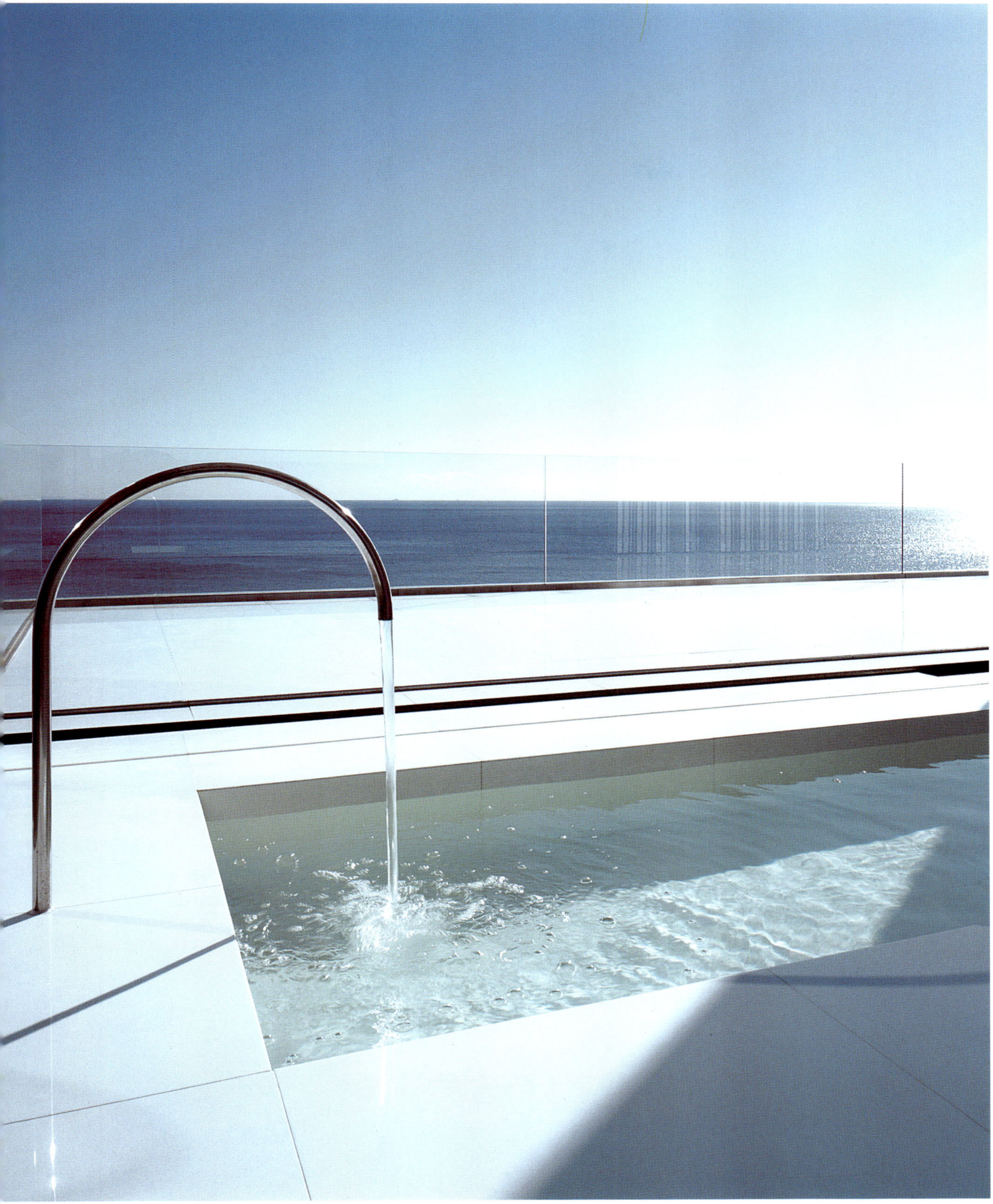

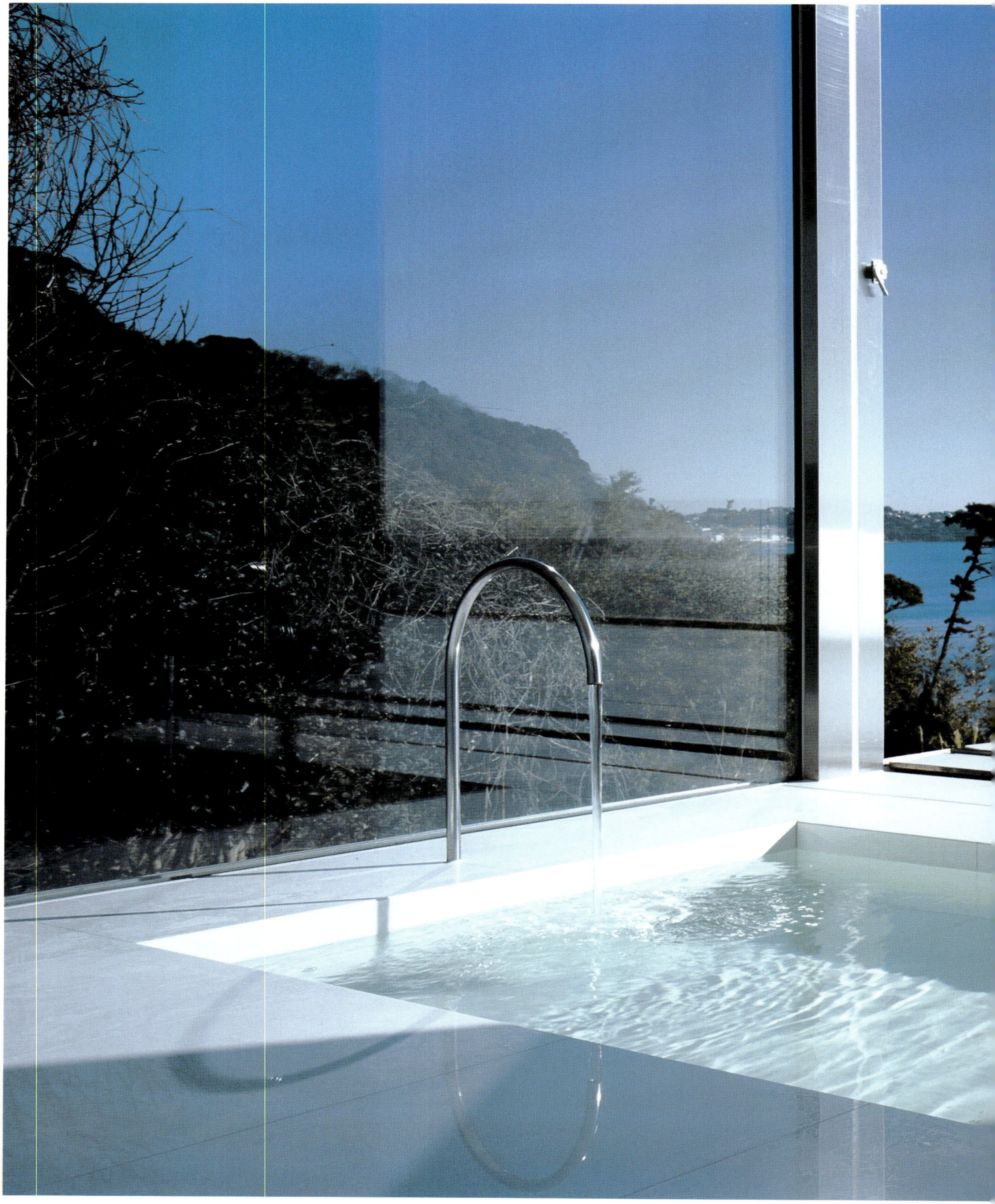

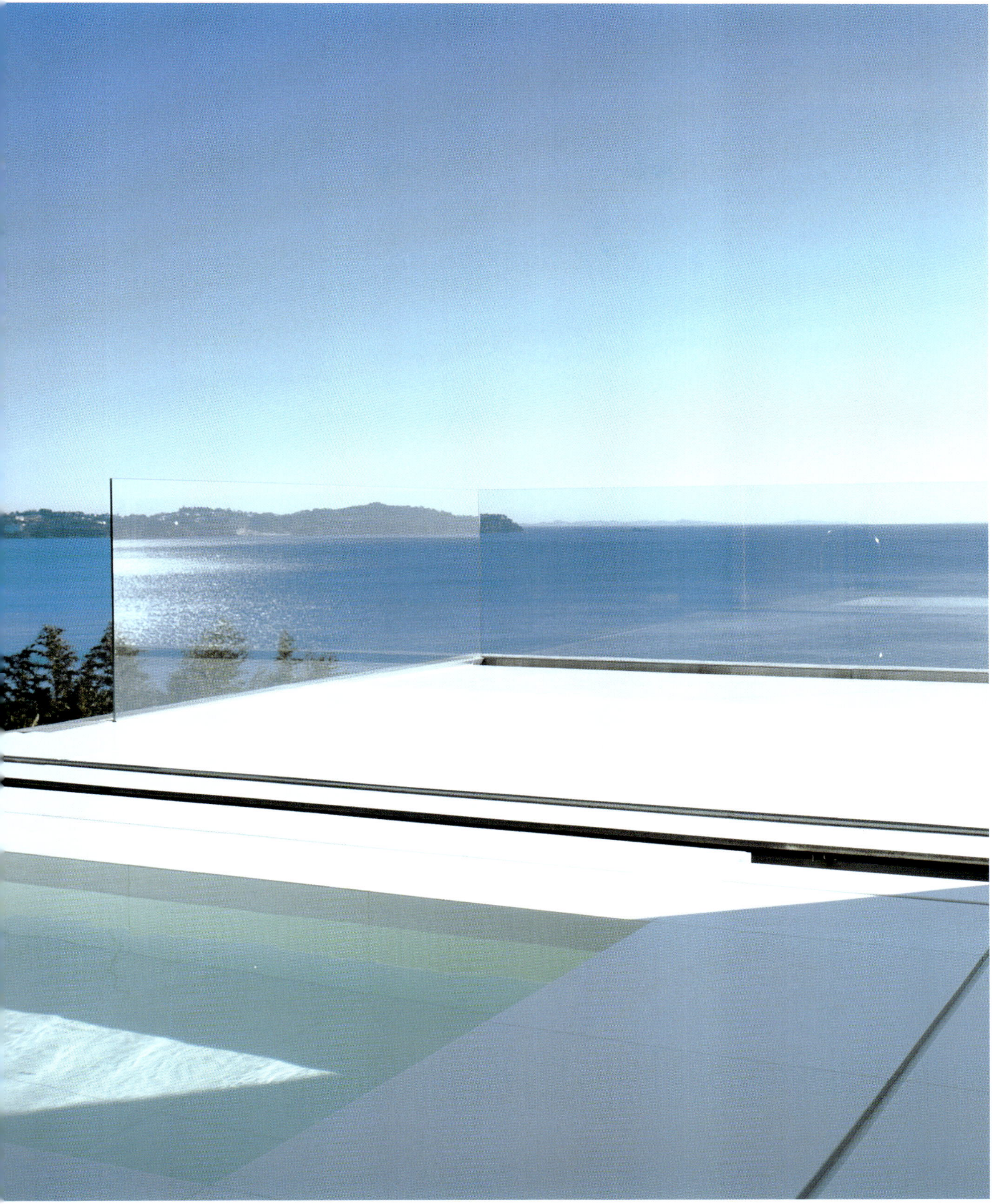

ネクサスを繋ぐ
JOINING NEXUS

アクアリウムはこの巨大ロフトの多様な空間を繋ぐ接続詞の役割を果たしている。繊細な線、さまざまな高さの組み合わせ、それらを優しく包むクリーム色、これらが独特な美しさを持つ洗練された空間を創りあげている。アクアリウムの全長は2m以上あり、リビングルーム、キッチン、そして小さな洗面所までをも繋ぐ結節点となっている。それはまた透明な窓でもあり、その向こうにあるもう1つの部屋へと開かれている。あらゆる部屋が水の持つ不思議な力と魚たちの動きの磁力で充満されている。

The aquarium of this magnificent loft acts as a joining element between different spaces. The elegance of the lines in this house, the combination of levels and the color cream, create a unique and distinguished space. The aquarium, that measures 7 ft, connects the living room, kitchen and even a small bathroom, while also creating a transparent window through which the room behind can be seen. All these places have been impregnated by the magic of water and the magnetism of the movement of the fish.

アイントホーフェンのロフト

NAT アーヒテクテン

アイントホーフェン―オランダ
撮影：ピーター・カイペルス

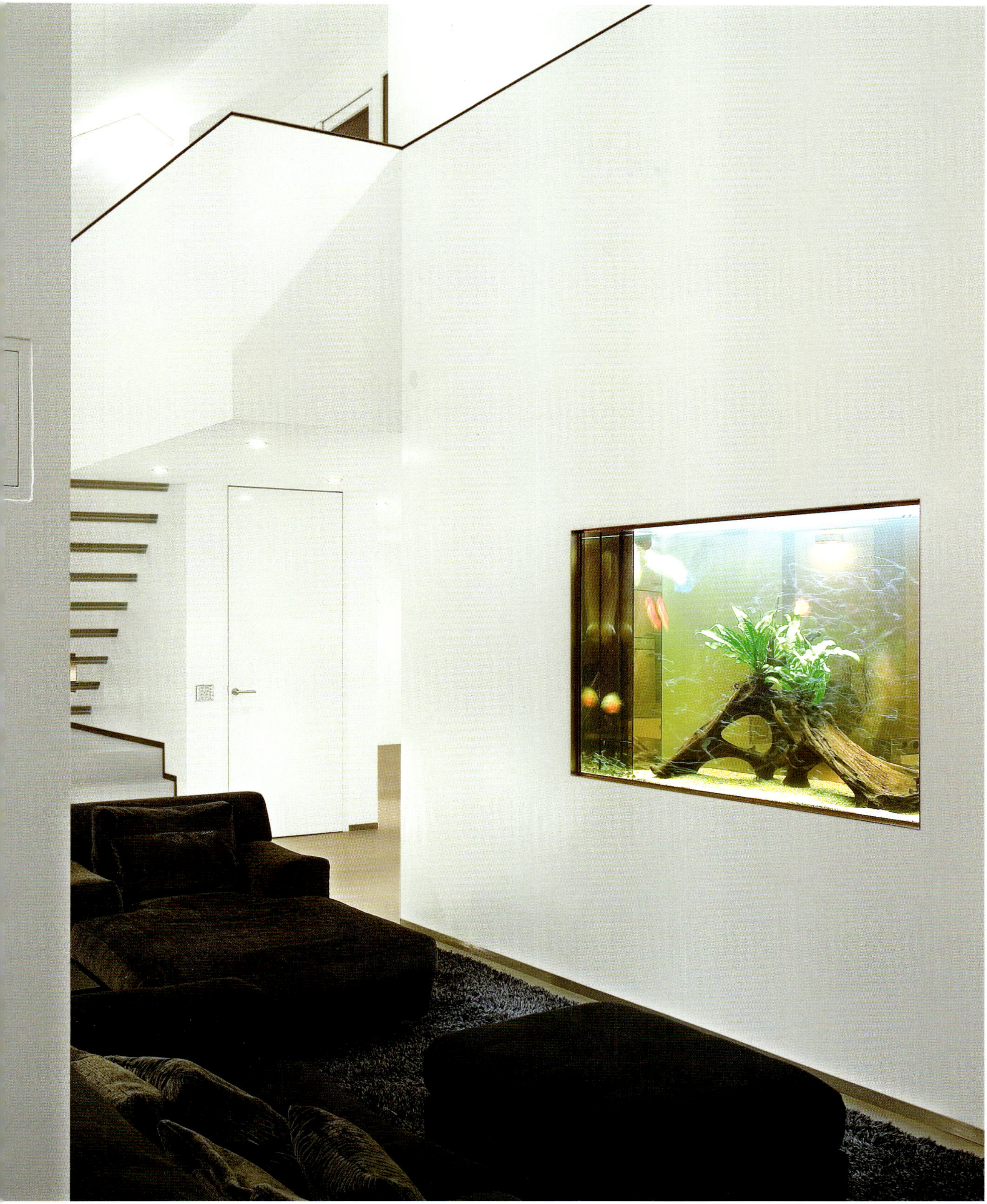

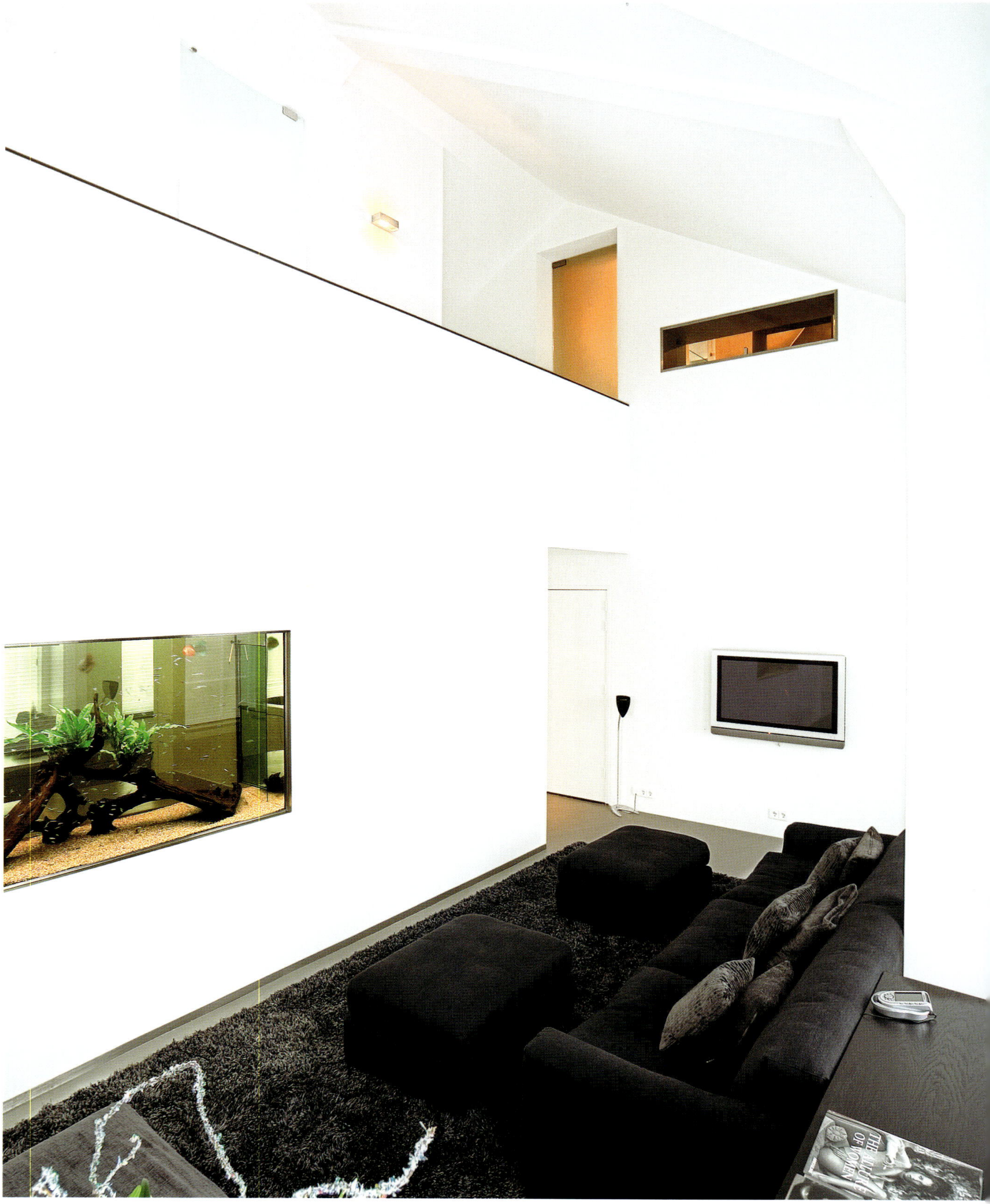

キッチンとリビングルームはアクアリウムで連結されているが、それぞれがまったく異なった雰囲気を持っている。アクアリウムはリビングルームに安息の気をもたらし、キッチンでは光源となっている。

The kitchen and living room are joined thanks to the aquarium, but they have different atmospheres. In the living room, the aquarium is an element providing tranquility, while in the kitchen it creates a point of light.

大西洋への窓
A WINDOW TO THE OCEAN

アクアリウムは自宅に持ち込むことのできる小さな水面下の世界。しかしそれは単なる人間の欲望の対象なのではなく、この地球のどこかにある未知の純粋な自然へと開かれた窓であり、小さな生態系である。それは見る者に生命の源である海の底を体感させ、畏敬の念を抱かせる。アクアリウムが明るい色に満ちた単調な世界ではなく、魚や他の生物が休息することのできる陰影のある世界であることは知っておく必要がある。所有者はこの小さな生態系全体に責任を負っている。

Aquariums form small underwater worlds that man has been able to bring into his home. But they are not only man's objects of desire, they are also windows to a wild and unknown world that takes place within our environment like small ecosystems. Aquariums can help us to better understand and respect the underwater world. It must be understood that an aquarium is not only a place full of bright colors, it is also a place where fish and other living beings reside, for which the owners must accept responsibility.

持続可能な未来へ

制作者不詳

サンパウロ―ブラジル
撮影：トゥッカー・ライネス

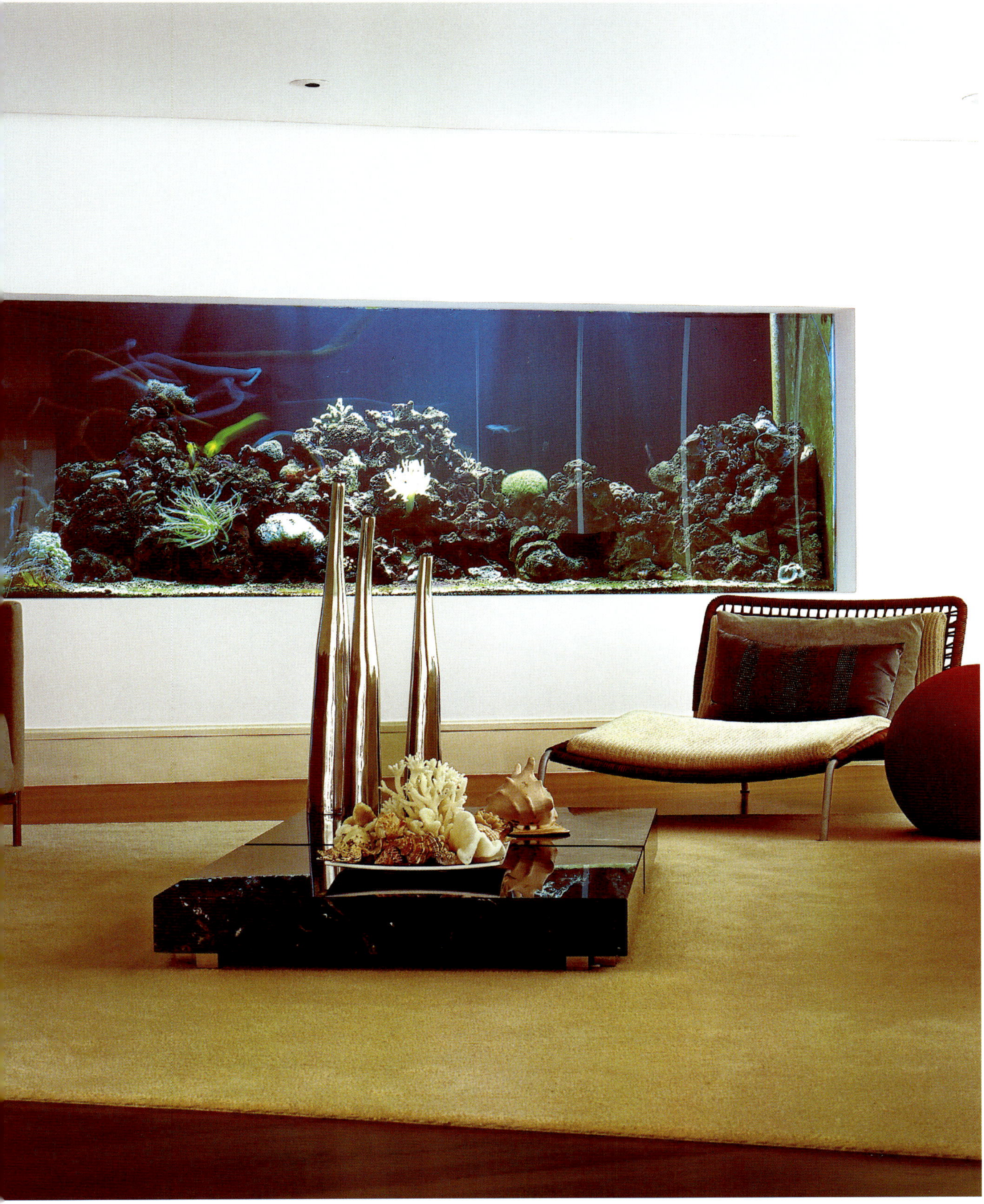

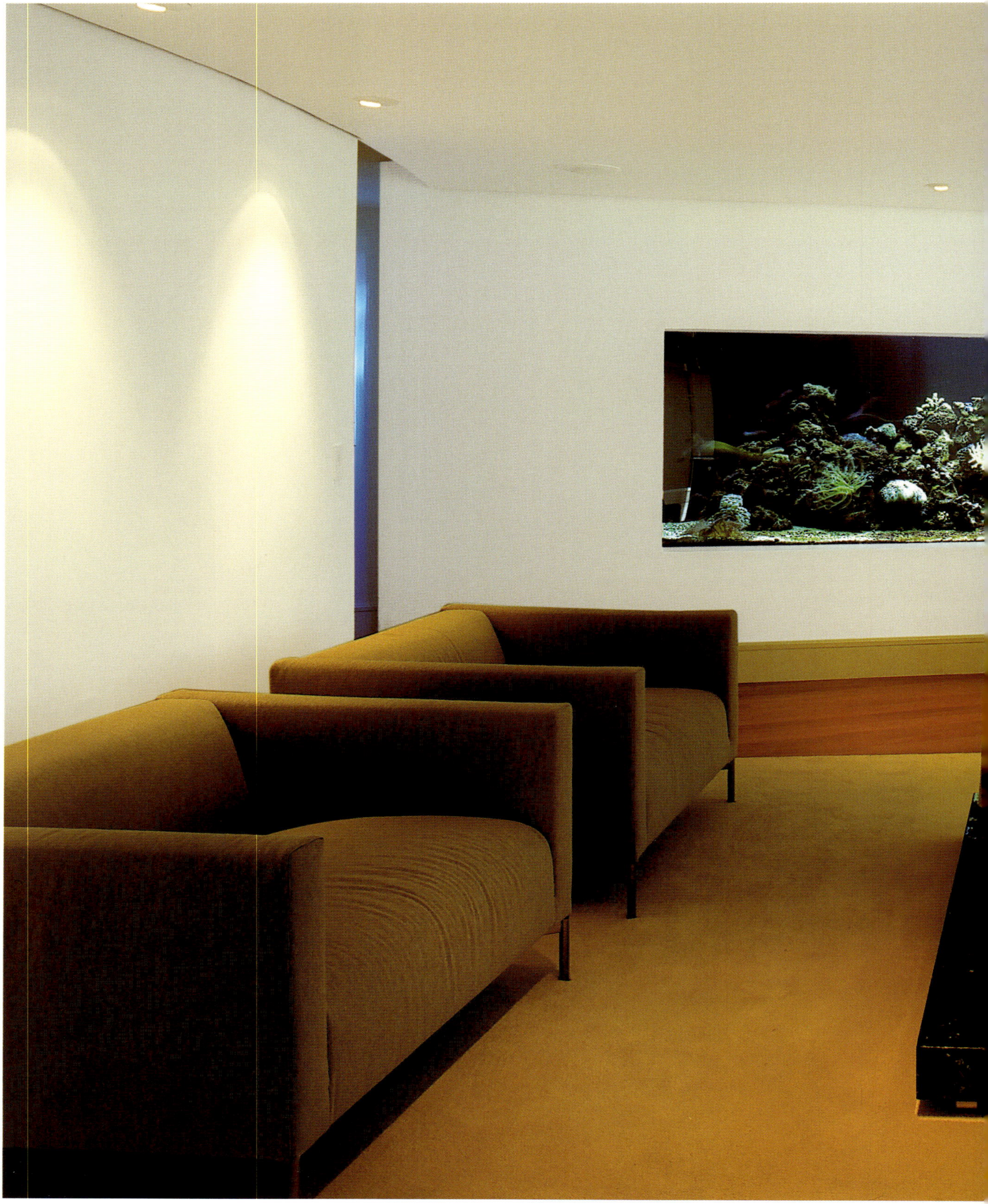

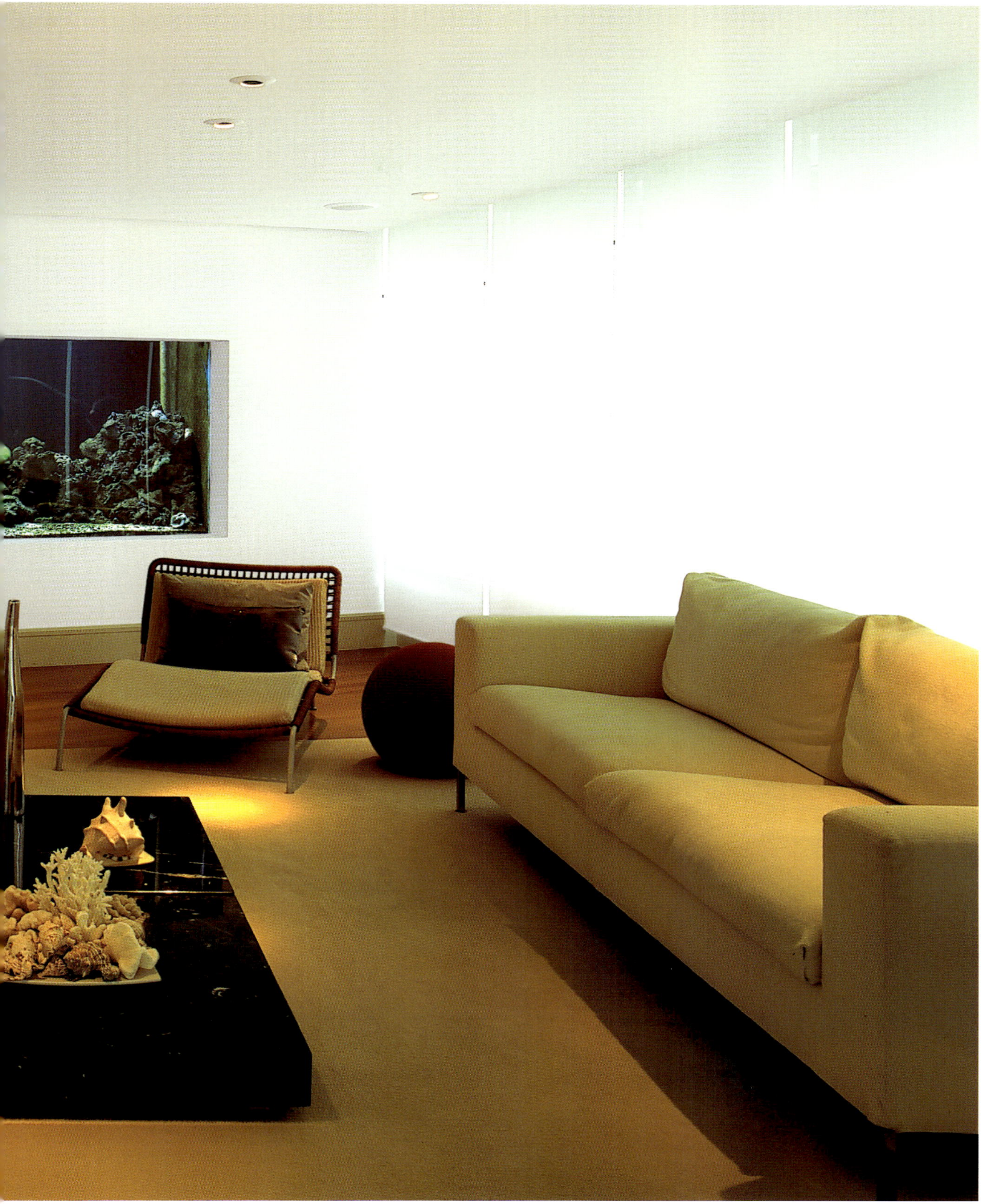

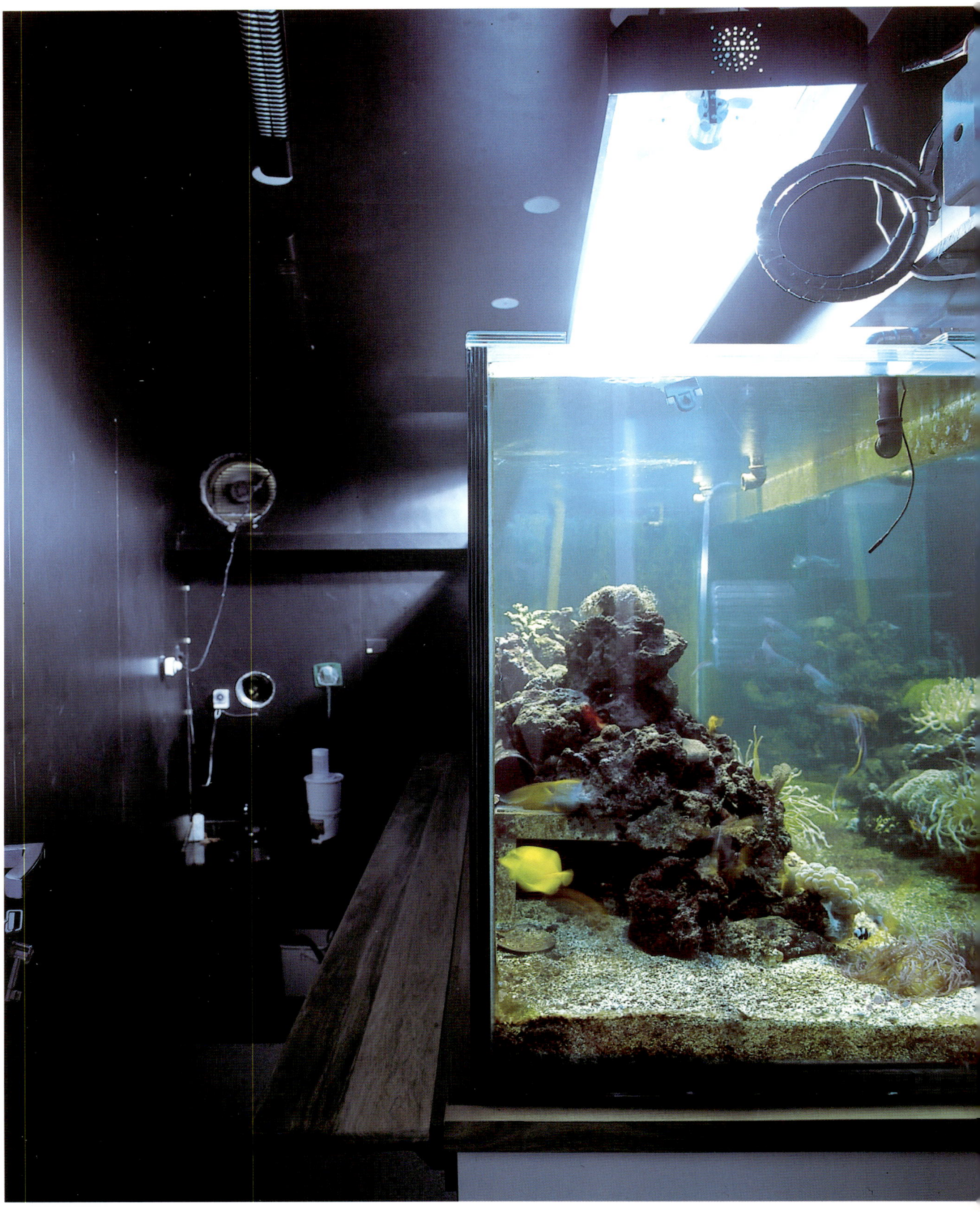

アクアリウムを維持することは見た目ほど簡単ではない。それは複雑な生態系であり、最適な水温の維持、照明の調節、フィルターの清掃、自動給餌システムなど多くのことに目を配っていなければならない。

The apparent simplicity of aquariums hides complex systems, which, among other functions, achieve the appropriate water temperature, provide lighting, clean the filters and automatically feed the occupants.

マジック・イン・ザ・ウォーター
MAGIC IN THE WATER

　アクアリウムは不思議な生き物に満ちた小宇宙であり、それ自身の律動を有している。昼間観察すると、魚やサンゴなどさまざまな種が水中をおもいおもいの姿で動き回っているのを見る。しかし夜が訪れると、自然と同じようにこの宇宙の主役は交代し、昼間には見られなかった光景が現れる。人間が眠っているとき、この魔法の世界を含む室内の様相は一変し、秘密の宇宙が出現する。

Aquariums are small worlds full of bizarre inhabitants and their own rhythm of life. When observed during the day we see different species of fish, corrals, etc., moving in their own ways through the water. When night falls, just as in nature, the stars of this space change, and are not as they previously appeared. While we sleep the interior of this magical world transforms into an entirely different, secret universe.

海底に眠る

D&Dアクアリウム・ソルーションズ

ロンドン―イギリス
撮影：カルロス・ドミンゲス

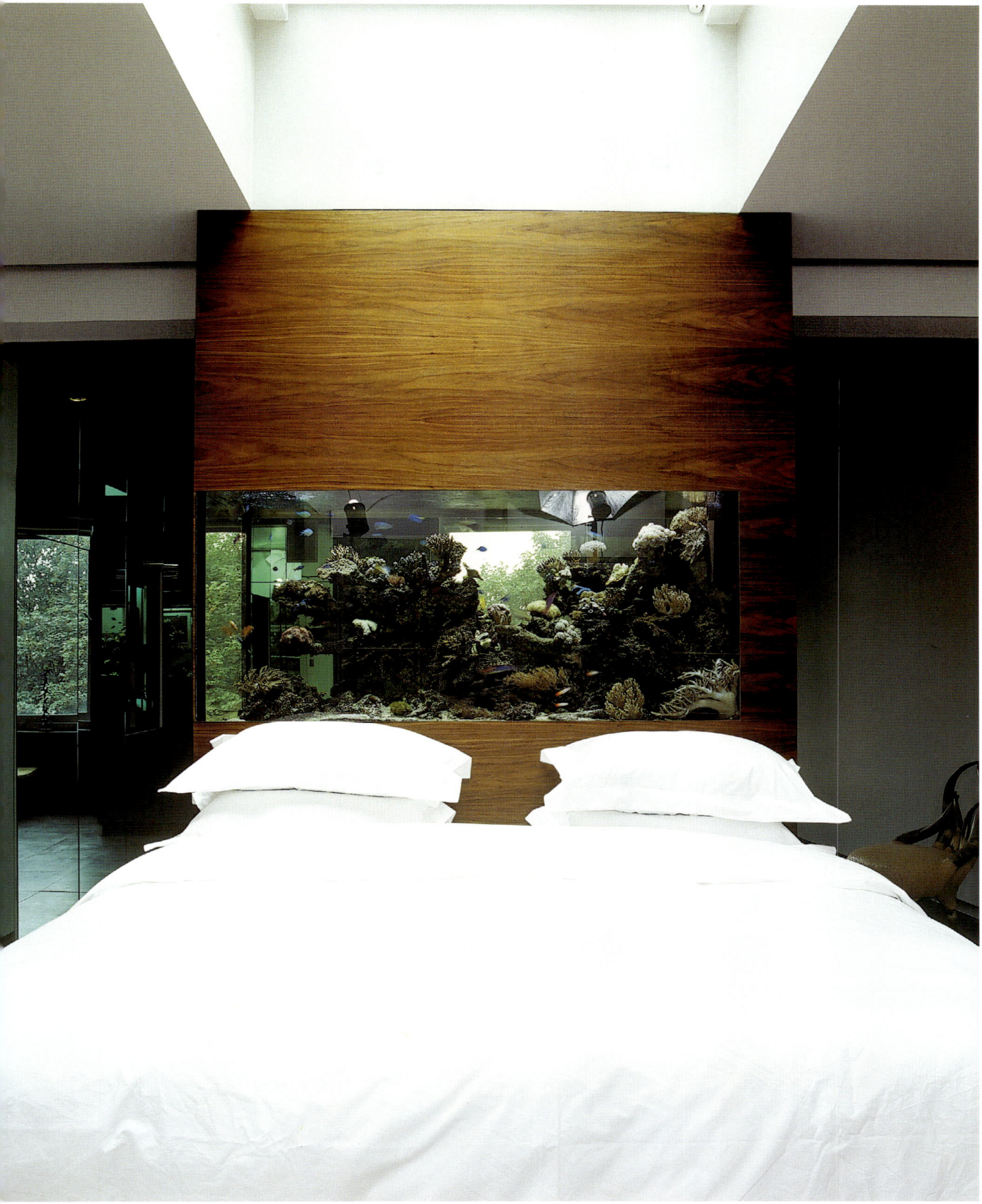

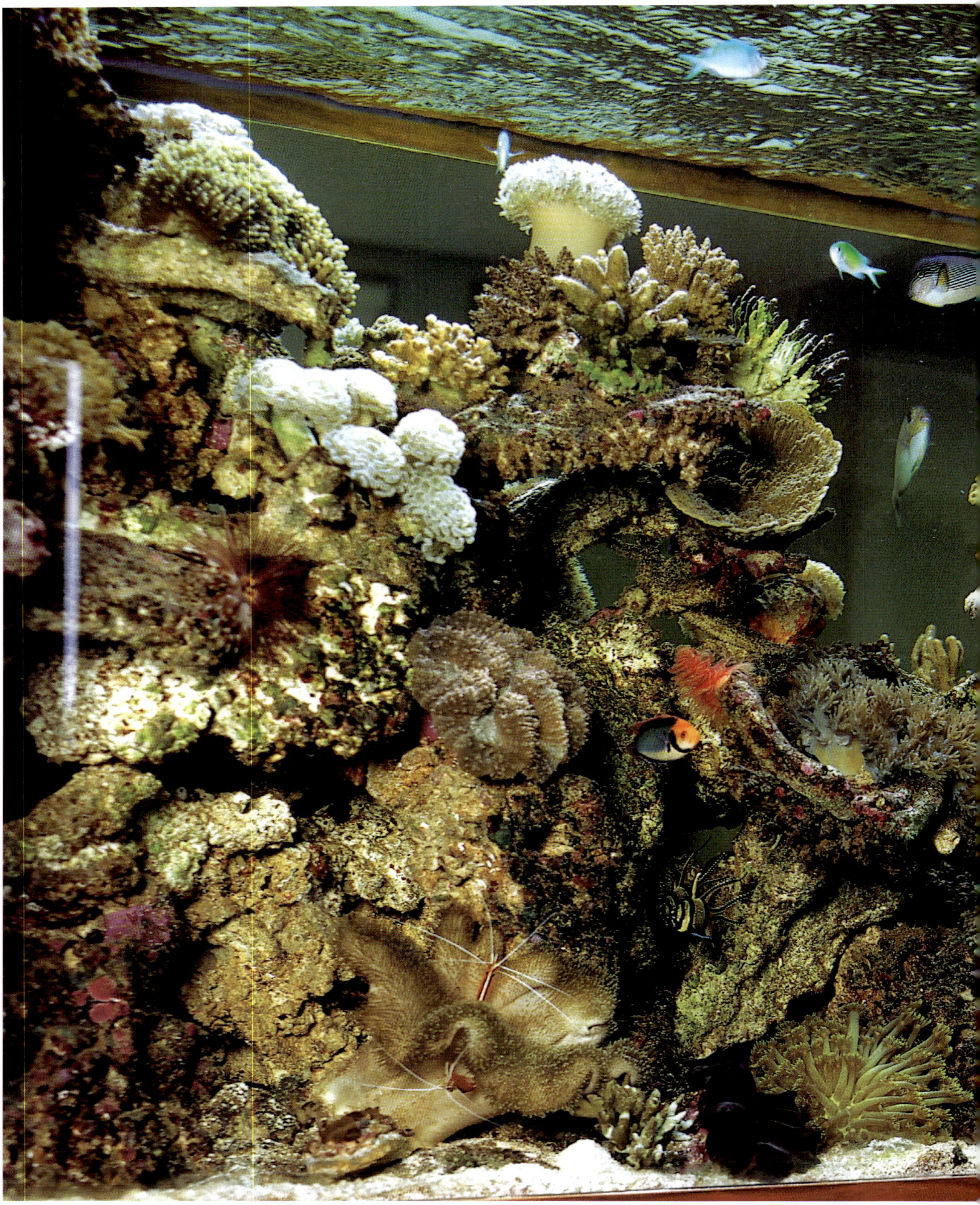

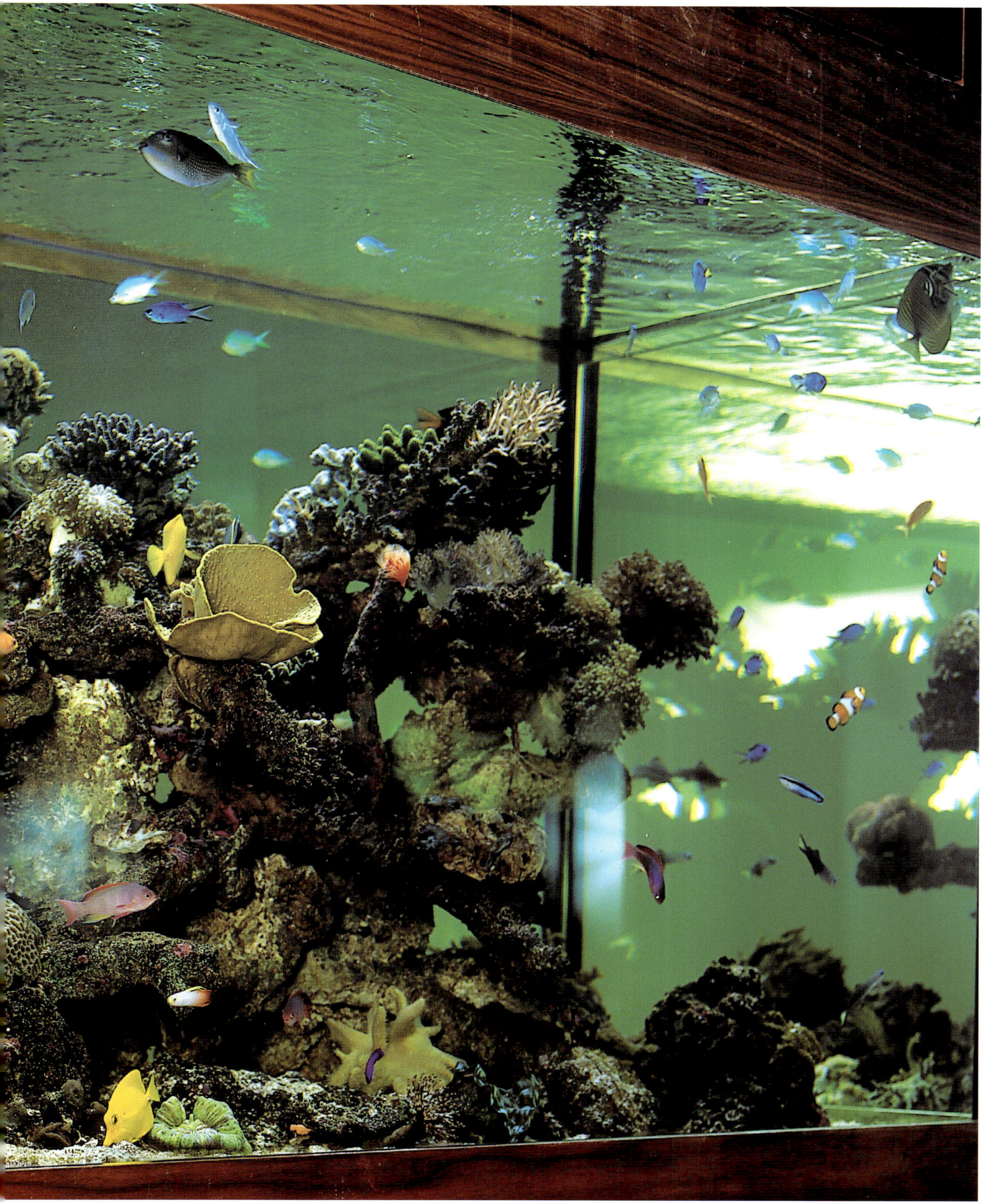

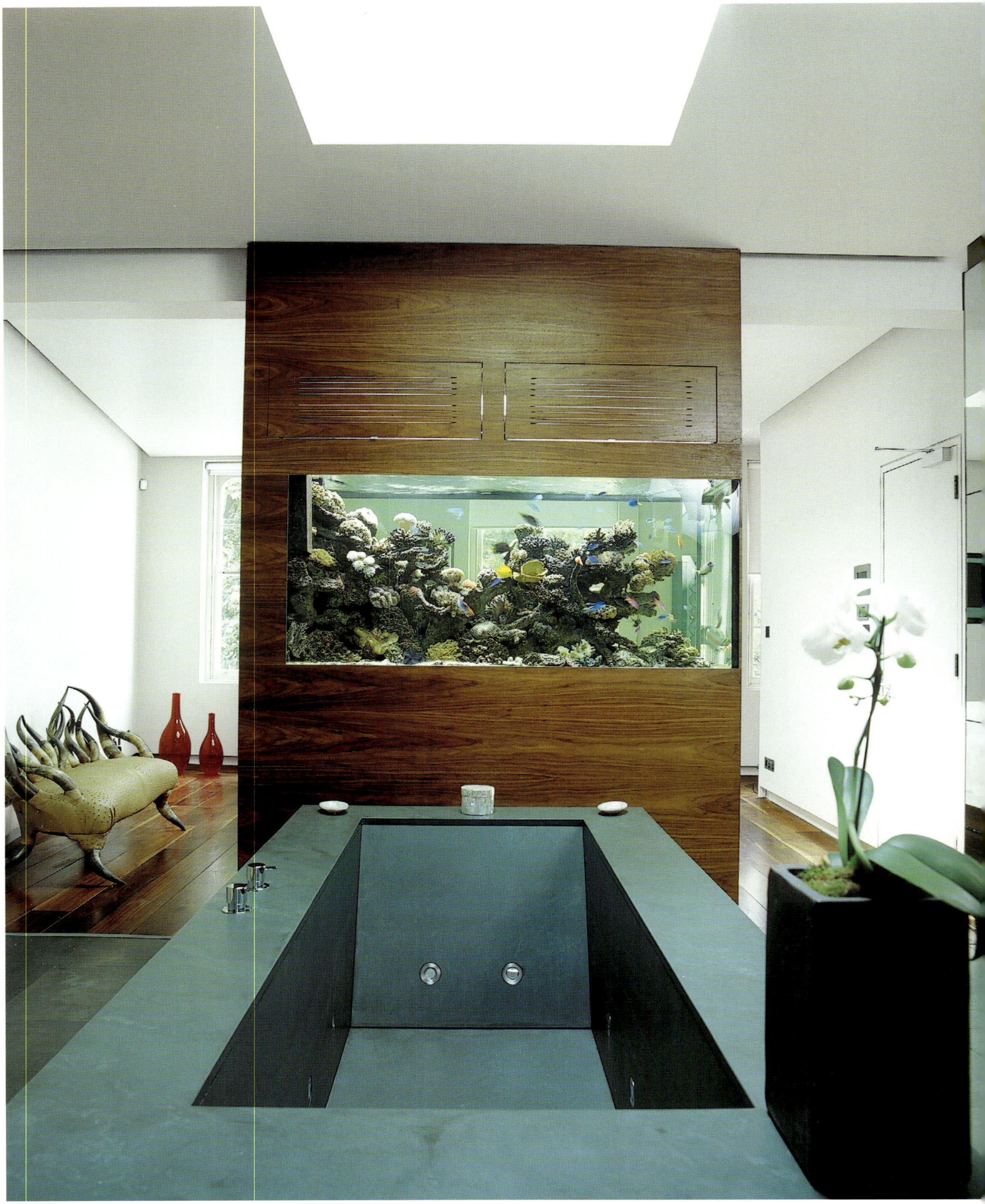

海底に眠る | 219

コーナー・オブ・ピース
CORNER OF PEACE

　コンクリート、漆喰、石、木の4つの材料によって構成されているこの住宅のコンセプトは、安息と瞑想の空間。ポーチと開放的な中庭は、微風を招き入れることができるように配置されている。その一角に、静かに水をたたえ光を映す小さな池がある。その池は見る者に建築と自然が共存することの意味を悟らせる。そこでの主役は水である。水面に浮かぶ睡蓮と池の周囲に敷かれた玉石が、このうえなく平和な空間を創りだしている。

The materials used in the construction of this residence are basically concrete, plaster, stone and wood. The house was conceived as a space for rest and meditation. Porches and open courtyards have been arranged in order to receive the breeze. In one of the corners is a mirror of water, a small pond where one can feel the relation between architecture and natural surroundings and where the water plays the starring role. The water lilies and stones that set its boundaries create a peaceful space.

カサ・マルドナド

アルベルト・ブルクハルト

アナポイマ―コロンビア
撮影:ジャン・マルク・ブルシュレーガー

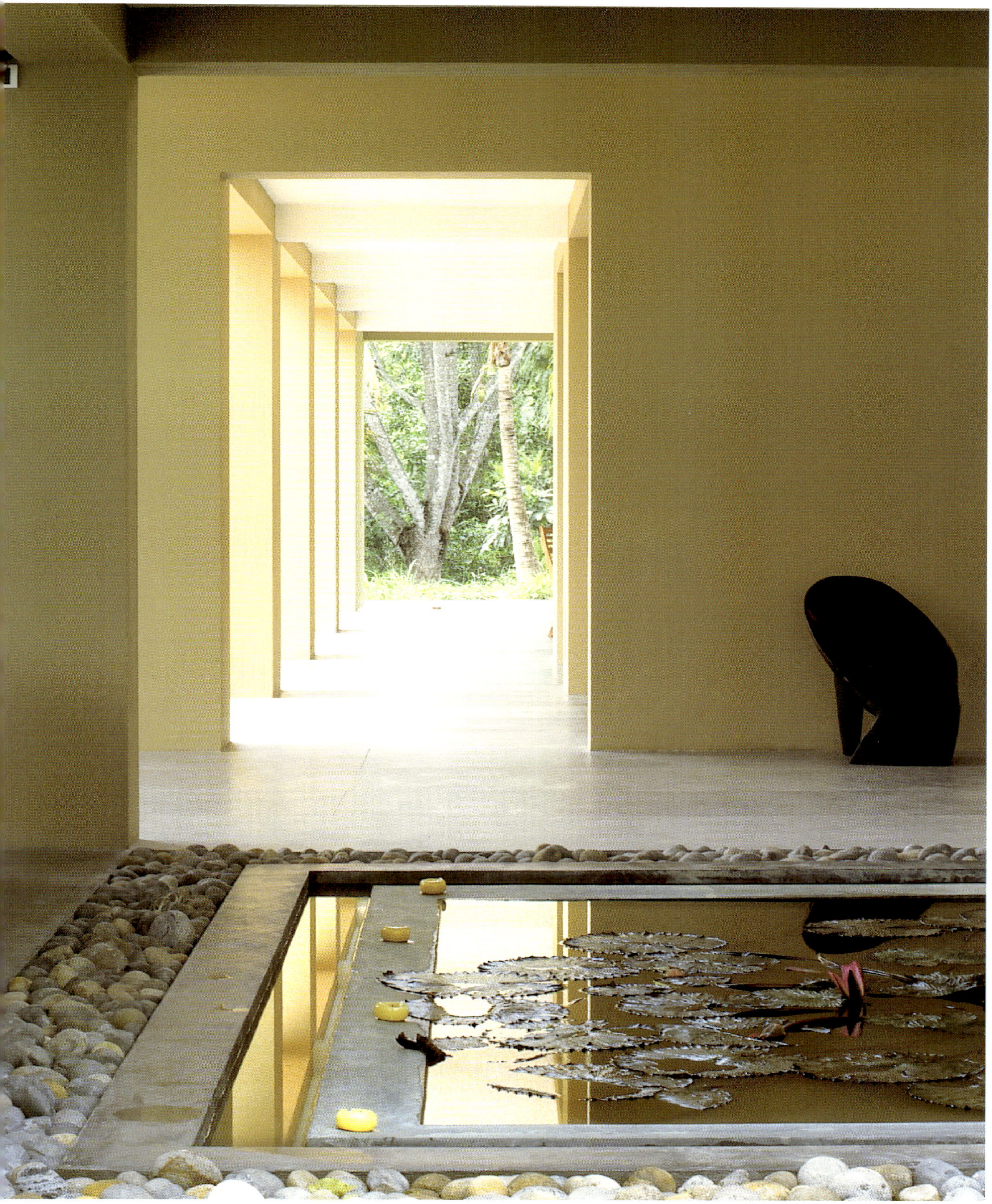

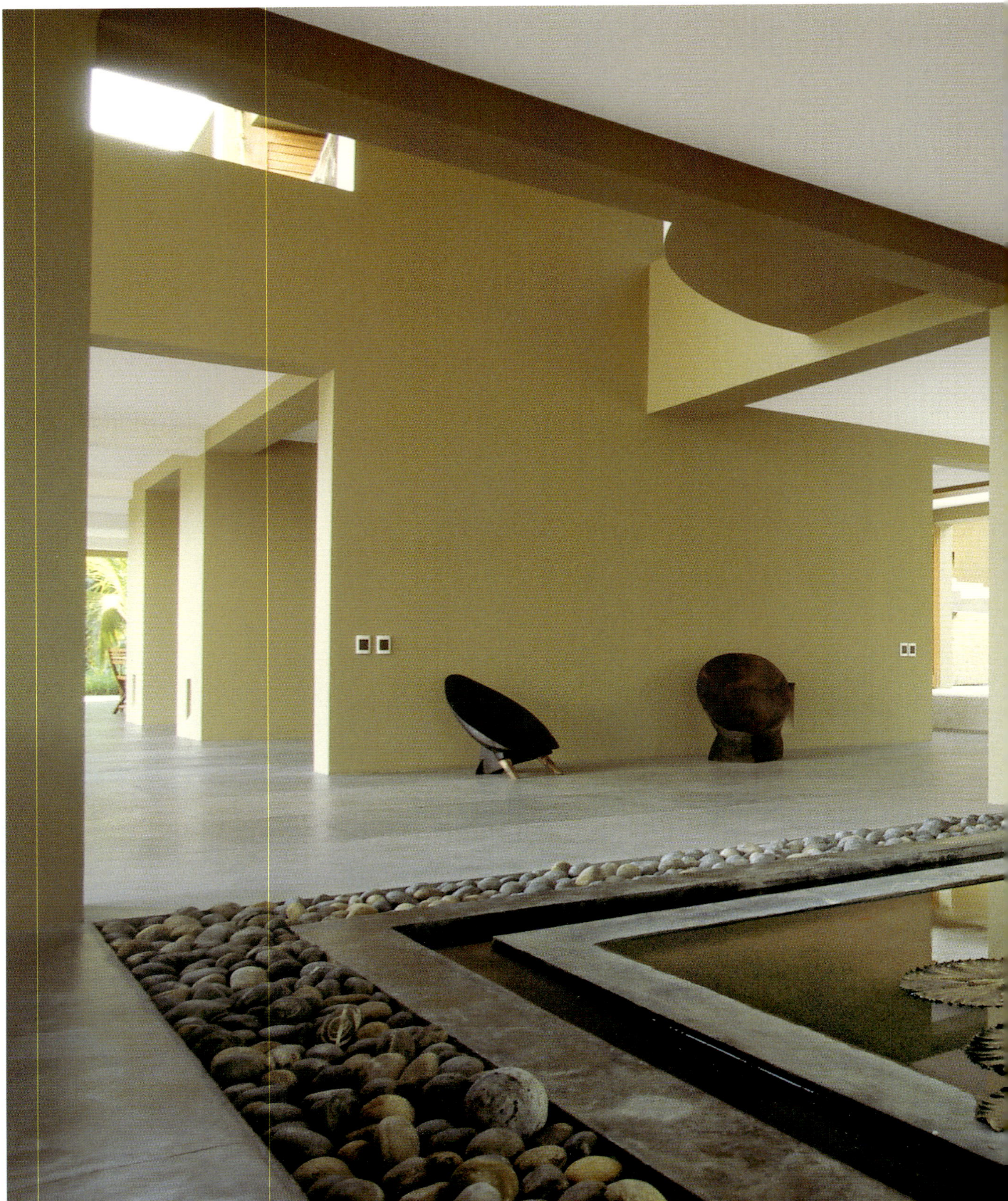

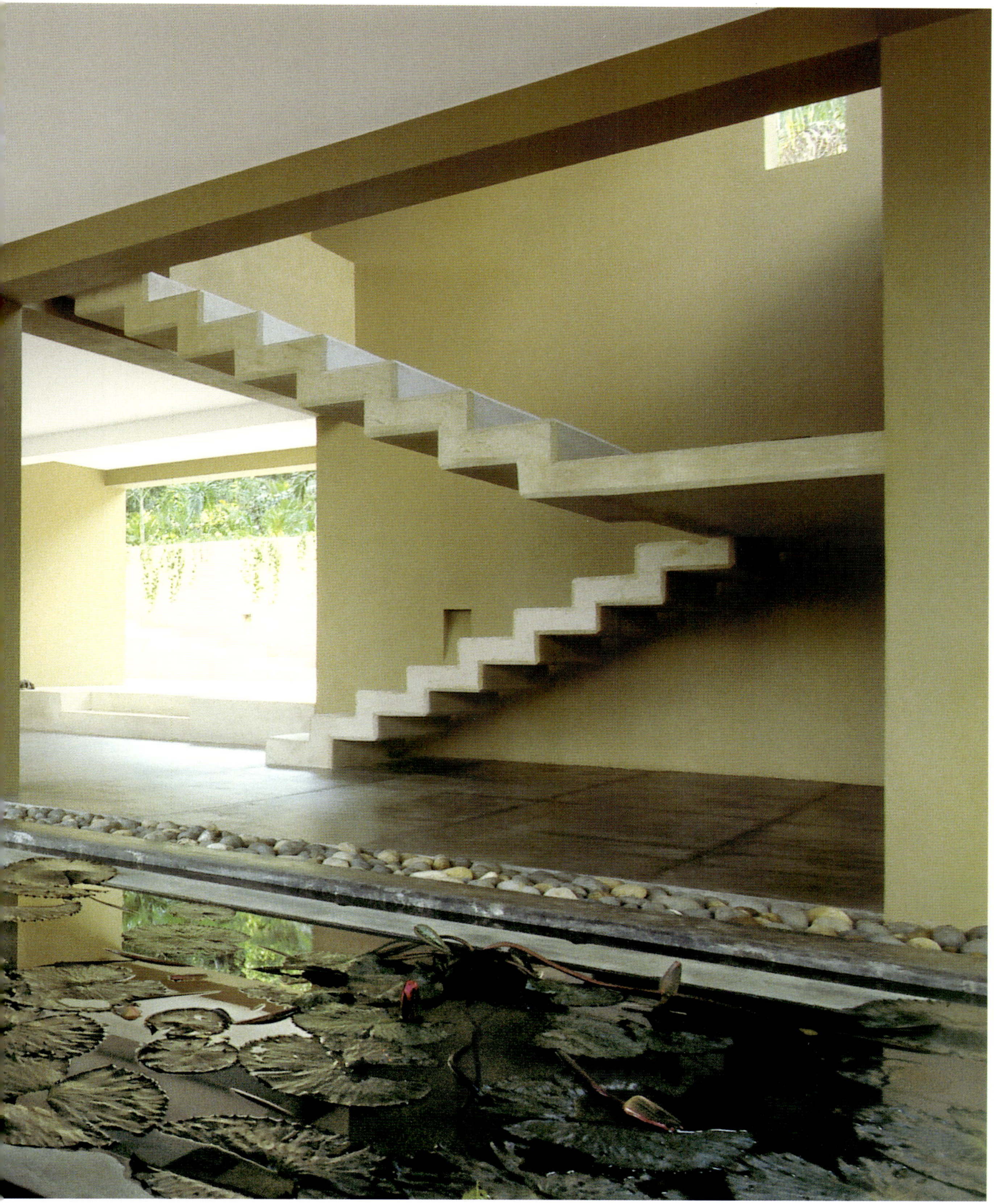

復活した伝統
RESTORED TRADITION

　この広いマンションのレイアウトは独特だ。部屋は中央に集められ、その周囲に回廊が走っている。特に目をひくのはスパのある空間で、スカンジナビア・デザインの伝統的な様式と現代的な様式とが見事に組み合わされている。スカンジナビアの伝統であるサウナが、現代的な線とデザインによってマンションに復活した。ミニマリスト的な線、楕円形のバスタブ、自然光、これらが平和を呼吸することができる安らぎの空間を創りだしている。

This large apartment has a unique layout. The rooms are in the center and corridors run down the sides. The spa is one of the most notable spaces, combining traditional and modern Scandinavian design.
The sauna is the traditional element but its shape and design are modern. The minimalist lines, the oval bathtub and the natural light, are some of the elements that create an atmosphere of relaxation where one can breath in peace.

ストックホルムのマンション

クラーソン・コイヴィスト・
ルーネ・アルキテクトコントール

ストックホルム―スウェーデン
撮影：エイク・イーソン・リンドマン

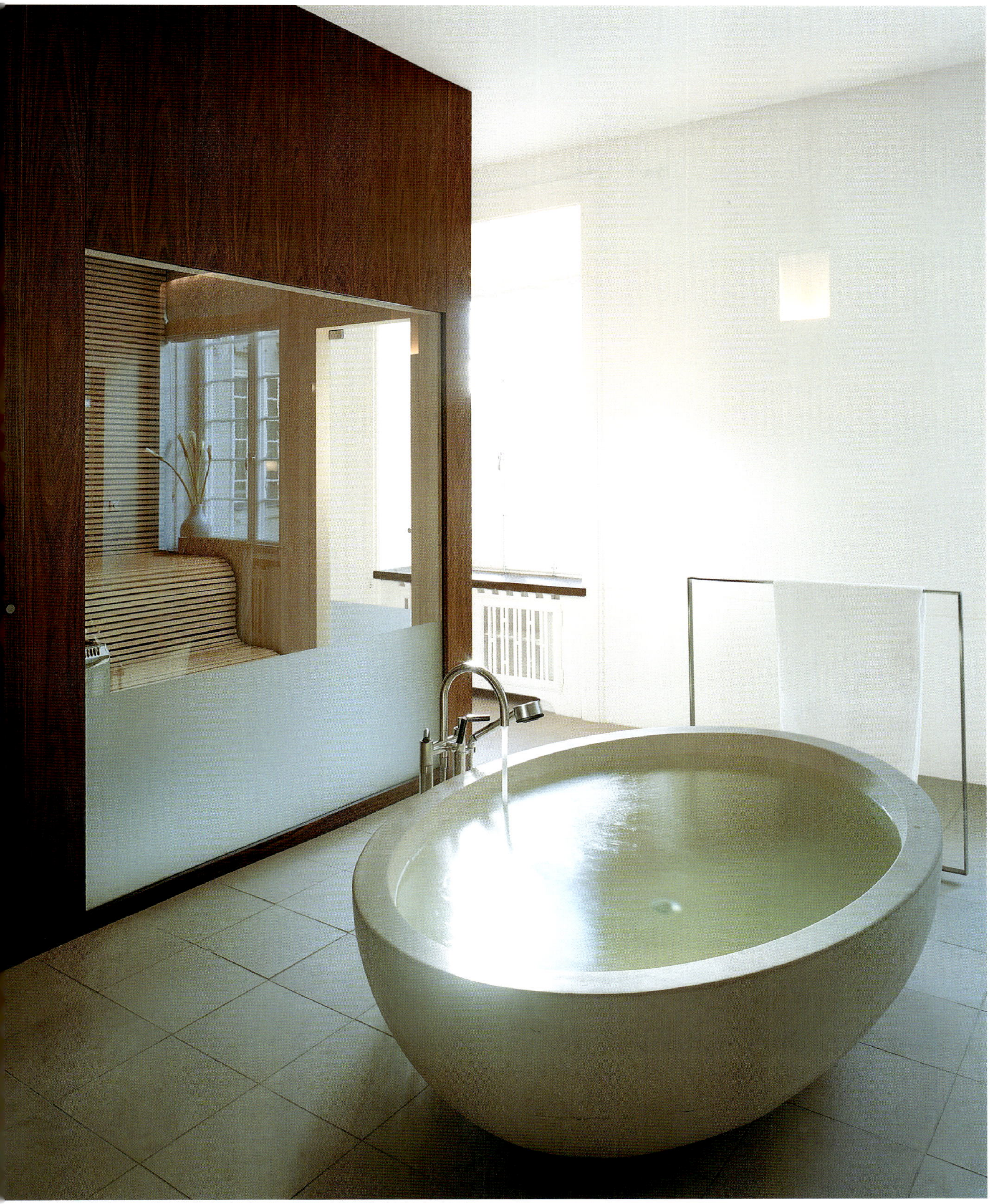

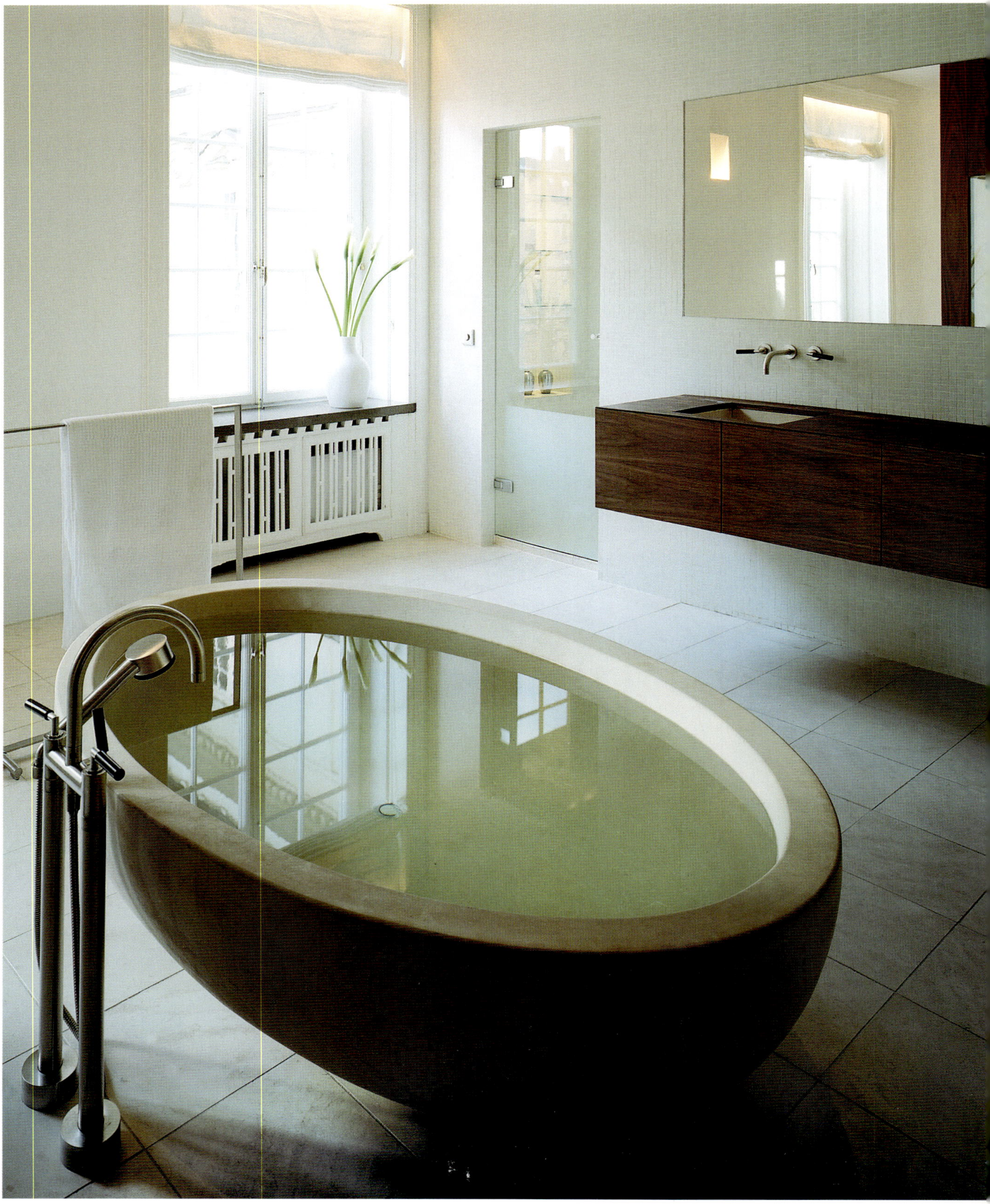

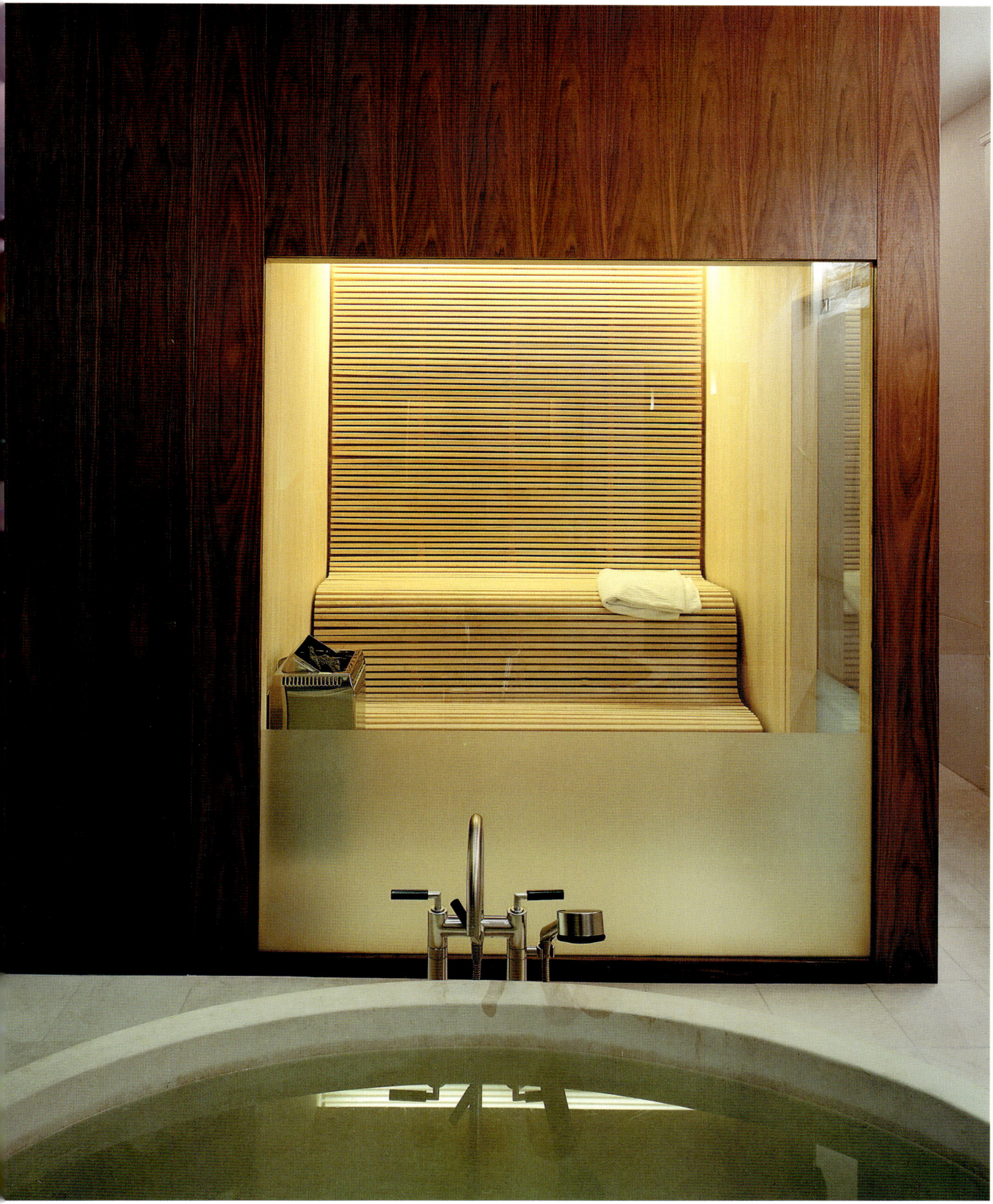

メディテーション
MEDITATION

　ヨガとメディテーションの熱心な実践家であるオーナーの哲学にそってこのマンハッタンのマンションの室内は設計された。デザインは室内に豊富な自然光と、線で構成された簡潔さをもたらした。なかでもバスルームはこの住居の最も重要な空間。水はリラクゼーションと休息をもたらし、自分自身に回帰する時間を与えてくれる。よく考えられた照明計画がもたらす光と影、無駄な装飾を省いた質実な家具、それらが瞑想のための完璧な空間を創造している。

The design of this Manhattan apartment was meant to follow the life philosophy of the owner, a keen practitioner of yoga and meditation. The design gives the interiors ample natural light and simplicity through the lines. The bathroom is one of the most special rooms in the house. Water is the element used to achieve relaxation and rest, as well as giving us time to ourselves. The decor's light shades and the elegant austerity of the furniture create the perfect atmosphere for rest.

セントラルパークのスパ

ボネッティ・コザルスキー・スタジオ

ニューヨーク―アメリカ
撮影：マテオ・ピアッツァ

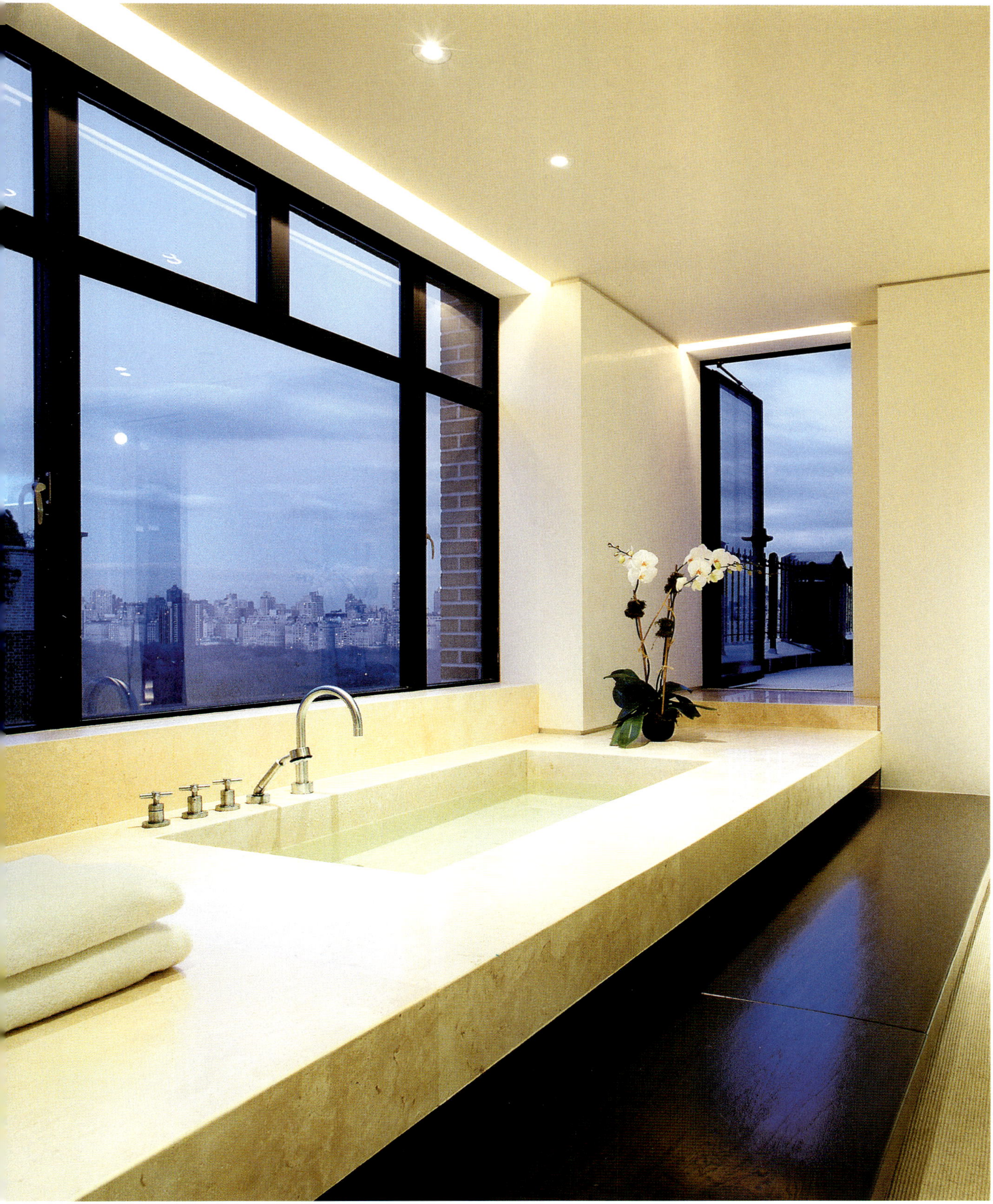

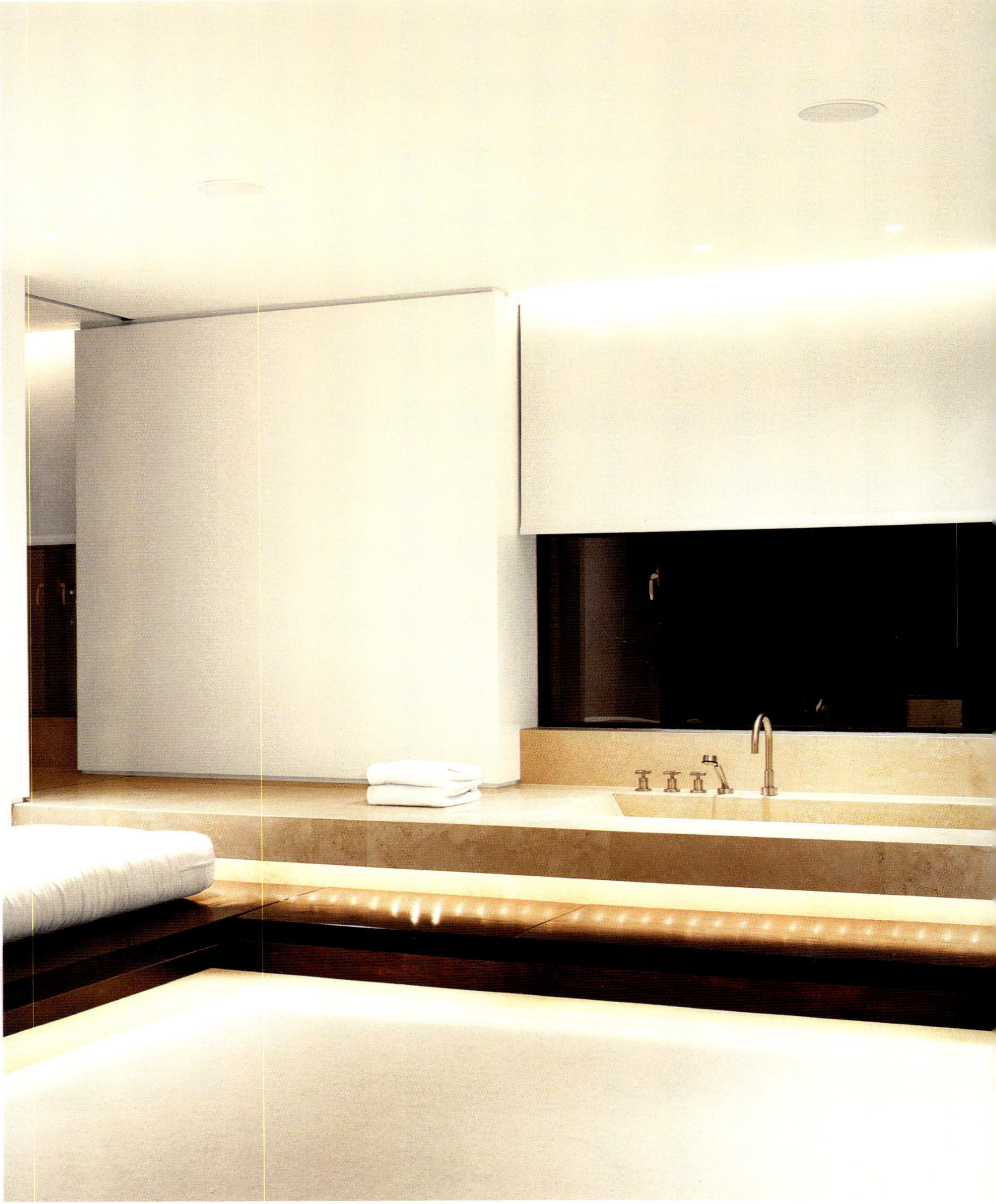

マンハッタンの超高層ビル群を眺めながらゆっくりと身体を伸ばせる大きな浴槽、マッサージ機能付きのジェットシャワー、これがこの劇的なバスルームの2大要素。片隅に敷いてある簡素なフトンが、もう1つのリラクゼーションと休息の場を提供する。

A large bath with views of the skyscrapers and a hydromassage shower are two important elements in this spectacular bathroom. In one corner is a comfortable futon constituting an additional relaxation and rest area.

オリエンタル・リラクゼーション
ORIENTAL RELAXATION

お風呂は日本人があみ出した究極のリラクゼーション。家族全員で使うことができるようにデザインされたお風呂のお湯には、石鹸、塩、その他の芳香剤は入れない。お風呂は、シャワーできれいに身体を洗った後に浸かり、身体と心を浄化する場。お湯のここち良い温もりが身体の毒を排出させ、筋肉の疲れをほぐし、心身ともに安らぎを与える。材料の選択（イペ材とスレートのタイル）、絶妙な空間レイアウト、これらが質実剛健で厳かな雰囲気を醸しだしている。

The ofuro is a Japanese practice dedicated to relaxation. This bathroom, designed to be shared by the family, does not use soaps, salts or any other aromatic substance. The ofuro, whose prime objective is to cleanse body and soul, is used after washing in a shower. The water temperature eliminates toxins, relaxes muscles and stimulates relaxation. A serene environment has been created thanks to the materials (ipé wood and slate tiles) and the elegant layout of the spaces.

お風呂

バーバラ・シンドリュー／
CADインテリオリスモ

バルセロナ―スペイン
撮影：ニューリア・フュエンテス

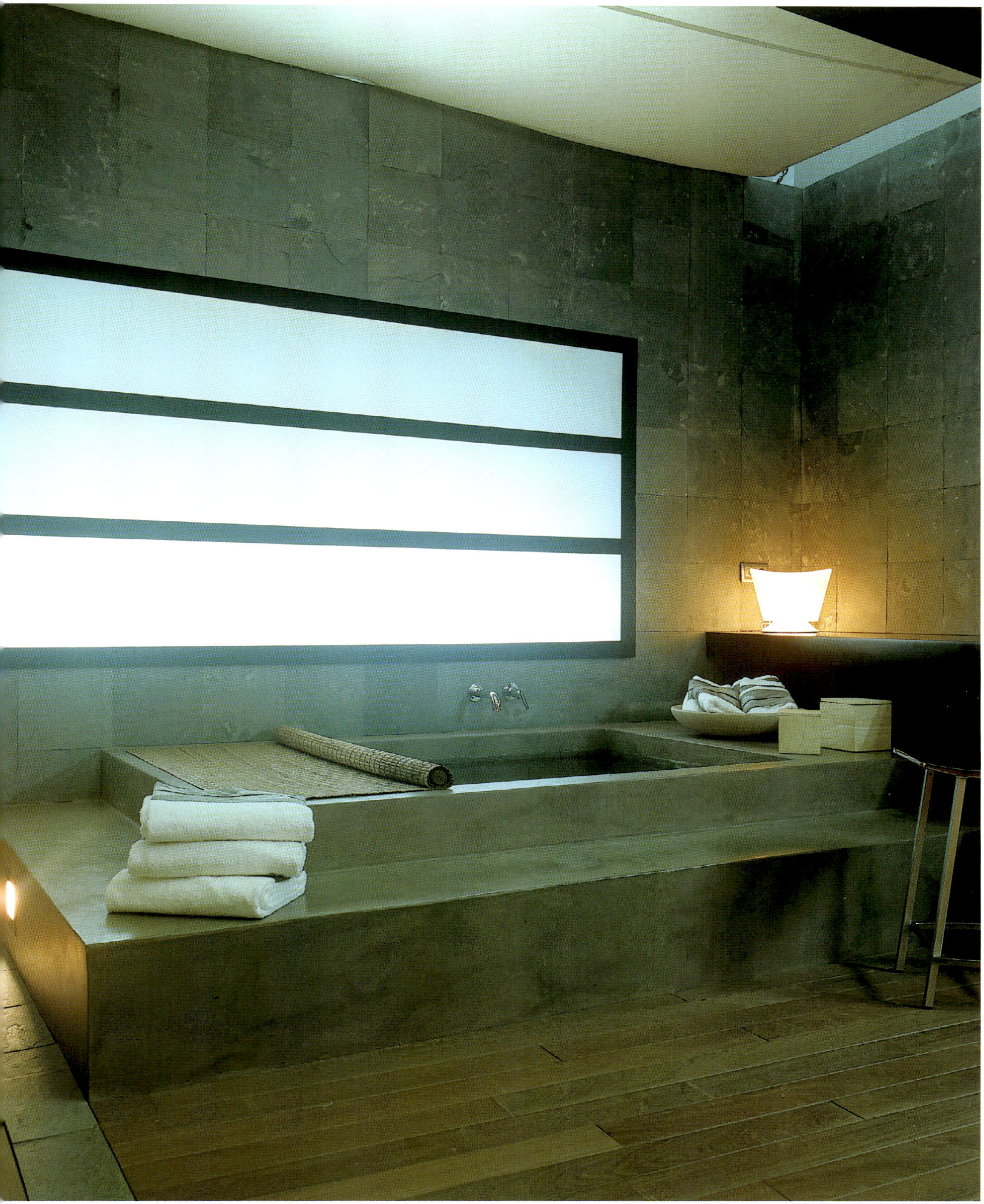

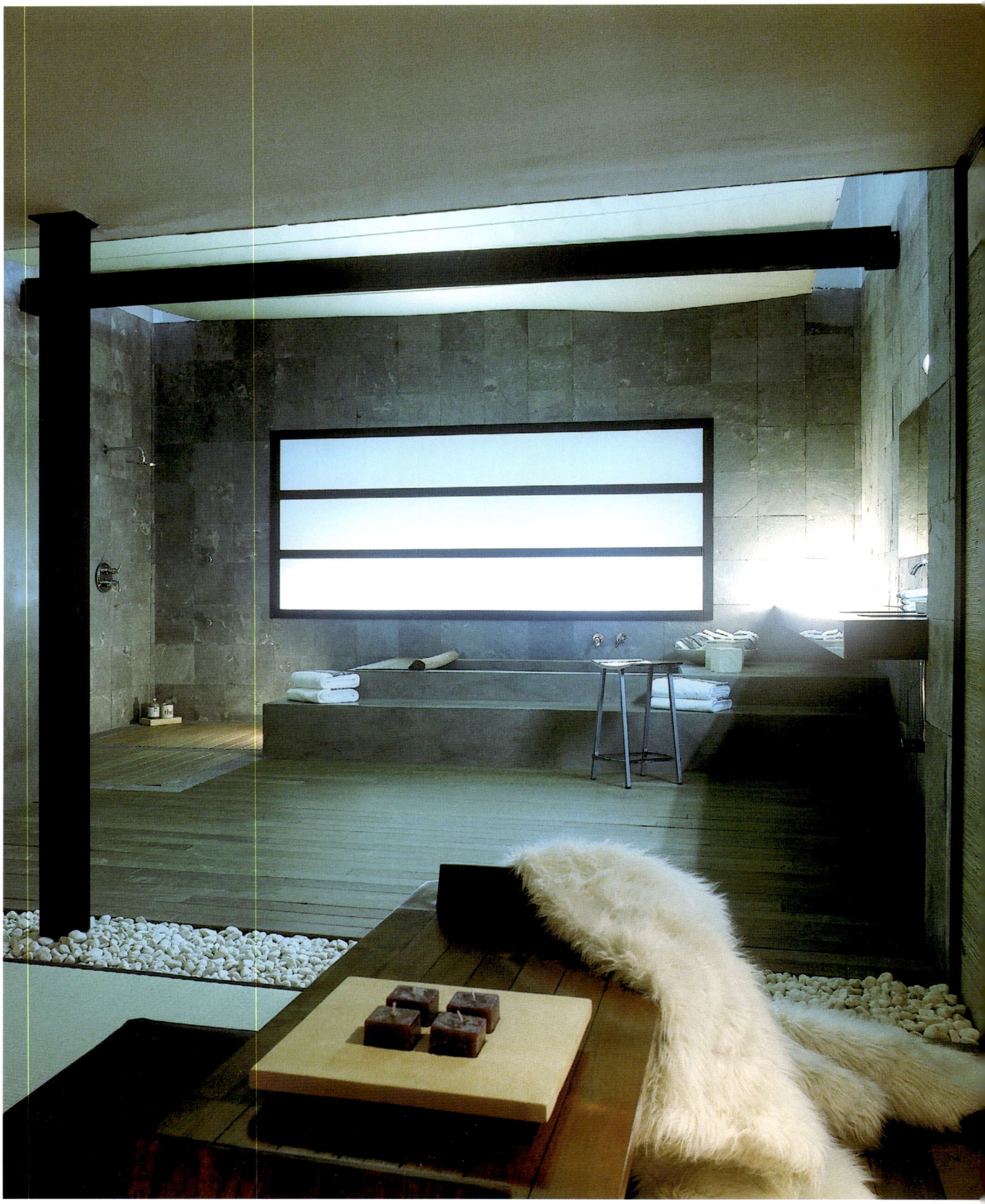

高い天井、広い床、大きな窓、これらが簡素だが厳粛な空間を創りだしている。お風呂の横には日本と同様に洗面台が置かれ、浴室の隣には浴衣を羽織ってゆったりと休息できる畳の間が用意されている。

The size of this space creates a serene and simple environment. The ofuro also has traditional elements of a bathroom, such as the sink, and an adjacent room designed for rest and relaxation.

ピース・イン・ザ・マウンテンズ
PEACE IN THE MOUNTAINS

　ブラジル山岳地帯にあるこの住宅の1階には巨大なスパがある。住宅正面は3枚の大きなスライド式ガラスパネルになっており、その透明性のため常にポーチや屋外空間が眺められる。スパにはサウナもあり、そこからもこの巨大空間にあるその他の施設、ジャクジーや細長いプールを見ることができる。木材と地元から産出された本石が、空間に強さと温もりを与え、巧緻な照明デザインが親密で居心地の良い空間を照らし出している。

On the ground floor of this house, located in a mountainous region of Brazil,
is a magnificent spa. The main façade consists of three sliding glass panels. This transparency gives a constant view
of the porch and the house's exterior. The spa includes a sauna from where the rest of this area, a Jacuzzi and an elongated swimming pool, can be seen. The wood and local stone lends strength and warmth, and the lighting creates
an intimate, cozy atmosphere.

ハウスBR

マルシオ・コーガン

アララス—ブラジル
撮影：ネルソン・コン

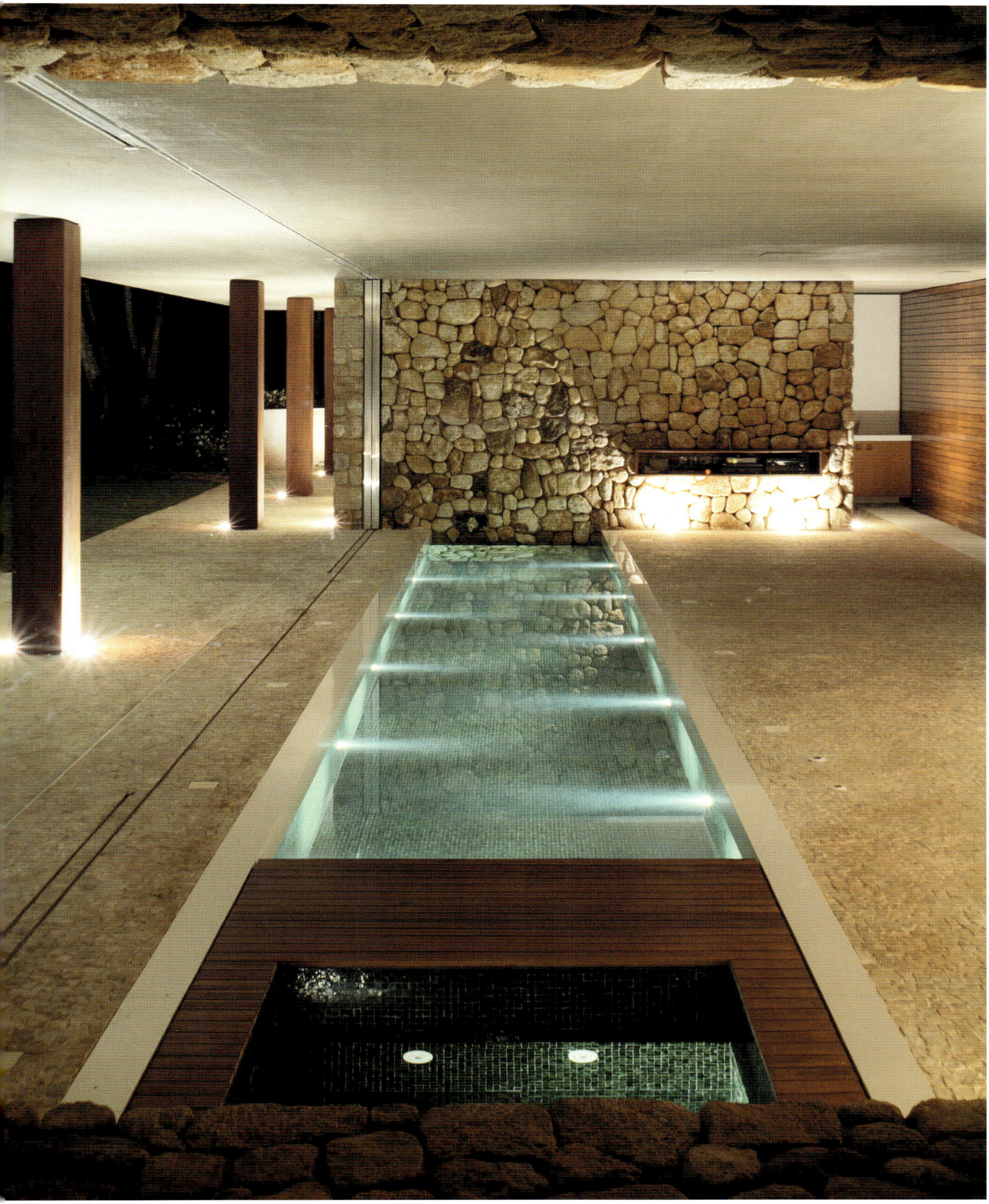

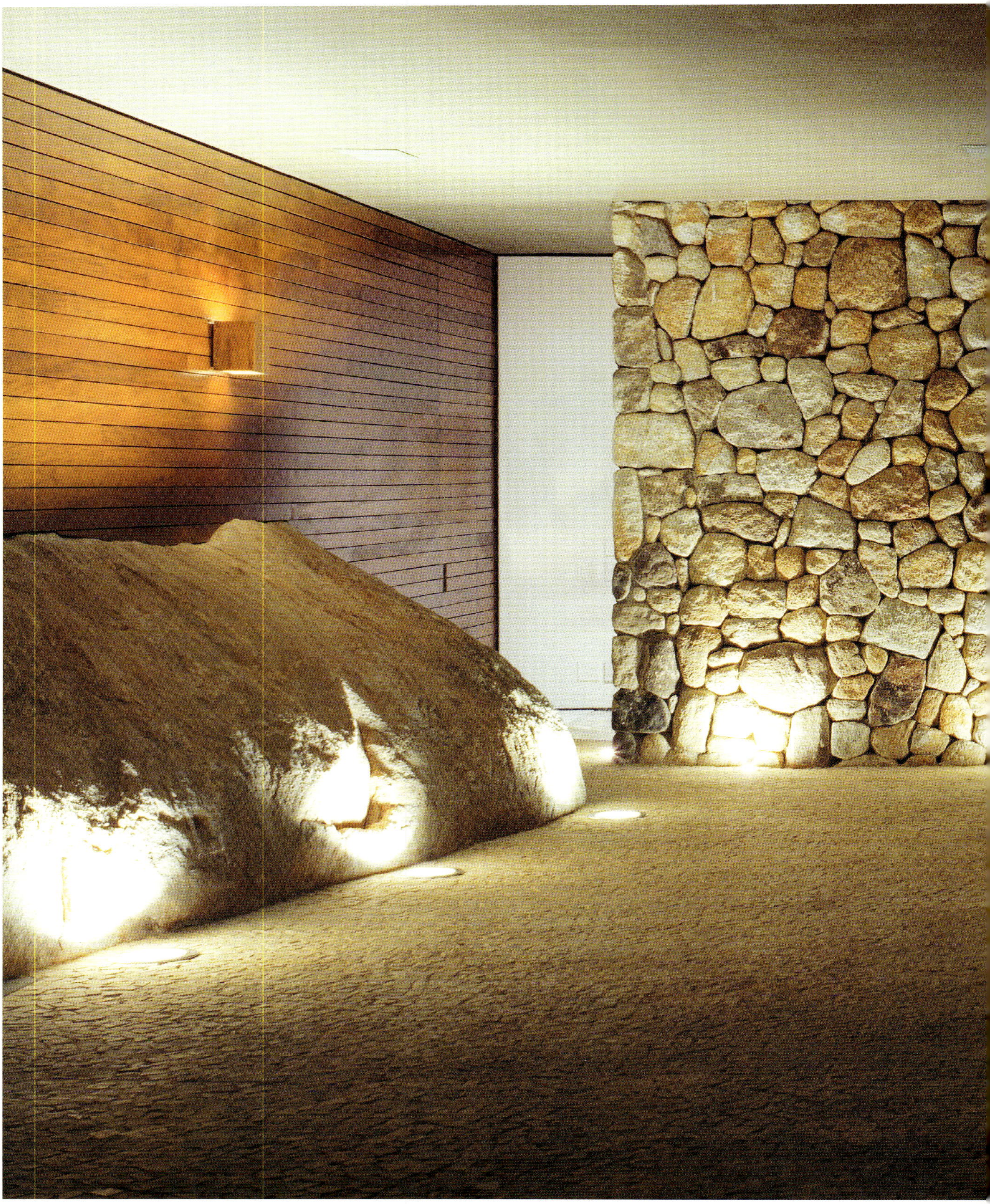

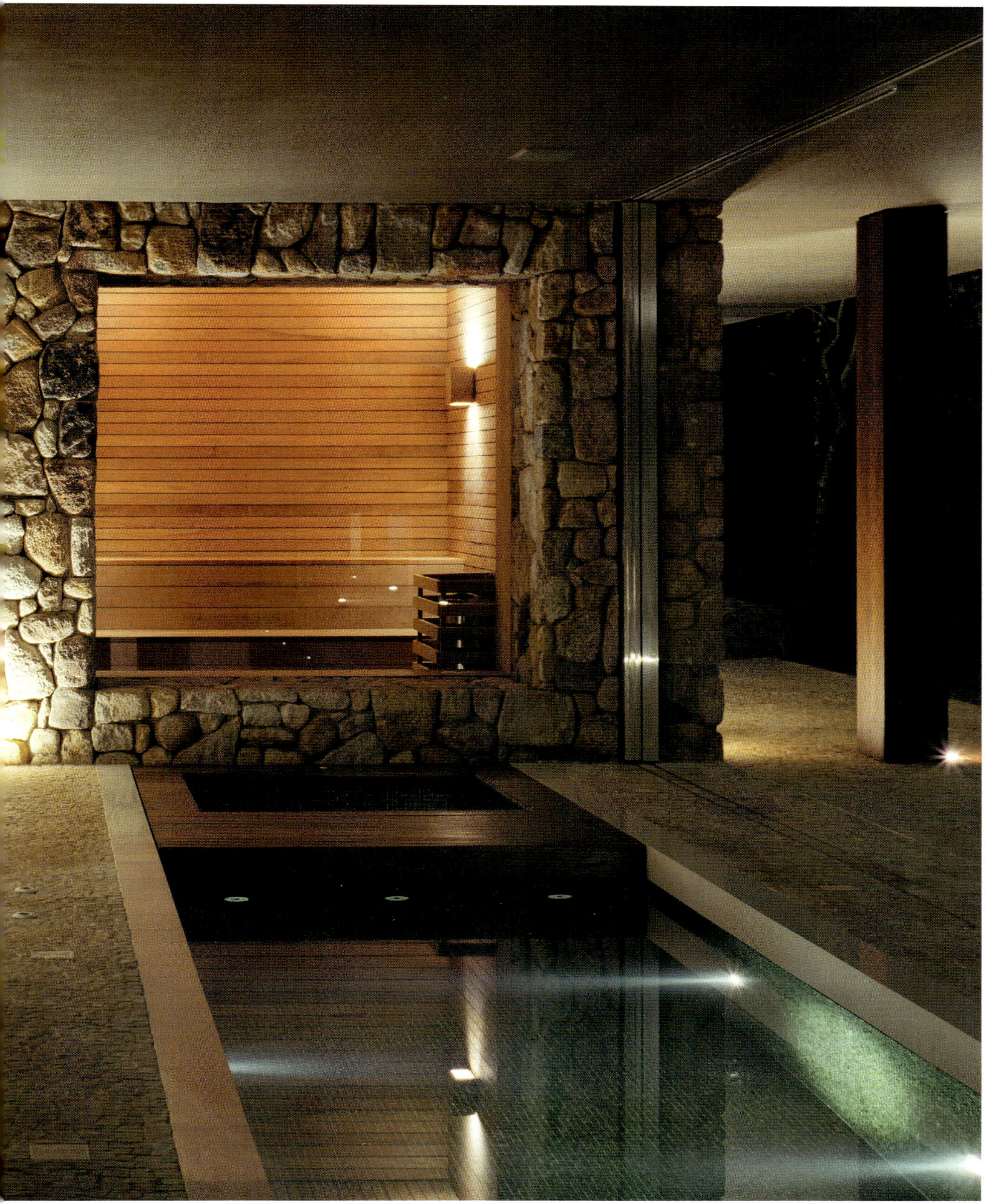

ミニマリストの泉
MINIMALIST FOUNTAIN

　この住宅の屋外空間を設計するにあたり、施主は2つの要望を建築家に伝えた。1つは疲れた身体と心を癒す休息の場所であること、もう1つは顧客や友人を招いたパーティーができる空間があること、というものであった。その要望に応えてできあがったのが、この広がりのあるテラス。ジャクジーがあり、泉があり、小さな池がある。その小さな池は壁のすぐ横を流れ、土塀と掘割といった城下町の佇まいを連想させる。コンクリートなどの使用されている材料、簡潔な線、それらがこの住宅を静かなミニマリスト的な建築にしているが、それだけではない現代的な洗練された感覚も付与している。

To design the exterior space of this house in Tokyo the owner set two premises: to create a place of rest and provide a space for organizing parties for clients and friends. The result is a spacious terrace with Jacuzzi, a fountain and a small pond that flows next to one of the side walls and evokes Japanese aesthetics.
The materials used, such as concrete, and the architectural lines define a serene and minimalist construction, but one with a markedly modern atmosphere.

青葉台の家

岡田哲史建築都市計画研究所

東京―日本
撮影：岡田哲史建築都市計画研究所

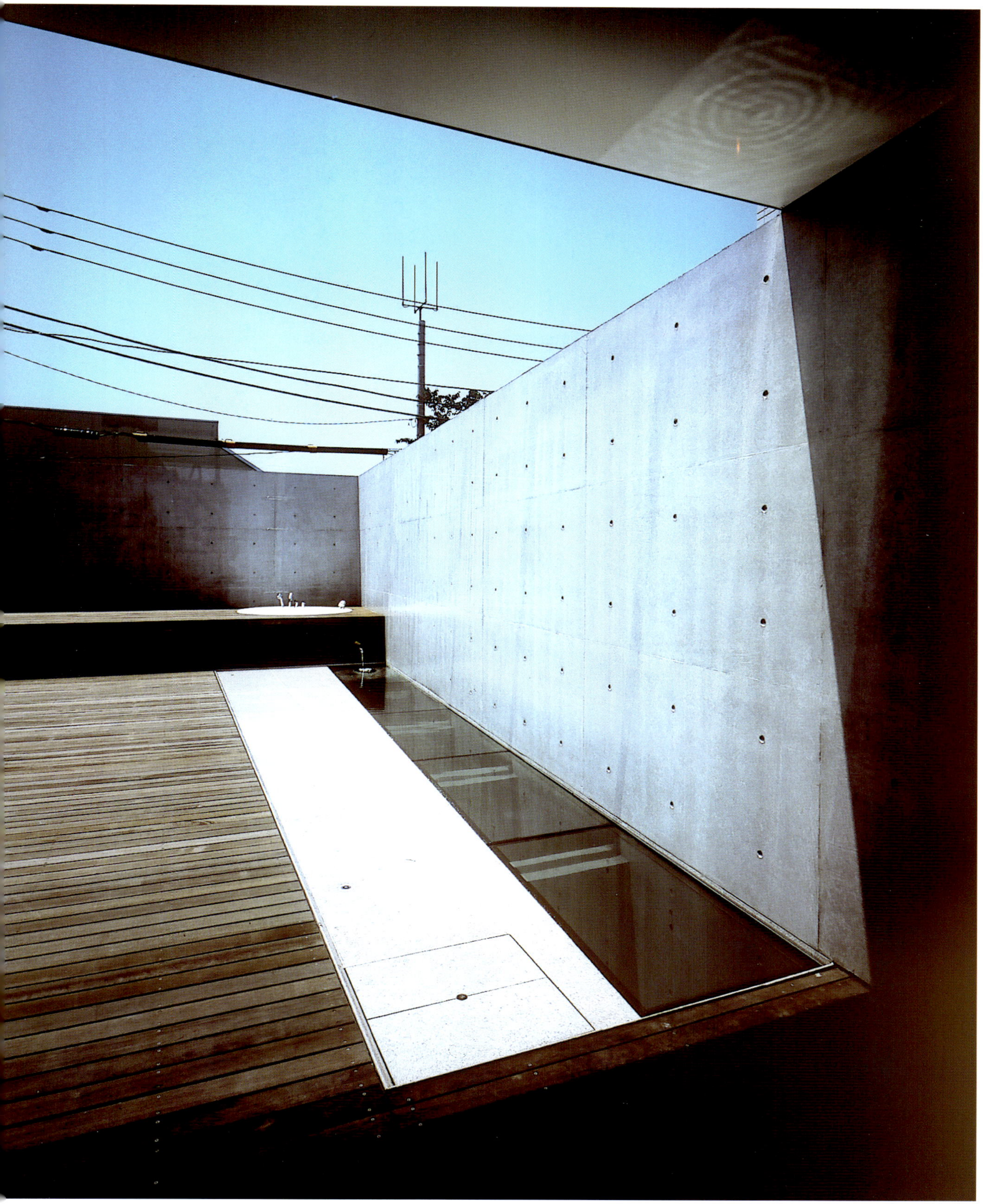

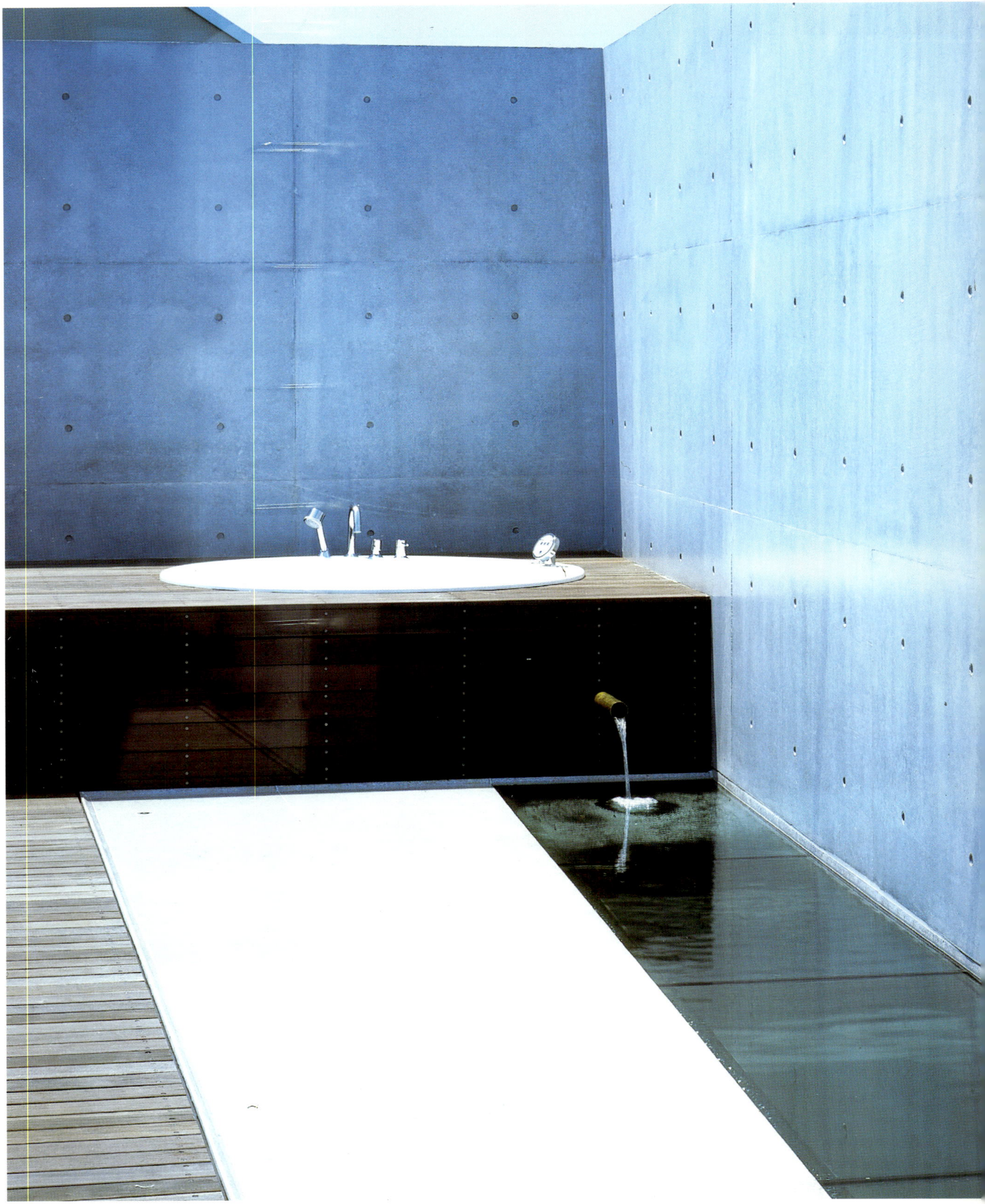

青葉台の家 | 243

幸福の感覚
SENSATION OF WELL-BEING

　以前ガレージであった場所は改築され、室内プールとその隣にジムが設けられた。この改築は、新たな所有者一家の人生観、すなわち何よりも健康が大切という優先順位に従って決定された。改築によって造り出された、直線が清潔で美しい広々とした居心地の良い空間は、いやがうえにもリラクゼーション効果を高める。木は空間に安らぎと温もりを与え、水は空間に静かな再生の気をもたらす。

The indoor swimming pool and the adjacent gymnasium and sauna built in this house are located where the garage had been. The change in use of this area
is evidence of the owners' lifestyles and the priority they give to health and well-being. The renovation has created a large, cozy space, of clean, straight lines, which encourage relaxation. The wood creates a comfortable and warm environment and the water provides a calm, refreshing atmosphere.

パリ郊外のプール

ギレム・ルスタン

イル・ド・フランス
撮影：ダニエル・モーリネ

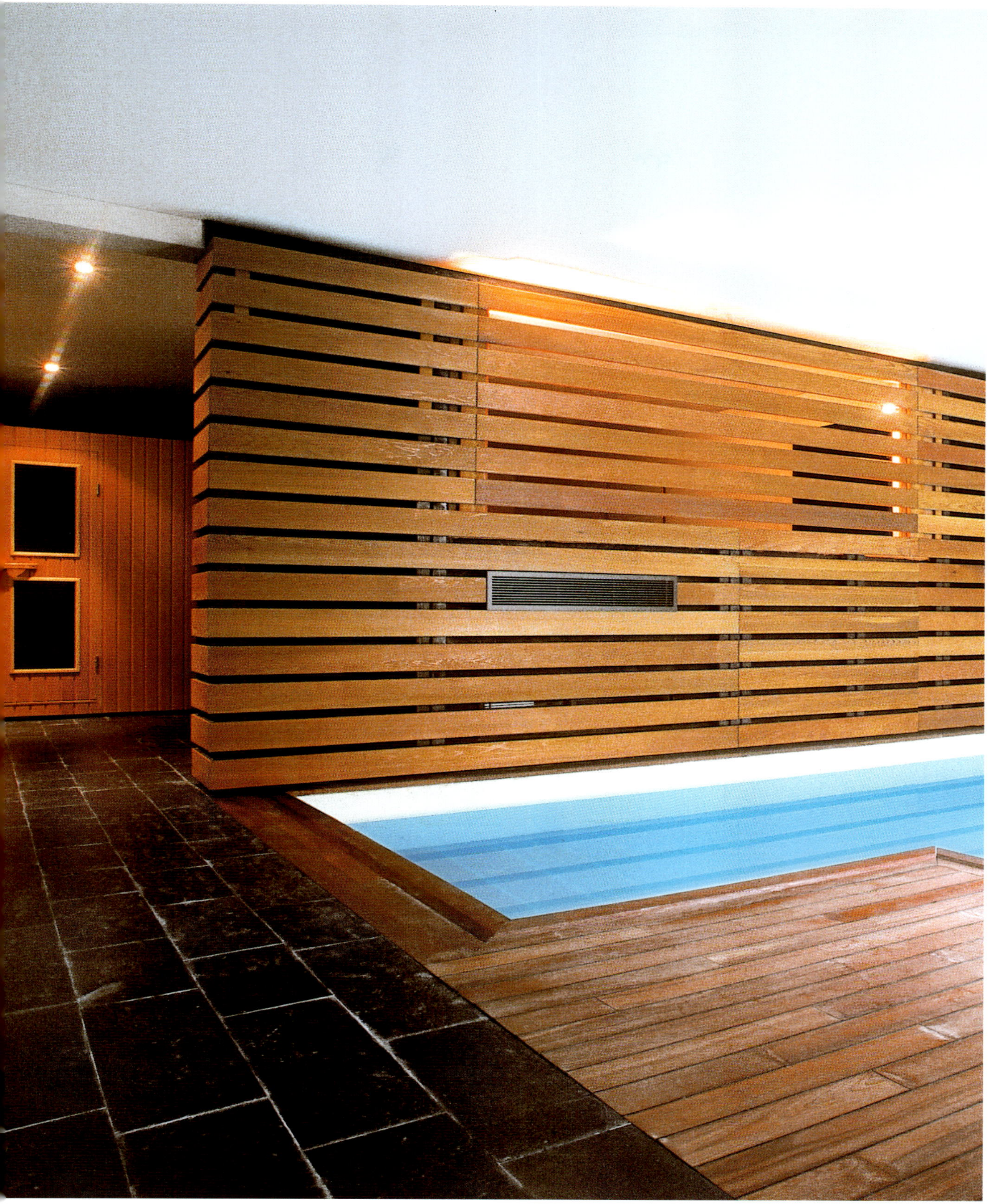

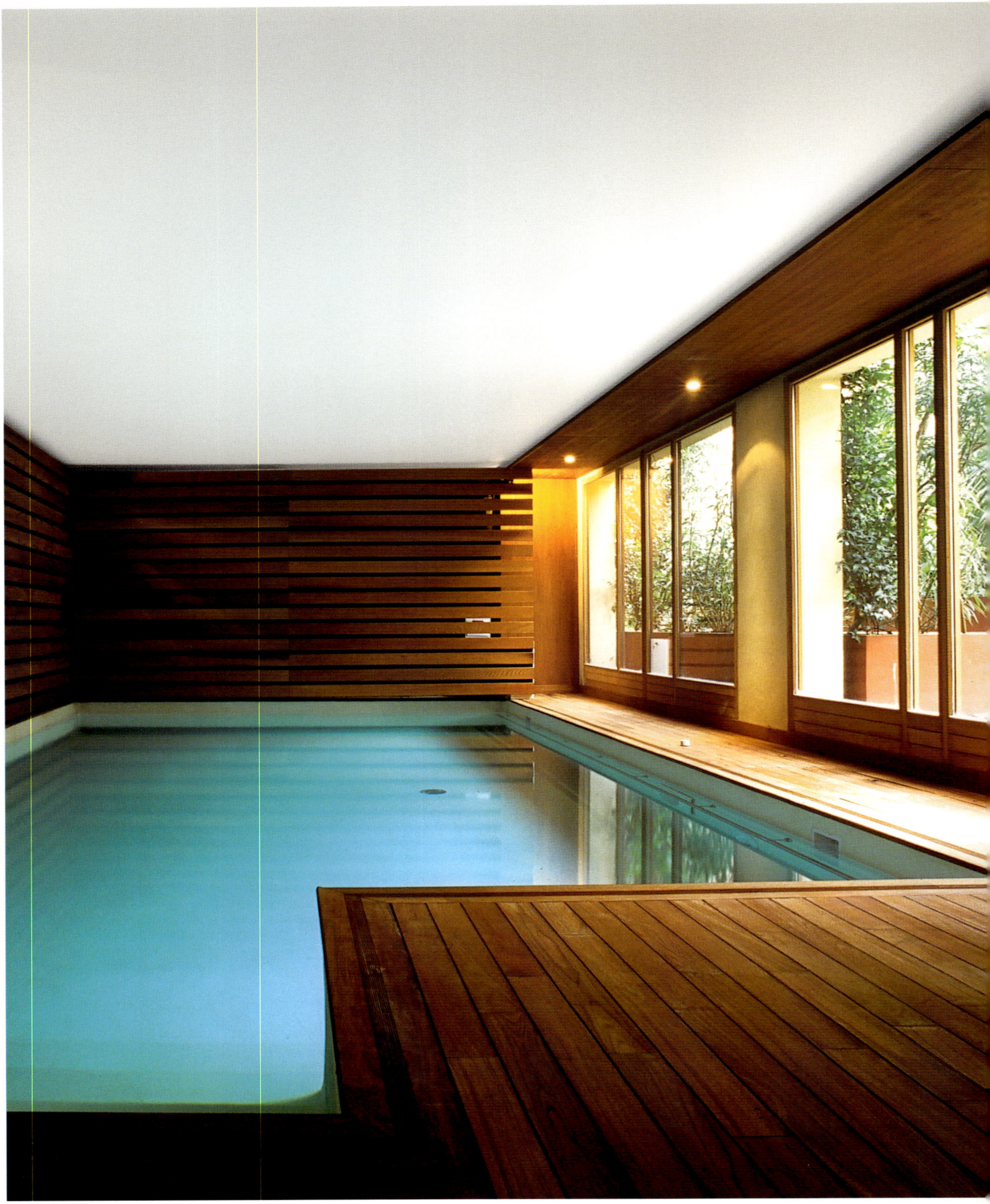

内壁とプール端の床には、垂直・水平の両方向に厚板がプールに平行に張られており、それが空間を軽く躍動感のあるものにしている。大きな開放的な窓からは自然光がたっぷりと注ぎ、水面と部屋全体を明るく包み込んでいる。

The wood that covers the walls and the edges of the pool is arranged in strips. This creates a light, dynamic space. The large window gives natural light to the room and lights up the interior.

スパ・フォー・ザ・ファミリー
SPA FOR THE FAMILY

　この住宅のプールとスパは中庭の比較的狭い場所に設置されているが、ミニマリスト的な合理的デザインのせいで実際よりもかなり広く感じられ、夜間照明に浮び上がった景観は非常に魅惑的である。プール端の石灰岩を積み上げて造られた壁には優美な滝があり、そこから流れ落ちる水が常にプールを満たしている。巧妙に配置された植物が楽園にいるような豊穣な感覚をもたらす。プールに隣接して、もう1つの楽しみであるジャクジーが設置されている。

The swimming pool and spa of this residence are situated in a small space in the courtyard, although a minimalist and rational design makes it appear larger, and the night lighting especially attractive. A waterfall, built with limestone, flows elegantly from one of the side walls of the swimming pool. A finish of strategically placed plants creates the sensation of a paradisiacal garden. The Jacuzzi, another of the attractions, is on one side.

ライスターフィールドのプール

アロハ・プールズ,
クリエイティブ・アウトドア・ソルーションズ

ライスターフィールド―ビクトリア州―オーストラリア
撮影：ティム・ターナー

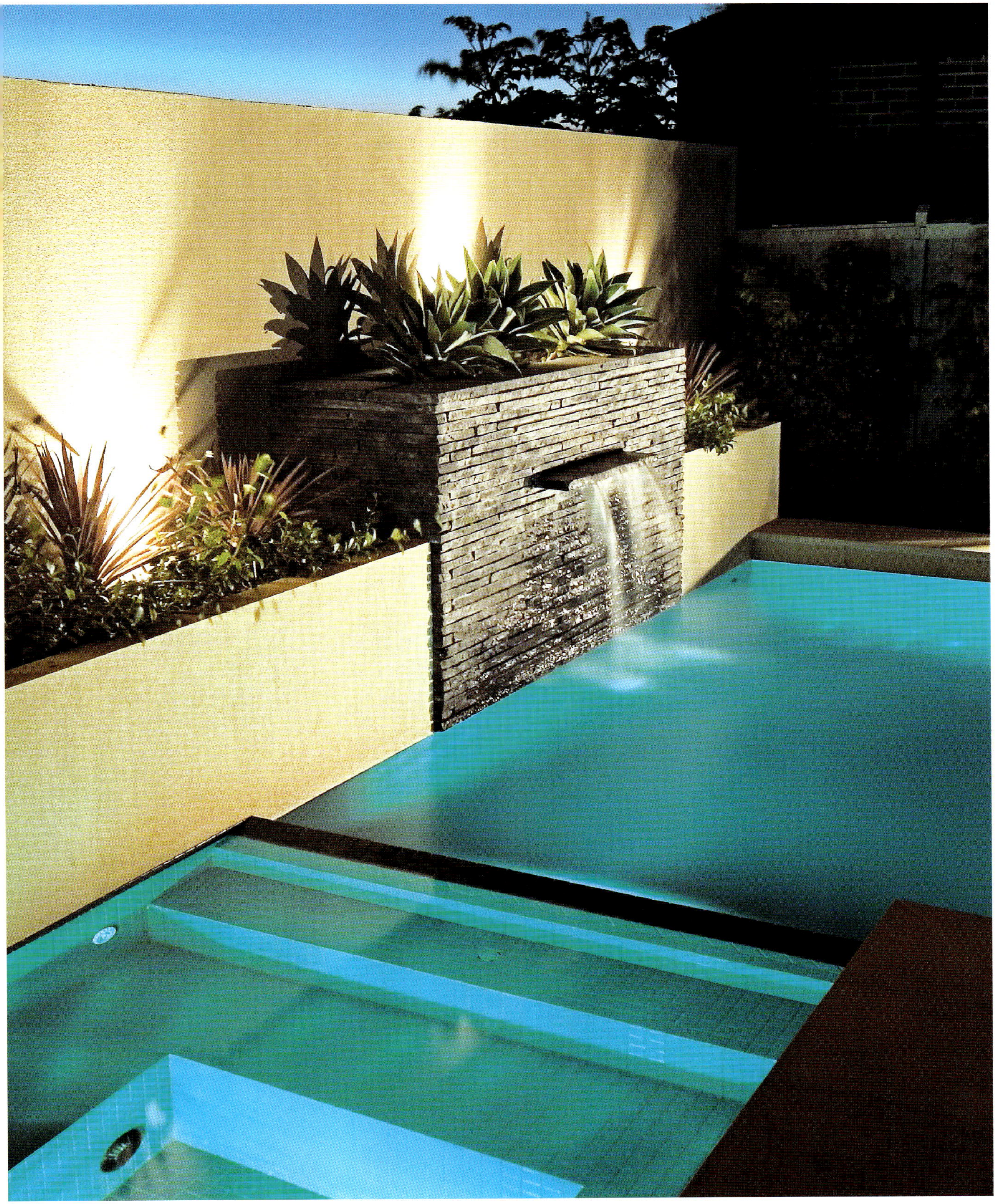

アーバン・オアシス

URBAN OASIS

　庭が住宅を優しく包み込み、小さな都会のオアシスが誕生した。庭に許された面積は比較的狭いものであったが、それを逆手にとり、垂直方向に壁に植物を多く配し、石と水と植物のテクスチュアを際立たせることによって深みのある屋外空間ができあがった。石積みの壁の上方に独創的な湧き水の泉が造られ、そこからしたたり落ちる水はいったん平たい石の台に受け止められ、そのあと滝となって小さな池に流れ落ちる。その池には石のスラブが敷かれ、その上を飛び石伝いに渡ることができる。

This garden surrounds a single-family residence and its aesthetics make it appear as a small urban oasis. Since the space available for a garden was so small, there
is more vegetation on the walls and many combinations of textures between the stone, vegetation and water.
On the wall is an original vertical fountain. The water flows to a stone platform forming a waterfall that drops to a small pond that can be crossed thanks
to large stone slabs.

水と石と植物と

フォークナー & チャップマン・ランドスケープ・アーキテクツ

ブライトン―オーストラリア
撮影：シャニア・シェゲディン

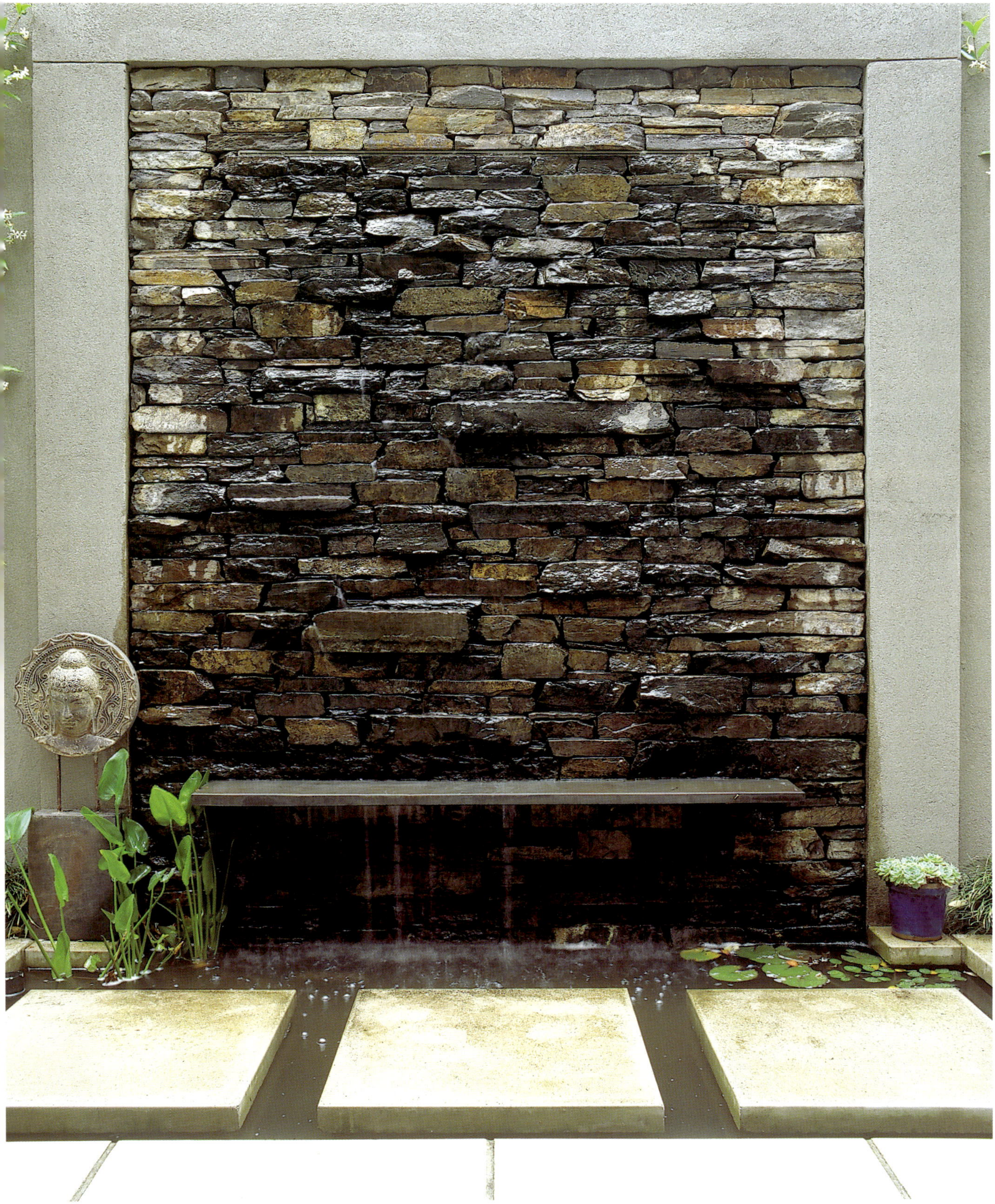

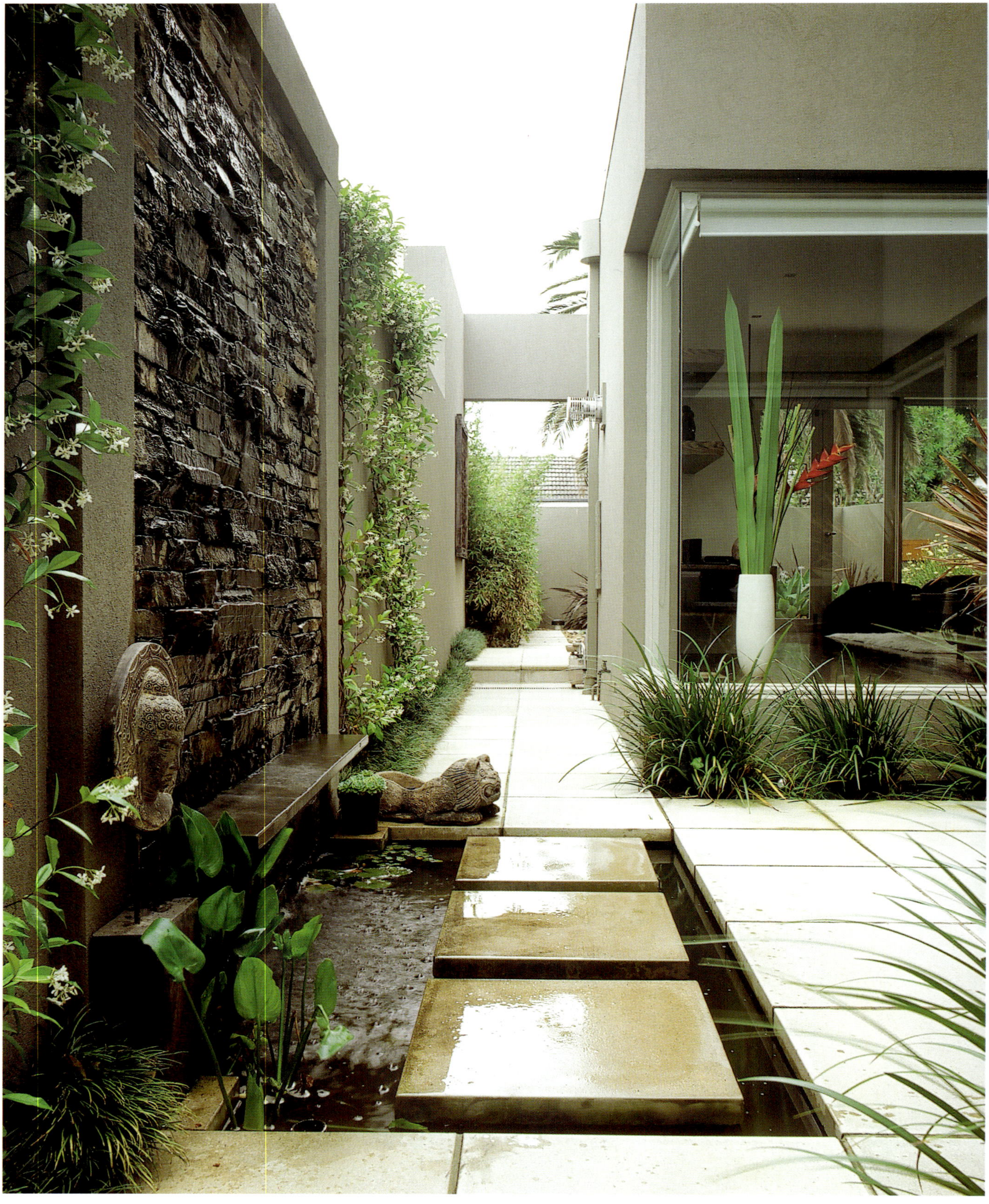

壁はつたと野生のブドウで覆われ、テラスには棕櫚、潅木、盆栽が調和よく配され、池には睡蓮が浮かぶ。清々しさに満ちた外部空間が室内に生き生きとしたエネルギーを注ぎ込む。

The walls of the terrace are covered in ivy and wild vine.
The rest of the garden is decorated with palms, bushes and bonsais.
The result is a space full of freshness that also brings vitality to the house.

ウォークウェイ・オン・ザ・ウォーター
WALKWAY ON THE WATER

マイアミのとある住宅、その南向きの一角に、じっと立ち止まって眺めたくなる浅い池がある。壁面を流れ落ちる滝の水が空間を区切り、その水は池に置かれた数枚の石のスラブによって循環させられる。池の周囲にはフロリダ半島特有の植物が植えられ、それらが鮮やかな緑と自然の芳香をもたらす。巧緻な空間の組織化と植物の配置、住宅設計においていかにランドスケープ・アーキテクチュアが重要であるかが実証された庭だ。

This pool is situated in a Miami residence.
A shallow pond sits noticeably in a space at the South facing part of the garden. The water comes from a waterfall on a wall that sets the boundaries to the space. Stone slabs have been placed to circulate around the water and local vegetation has been planted to provide freshness and natural fragrances. The lushness of the plants and the organization of the space show the importance of landscape architecture
in residential projects.

八つ橋のある庭

ジャングルズ・ランドスケープ・アーキテクチュア

キーウェスト—フロリダ州—アメリカ
撮影:レニー・プロボ

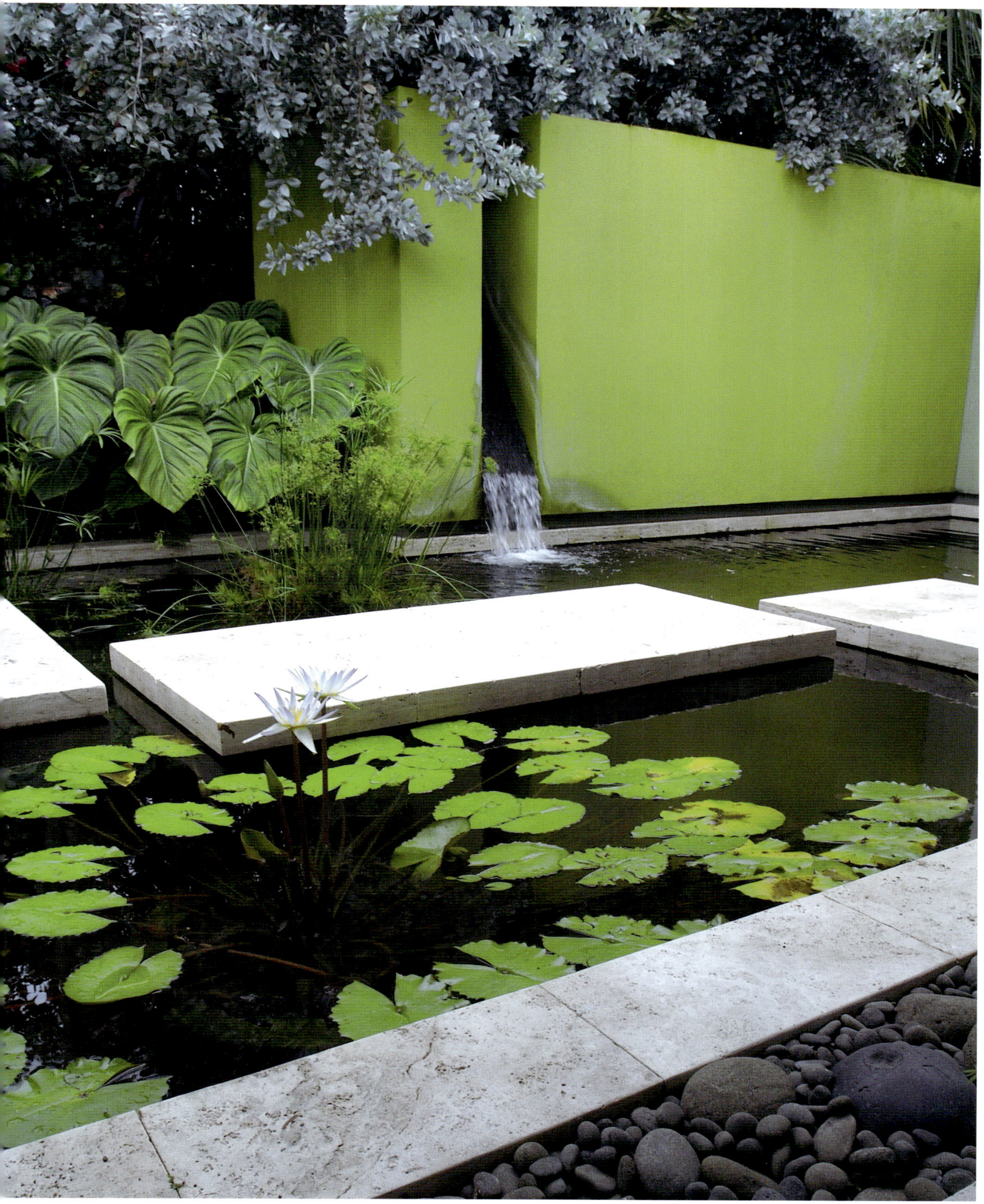

滝は心を休める音色を奏でながら水を循環させている。その水の音と豊かな濃い緑が、深い森の奥に入り込んだときのような静けさと平和の感覚をもたらす。

The waterfall creates movement in the water producing relaxing sounds. The water creates these sounds, which, together with the dense vegetation, provide a deep sensation of calm and peace.

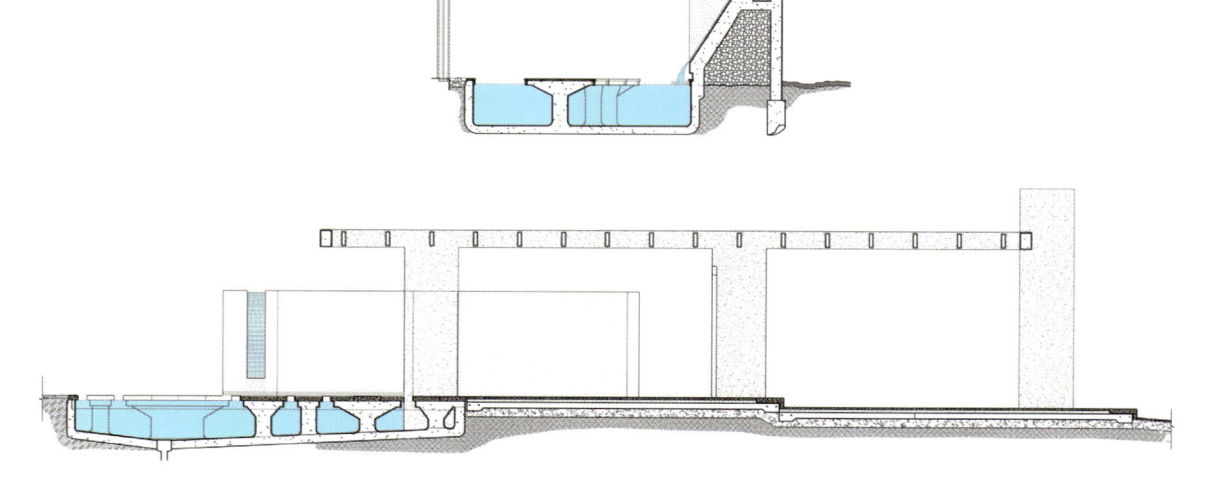

八つ橋のある庭 | 257

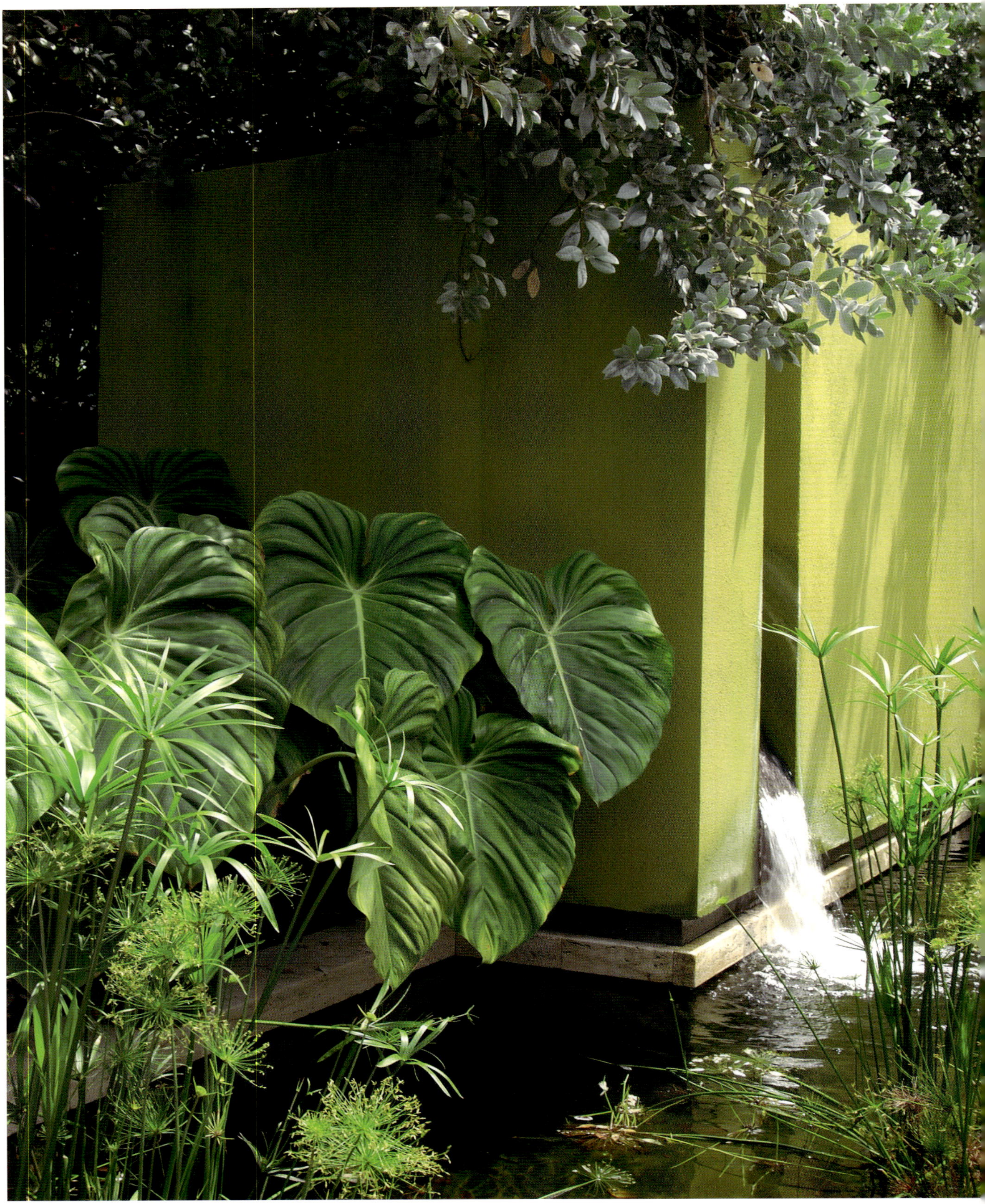

庭の境界を画す壁は歳月とともに周りの空間になじんでいくように緑色に塗られ、そのまわりを地元の植物であるブーゲンビリアや野生の花々が囲んでいる。池にはパピルスが伸び、睡蓮が浮かぶ。

The wall that delimits the garden has been painted green to integrate it with the space. Bougainvilleas, a native tree, and wild flowers grow around it. Bamboo and water lilies grow in the water.

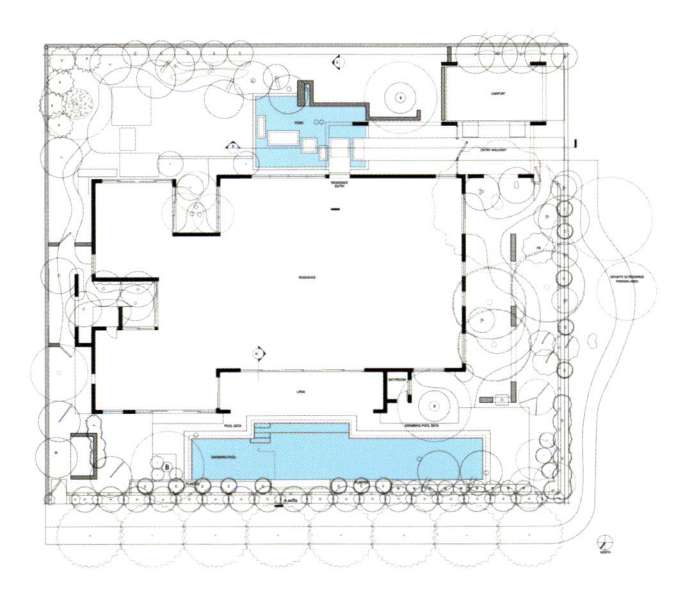

沈黙の庭
GARDEN OF SILENCE

　敷地の一角に個性的な庭がある。木々に見守られながら、たおやかなコンクリートの壁面に寄り添うように細長い池が造られている。その池は浅く、それゆえ、深さではなく平面が強調された彫刻的要素として存在している。実際この庭全体が玉砂利に覆われた広い平面になっており、その平面に浮かぶ滑らかな床の島にテーブルと椅子が置かれている。さまざまな素材が生みだすコントラストがこの庭を独特の詩的空間にしている。

This garden is located in one of the corners of the plot where a house stands. Surrounded by trees and parallel
to an elegant concrete wall, is a small rectangular pond. This pond is very shallow and therefore acts as a sculptural element within the garden. Practically the entire space is covered in gravel, except a small island of smooth flooring with a table and chairs. The different materials create a strong aesthetical contrast.

庭の一隅

ダルデレ

スイス
撮影：ダルデレ

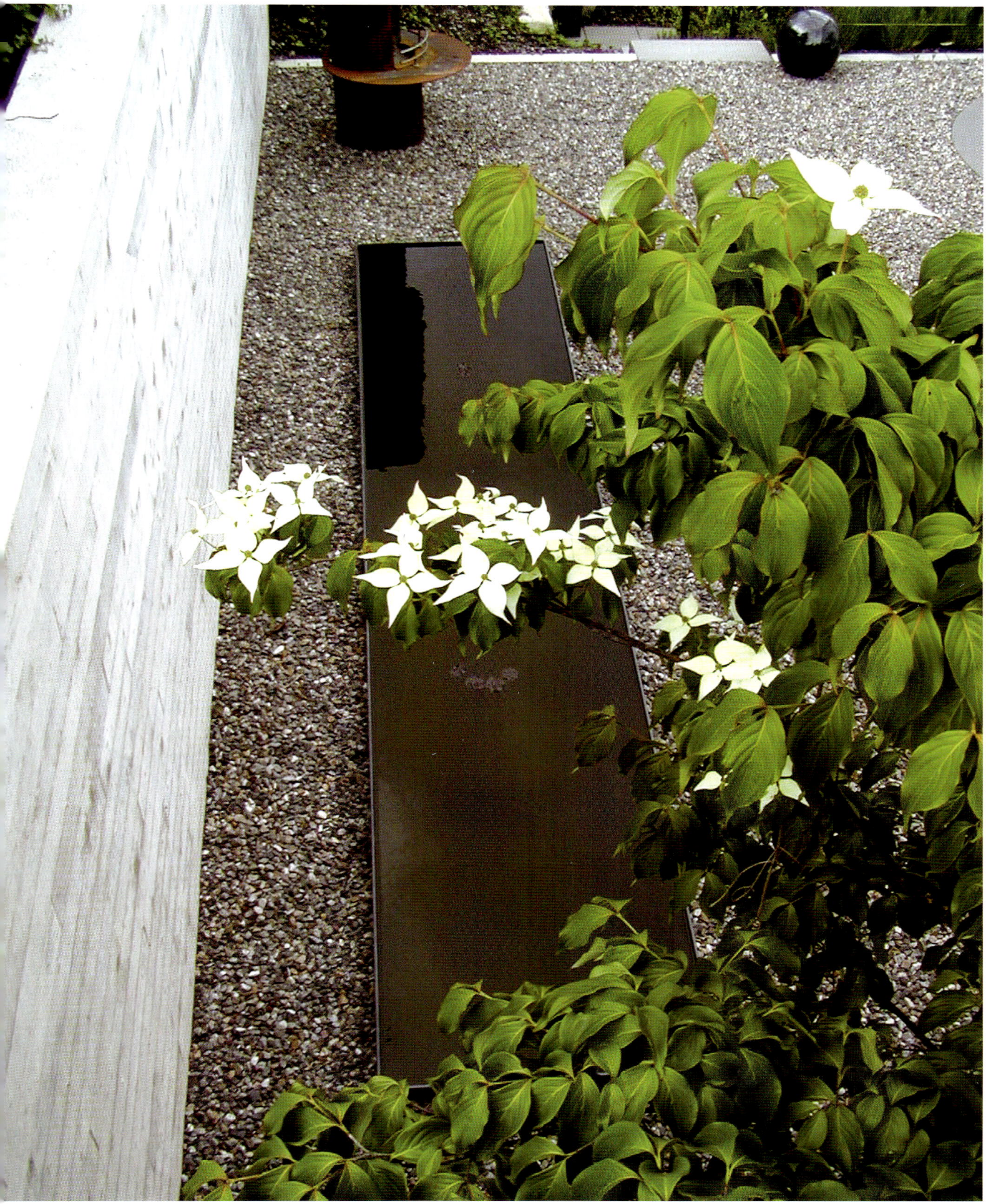

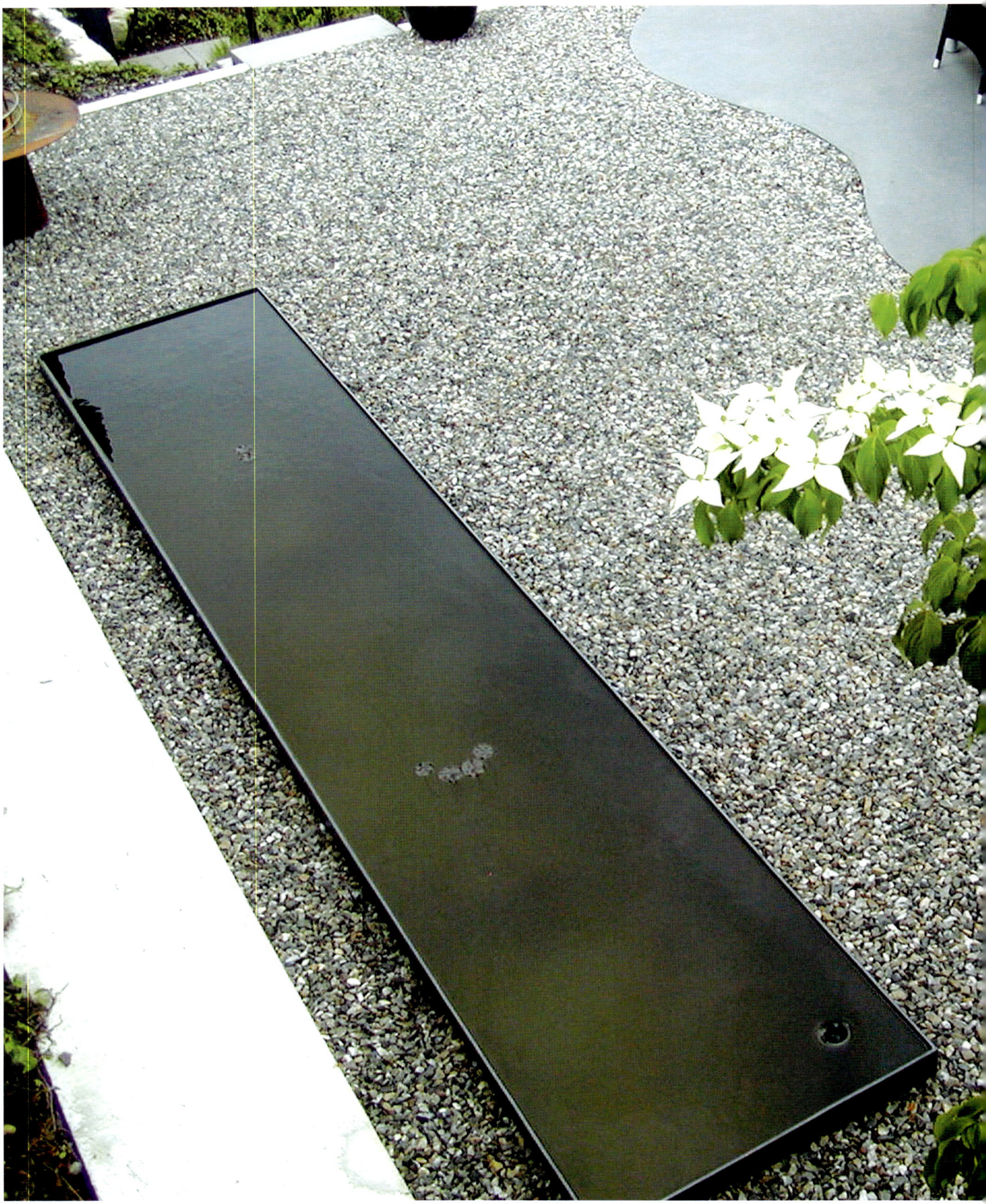

小さな島にテーブルと椅子が置かれているということは、この一隅が最もよく家人に親しまれているということを物語っている。現代詩のようなミニマリスト的空間。植栽、玉砂利、黒い池、これらが静かに存在の意味を問うている。

The small island with table and chairs indicates that this is the most used outdoor area. This area is aesthetically minimalist and highly poetic. The trees, the gravel and the pond create a calm place.

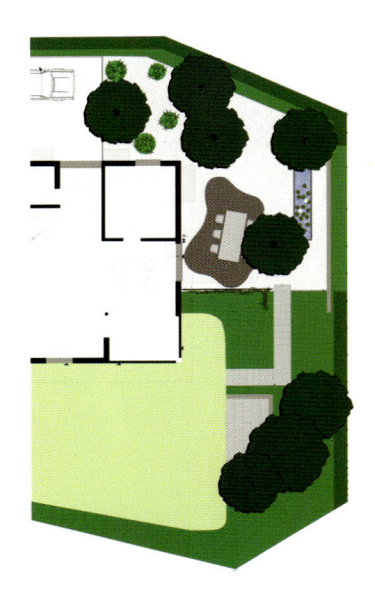

水上に浮かぶ家に暮らす、これは誰もが経験できることではない。水上に家を建てることは建築家にとってけっしてやさしい仕事ではないが、逆にそれは革新的な素材を駆使して独創性に富むプロジェクトを実現するまたとない機会でもある。

この章で紹介する住宅は、どれもみな常識の枠を抜け出し、オーナーにより自由でより独立的な生活様式の舞台を提供する。

Living in a floating house is a unique experience. This type of construction surrounded by water, presents the architect with a true challenge and the opportunity to develop audacious projects using innovative materials.
The houses presented in this chapter move away from conventionalisms providing their owners with a freer and more indepenent lifestyle.

夢
としての水

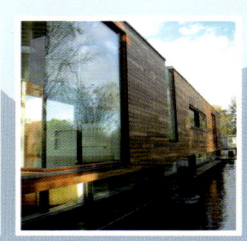

ウォーキング・オン・ザ・ウォーター
WALKING ON THE WATER

　この住宅はスウェーデンの東海岸に浮かんでいる。この種の住宅が快適で広々としていることは言うまでもないが、それ以外にも、水の眺め、周囲の景色、静寂さなど、まだまだ多くの長所がある。

　フローティングハウスの必要条件は安定性である。構法は現在特許権を取得しているが、コンクリートによるアウターシェル構法で、十分な安定性が確保されている。空間は光に溢れ、階層構造になっているため想像以上に広々としている。

This floating residence is situated on the East coast of Sweden. This type of house
is no stranger to comfort or large spaces, and also includes added advantages such as the views of the water and surrounding scenery or the tranquility.
The volume of the house had to be stable. The constructive method, which has now been patented, used concrete and an outer-shell design that provided the required stability. The resulting space is bathed in light and very spacious, thanks to the different levels.

ナクロスの別荘
スタファン・ストリンドベリ

カルマー――スウェーデン
撮影：ジェームズ・シルバーマン

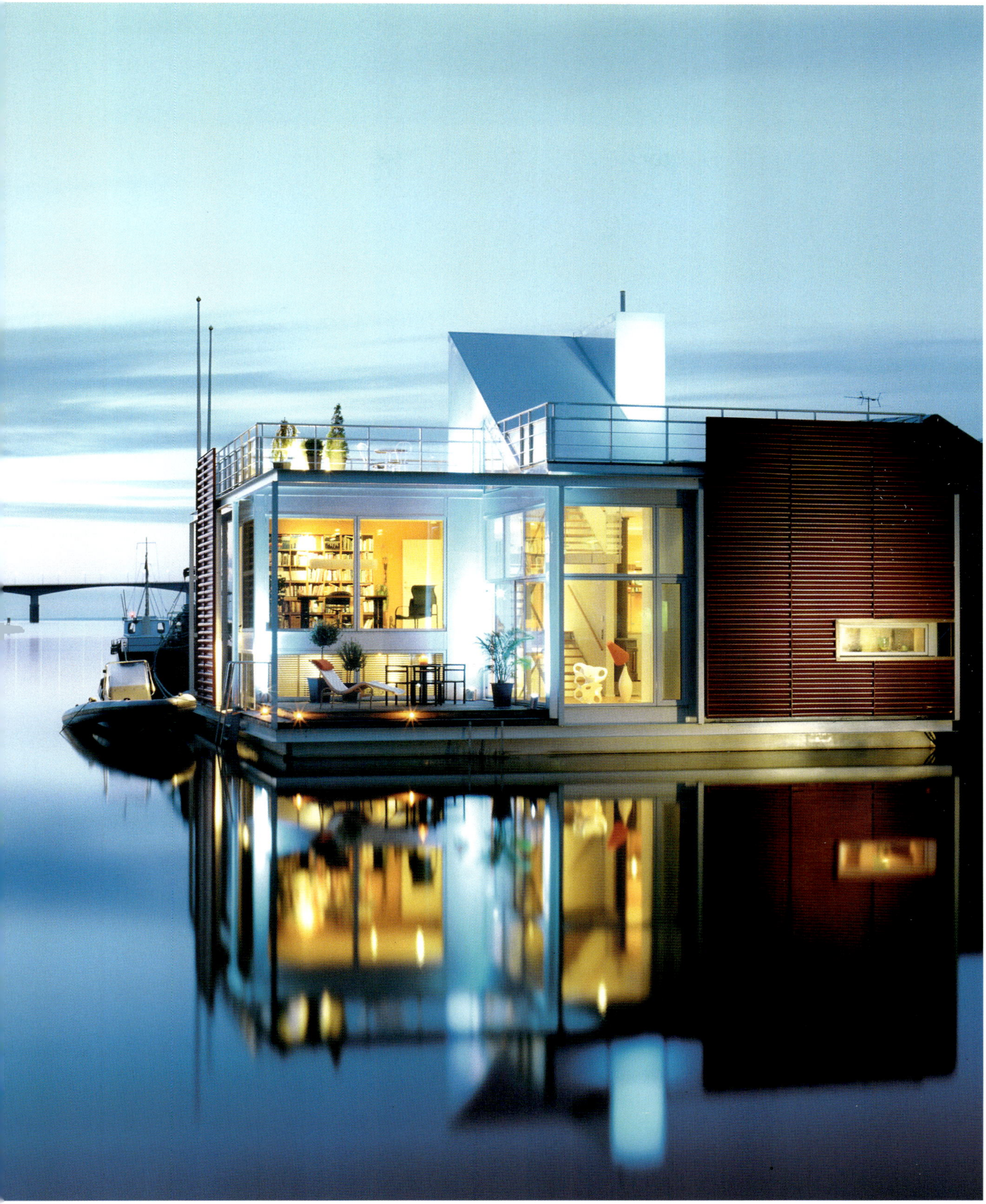

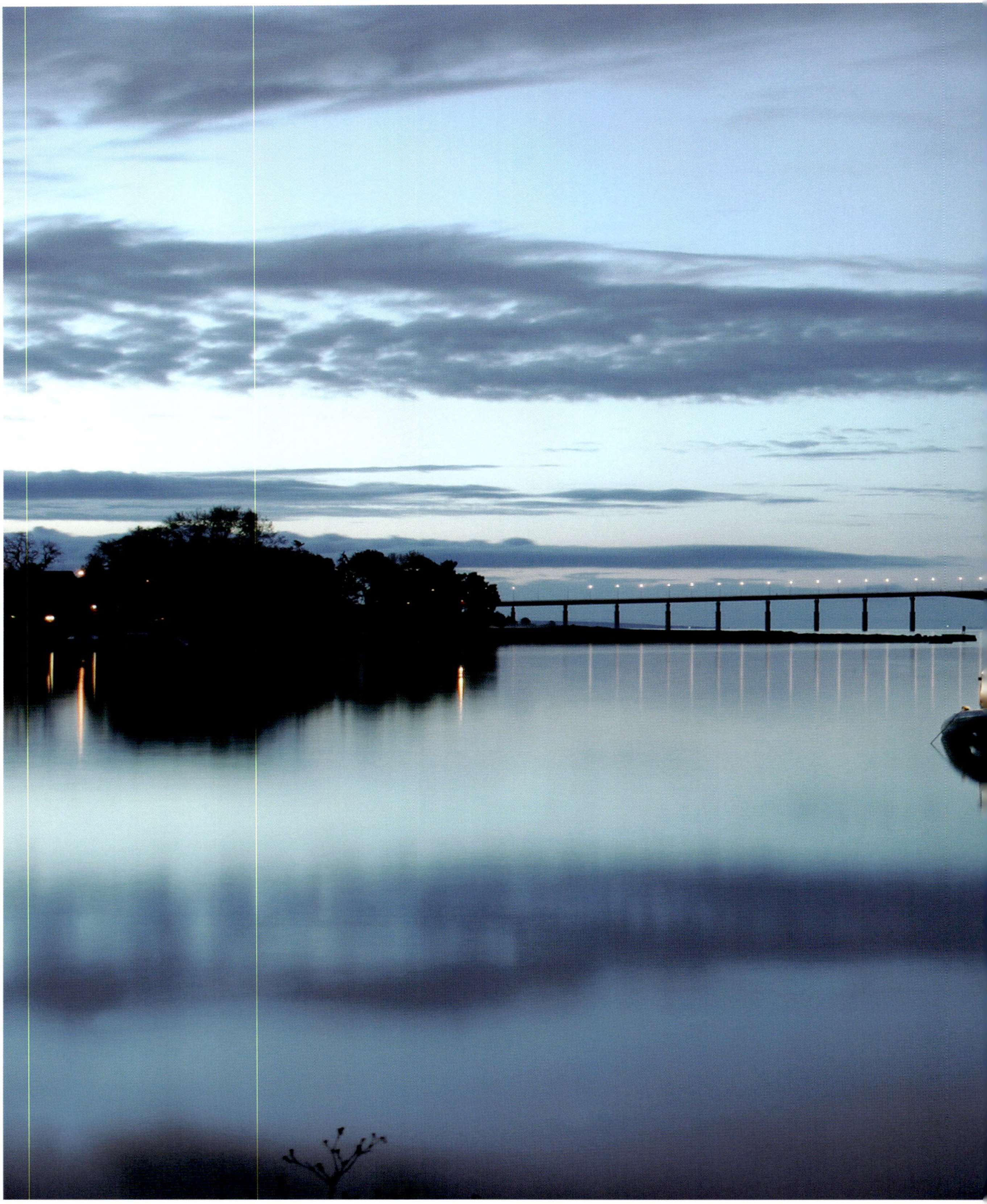

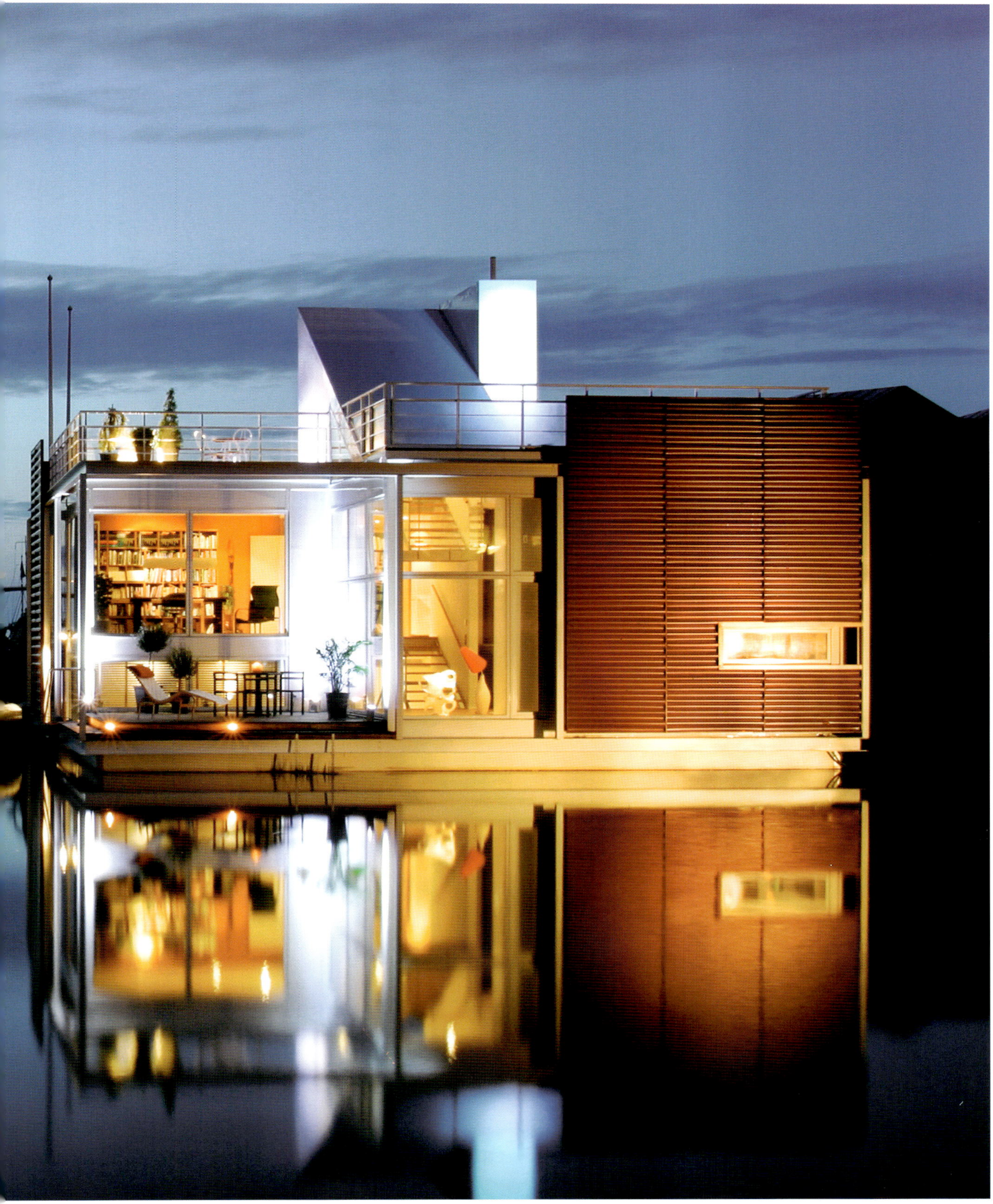

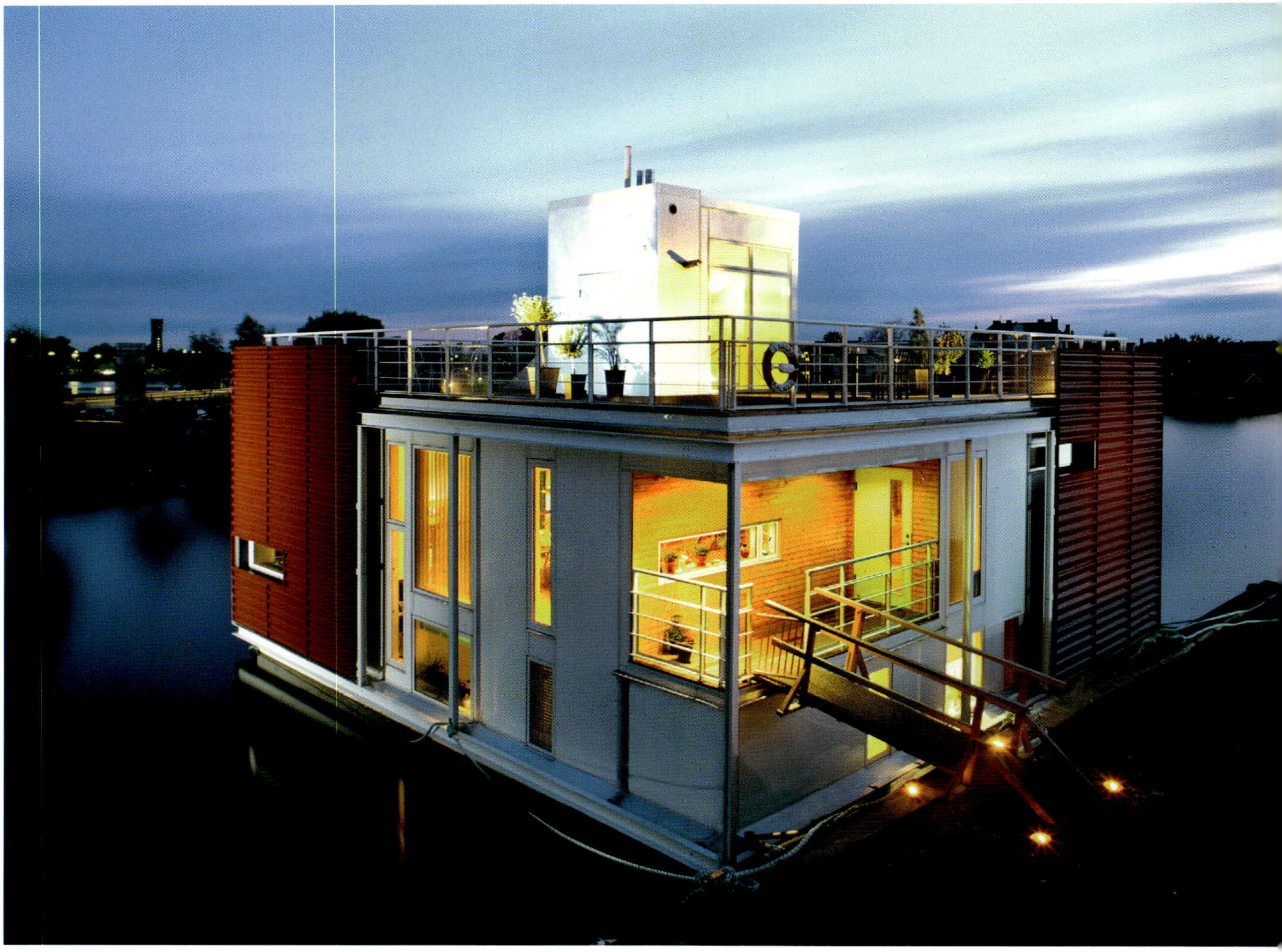

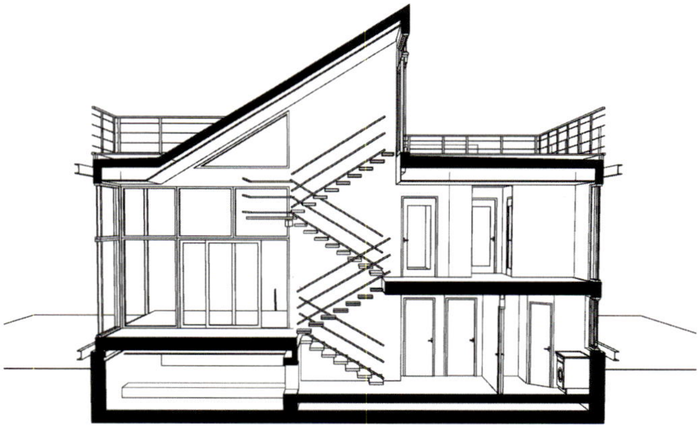

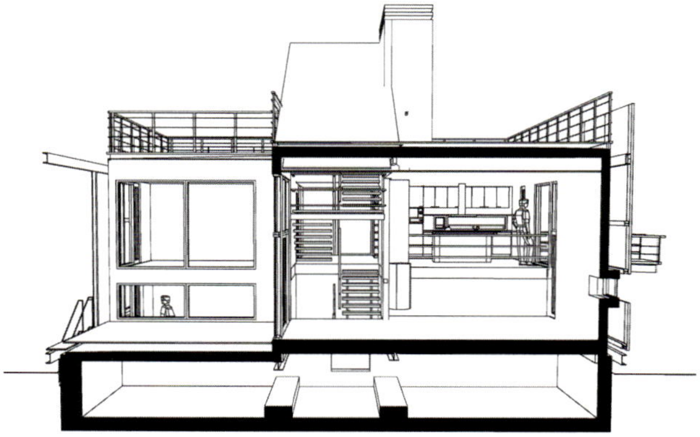

屋上はテラスになっており、タラップを昇って玄関を開けると、そこがキッチンと書斎になっている。そこから1段階段を下りた所が大きなリビングルームになっている。寝室はさらにその下にある。

The terrace is on the upper level, although the main entrance is at the level of the kitchen and study. The first flight of stairs descends to the large living room. The bedrooms are on a lower level.

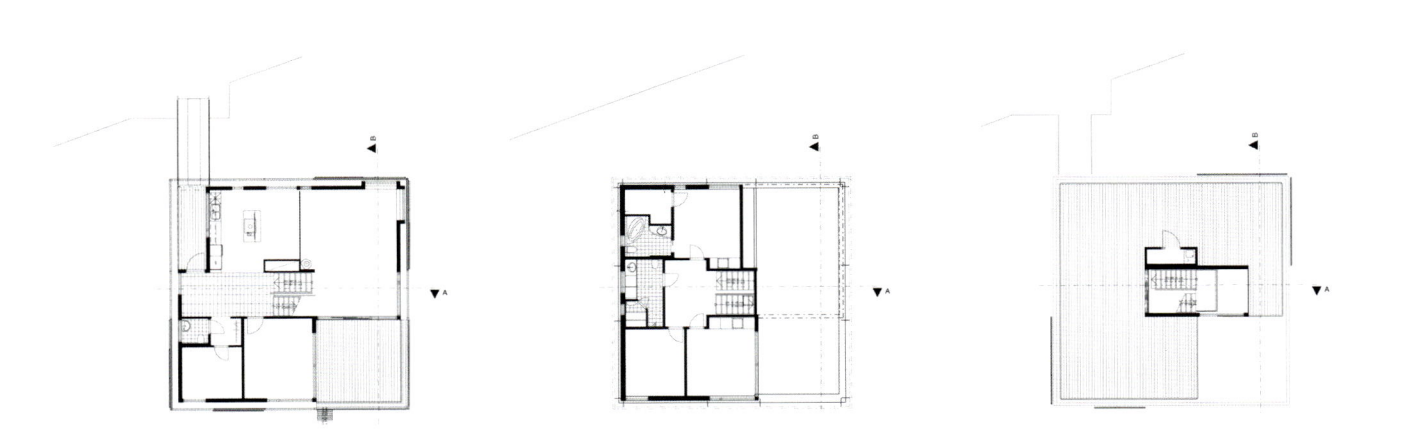

デイリーライフ・オン・ザ・ウォーター
DAILY LIFE ON THE WATER

ボートハウスやフローティングハウスで暮らすことはオランダでは珍しいことではないが、この住宅はより現代的な生活様式に適合されている点でこれまでのものとは違う。若い世代用にデザインされたこの住宅には、陸地に建てられている住宅の持つすべての機能が備わっている。2階建て構造になっており、水面より上の階が昼間過ごす空間で、リビングルームやキッチン、書斎などがある。その下、水面下の部分が、寝室、バスルーム、そして遊戯室になっている。

In Holland it is not unusual to live on a boat or a floating house, although these houses are adapted to a more modern lifestyle nowadays. This floating house, designed for a young family, has all the household commodities of a traditional home. It is organized on two levels; one of which groups the daytime areas: the living room, kitchen, study etc., and the other, located just below the flotation line, houses the bedrooms, bathrooms and a games area.

水上住宅

バネケ, ファン・デル・ホーベン・アルヒテクテン

ルーネン―オランダ
撮影：バネケ, ファン・デル・ホーベン・アルヒテクテン

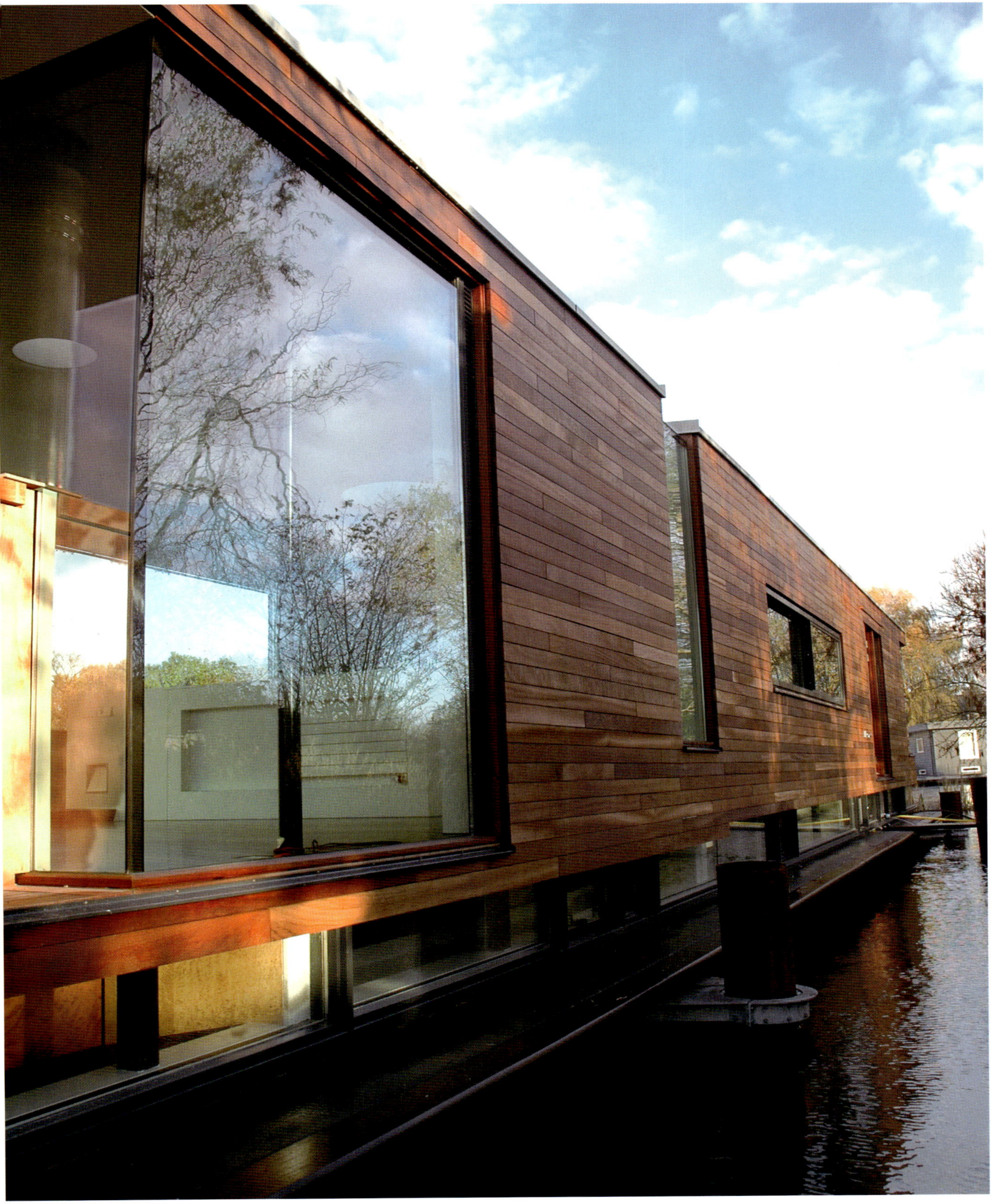

274 | 夢としての水 | Dream it

大きな窓と屋根に設けられたさまざまな形と大きさの開口部のおかげで、住宅のどの部分にも自然光が届く。内装に用いられている建築材料は、どこか客船のものを思い出させる。

Natural light reaches every part of the house thanks to the large windows and the openings of different shapes and sizes in the roof. The materials used inside recall those used for sea craft.

ウォーター・フォー・ライフ
WATER FOR LIFE

　水上に浮かぶ基台の上に家を建てることは、決してたやすい仕事ではない。構法上の課題は言うまでもなく、種々の特殊な要件を満たした上で、格段の安定性と絶縁性を確保していなければならない。このフローティングハウスはさまざまなヴォリュームを結合させてできており、それらが通路で結ばれている。白く塗装されているのが主要なヴォリュームで、ファサードは全面ガラスウォールになっており、水面の向こうに港の風景が一望できる。その他のヴォリュームがその周囲に接合され、甲板が屋外庭園の役目を果たしている。

Building a house on a platform in the water is no easy task. Apart from the technical aspects a house must employ, other specific requirements are added, such as particular stability and insulation.
This floating house consists of various volumes joined together, accessed via a walkway. The largest of them, which is painted white, has a glass wall that looks towards the water and the port; the others are situated around this one. The exterior spaces act as terraces.

シアトルのハウスボート

ジェニファー・ランドール
建築設計事務所

シアトル—ワシントン州—アメリカ
撮影：ジョルディ・ミラーレス

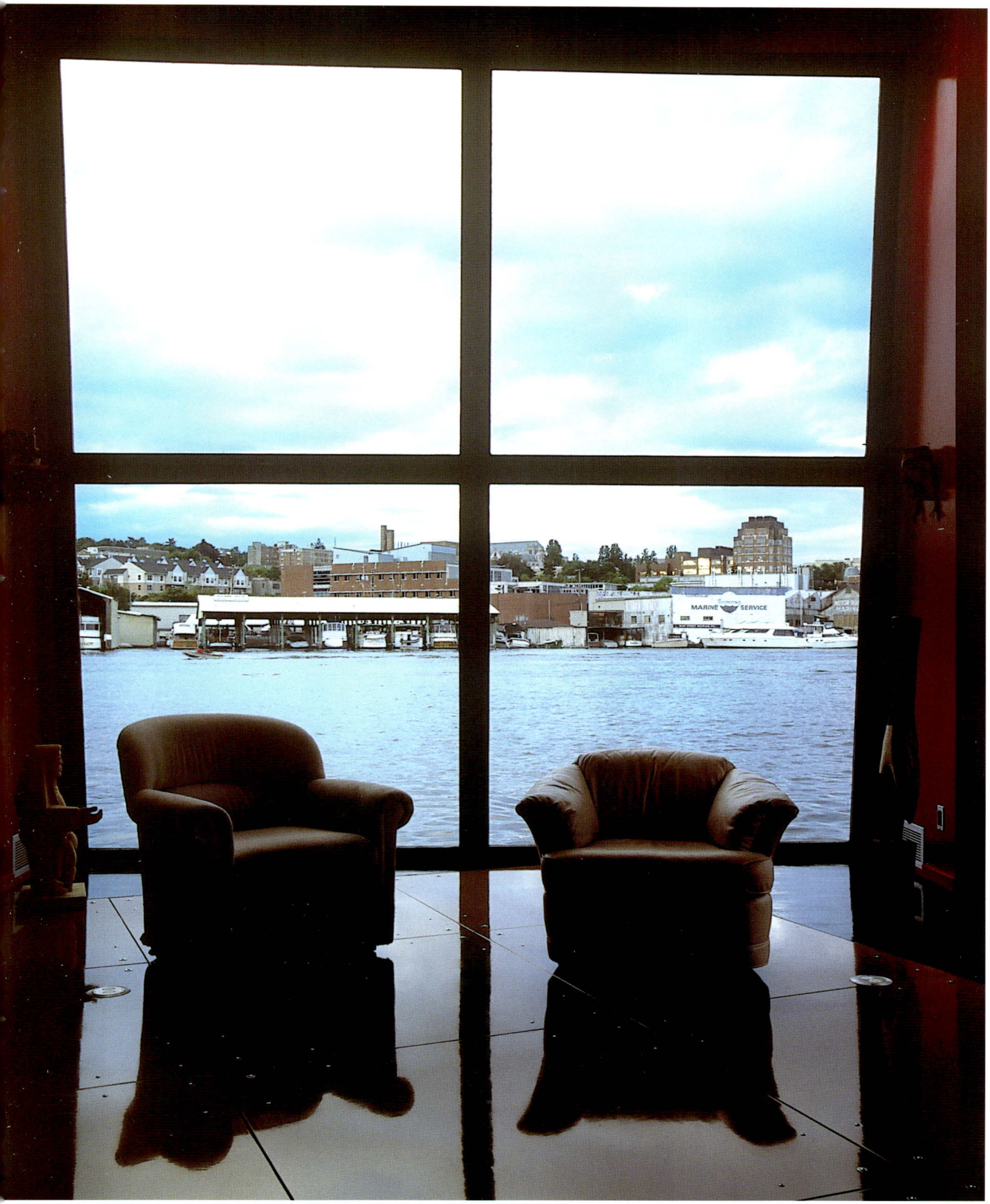
MARINE SERVICE

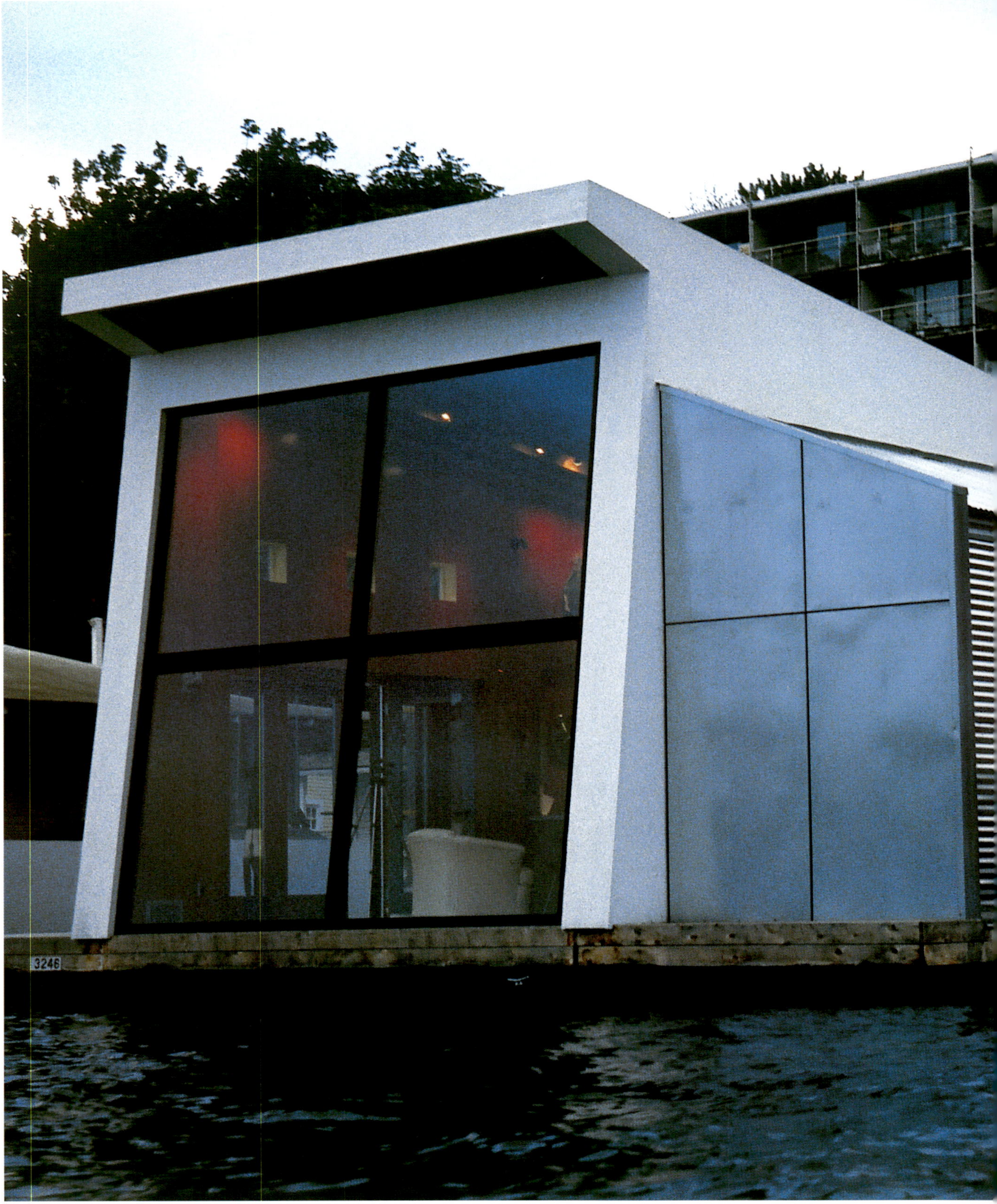
3246

カヌーとボートが引き揚げられている甲板に立つと、湖の全景が広がり、まだ見ぬ大物との遭遇が期待される。大きな窓から大量の光がリビングルームに届けられ、薄暮の残光までたっぷりと味わうことができる。

The exterior areas act as terraces where the views over the lake can be appreciated and where the canoes and launches are kept.
The large window allows a lot of light to enter the living room, even when there is no sun.

概念の見直し
REVIEWING CONCEPTS

　このボートハウスの目的の1つは、フローティングハウスの概念をもう一度見直し、その新しい可能性を探ることであった。もともとオーストラリア様式のフローティングハウスは、船台の上に支えられた木造の建造物を基礎にしていた。このボートハウスも船台の中心に木造の小さな屋形を建てているが、日本の障子の考え方を取り入れてその周囲をガラス張りのスライディングドアとすることによって、広い室内空間を享受することができ、360度の展望が得られた。キッチンとダイニングルームを前方に、寝室とバスルームを後方に配置した。

One of the objectives of this project was to redesign the concept of the floating house. The typical Australian model of the floating house is based on a wooden structure supported on pontoons. On this occasion a small pavilion has been built in the center of the platform. Most of the doors are sliding and made of glass, which make the most of the space and offer 360º views. The kitchen and the dining room are situated at the front of the house and the bedrooms and bathroom at the back.

ボートハウス

ドリュー・ヘス

シドニー―オーストラリア
撮影：ブレット・ボードマン

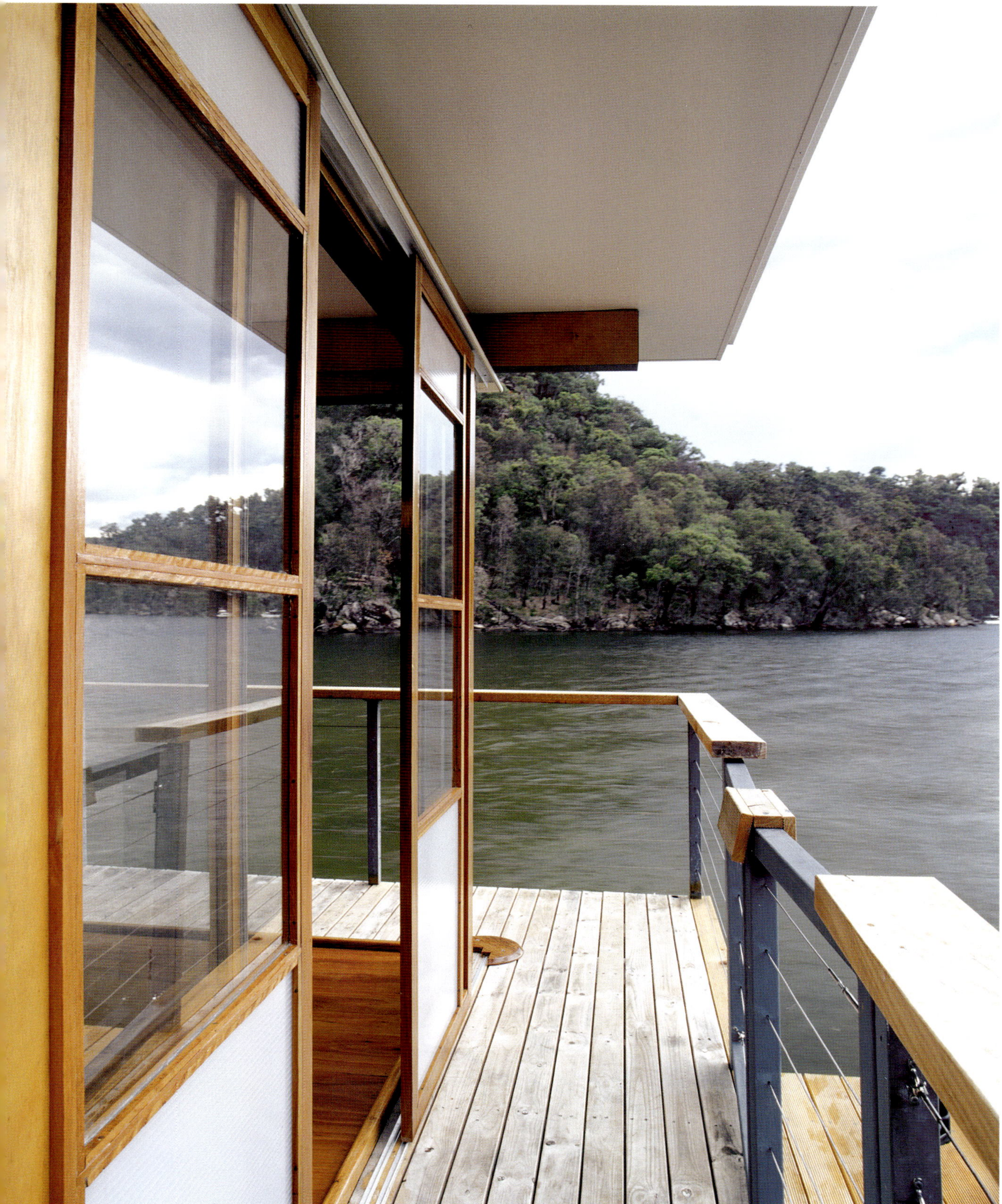

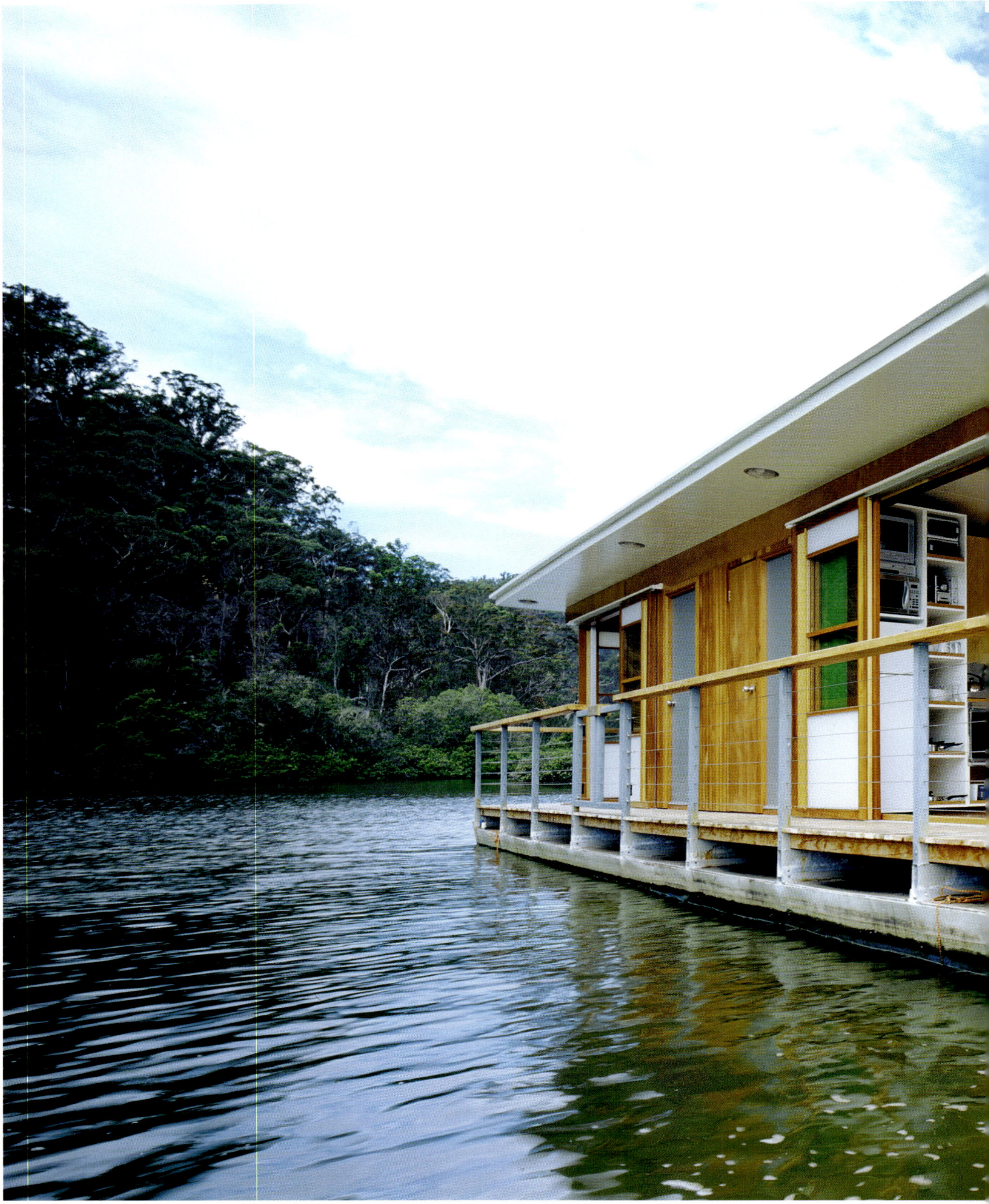

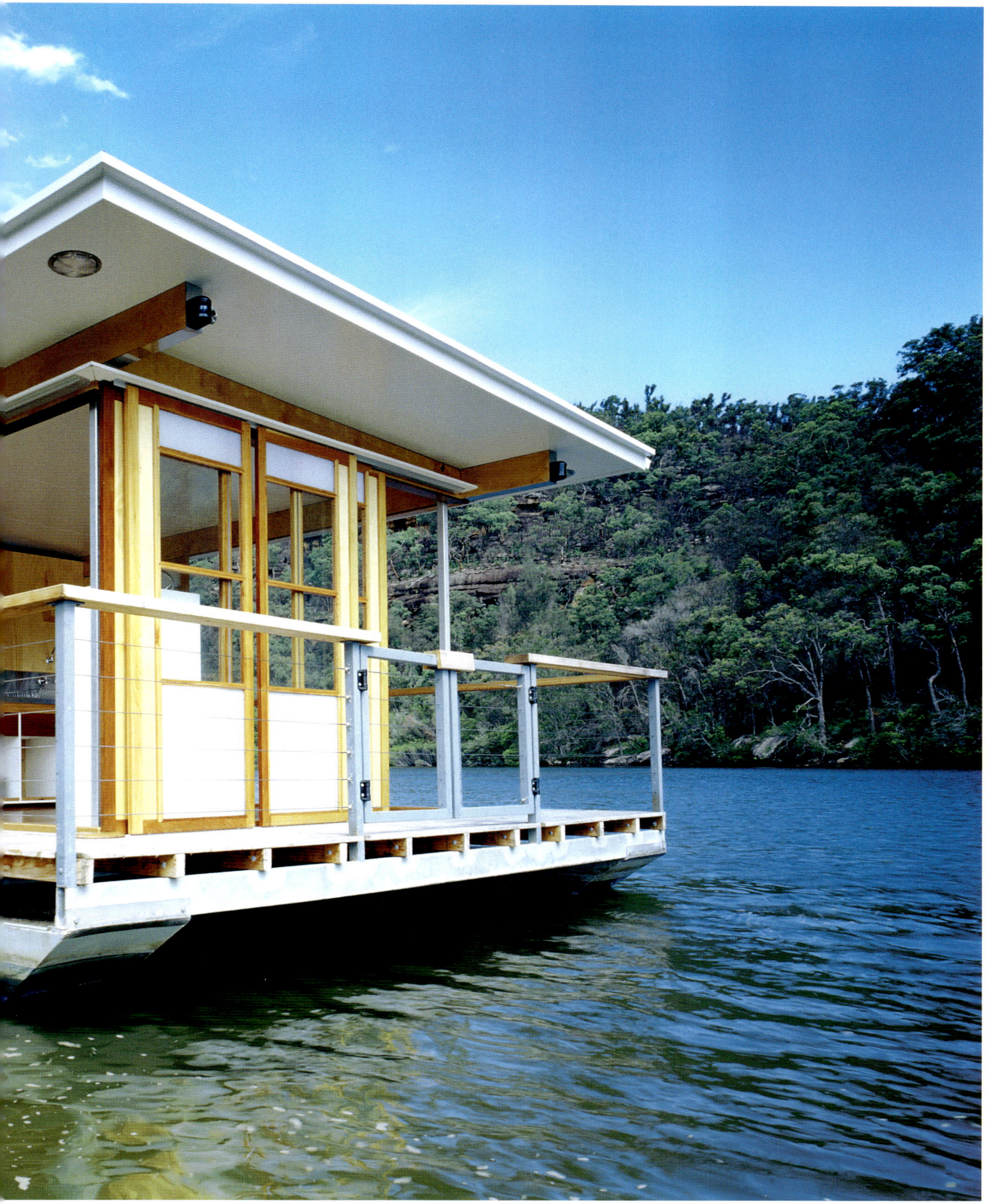

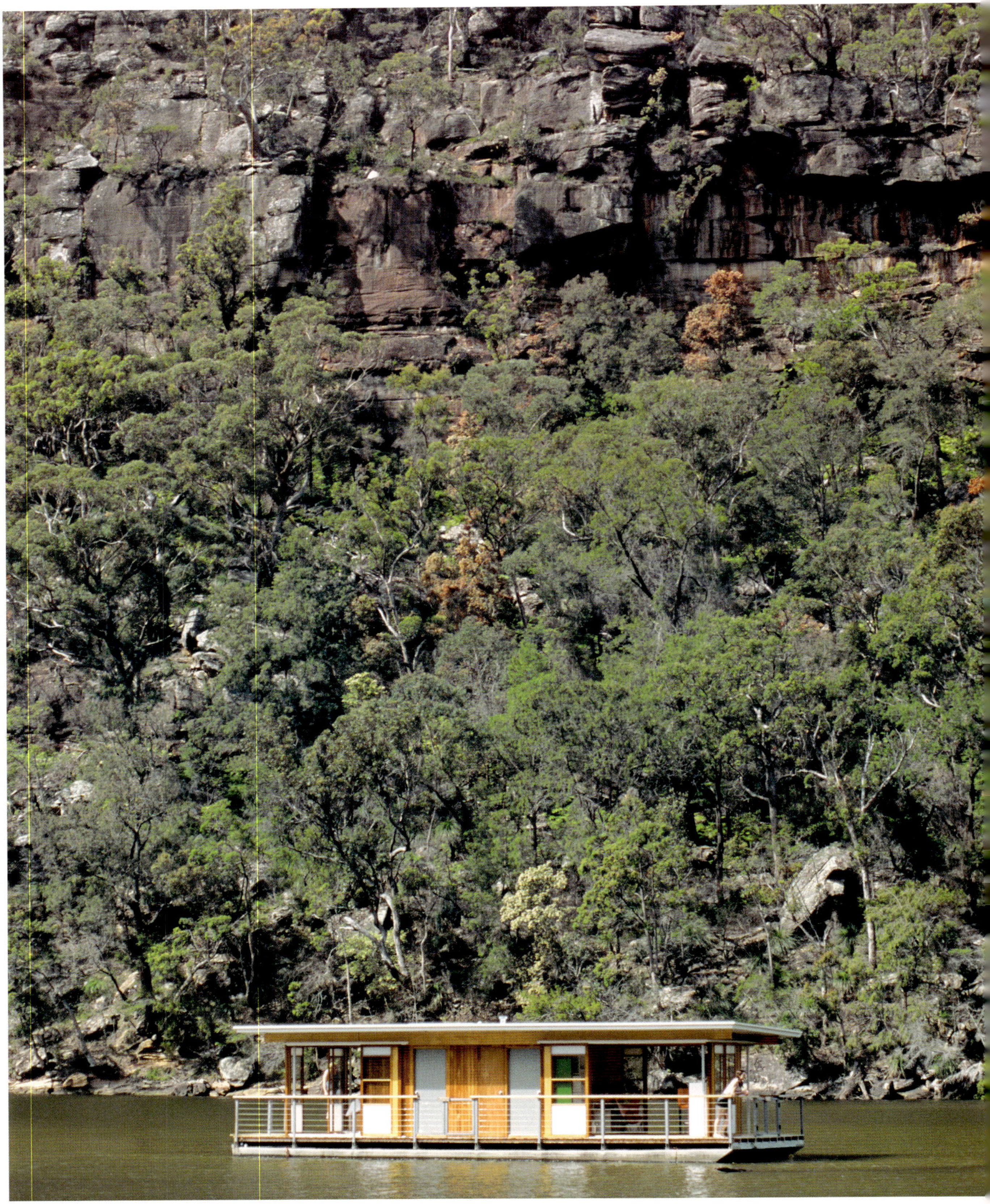

船台の周囲に手すりを渡すことによって安全性が確保され、同時にそれが甲板を部分的に屋根に覆われた回廊とすることによって、室内と外界とのより高次元での交流が可能となった。

A railing guaranteeing the occupants' security surrounds this floating house. Thanks to the layout a partly covered corridor allows a greater level of interaction with the exterior.

作品・建築家一覧 Directory

フローティングハウス・ムソカ	12	シム & サットクリフ・アーキテクツ 441 Queen Street East Toronto, ON M5A 1T5 Canada T. +1 416 368 3892 F. +1 416 368 9468 www.shim-sutcliffe.com	
ランドバーグ・キャビン	18	ランドバーグ・デザイン 2620 Third Street 94107 San Francisco, CA, USA T. +1 415 695 0110 F. +1 415 695 0379 www.lundbergdesign.com	
メゾン・ペレ	22	L-アルシテクト Côtes de Montbenon 23 CH 1003 Laussane, Switzerland T. +41 21 312 26 22 F. +41 21 312 15 54 info@l-architectes.ch	
バジル邸 エリー・サーブ邸 プライベート・レジデンス	30 136 166	ウラジミール・ジュロヴィッチ・ランドスケープ・アーキテクチュア Rizk Plaza, 1st floor. Broumana Lebanon www.vladimirdjurovic.com	
ハウス・ベイフェ	38	クラエ & ジャメイン・ソシエ・アルシテクト Rue de la Tannerie 1 B-4960 Malmedy, Belgium T. +32 (0) 80672203 F. +32 (0) 88067205 www.crahayjamaigne.com	
レイクサイド・レジデンス	44	オーバーランド・パートナーズ 5101 Broadway San Antonio, TX 78209, USA T. +1 210 829 7003 F. +1 210 829 0844 www.overlandpartners.com	
サマーハウス	50	トット・サンダース サンダース・アーキテクチュア Vestre Torggate 22 NO-5015 Bergen, Norway T. +47 55 36 85 06 F. +47 97 52 57 61 post@saunders.no トミー・ウィルヘルムセン Pedersgaten 32 4013 Stavanger, Norway M. +47 917 444 76 tommie@online.no	
チキンポイント・キャビン	54	オルソン・サンドバーグ & クンディック・アレン・アーキテクツ 159 South Jackson Street, 6th floor Seattle, WA 98104, USA T. +1 206 624 5570 F. +1 206 624 3730 www.olsonsundberg.com	
ボート・ドック ゲストハウス 歩道橋	58 62 186	ミロ・リベラ・アーキテクツ 505 Powell Street Austin, Texas 78703, USA T. +1 512 477 7016 F. +1 512 476 7672 www.mirorivera.com	
ザ・スフィンクス	68	ノイトリング・リーダイク・アーキテクツ P.O. Box 527 3000 AM Rotterdam, Netherland T. +31 (0)10 404 66 77 F. +31 (0)10 414 27 12 www.neutelings-riedijk.com	
桟橋の家	74	オニキス Papiermolenlaan 3/15 Postbus 474 9700 AL Groningen, Netherland T. +31 050 5290252 F. +31 050 5290282 www.onix.nl	
缶詰工場ロフト	78	ターナーヘクト・アーキテクチュア 2 Bryant Street, suite 100 San Francisco, CA 94105, USA T. +1 415 979 1500 F. +1 415 979 1530 www.tannerhecht.com	
X氏邸	84	バークレイ & クラウス・アーキテクチュア 7, Passage Saint Bernard 75011 Paris, France T. +33 (0) 1 49235136 F. +33 (0) 1 48078832 www.barclaycrousse.com	
ヴィラ +	88	ハイメ・サナウーハ・アソシアードス Fernando el Católico 34, bajos 12005 Castellón, Spain T. +34 964 724 949 www.jaimesanahuja.com	
クロナキルティーの家	94	ナイアル・マクラフリン・アーキテクツ 39-51 Highgate Road London NW5 1RS, UK T: +44 (0) 20 7485 9170 F: +44 (0) 20 7485 9171 www.niallmclaughlin.com	
ポルタス・ノヴァス グラスハウス	98 194	ファン・ロカ／アクアート、ヴィクトール・カニャス Water Shape Designer Costa Rica T./F. +506 675 0537 www.aquart.net	
水平線の家 風景のあるバスルーム	106 200	小川　晋一　都市建築設計事務所 Plaza Tower 3016 1-13-6 Kachidoki Chuo-ku Tokyo 104-0054, Japan T. +81 (0)3 3533 0070 F. +81 (0)3 3533 0021 www.shinichiogawa.com	
サ・リエラ	112	アルフォンソ・モラレス Pau Claris 173 2°1ª 08037 Barcelona, Spain T. +34 934 879 341 M. +34 687 729 746 F. +34 934 879 342 a.morales@coac.net	
ナムリー通りの家	118 176	ベドマール & シー 12a Keong Saik Road 089119 Singapur T. +65 62277117 F. +65 622 77695 www.bedmar-and-shi.com	
アイランド・モダン ウォークウェイ・オン・ザ・ウォーター	122 254	ジャングルズ・ランドスケープ・アーキテクチュア 242 SW 5th Street Miami, FL 33130, USA T. +1 305 858 6777 F. +1 305 856 0742 www.raymondjungles.com	
カサ・マルドナド ピエリーノ邸 コーナー・オブ・ピース	124 132 220	アルベルト・ブルクハルト Cra. 9 75-50 Apt. 502 Bogotá, Colombia T. +57 13 217 483 F. +57 13 417 008 alburcart@yahoo.com	

作品名	頁	設計者・連絡先
カブリー邸	128	ハビエル・プラナス／プラナス―トーレス建築設計事務所 Madrid, 6 2o 07820. Sant Antoni, Eivissa, Spain T. +34 971 340 445 F. +34 971 343 261 www.planas-torres.com
カルデラ湖のある家	142	GADアーキテクチュア 29 Broadway, suite 1707 New York, NY 10006, USA T. +1 917 579 4971 F. +1 646 258 1777 www.gadarchitecture.com
カサ・トーロ	146	アルヴァロ・レイト シザ・ヴィエイラ Rua do Aleixo, 53 CV A 4150-043 Porto, Portugal alvarinhosiza@sapo.pt
ウッドサイド・レジデンス ブドウ畑の池	152 180	ラツコー建築設計事務所 2815 18th Street San Francisco, CA 94110, USA T. +1 415 920 2800 F. +1 415 920 2809 www.lutskoassociates.com
リューティ	158	ドナルド・ヤコブ／ヤコブ・ラントシャフツアルヒテクテン Dornacherstrasse 192 CH-4053 Bassel, Switzerland T. +41 061 603 28 30 F. +41 061 603 28 31 www.gartenplan.ch
シューベルト邸	162	ホルガー・シューベルト／アーキシス 717 Tigertail Road Los Angeles, CA 90049, USA T. +1 310 471 0817 F. +1 310 471 0813 has@archisis.com
デザイナーの家	172	ブッジリビング・バンコク No. 7 Thonglor 25 Sukhumvit 55 Road Klongton-Nua, Wattana Bangkok 10110, Thailand www.budjibangkok.com
風景のあるラウンジ	198	デイヴィット・ラック・アーキテクチュア 7 Hardy Street, 3141 South Yarra, Victoria, Australia T. +61 03 98677509 F. +61 03 98677509 www.users.bigpond.com/david.luck
ネクサスを繋ぐ	204	NATアーヒテクテン Frans Halsstraat 26 b 1072 BR Amsterdam, Netherland T. +31 (020) 679 0750 F. +31 (020) 675 6444 www.natarchitecten.nl
マジック・イン・ザ・ウォーター	214	D&Dアクアリウム・ソリューションズ Unit CX, 11-17 Fowler Road Hainault Industrial State Ilford, Essex IG6 3UT, UK T. +44 020 8501 2492 F. +44 020 8500 9102 www.deltecaquariumsolutions.com
復活した伝統	224	クラーソン・コイヴィスト・ルーネ・アルキテクトコントロール Sankt Paulsgatan 25 118 48 Stockholm, Sweden T. +46 8 644 58 63 F. +46 8 644 58 83 www.claesson-koivisto-rune.se
メディテーション	228	ボネッティ・コザルスキー・スタジオ 270 Lafayette Street suite 906 New York, NY 10012, USA T. +1 212 343 9898 F. +1 212 343 8042 www.bonettikozerski.com
オリエンタル・リラクゼーション	232	バーバラ・シンドリュー／CADインテリオリスモ Edificio Torreón Tellinaires, 29, apto. 3 08850 Gavà Mar, Barcelona, Spain T. +34 93 633.23.54 F. +34 93 633.23.49 barbara@cadinteriorismo.com
ピース・イン・ザ・マウンテンズ	236	マルシオ・コーガン Al. Tietê, 505, São Paulo Cep 04616-001, Brazil T. +55 11 308 135 22 F. +55 11 306 334 24 www.marciokogan.com.br
ミニマリストの泉	240	岡田哲史建築都市計画研究所 16-12-302/303 Tomihisa, Shinjuku Tokyo 162-0067, Japan T. +81 3 3355 0646 F. +81 3 3355 0658 www.okada-archi.com
幸福の感覚	244	ギレム・ルスタン Atelier NordSud 7, Passage Saint Bernard 75011 Paris, France T. +33 01 43 55 80 04 F. +33 01 40 21 69 14 www.roustanarchitecture.com
スパ・フォー・ザ・ファミリー	248	アロハ・プールズ, クリエイティブ・アウトドア・ソリューションズ 15 Brett Drive Carrum Downs 3201 Victoria, Australia T. +61 (03) 9775 0033 www.aloha-pools.com.au
アーバン・オアシス	250	フォークナー & チャップマン・ランドスケープ・アーキテクツ 106 Cole St Brighton Victoria 3186, Australia T. +61 (03) 9596 0059 F. +61 (03) 9596 0159 faulkner@netlink.com.au
沈黙の庭	260	ダルデレ Gmbh Büro für Landschaftsarchitektur & Golfdesign Gewerbestrasse 12 8132 Egg b. Zürich, Switzerland T. +41 (0) 44 984 33 03 F. +31 (0) 44 984 09 50 www.dardelet.ch
ウォーキング・オン・ザ・ウォーター	266	スタファン・ストリンドベリ Strindberg Arkitekter AB Stortorget 38 S392 31 Kalmar, Sweden T. +46 480 144 53 / +46 70 633 37 37 www.strindberg.se
デイリーライフ・オン・ザ・ウォーター	272	バネケ, ファン・デル・ホーベン・アルヒテクテン Rapenburg 31 1011 TV Amsterdam, Netherland T. +31 (0)20 627 2132 F. +31 (0)20 620 0966 www.bvdh.nl
ウォーター・フォー・ライフ	276	ジェニファー・ランドール建築設計事務所 1100 East Union Street, Studio 1B Seattle, WA 98122, USA T. +1 206 323 1520 F. +1 206 325 2306 jr@jrdesigns.com
概念の見直し	280	ドリュー・ヘス 6/110 Kippax Street Surry Hills 2010, Sydney, Australia T. +61 414 491 270 drewheath@ozemail.com.au

Idea
Mariarosaria Tagliaferri

Realization
LOFT Publications

Editor
Cristina Paredes

Editorial coordinator
Catherine Collin

Graphic design
Mireia Casanovas Soley

Layout
Ignasi Gracia Blanco

Publishing Director/Direttore editoriale/Director editorial: Alberto Dragone
Editorial coordinator/Coordinamento editoriale/Coordinador editorial: Stefano Delmastro, Paola Morelli
Copy Editing/Editing/Corrector: Vanina M. Carta
Editorial Assistant/Segretaria di redazione/Secretaria de redacción: Anna Gribaudo

© Edizioni Gribaudo srl
Savigliano (CN)
Japanese translation rights arranged with Edizioni Gribaudo srl, Savigliano
Italy through Tuttle-Mori Agency, Inc., Tokyo

現代建築家による木造建築
世界から蒐集した
美しい癒しの住宅集

編集：ナチョ・アセンシオ

世界の著名建築家による最新の木造建築を、500枚超の美しい現地写真と200枚に及ぶ設計図面で紹介。地形学的パラメーターに基づいて編集、建築業界の最先端の流れを明らかに。天然木材の美しさと機能性を併せ持った究極の集大成。

本体価格3,600円

世界木材図鑑
世界中で最もよく使用されている
用途の広い木材150種を厳選

エイダン・ウォーカー：総編集
ニック・ギブス／ルシンダ・リーチ他：共著

序章では木の組織・生長過程や製材方法等、また森林保護について。木材一覧では、世界で最も使用されている樹種150種について豊富な情報を提供、精緻な写真も掲載。木材の美しさを愛する全ての人々に捧ぐ総括的木材図鑑。

本体価格4,800円

水のヒーリング
水の本質を知り、
人体とのバランスと健康に活かす

チャーリー・ライリー 著

身体を癒し、健康を維持するための水を使ったヒーリングを紹介。また、人間と水との関係の歴史をたどり、太古の治療を目的とした儀式や、最近の科学的研究、水の持つ記憶についてなどの研究を取りあげる。

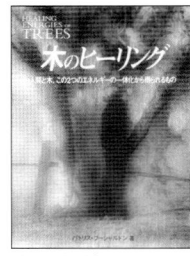

本体価格2,920円

木のヒーリング
人間と木、この2つのエネルギーの
一体化から得られるもの

パトリス・ブーシャルドン 著

人は、木から心・体・魂にエネルギーをもらい、癒す事ができる。木と交流するエクササイズ等を紹介。

本体価格2,920円

Architecture Water
水建築

発　　行	2007年10月20日
本体価格	3,600円
発行者	平野　陽三
発行所	産調出版株式会社

〒169-0074 東京都新宿区北新宿3-14-8
TEL.03(3363)9221　FAX.03(3366)3503
http://www.gaiajapan.co.jp

Copyright SUNCHOH SHUPPAN INC. JAPAN2007
ISBN978-4-88282-624-8 C3052

編集制作：マリアロザリア　タリアフェッリを主としたチーム

翻訳者：乙須 敏紀（おとす としのり）
九州大学文学部哲学科卒業。訳書に『現代建築家による木造建築』『屋根のデザイン』『世界木材図鑑』（いずれも産調出版）など。

落丁本・乱丁本はお取り替えいたします。
本書を許可なく複製することは、かたくお断わりします。
Printed and bound in Italy